Dec 16th 1957.
"Thanks for 13 Happy Years."
Connie

The Jazz Makers

Books Edited by ∗ Nat Shapiro and Nat Hentoff

HEAR ME TALKIN' TO YA

THE JAZZ MAKERS

The
Jazz
Makers

* * * * *

EDITED BY

Nat Shapiro

and

Nat Hentoff

Rinehart & Company, Inc.

New York   Toronto

Grateful acknowledgement is made to Doubleday and Company, Inc., New York, N.Y., for permission to quote excerpts from: LADY SINGS THE BLUES, copyright © 1956, by Eleanora Fagan and William F. Dufty, in the chapters on Billie Holiday and Lester Young.

Published simultaneously in Canada by
Clarke, Irwin & Company, Ltd., Toronto

To *all* the jazz makers

Preface

   The Jazz Makers tells of the lives and works of twenty-one jazzmen. Neither the editors nor the contributors are ingenuous—or unwary—enough to claim that these are *the* most influential figures in the history of jazz. We feel that the musicians included in this assembly are certainly *among* the significant enrichers of the jazz tradition, and that a knowledge of their collective body of work is vital to an understanding of the nature and development of the jazz language.

   The selection of the 21 (a figure dictated by editorial considerations) occurred after several hours of spirited discussion among most of the collaborators. When the final vote was taken, those musicians represented in this book were those who led the ballot. Since each of the contributors painfully witnessed omission of at least one choice apiece, all are aware of the equal right to inclusion in a book of this nature of several other jazzmen. Jo Jones, Sidney Bechet, Erroll Garner, King Oliver, Sid Catlett, Johnny Dodds, Jimmy Blanton, Mary Lou Williams, and more deserve—and require—a place in any assessment of those whose lives became part of jazz.

   We hope that a future volume will allow us to write at length and in a similar context of many of those who have been omitted. We must also make clear that the intent of this volume is to bring the story of jazz *up to* the multi-directional modern movement, but not to try to include more than the two key representatives of the beginnings of modern jazz—Charlie Parker and Dizzy Gillespie. We expect that the most effective means of presenting a relatively cohesive perspective of modern jazz is a book that will deal entirely with the major modernists—Thelonius Monk, Gerry Mulligan, John Lewis, J. J. Johnson, Sonny Rollins, and others.

   There was no predetermined formula in the preparation of these chapters. In jazz particularly, form follows function. Each writer determined for himself the most illuminating way of handling his subject. Some chose to bear strongly on biography; others were more concerned with analysis of the musical achievements of the man. Several combined both approaches.

   The main goal for all, regardless of individual differences in emphasis, was to try to communicate something of the personality of each of these jazz makers. As Charlie Parker once pointed out, "Music is your own experience, your thoughts, your wisdom. If you don't live it, it won't come out of your horn."

We feel that in coming to know these musicians as they are (or were) at all hours of the day—and not just on the bandstand or in the recording studio—you will also understand much more of their music.

About the Authors

NAT SHAPIRO, co-editor of "Hear Me Talkin' To Ya," is Co-ordinator of International Artists and Repertoire for Columbia Records. For the past ten years, he has been active in the commercial music business as a publicist, music publisher, and part-time writer. He is currently at work on a new book about the musical theatre in the United States and, along with co-editor Hentoff, is planning a sequel to "Jazz Makers" which will be concerned with the leading figures in modern jazz.

NAT HENTOFF, co-editor of "Hear Me Talkin' To Ya," was for four years Associate Editor of *Down Beat*. He has contributed to the *Saturday Review, Hi Fidelity, Chicago Review, Commonweal*, and is American correspondent for *New Musical Express* (London) and *Jazz Hot* (Paris). He is currently writing a book on the blues.

CHARLES EDWARD SMITH has been described as the "dean of jazz critics." He wrote the first serious study of jazz to be published in the United States, the first article on the subject to appear in a national popular magazine, and was co-editor of "Jazzmen" and editor of "The Jazz Record Book." He is a frequent contributor to *The New York Times Book Review, Esquire,* and the *Saturday Review.*

JOHN WILSON is a jazz critic for *The New York Times* and *Hi Fidelity.* He conducts the radio program "The World of Jazz" on WQXR in New York and has been on the staff of *PM, Theatre Arts,* and *Down Beat.*

GEORGE HOEFER has conducted the "Hot Box" column in *Down Beat* for more than 20 years and has written for *Esquire, Metronome, Tempo,* and other jazz publications.

BILL SIMON is an Associate Editor of the show business trade publication *The Billboard,* was formally a popular record reviewer for the *Saturday Review* and is American correspondent for the English music journal, *Melody Maker.*

ORRIN KEEPNEWS is co-editor of "A Pictorial History of Jazz" and former Associate Editor of *The Record Changer*. He is currently associated with Bill Grauer, Jr. in the direction of Riverside Records.

LEONARD FEATHER, author of "The Encyclopedia of Jazz," "Inside Be-bop," and other books, is perhaps the best known and most prolific writer on the subject. He has contributed to *The New York Times, Look, Redbook, Metronome, Esquire, Down Beat, Playboy,* and many publications abroad. He is also active as a musician and composer, concert producer and moderator of his own popular network radio show, "Platterbrains."

GEORGE AVAKIAN has been writing about—and, as an artists and repertoire executive at Columbia Records, producing—good jazz for nearly two decades. *Down Beat, The Record Changer, Metronome, Tempo* and *Mademoiselle* are a few of the publications for which he has written. The choicest examples of Avakiana, however, are to be found in his record notes for such worth-while sets as the Louis Armstrong, Bix Beiderbecke and Bessie Smith albums for Columbia.

Contents

Preface		ix
About the Authors		xi
Jelly Roll Morton	Orrin Keepnews	3
Warren "Baby" Dodds	Nat Hentoff	18
Louis Armstrong	George Avakian	49
Jack Teagarden	Charles Edward Smith	59
Earl Hines	John S. Wilson	80
Bix Beiderbecke	George Hoefer	90
Pee Wee Russell	Charles Edward Smith	103
Bessie Smith	George Hoefer	127
Thomas "Fats" Waller	John S. Wilson	141
Art Tatum	Orrin Keepnews	151
Coleman Hawkins	Leonard Feather	163
Benny Goodman	Nat Shapiro	175
Duke Ellington	Leonard Feather	187
Charlie Parker	Orrin Keepnews	202
Fletcher Henderson	John S. Wilson	218
William "Count" Basie	Nat Shapiro	232
Lester Young	Nat Hentoff	243
Billie Holiday	Charles Edward Smith	276
Roy Eldridge	Nat Hentoff	296
Charlie Christian	Bill Simon	316
John "Dizzy" Gillespie	Leonard Feather	332
Index		349

The Jazz Makers

Jelly Roll Morton

* * * *

By Orrin Keepnews

> ". . . And when I die, you can bury me
> In a box-back coat and Stetson hat;
> Put a forty-dollar gold piece in my watch fob,
> So the boys'll know I died standin' pat."

The words of the old, traditional song refer of course to some anonymous gambler; but the sentiment expressed could not have been any more directly applicable to Jelly Roll Morton if they had happened to be among the very many words he spoke about himself during his turbulent life. Jelly himself did speak of a fervent early desire to own "a hat with the emblem Stetson on it." A photograph taken in Chicago in the early nineteen twenties shows him resplendent in box-back coat; even when he was down in his luck, in Washington in the late nineteen thirties, his watch fob was gold. When he died, however, he was buried in more conventional attire and, it is sadly and reliably reported, the celebrated diamond he had worn in a front tooth for many years was unaccountably missing. Nevertheless, there is no doubt that Morton died as he had lived: planning a big comeback, blaming only his ill health for holding him back, convinced that he was being cheated by music publishers, and doing all he could to show that he held—or at least shortly would hold—a hand with which he could safely stand pat.

"Good music," Jelly Roll had told perhaps the closest friend of his last years, Roy Carew, "doesn't get old." And there is reason to believe that he was right. At the time of his death it may have looked as if he had been bluffing and his bluff had been called: he was broke and embittered; his kind of music was largely being overlooked. But in the years since he died there has been a very

3

extensive resurgence of interest in traditional New Orleans jazz, and Morton has been one of the principal posthumous beneficiaries of this movement. Many jazz writers have analyzed his recorded work and found it (particularly the best of the Victor *Red Hot Peppers* material) worthy of the highest praise; and his influence has been newly felt in the music of young jazzmen deliberately seeking to carry on in the spirit of early jazz. It would be overdoing it to claim that Morton's greatness is unanimously accepted. There are those who consider him to have been a greater braggart than anything else; although he died in 1941, some musicians who disliked this unparalleled egotist with passionate intensity have not yet reached a state of being able to hear his music with anything like objectivity. But the consensus would probably go along with the statement once made by Omer Simeon, the New Orleans-born clarinetist who played on some of Morton's most celebrated recordings: "One thing . . . about Jelly, he would back up everything he *said* by what he could *do*."

One other thing is certain. For better or for worse, like him or not, this Morton was an original. There are many musicians whose life stories have been legendized, embellished and refurbished—by themselves or by others. There are many whose abilities and contributions to the mainstream of jazz have been hotly debated. There are many who have praised themselves with brash self-confidence, many whose careers have taken them from obscurity to the top and back again. But there was only one Jelly Roll Morton. And, as has been true of "unique" individuals in many fields of endeavor, a good part of his uniqueness can be attributed to what might be called a sort of personalized universality. Gambler, flashy dresser, ragtime pianist, footloose traveler, band leader, pool shark, arranger, bordello "professor," ladies' man and composer of many tunes that became firmly established jazz standards, Ferd Morton packed into his approximately fifty-five years of life just about all the ingredients that are to be associated with the gaudy, bawdy, flamboyant, earthy, and richly musical aspects of the New Orleans red-light-district origins of jazz.

"Approximately fifty-five years" is about as close as one can hope to come to his precise age. He died, in Los Angeles, on July 10, 1941, but the date of his birth was variously given by Morton himself as 1885, 1886 and 1890. His name was, to begin with, Ferdinand Joseph LaMenthe; he has claimed that "Morton" was his own invention ("for business reasons . . . I didn't want to be called

Frenchy"), but research by Alan Lomax has established that this was actually the family name of "a nice type of fellow who did portering jobs" (as an uncle of Jelly Roll's put it), and who married Jelly's mother after the irresponsible Mr. LaMenthe left her. It might be thought that when a man's spoken autobiography exists in sufficient detail to make up a dozen long-play records, his story would be in clear focus. But discrepancies like the rather basic LaMenthe-Morton matter serve to point up that the extensive recordings made by Jelly for the Library of Congress in May of 1938 are much more valuable for recreating the aura of early jazz as recalled by one of its most colorful practitioners than for determining cold, hard fact. Actually, it would appear that Lomax, who was responsible for the recording, was at first primarily interested in setting down a firsthand recollection of New Orleans in the days when jazz was first taking shape, rather than being concerned with the personality and career of his subject. But inevitably and characteristically, Morton took over. (A decade later, Lomax put together a book titled *Mister Jelly Roll,* which combines an edited transcript of Morton's words with the results of further search among family and fellow musicians for opinions and for corroborative—or differing—fact. Consequently, anyone who cares to delve into matters concerning Jelly Roll, particularly in his younger years, would find it both difficult and rather pointless to avoid being indebted to Lomax.)

Putting together the data available from Morton, Lomax, various veteran musicians, jazz historians and other first- and second-hand reporters on the Storyville scene, plus such documentation as the *Blue Books* that advertised the better-type New Orleans houses of joy—putting together all this and no more than a grain of salt, one can arrive at a reasonably firm picture of the setting from which this controversial titan of jazz emerged.

"Storyville," a place name that (you might say) every schoolboy should know by now, was the legally fixed area within which prostitution flourished in New Orleans between 1896, the year in which Alderman Sidney Story unwittingly immortalized his name by sponsoring a city ordinance, and November 14, 1917, the date on which the mayor obeyed the close-down edict of Secretary of the Navy Josephus Daniels. The attempted solution of an ancient problem which had satisfied a city with a basically Old World culture and viewpoint had become untenable when war brought young men from all over the nation within its range. But during its twenty-one years of existence, the thirty-eight-block Tenderloin District adjoining Canal Street was obviously quite something. It was, as the 1906 *Blue Book* put it, "the only district of its kind in the States set aside for the fast women by law," and its gamut included, as Morton has said, everything from "creep joints (and) cribs" to "the mansions where everything was of the highest class." Photographs of the lavishly appointed dining room at Miss Josie Arlington's still exist, and they are as impressive as a *Blue Book* description of Madame Lulu White's establishment (". . . some of the most costly oil paintings in the Southern country. Her mirror-parlor is also a dream"). Inevitably, Storyville also housed a multitude of assorted saloons, gambling joints, dives and cabarets, and in all of these there was music. Jazz was obviously not "born" in New Orleans in any single sudden lightning flash; and there is no room here to do any more than acknowledge as accepted fact the myriad sources —religious and profane; African, European and indigenous American—from which this singular musical form slowly developed itself. But Storyville, although it undoubtedly couldn't have cared less, was clearly a vital catalyst. New Orleans, a bustling metropolis at the mouth of the Mississippi, drew to itself musicians (as well as a good many others) from all over the South. And New Orleans, a city with a rich French-Spanish "Creole" cultural heritage, was highly conscious of music. That tells the story quickly, but it should make it easy to understand how the young Creole LaMenthe boy, brought up with music all around him and fascinated by the sights, sounds and mystery of the District ("I liked the freedom of standing at a saloon bar, passing along streets crowded with men of all nationalities and descriptions"), needed little urging to use his ability as a pianist to make himself part of that surging, richly flavored life.

Morton has specified "the year of 1902" (when, by any count, he was no more than seventeen) as the time when he first "happened to invade" the District, and there is little doubt that he quickly became a figure of some musical importance. Bunk Johnson has been quoted as saying that Jelly was even more noted than a legendary pianist like Tony Jackson, because "Tony was dicty" (that is, a bit pretentious for some tastes), while Morton from the very first played "barrelhouse music . . . the music the whores liked." Jelly Roll himself was somewhat more diffident about comparisons with Jackson, a pianist from whom he learned much and for whom he appears to have had great respect. Years later, in a letter to Roy

Carew, which is generally notable for its lack of the usual Morton self-esteem, he referred to Jackson as the "world's greatest single-handed entertainer," and claimed that he decided to concentrate on playing "something truly different from ragtime" because he felt inferior in that genre to Jackson and several other highly regarded piano men of the day, all of whom were, Jelly Roll wrote, "much faster in manipulation" than he. Jackson was a singer and composer as well (*Pretty Baby* was his best-known number although, typically enough, he reportedly sold it outright for a small sum long before it became a hit), and Morton, who remained quite proud of having once beaten him in a piano-playing contest, was given to explaining that he won by unnerving Jackson: he repeatedly whispered, "You can't sing now," while Tony was playing.

One early result of Morton's new career as a sporting-house pianist was the severing of family ties. His mother had died, and the grandmother who had raised him apparently refused to have anything more to do with him when she learned how he was earning his living. Also, pianists tended to be loners by trade: they obviously didn't march in parades; many bands didn't use them at all; and so the most usual job was solo work in the parlor of a house. Thus it was not surprising or unusual that Morton left New Orleans after a while and wandered throughout the South, playing piano and shooting pool. Jelly Roll himself would have reversed the order of listing those activities: in the Library of Congress recording he can be heard claiming—how seriously is anyone's guess—that he "wanted to be the champion pool player in the world," and only used the piano "as a decoy," getting jobs in honky-tonks with an eye to being invited into pool games by the local "suckers." He was back in New Orleans at times, but after 1907 apparently never returned there. It is not really possible to draw a clear picture of his itinerary during the next several years, since the only firsthand account is the one he supplied to Lomax long after the fact and, although this is sometimes full of minute detail, it is thoroughly convoluted and full of digression and not necessarily to be taken as gospel.

However, it is relatively easy to establish a general pattern and make certain basic conclusions. He played, gambled, hustled pool and lived as high as possible (by his own account: "I had the bad habit . . . of being a big spender when I had money," and there was "a new girl in every town"), in a wide variety of towns, good and bad. The bad would include Helena, Arkansas, where, he said, a policeman told him, "A musician don't mean anything down here. We put more of *them* in jail than anybody else. . . ." The good would include Chicago where, in 1907, "there were more jobs than I could ever think of doing," and, about five years later, he managed and played at the Elite club until the Original Creole Orchestra hit town from New Orleans and was such a powerful attraction (its trumpet player, Freddie Keppard, was rated by Jelly as superior to King Oliver and Louis Armstrong) that business at Morton's place "went to the bad."

In between, before and thereafter he turned up in New York (James P. Johnson recalled hearing him there in 1911); Memphis (he had a run-in there with W. C. Handy in 1908); Houston, where he ran a tailor shop for a while; St. Louis; Los Angeles. He was writing music—enough musicians have recalled hearing his *Jelly Roll Blues* way back then to support his statement that it was originally written in about 1905; and he was working in vaudeville and in minstrel shows. This last point has its significance: Morton's greatest success, in the 'twenties, came as a band leader; the standard and generally accurate picture of him as a solo pianist in earlier years does not supply any real explanation of what should actually be considered a marked change in musical *thinking*—from soloist to bandsman. Morton himself credited the depression of 1905 for his having "learned the band business." In that year, "the work in the high-class mansions fell off" in New Orleans and he had to take a variety of "small-time band jobs," sometimes even playing trombone or drums in those endless streams of parades organized, by the countless societies and clubs supported by the city's Negro population, to celebrate all manner of social events (including the funerals of members). That background, plus a reasonable amount of formal musical training as a boy, apparently made it easy enough for Jelly Roll to pick up band jobs as he moved about—something that would not have been that easy for most sporting-house "professors."

In about 1917, Morton was in Los Angeles, which was to be his base for the next five years. According to his story, he was a fabulous success, not only musically, but as the owner or manager of cabarets, a gambling palace, a dance hall and other enterprises. Anita Gonzales, a girl from New Orleans (her brother was Bill Johnson, who played with King Oliver's Creole Jazz Band), became his wife during this period. Anita obviously had some money of her own (some stories have it that she paid for the famous diamond that adorned his gold front tooth), and she bought a "hotel" in Los Angeles. There are quotation marks around the word because the difference between her mention of it (when Alan Lomax interviewed her years later) and Morton's description seems to cast a revealing ray of realism. As noted by Jelly Roll, it seemed a part of a grandiose pattern of business success; Anita's words indicate something more like a small rooming house that didn't pay off too well. Unquestionably Morton worked regularly, up and down the coast, probably as far north as Canada and certainly as far south as Tia Juana (his *Kansas City Stomps* is named for a bar in that town, and *The Pearls* was inspired by a waitress at the bar). What can be questioned is whether his playing actually attracted the "movie trade," whether he actually vacationed in Alaska with "diamonds pinned to my underwear," whether "Anita had three or four fur coats and I had plenty clothes, plenty diamonds," whether it was really the politically powerful enemies and jealous rivals he later complained of so darkly who cost him bookings and squeezed him out of ownerships.

But if one is inevitably moved to question and minimize, it must be done carefully and within limits. The man did build an impressive musical reputation; he did wear diamonds and the sharpest of clothes; a decade later, in New York, he did keep a thousand-dollar bill (or at least some very large denomination) on hand to flash at anyone who wondered out loud if he were doing well. These things were not inventions, and if the way he dressed and spoke was designed to advertise himself and magnify his success to the utmost, it was no more than an inevitable and readily understandable outcome of the way of life he followed (a self-chosen way, it is true) since he was barely out of short pants. Wilbur de Paris, who knew him well in New York in the 'thirties, is emphatic about describing him as "sensitive, a gentleman," who, although he had lived in a sporting-house environment, "was no roughneck." If this description seems at variance with the standard picture of a flamboyant, argumentative Morton, note that de Paris knew him better, and differently, than most. He rarely worked for Morton; primarily he knew him as his neighbor in a brownstone rooming house on a Harlem side street, a man with whom Morton talked about other, more casual things than music, a man whose second wife had worked for a "plantation show" run by Wilbur's father. In short, a man Morton might have felt little need to dazzle and impress. The only other man who knew Morton in something of the same way in his later years was Roy Carew, a white man who had worked in New Orleans in the early part of the century and had known Tony Jackson then. He met Jelly Roll in Washington in the late 'thirties, and the first basis of their close relationship was that Carew could "talk to him about Tony and about the old days." To Carew also, Morton was a sensitive, relatively quiet man: "He was no braggart to me."

It is certainly reassuring to anyone who feels that there is depth and warmth in Jelly Roll's music to find evidence that the face he turned to the outside world was not his only face. As for the nature and derivation of that public face, de Paris provides an important clue by pointing out that the diamond in the tooth, the extravagant dress and mannerisms, were by no means an individual affectation limited to Morton alone. They were, on the contrary, more in the nature of a uniform: it was by such means that all "sporting gentlemen—and that included pimps" of the early nineteen hundreds announced to the world that they were in a state of affluence. Morton, in 1902, had surely not become a professional musician solely because of some abstract love of music. It was rather that this was the way of moving into a setting that this teenage boy found immensely glamorous and attractively free and easy. It began by being all mixed together—the music, the gambling, the women and all the rest of it—and there was never any reason or occasion for things to become much different. Young Ferdinand Morton went into that world alone; his grandmother quickly made it impossible for him to back out (in the unlikely event that he would have wanted to back out). So the only place to try to go was up, and the only standards to use were those of his environment. (Jelly Roll's manner of speaking, it has been said, had its only counterpart in the rococo prose style of the advertisements in the Storyville *Blue Book.*)

He took on new names: he was known as, or called himself, The Winding Boy (*not* "Wineing," which was what he tried to tell Lomax many years later) and, of course, Jelly Roll. Both terms have clear connotations of sexual prowess. When he was setting himself down for posterity via the Library of Congress, it may have seemed somewhat more respectable to claim that one nickname was associated with drink and the other with a bakery, but in Storyville, where sex was the pivot point, how better to proclaim yourself a man among men than by being called by names like these? In his travels this pianist-gambler-pool shark had to ply his trades in the toughest joints in town; in most cases he must have come into town a stranger and alone, and (judging both from his own stories of encounters with men like Bad Sam, "the toughest Negro in Memphis," and from what is known about such towns in those days) if he were to thrive, or even survive, it was clear that he had to talk, bluff or play—or perhaps all three—himself into a position of acceptance.

Pianist Don Frye recalls meeting Jelly Roll in 1923, when Morton was briefly working in Kentucky with Fate Marable, most celebrated of river-boat band leaders. This would have been when Jelly was first making Chicago his base of operations, after leaving California; and Frye remembers that he "made a big splash in the Midwest," as much because of his singing, his clothes and his personality as because of his playing. "He was a big talker, with stories about gambling in buffet flats, and music and everything else" all mingled together; "he jumped about in his conversation as if it was all the same in his mind. . . ." As, of course, it was. Although, in all fairness, even if music had not necessarily been his sole motivation at the start, it was by this time rapidly becoming the key to his whole existence. Alan Lomax, in his book, attributes Morton's great productivity during the Chicago period largely to that city's being too well gang-organized to enable Jelly Roll to get into his usual business side lines of running gambling joints, managing clubs and the like—which may have truth in it, but seems sorely to overdo the sociological-realism approach. To credit nothing more than the absence of business distractions for the intensity of the most successful *Red Hot Peppers* recordings is to take far too dim a view of musical creativity.

Of course, as far as "business" is concerned, it was in Chicago in the 'twenties that jazz itself first became any sort of business: the era of the phonograph record was under way; jazz compositions were being published and sheet music sold; for the first time a musician could earn money from jazz in other ways than just playing in joints. Morton may have left Los Angeles because of a fight with Anita, or because of an awareness that Chicago was the new hub of the jazz world, or because (as he later told it) he wanted to straighten out the matter of his associates, the song-writing Spikes brothers, taking partial credit for *Wolverine Blues,* which had been taken over for publication by the Melrose firm in Chicago. At any rate, that city became his home for the next half-dozen years.

At first he does not seem to have fitted in too well: for one thing, men like King Oliver and Jimmie Noone were already well established as top public favorites; for another, New Orleans musicians are a traditionally clannish crowd, and the newly arrived Morton was not only a known lone wolf but also a man who had been geographically dissociated from New Orleans for a good many years. It is a fact that he never had a band booking in Chicago itself (which may well be because this aggressive, vehemently outspoken fellow, the very antithesis of a "good darky," offended the local gang lords). But in all other respects, Jelly Roll was not to be denied. The Melrose brothers, who had done well with *Wolverine*, were publishing and pushing the compositions that many consider to be his real, lasting contributions to jazz: *King Porter Stomp, The Pearls, Milenburg Joys* and others, several of which he may have written years before, but which were now first being formally set forth, earning royalties and adding greatly to his reputation. Walter and Lester Melrose were probably responsible for his first important recording sessions, too. They placed quite a few of their tunes and artists with the Gennett company, in whose studios in nearby Richmond, Indiana, some of the most impressive early jazz records were made (Oliver, Morton, the New Orleans Rhythm Kings). Most of Jelly's major compositions were first recorded as piano solos for Gennett, in 1923 and '24. One of these sessions, on June 9, 1924, is notable as a monumental example of hard-working productivity: on this one day, no less than eleven numbers were recorded, ten of which (one was not released and the master has most probably been destroyed) remain treasured items to collectors of traditional jazz.

By the mid-'twenties, the major record companies had discovered that jazz, designated as "race records" and aimed primarily at the Negro market, could be quite profitable, and a good deal of such material was being issued. It is open to question whether the powers at Victor, arranging for Morton to make some records, considered that they were taking a step of any great consequence. Omer Simeon, clarinetist on Morton's first Victor sides, has said that "Those people . . . treated Jelly like he was something special. . . ." On the other hand, Morton, who had been held back by a period of illness and had hardly been setting Chicago on fire, may have seemed no more than another local band leader of moderate fame and good publishing connections. (Significantly, all selections on the first *Red Hot Peppers* sessions, even those not written by Morton, were

Melrose-owned, and the recording sheets list his address as in care of the publishing company.) But in any event, Jelly Roll appears to have approached the occasion like the momentous one it turns out, in retrospect, to have been. Ignoring the now-anonymous men with whom he had been playing club dates, he turned to top men of the New Orleans school: Simeon, Kid Ory, Johnny St. Cyr (on slightly later dates he used Johnny and Baby Dodds). According to Simeon, "I knew he was a big shot and one of the pioneers of jazz, so I was real excited," and even if that is a statement colored by the intervening years, the ten selections recorded on September fifteenth and twenty-first and December 16, 1926 (as well as several others made in the next few years) would seem to have been worth getting excited about. Accounts of those first sessions by St. Cyr and Simeon indicate that, on these occasions at least, Jelly was a master of tact. ("Very jolly, very full of life all the time, but serious," Simeon has said. "We used to spend maybe three hours rehearsing four sides . . . he'd give us the effects he wanted" but "The solos —they were ad lib. . . . Jelly had his ideas and sometimes we'd listen to them and sometimes, together with our own, we'd make something better." To St. Cyr, "Jelly was a very, very agreeable man to cut a record with," largely because he would let his men take breaks and choruses as and where they felt they best could: ". . . he'd leave it to your own judgement . . . and he was always open for suggestions.")

It may have been that Morton knew he could get nowhere playing the dictator with the men he had chosen, or simply that he had the taste to know that these men had to be eased and gentled into the delicate combination he needed: enough skill and enough rehearsal time to do justice to his material as written, and enough improvisational talent and the right frame of mind to develop the right sort of solo work from the base he was providing. The results have been called the finest recordings of New Orleans jazz ever made: to cite just one example, Rudi Blesh, in his book *Shining Trumpets,* devotes nine pages to the 1926 recordings without ever dropping below a superlative ("the qualities of classic jazz in their fullest development . . . incredible masterpiece"). Actually, this is not New Orleans jazz so much as it is Jelly Roll's jazz: obviously firmly based on the New Orleans pattern, but with a rich complexity, a showiness, a range from brashness to poetry, from naïveté to sophistication, that reflect this man and therefore cannot be exactly duplicated by anyone else.

During the rest of the 'twenties, Morton rode high. His records sold well enough for Victor to bill him as "Number One Hot Band," and he toured successfully through the Midwest, always using the *Red Hot Peppers* name, but never the same musicians as on his records. This distinction is no real matter of mystery: his recording bands were made up of men too much in demand in Chicago to go on the road; and undoubtedly too expensive, too unlikely to subject themselves to Morton's strict handling of his bands (unlike the co-operative spirit of the first record dates, Jelly Roll as an everyday leader was, according to Wilbur de Paris, a "disciplinarian," with "very little patience with out-of-line guys").

There is no doubt about this being a diamonds and rich clothes period for Morton. But, at the very end of the 'twenties, he moved his headquarters to New York, the new center of the jazz world, and then very suddenly he was on the down grade. "It was still good times when Jelly came to New York," de Paris has noted, but the music was beginning to change. "He was nothing special: Henderson and McKinney were *the* bands, and Jelly was just another leader making gigs." In New York the Peppers' records had not stirred up "*that* much fuss"—this was a city with its own Negro jazz traditions (Harlem stride piano; the big-band pre-swing style of Henderson and, later, Ellington), and New Orleans jazz and its practitioners were never really idolized in the big town. New York musicians were much more likely to note that, in terms of technique, Jelly was "a bit backward, like many of the old-line New Orleans men." When the 'thirties came, Morton was in his own mid-'forties, which is no age for change, even in a man much less supremely self-confident than Jelly Roll. His Victor contract was ended after 1930 (he did make eight more sides for that company in 1939, but those were nine long years); he was not working frequently enough to hold to-gether a regular band. This was the time of the Depression, of course, and it was not merely that Morton's jazz was rapidly going out of style: very few jazz musicians could say they were doing well in those years. But Jelly took it all very personally: a monumental bitterness took hold of him. Publishers were cheating him on roy-alties, were stealing his tunes; ASCAP and the booking agents were conspiring against him; an evil West Indian (he told Lomax) had put a spell on him. By no means did he agree that he or his music had had its day; de Paris describes Jelly's principal feeling at the time as one of "frustration"—he did not have enough chance to play, to express his ideas as a band leader, and he still felt he had so much more to say.

Morton had always been disliked and feared by many people. He was certainly not a considerate man. Little stories that could sound funny must have seemed tragic to those involved: Lil Armstrong recalling how frightened she was, as a youngster demonstrating sheet music in a store, the day Jelly Roll came by and sat down at her piano to give her "a lesson"; the three New Orleans musicians who were invited to join him in California (one was Buddy Pettit, a trumpeter Jelly has rated as second only to Keppard) and who soon "blew up, threatened to kill us" and headed back home because Morton made fun of their "antiquated" clothes and their down-home habit of bringing a bucket of red beans and rice and cooking dinner right on the job. Now that he was on the way down, more than a few people were ready to strike out at him and ridicule him: Harlem musicians delighted in standing near him on the street, making deliberate misstatements about the old days, knowing that this would quickly provoke him into futile rage.

In 1937 he was in Washington, part owner of a small and never very successful club variously known as The Jungle Inn, The Music Box, The Blue Moon Inn. It was here that Carew knew him as a neatly dressed man who liked to talk about the old days. Carew was one of the few who knew directly from Morton himself that he was badly off. (He told of refusing offers of money from men who had known him when he was on top: "I wouldn't let them know I needed help.") But he still had not lost the habit—or was it the compulsion—of being bluntly outspoken about other people's musical or personal shortcomings; he still planned grandly for the future; and at times he could still play up a storm. Pianist Billy Taylor, then a student in Washington, tells of going with a friend to hear this relic, "mostly for laughs;" someone tipped off the fact that there were skeptical musicians in the house, and Jelly proceeded to put on a dazzling and impressive exhibition. And of course the 1938 Library of Congress recordings bear permanent witness that he could still talk of his own greatness with unflagging conviction.

One of the last instances of the old flair came earlier in that year, when Robert Ripley made the mistake of introducing W. C. Handy, on the "Believe It or Not" radio program, as "the originator of jazz and the blues." Morton had always been particularly contemptuous of Handy as a man who couldn't play jazz and who, above all, had made money by converting folk material to his own use. Jelly Roll's written rebuttal, which was published in *Down Beat,* branded Handy as "the most dastardly impostor in the history of music" and included the celebrated phrase that (even if it is assumed not to have been intended as literal truth) is breath-taking in its assumptions: "I, myself, happen to be the creator (of jazz) in the year 1902." This at least put Jelly back into the limelight for the moment, and he made another brief stab at New York. There were some records—some of them good, others indifferent or less— and a scattering of one-shot jobs. But it was all rather artificial; people seemed to be paying attention to Jelly, not as a currently active musician, but rather on the somewhat unflattering premise that a surprisingly still-surviving founding father should not be ignored. This flurry of interest could not last long; Wilbur de Paris gauged its decline by noting that Morton could be found in the pool hall more often than in the nearby rehearsal hall. Then, too, there were asthma attacks; after one particularly severe one, he spent a month in the hospital.

In 1940, he learned that his godmother was dying in Los Angeles; there is reason to consider this just a good excuse for taking to the road again; in any case he did proceed to drive there from New York. There was a half year of little money and various plans: in January, 1941, a royalty check for fifty-two dollars arrived from Melrose and he talked of suing them; he informed Roy Carew that he was going to appear on an Orson Welles radio show (part of the series that did succeed in sparking Kid Ory's considerable comeback). But he also wrote to Carew that "my poor health is spoiling everything;" he would be up and about for only a day or two at a time, and then the "heart trouble and asthma" that were the cause of his death would have him in bed again. He died in Los Angeles Hospital on July 10, 1941. Kid Ory and members of his band were the pallbearers, but the ceremony was a Catholic high requiem mass, which (although he had been nominally a Catholic all his life) hardly seemed the most fitting final gesture.

It is clear that Jelly had a great capacity for annoying people, and that at times it kept them from granting him his due. (Duke Ellington has been quoted as making the bitter statement: "Sure, Jelly Roll Morton has talent . . . talent for talking about Jelly Roll Morton."—which seems something less than a fair appraisal.) But it also is clear that all the traits and the trappings that disturbed

many (though certainly not all) of his contemporaries were funda-
mental parts of the man and of the way of life he chose; they were
a facet of the whole man, and he would not have been *himself* without them. Put it this way: a more sedate Morton, without diamonds
or the name "Jelly Roll" or the bravado to have his business cards
carry slogans like "Originator of Jazz—Stomp—Swing" and "World's
Greatest Hot Tune Writer"—such a man could not have written
The Pearls or *King Porter*. And, all things considered, it was much
better to have had it the way it was.

SELECTED DISCOGRAPHY—JELLY ROLL MORTON

Jelly Roll Morton: New Orleans Memories, Commodore 30000

Jelly Roll Morton: Classic Solos, Riverside 12-111 (Reissues of Gennett
material)

(NOTE: The amount of Morton material available at any given time
fluctuates widely, since from time to time reissues of various "Red Hot
Peppers" selections can be expected, on Victor or subsidiary labels. Also,
the Library of Congress recordings, unavailable at this writing, may be
reissued shortly on Riverside.)

Warren "Baby" Dodds

*   *   *   *

By Nat Hentoff

During the summer of 1956, a number of jazzmen gathered at Music Inn in the Berkshires to exchange musical ideas, memories and hopes. Max Roach, considered by many young musicians the most influential drummer to have grown along with modern jazz, was remembering an evening eight or nine years before at which a modern combo that included Charlie Parker and himself was playing opposite a New Orleans unit with Baby Dodds on drums.

The occasion was a New York *Herald Tribune* Youth Forum; the site was the ballroom of the Waldorf-Astoria. Max recalled his shock of belated recognition that the New Orleans band sounded fuller than his. More, he felt, was happening in terms of the busier, roughly polyphonic interweaving of the voices within the older combo as contrasted with the largely unison ensemble playing of the modernists.

He was also struck with the range and constant shifting of tonal colors Baby Dodds himself displayed as he moved all over his set, and as he continued to vary the sound of his beat according to soloist, development of solo, and other changing contextual needs within a single piece.

Unfortunately Max's recognition of the continued vitality and imaginative resources of Baby Dodds's drumming has not been contagious. Except for specialists in New Orleans jazz, Baby is usually quickly categorized by most jazz listeners, some critics, and many younger musicians as one of the "old cats" who was, to be sure, important in the early years of jazz but whose work must now be considered dated, considerably more interesting from a historical than from a musical viewpoint.

Increasingly overlooked have been the intrinsic values of Baby's style; his developed insights into the basic nature of jazz drumming;

elements in his work that, in a sense, helped to form certain aspects of modern jazz percussion; and his deeply direct influence on the course of jazz drumming in the 'twenties and 'thirties.

It was Baby more than anyone else who indicated by continuous example in the formative period of traditional jazz that a drummer, as he once said firmly, *"must* be a *musician.* You can't be just anybody. Anybody can't drum. Anybody can *beat* a drum, but anybody can't drum."

Baby wasn't and isn't just anybody.

The basic source for biographical material on Baby Dodds is his own autobiography as taped by Larry Gara and later printed in part in Sinclair Traill's English monthly, *Jazz Journal,* from May, 1955, until the end of that year. Two chapters from this autobiography have been published in expanded form in the first number of the *Evergreen Review,* and it's to be hoped that all of the material will soon be published in book form. I have quoted heavily from this chronicle in the pages ahead and am grateful to Larry Gara and the *Jazz Journal* for permission to do so.

Warren Dodds was born in New Orleans on Christmas Eve, 1894. His nickname came about because: "My name was the same as my father's. . . . My mother would call 'Warren,' and I would answer. She'd say, 'I'm calling your father.' Then she'd say 'Warren' and my father would answer and she'd say 'I'm calling the baby.' That's where baby came in."

His older brother by two years, Johnny, was to become the best-known (and to many, the best) of the New Orleans clarinetists. Like many New Orleans children, the brothers invented their first instruments from scrap material at hand before they earned—or were given by their parents—the money for real instruments.

The family was a musical one, and Baby, as quoted in the *Evergreen Review,* says: "When I was little I was inspired by music all around. . . . My father and his brother used to play violin. One of my sisters played a melodeon, and my father and sister also used to play harmonicas. My sister used to play some blues and I tried to pick it up. The rest of the family didn't know it because I would get off by myself and try to play different things my sister played. But I didn't think I was so good with it and I gave it up. My dad also played quills. He took green bamboo reeds and removed the soft spongy material in them. That would leave a clear hole in the reed and then my father would cut them down to about three to six inches, each one a little longer than the other. Then he would put a plug in the top and cut it down, like any other whistle, and he would blow these quills and make very nice music. There was one quill for each note of the scale and he could play almost anything on them. It sounded just like a flute but there was no fingering. I made myself a little set of quills and my father helped me but I didn't make out so well on them. My father was very religious and he only played and sang hymns and sacred music. In fact, everybody in the family used to sing. It was the most beautiful quartet you ever heard, to hear that outfit sing. I could sing soprano or tenor and my brother John used to sing real high tenor. And do you know what took it away from him? Clarinet! And do you know what took mine away? Whiskey!"

Fred Ramsey Jr. in *Jazzmen* tells of how "Johnny and Baby had been pretending that they had a band of their own. Johnny had a toy whistle; Baby had a pile of tin cans, his first set of drums."

When the penny whistle broke, Johnny's father surprised him into exaltation by bringing home a real clarinet.

For Baby, the road to being taken seriously was harder. First he wanted to play flute. ("I don't see how in the world I ever wanted to play the flute, because there was no field for colored people in classical music.")

"I wanted a real drum set," he recalled when talking to Gara. "I told my father and he said, 'You don't get any drum. How on earth could we stand all the noise! It's bad enough around here now. You'd chase everybody out of the neighborhood.' I thought that was very bad. It hurt me and I couldn't understand why he would buy my brother a clarinet and not buy me drums. I knew drums would not cost as much.

"Of course, in those days," Baby continued, "any child who turned out to be a musician was considered no good. As a musician one had to play in places where there was liquor and the chances were he would drink a lot. And I had been drinking before I started playing music (professionally). It wasn't that I had anything on my mind, or drank to drown my troubles, but I used to love the taste of liquor and always have. Then again we had to play in the Tenderloin District. We were looked upon as nobody."

Baby did make a more complex home-made model in time. "I took a lard can and put holes in the bottom and turned it over and took nails and put holes around the top of it. Then I took some rounds out of my mother's chairs and made drumsticks out of them. Sometimes we used to go in the back yard, to our back place. There was a baseboard and I used to kick my heels against the baseboard and make it sound like a bass drum, using the can as a snare drum. With a clarinet it sounded so good that all the kids in the neighborhood came around to get in on the fun."

When Baby was sixteen, he took a job with a white family as combination butler-salad-fixer-cleaner, and saved his money for sixteen months to get his first drum.

"I got only four dollars and six bits a week but managed to save around ten or twelve dollars to buy my first drum. It was a single-head snare drum. I also got some sticks and little different things, but it took so long to save up enough to get more drums that I got a job at Mentes bag factory. While working there I bought the rest of my drum set one piece at a time. I bought a bass drum, which was a big high thing with ropes like the drums they used in school bands. I had to pull them to tighten, and after they were pulled awhile, the ropes got slick. Then I would let my fingers slide on the rope. It cost me about ten dollars. It was a big narrow thing and I had no cymbal, foot pedal or anything else. Finally I got a foot pedal, put the set together, and by gimmy, I come to make a noise!

"I amused the kids in the neighborhood and was real satisfied with myself. Then I added little traps that I needed like a cymbal, wood block, and a ratchet and whistles and things of that sort. I got them all second hand at a pawnshop but they were as good as new to me. I loved them as much as if they had just come from a factory. It was the hard way and the best way since I knew that I had to take care of them.

"Of course, a great deal about drumming I had to work out for myself. When you work at something daily that's yours. I taught myself how to tune my drums and how to put the heads on and tuck them in. The skin was wet when I got them and I learned how to trim the edges and then tuck the heads on. Today they have regular tuckers but when I started we used to tuck them on with a spoon handle. We had to tuck it very tight. And today they don't sell drum heads that you have to wet. They are on the hoop when you buy them. Then we had to put them on the hoop. All those things I had to learn by myself. But when you want to be a drummer, nothing's too hard."

Baby's first inspiration was Mack Murray, whom he heard when he was about fifteen and before he had his own drums. "He played in street parades and in the Robichaux band," Baby told

Gara. "When playing for dancing, Mack Murray used a very small
snare drum which looked like a banjo. . . . He used ebony sticks
and you would never know that they were so heavy. He played beautiful drums. When he made a roll it sounded like he was tearing
paper."

Another New Orleans drummer who impressed Baby was the
Creole, Louis Cottrell, whom Preston Jackson once called "the
father of all the drummers." Baby picked up some pointers from
Cottrell, but he learned his first rudiments from Dave Perkins. "He
had an awful big class and taught all kinds of drumming to all
colors although he was in a colored neighborhood. But he taught
me individually and I paid him by the lesson rather than go in
the class."

Baby, then as always, was independent: "Perkins gave me a
drum pad to use, but he didn't want me to use a bass drum. Well,
he didn't know I owned one so I practiced there with the pad, and
I'd go right home at night and execute what I knew on both bass
drum and snare. I got along so well Dave wanted to know if I
played anywhere or if I had a bass drum. I told him I didn't have
any and he said, 'No, I don't want you to touch it.' I stayed with
him at least a year and after I got so far advanced and did so well
on my bass drum, I went to another teacher."

The next teacher, Walter Brundy, taught Baby the funda-
mentals of reading music. "I found out that everything I had been
doing was wrong. He taught me that the right hand was 'mammy'
and the left 'daddy,' and I soon learned how to get my two hands
working differently. This was, of course, after I mastered having
both hands doing the same thing."

Baby also observed a drummer called Paps who had traveled
in tent shows, and he learned his famous press roll from Henry
Zeno, Henry Martin and Tubby Hall. His early practical apprenticeship included street-parade work with Bunk Johnson's band and
some sitting in with Armand Piron's small unit. A very early job
was with Willie Hightower's band, The American Stars. "We played
little ice-cream-party dates, and at first all I got was ice cream. . . .
I didn't even look for any money and didn't think I was good
enough to get money."

The time of apprenticeship was sometimes very trying. In the
section of his memoirs printed in the *Evergreen Review,* Baby relates: "Sometimes I would go around to dances in New Orleans
where my brother was playing with Ory. I used to go to the drum-

mer, Henry Martin, and get him to let me drum. He would get up
and I would sit down in the band. And then the band fellows would
look around and see it wasn't the same style of drumming. My
brother and Ory and the others didn't think that I was capable or
good enough to play in that band, and they'd walk off the stand one
by one, until all the fellows were off but the bass player and me.
The bass player was Eddie Garland, and the next thing he would
be laying the bass down, and I'd know there was nothing for me
to do but get down. And when I'd get down the band would all
come back again. It was very embarrassing. They pulled that quite
a few times, made me feel awfully bad. I was determined, though.
I felt as though a baby must crawl before it can walk, and I felt
that I wasn't quite ready to walk yet and just took it for granted.

"And for an encouragement I would go around and do the
same thing all over again. That gave me ambition to learn. I was
trying to play with someone who was capable of playing. And many
times later I returned the compliment. But I never did get over the
feeling I had towards Ory. Later I played with him on the West
Coast but I never got close enough to Ory to know him. It's a respect
that I gave him that I perhaps wouldn't give anyone else.

"The musicians of those days were remarkable men. When the
leader of an orchestra would hire a man, there was no jealousy in the
gang. Everybody took him in as a brother, and he was treated accordingly. If a fellow came to work with anything, even a sand-
wich or an orange, the new man would be offered a piece of it.
That's the way they were. They believed in harmony. That's how
they played music, in harmony. And that's the way the fellows
were, those oldtimers. And I was young and I had to give them a
lot of respect. If those men would happen to like you enough to
pick you up, they would either make a musician out of you, or
you wouldn't be any musician. In their way, they were rough, but in
a way they weren't rough. Everything they told you they would make
you do for your own benefit. But I used to try to drum and I'd drum
my best and they knew I was doing my best and they all said the
same thing. They said, 'Someday he's going to be a good drummer
because he pays attention. He wants to learn.' And I did."

And Baby tells of another lesson, this one from parading:
"With the brass band I only had one drum, the snare drum. Someone else played the bass drum. . . . Sometimes the groups would
have several bands in a parade. Then the main band had to start
first and finish last and all the other bands had to go through this

leading band at the end of the parade. Of course the head band
would always be the best. And it was one of the most exciting things
I ever did to play music and go through another band that was playing. The main band was lined up on both sides and we had to go
between them and keep playing.

"I remember the first time it happened. I don't remember who
was drumming in the main band, but I think it was Ernest Trepagnier
who was beating bass drum. The snare I don't remember. But my
snare was a four-inch drum, and this fellow had a six-inch snare
drum. When we got going through I couldn't hear my drumming
any more so I didn't know what I was doing. And I picked up with
the other drummer, who was playing six-eight in contrast to the
two-four time we had been playing.

"I should have displaced the other fellow's drumming with
concentrating on what I was doing, but that time I heard the other
guy's part and not my own, and of course we were playing altogether
different numbers. But it's those experiences which make you know
what music is, and it's the hard way of learning."

Baby's first job in the Tenderloin District was at the Few-clothes
Café with Roy Palmer who had played trombone with him in the
Hightower band.

"In those days we used to play all kinds of numbers. New Orleans is a seaport town and boats would come in from all parts of
Europe. Many of the fellows had been on boats for three to five
months when they came in and they were glad to find a dance hall
and fast women in the district. Then we'd play *Over the Waves* for
the sailors and different nationality songs. The men would pay for
them because they hadn't heard their native songs in the United
States before. We'd also jazz up songs like *In the Shade of the Old
Apple Tree*. We used to take waltz tunes and change them into
four-four time. And *High Society* we always played as a straight
march. Now they play it as a jazz number.

"We played what was later called ragtime but was then called
syncopation. It was picked up off Scott Joplin. It was called syncopation before I even started playing. . . . And we always stressed
the melody. That's the secret of jazz music, to carry the melody
at all times.

"On New Orleans dance dates we also had to play mazurkas,
quadrilles, polkas, and schottisches. There were certain halls in New
Orleans where you had to play all those things. Some of the Creole

people went only for that music. If you couldn't play them you just didn't get the job.

"Of course we also played the blues. Some of the guys would come in and drink with women and they would be blue about something, and they would ask us to play the blues. The blues that were popular were the *Memphis Blues,* the *St. Louis Blues,* and *Careless Love. Bucket Got a Hole in It* was also a blues type of number and *Ace in the Hole* was another. The blues played in New Orleans in the early days were very, very slow, and not like today, but with a Spanish rhythm."

After another job in the district (Storyville), Baby rejoined Hightower. "I was glad to get away from the district anyway. I didn't like that sort of life. Furthermore, I had a girl in the district who wanted to cut my throat." He soon experienced a particular kick because they played a job that Kid Ory (with Johnny Dodds in his band) had just left. "All I wanted to do was to get a chance to play where my brother used to play."

Baby was with the Hightower band off and on for several years. "It was when I was working with Willie Hightower's outfit that I first realized how important drums were to a band. Sometimes when I had to go out and happened to hear the group start to play, I could feel that something was missing. And the greatest satisfaction of my entire musical career was knowing that I belonged there."

Several times during his New Orleans career, Baby played with clarinetist Big Eye Louis Nelson. In describing the relationship between them, Baby also indicates the social gulf between the uptown New Orleans Negroes and the lighter Creoles: "He lived downtown and I lived uptown. He was on the north side of town and I lived on the east side. In other words, he was a Creole and lived in the French part of town. Canal Street was the dividing line and the people from the different sections didn't mix. The musicians mixed only if you were good enough. But at one time the Creole fellows thought the uptown musicians weren't good enough to play with them, because most of the uptown musicians didn't read music.

"In those days," Baby said, "the instrumentation was different. When I first started out they had no piano. They mostly used bass viol, guitar, clarinet, trumpet, trombone and drums. The guitar carried only rhythm in the bands. Actually you have a much sweeter jazz band when you have a guitar and no piano. In that way the drums couldn't outplay the other guys, because the drummer had to keep in touch with the guitar." (Baby bears out Gerry Mulligan's assertion that his initial pianoless quartet had sound historical roots in jazz history.)

"In many places they had nothing but just piano and drums. In fact, on one occasion, I had to play a whole evening with nothing but drums and trombone. That was with Jack Carey. We had a date to play uptown in what they called the Irish Channel. The Irish people liked the colored music and they hired Jack Carey's outfit. He had no regular drummer but would hire individuals for different dates, and that time he wanted me to play with the group.

"It had rained in the afternoon and only Jack Carey and I showed up with our drums and trombone. Well, those Irishmen were very tough on colored fellows and we wanted to avoid a misunderstanding. After waiting a half hour we noticed that a lot of the Irish fellows were getting drunker and we knew what would happen if the music didn't start soon. So we began to play that way and played the whole dance through. Carey played a rough tailgate trombone and they liked it very much."

Baby in time replaced Henry Zeno, who had died suddenly, with Frankie Dusen's Eagle Band which included Bunk Johnson. He played many funeral parades as well as on advertising wagons. "We would start out about two o'clock in the afternoon and wouldn't get back till around five. When some other outfit was also advertising and we met each other along the street in those wagons, it used to make it very interesting. The guys would put the wheels together and tie them so the band that got outplayed could not run away. That made us stay right there and fight it out. And we used to draw quite a crowd of people in the street that way.

"I'll never forget one time when we were stopped on the streets. I was playing with Jack Carey on that occasion. . . . Jack Carey played trombone, his brother Mutt, cornet, and Carey's nephew, named Zeb, clarinet, and we ran across Ory's band. Quite naturally the Ory band had the best of it all. Besides Ory, my brother was in that band, and Joe Oliver. Of course we didn't have a chance, but we had to stay there. When we played a number there wouldn't be much applause, but when Ory played we would hear a lot of people whistling and applauding. When we heard that quite naturally our courage went down and we wanted to get away. But the wheels were tied together. It lasted about an hour and a half or two hours and it was very discouraging. I wasn't so good. I was just starting and Ory's drummer, Henry Martin, was a finished musician, but those things are what made us want to become good musicans because it made us know what we had to do better."

As Baby Dodds improved, he joined Sunny Celestin, with whom he also sang occasionally. While with Celestin at a place called Jack Sheehan's, Baby devised what came to be his best-known visual-aural invention, the shimmy beat. "It was wartime, around 1918. One night a French soldier came in. When he heard the music he couldn't dance to it, but he just started to shake all over. That's the way it affected him. I saw him do it and I did it too. The people got such a kick out of seeing me shaking like him that they all came around and watched. Then when I saw that it caused such a big sensation and brought credit to myself and my drumming, I continued it. I used to shimmy and at the same time I used my press roll and a full beat. It was perfect. I slapped my left foot, the right foot was busy, and it worked very nicely. I used it ever since that time and it became a specialty with me."

Toward the end of 1918, bassist George "Pops" Foster was instrumental in Baby's getting a job playing on the river boats. Louis Armstrong went with him and they worked on the boats until September, 1921.

"The boats," Baby explained to Gara, "belonged to the Streck-fus line. They had jazz bands for dancing on all their boats. We would leave New Orleans around the fifteenth of May and head up the river for St. Louis. We played in St. Louis from about the fif-teen of June until the fifteenth of September, but we also took trips out to some towns farther up the river. We went all the way up to St. Paul and stopped in Davenport, Dubuque and Keokuk, Iowa; LaCrosse, Wisconsin; and Red Wing, Minnesota, on the way.

"In St. Louis they used to give colored excursions every Mon-day night. It was one of the most wonderful things you've ever seen carried on. The boat was packed and we got such a kick out of it because it gave us a free kind of sensation for working. We worked all the week for white people and this one night we could work for colored. It gave us an altogether different sensation be-cause we were free to talk to people and the people could talk to us, and that's a great deal in playing music.

"We were less tense because it was our own people. I especially loved it because I made a big sensation with my shimmy beat. I used to shimmy and drum at the same time, shake all over. The colored people had never seen anything like that. I used to have a bunch around me backed up five or six deep; and Louis Armstrong would have a bunch five or six deep backed up around him. It was a wonderful thing, and we were the two sensational men on the boat, Louis and I.

"The bosses demanded discipline," Baby said. "I remember once when I was in Keokuk, Iowa, I got into a humbug. We all piled off the boat one day and I got so drunk I couldn't see. They were using this homemade beer, they used to call it 'bust-head' in Keokuk, and I came back to the boat so drunk with the stuff that I just couldn't walk up the gangplank. They tied me to a post and one of the bosses said I should have been horsewhipped. I said: 'Yeah? I'll bet it would be the worst horsewhipping you ever saw if you'd left me alive when you got through.' They were kind of shy of me. I didn't care about anything in those days so maybe I would have done something. I don't know.

"But my heart was in my music, and that was some of the sweetest music I ever played. It was a wonderful outfit. Besides the standard jazz and popular numbers we played classical numbers and also played for ordinary singing. The Marable band was the first big band that I worked with. The leader was a very light-colored man with red hair. He was a pretty stern fellow who kept strict order. Marable had worked for Streckfus so long, and he looked so white that people used to say he was Streckfus' son . . .

"Often when we went to a town nobody would dance. Then when we'd go back for a second trip that same day, the boat would be packed. My God, you couldn't get them off the boat; the boat was packed to capacity. I think the first time it was a surprise for the people . . . They'd advertise before we got there that we were colored. . . . They had never before seen Negroes on the boat. They saw Negro roustabouts but had never seen a Negro with a tie and collar on, and a white shirt, playing music. They just didn't know what to make of it. But they really liked it."

About Louis on the boats, Baby remembers: "Louis was especially versatile. Once Streckfus bought some trick instruments for the different people in the band. He bought Louis a toy slide trumpet and me a slide whistle and different little trinkets that were to go with my drums. That's what they call traps. A snare drum isn't a trap drum. Rather traps are such things as blocks, triangles, slide whistles, horns, tambourines, cocoa blocks, and things like that. In those days nobody handled these traps but the drummers. And if you couldn't handle the traps you didn't get a job. Well, Streckfus bought this slide whistle for me but I didn't even look at it. Louis did. He played it and years later he used it sometimes with the Oliver band."

Baby's confidence grew on the boats. There were daily rehearsals, a flow of new music, and the Streckfus' perfectionism. He recalls an event in St. Louis. One of the protagonists was a drummer, Red Muse, "who was supposed to be very sensational. It was a place called the Chauffeur's Club, a night club joined to a hotel. I was with Fate Marable and everybody was hollering when we came in the place. His drumming was very sensational, very good. He'd throw up sticks and things like that. I was actually afraid to sit down there. But one night Fate played piano, and Louis played trumpet and I played drums, and we broke up the place. . . . I shimmied when I drummed and that took the eyes of the people."

Finally, Louis and Baby left the boats "because of a misunderstanding we had with our bosses." The Streckfuses wanted them to beat a different time because some of the older people couldn't dance to their music. Baby joined King Oliver. Oliver, then in San Francisco, had Johnny Dodds in the band and his drummer, Minor Hall, had just left. Johnny advised against the hiring of his brother, protesting that Baby didn't play enough drums, never would, and besides, drank too much. But on the recommendation of Davey Jones, who had worked with Baby on the boats, Oliver sent for the younger Dodds.

In his interview with Gara, Baby remembered proudly: "When I got there the first piece of music they put in front of me was *Canadian Capers*. I asked Joe how he was going to play it. He said from the left-hand corner to the right-hand corner; from top to bottom. The trio was in the middle of the number. I said 'Kick off,' and Joe kicked off. I read that piece of music down, from side to side and went back to the trio. I had played that number once and knew it, so I began playing my own style of drums. It was a jitney dance hall where everybody paid to get in the ring and dance, but people began leaving the ring to come over to the bandstand. Some even asked who I was and where I came from. Quite naturally it made Joe Oliver feel very happy to see people leave the dance floor and stop to listen to me.

"Davey Jones said to Joe, 'I told you so.' My brother was dumbfounded. He later told me, 'You surprised me. How did you learn to drum like that?' I answered him, 'That was my inspiration, to show you someday that I could drum. And I did.' "

While on the Coast, Baby also worked intermittently with

Kid Ory. Oliver, the Dodds brothers and Ory then took over an Oakland dance hall; and in 1922, King Oliver led the band back to Chicago and the Lincoln Gardens (called the Royal Gardens when Oliver had worked there before). Louis Armstrong joined on as second cornet in 1923.

This was the King Oliver Creole Jazz Band that was in retrospect to be recognized as the classic jazz band of the 'twenties, the unit that first helped make the reputation of Louis outside of New Orleans, and that was to influence a long second line of Negro and white musicians.

In his chapter on King Oliver in *Jazzmen,* Fred Ramsey writes: "There were no waltzes played at the Lincoln Gardens, the customers liked the Bunny-hug, the Charleston, the Black Bottom. A stomp ended; a minute's silence broke in on the din, then Joe tooted a few notes down low to the orchestra, stomped his feet to give the beat, turned around, and they were off on a new piece, first impatient for a release from the stiffness of the opening bars, then relieved to be tearing through fast and loud in their own way. Lil Hardin bit hard on her four beats to a measure, while the deep beat of Bill Johnson's string bass and the clearly defined foundation of Baby Dodds' drum and high-toned, biting cymbal filled out the 'bounce' and kept the others sweeping forward. This motion led to a climax, a point beyond which the breathless pace of the music seemed doomed to fall, unless something would intervene. Then Joe and Louis stepped out, and one of their 'breaks' came rolling out of the two short horns, fiercely and flawlessly."

"It was merely a hall with benches placed around for people to sit on," Baby remembers. "There was a balcony with tables on one side and the whole interior was painted with lively, bright colors. I would judge that the Gardens held about six or seven hundred people and many a night I've seen it filled up. When it was full there would be a lot of people on the floor but dancing was nearly impossible because they used to bump into each other, and of course, that's not dancing. But the people came to dance. One couldn't help but dance to that band. The music was so wonderful that they had to do something, even if there was only room to bounce around. . . .

"I used to hate it when it was time to knock off. I would drum all night till about three o'clock, and when I went home I would dream all night of drumming. That showed I had my heart in it, and the others had the same heart that I had. We worked to make music, and we played music to make people like it. The Oliver band played for the comfort of the people. Not so they couldn't hear, or so they had to put their fingers in their ears, nothing like that. Sometimes the band played so softly you could hardly hear it, but still you knew the music was going. We played so soft that you could often hear the people's feet dancing. The music was so soothing and then when we put a little jump into it the patrons just had to dance. . . .

"We were all so ambitious. Somebody would suggest a number, and we would play it and experiment with different keys to see which would sound the best. Working with the Oliver band was a beautiful experience. . . . There was no individual star, but everybody had to come through. . . .

"Not all the people came to the Lincoln Gardens to dance. Some of the white musicians came to hear our band. Benny Goodman, Jess Stacy, Frank Teschemacher, Dave Tough, Bud Freeman and Ben Pollack used to come to listen. George Wettling came when he was still in knee pants."

Wettling remembers: "Baby had a better beat than anybody I'd ever heard. He really swung the band. And he'd play all over the drums. I was so pleased that when I went to England with Eddie Condon at the beginning of 1957, some of the collectors said that I reminded them of Baby. Baby was the greatest thing I ever heard.

"In those days," George continued, "young kids weren't around where jazz was played very much. For one thing, hardly any one was interested in that stuff. Why, over at the Lincoln Gardens there was the greatest band in the world and everybody was talking about Isham Jones! But Dave Tough, Bud Freeman, Muggsy and I would sit there all night.

"Baby would encourage us, and all of us interested in drums learned from him. He had a press roll that was better than anyone's. And he played *behind* the man, each man according to what he's doing, and that's a lost art.

"Baby put the drums in people's eyes and made it mean something. In the old days, they'd say anybody could beat a drum. But Baby proved what could be done with drums. Another thing I remember about Baby is he was always cheerful."

Tommy Brookins, later a vaudevillian and singer, remembered: "One of the things that struck me most at the Royal Gardens was the smile of Baby Dodds. When he played drums he had the most patched-up material for a drum set that I'd ever seen in my life, but he had a rhythm entirely his own, and I feel that as a drummer he has more personality than any other specialist on any other instrument. He was a man of natural playfulness, possessed by rhythm. Just to see him smile and to hear his beat would make you happy."

Baby influenced Wettling, Ray Bauduc, Wally Bishop, Ben Pollack, Zutty Singleton, Gene Krupa, and Dave Tough, among others. He in turn continued to be influenced by the men he played with.

He told Gara: "Joe was always making suggestions for the improvement of the band. In 1923 I used very heavy sticks. One day Joe told me, 'I want to try to get you to beat light,' and he bought me some wire brushes. It was a new thing and I was probably the first guy that ever worked with wire brushes in that part of the country. But I still beat heavy even with the brushes and Joe said, 'You'd beat heavy with two wet mops. Give me those things. Take your sticks back.' I didn't like the brushes and couldn't get anything out of them. It seemed lazy to me. But I realized that I should learn to beat lighter with the sticks. I worked on this and began getting very technical with the drumsticks. That is why I can beat so light now with sticks. Joe Oliver was the cause of that.

"I studied each player individually. I had to study their method of improvising and to know what they intended to do. And when the band came in as a whole, in ensemble, I had to do something different again. But at all times I heard every instrument distinctly. I knew when any of them were out of tune or playing the wrong note. I made that a distinct study. Those of us who worked with the King Oliver Band had known each other so long we felt that we were almost related. That outfit had more harmony and feeling of brotherly love than any I ever worked with. And playing music is just like having a home.

"We did a lot of kidding around in the Oliver band. Of course, Louis was the comical man in the band. My brother was serious but he had play days too. Sometimes Louis and I used to have some special fun while playing. Louis would make something on his horn, in an afterbeat, or make it so fast that he figured I couldn't make it that fast, or he'd make it in syncopation or in Charleston time, or anything like that for a trick. And I would come back with something on the snare drums, and with the afterbeat on the bass drum, or a roll or something. But I had to keep the bass drum going straight because of the band. I couldn't throw the band. Louis and I would throw each other and pick it up ourselves and keep the band going.

They would feel it, but no one in the audience knew anything about it."

Baby's pleasure in drinking continued during this happy time. "I had a lot of girl friends in those days . . . when I first went with the Oliver band every girl in the place wanted to talk to me but if a girl wouldn't buy me a pint of Old Taylor, she couldn't even talk to me. But if she bought me a pint of Old Taylor, I would give her my undivided attention."

It was at the Lincoln Gardens that Baby met his second wife Irene. "She had been at Lincoln Gardens listening to the band and dancing and was going home when I caught up with her at the corner of Indiana and Thirty-first streets. I had a lot of little toys which I had purchased for John's children. I carried them to work because I did not want to go back home before going to John's place. I had my arms full of toys, and I had been drinking, so naturally I dropped one of them. We were both waiting for the street car and Irene picked up the toy I dropped. I could hardly stand up and she sympathized with me and helped me on the street car. She carried some of the toys and thought it was a very nice thing for me to carry so many toys home for my brother's children."

The band finally disbanded because of money. The members —with Baby as chief instigator—suspected that King Oliver was taking more than his share of royalties from their records. The discord finished the unit. Baby played with King only once again—in 1925 when Oliver was heading a big band and the regular drummer, Paul Barbarin, fell ill.

Baby went to work under his brother at Burt Kelly's stables. He was fired after a year. "Kelly thought I was the rottenest drummer he had ever heard." Baby came back in 1928 "and Kelly was glad to hear my drumming. Johnny told the boss, 'Well, that's the same guy I had before; that's my brother.' In fact Kelly was so pleased that he had a light put on the post right by the drums. He said, 'We've got to see the guy that's doing so much drumming.' " In 1930, the government closed the room, accusing Kelly of having sold liquor, this being Prohibition time. Baby says it was a bum rap.

The Dodds brothers, after a period of unemployment in a city that no longer was nearly as jazz-prone as in the 'twenties, took work in a Chinese restaurant with Freddie Keppard on trumpet and Big Eye Lil on piano.

"I worked just as hard under my brother," Baby said in the

Gara interview, "as I did under anyone. He was very strict on me
and said, 'Now, because you're my brother I'm not going to be any
more lenient with you than anyone else.' I understood that and tried
to do my best to please him. But John didn't drink himself and he
was always on me for my drinking. I felt I had a right to lead my
own life and to drink if I wanted to, but I tried not to make him
angry or to displease him in any way. But playing with John was
a tough assignment for everyone. Sometimes John would order a
rehearsal and nobody would show up but him and me. I used to
drive him to the job so I was forced to be there. And when the fellows didn't come to rehearsals John would be very angry and tell
them, 'Well, now, since you weren't at rehearsal, you take the piece
of music home with you. You'd better know it when we get together and not make any mistakes.' And that's the way John was:
positive, very positive."

At the Three Deuces, Baby worked with Johnny's combo
downstairs and upstairs with the pianist, Cleo Brown; and when
Johnny was replaced by a Roy Eldridge unit, Baby just worked
with Cleo. Baby first worked the club in 1931 and was there again
in 1938. On Sundays for a time, Baby played with just guitarist
Lonnie Johnson. He still didn't use brushes. "I would have to play
along and try to do as much as I could to fill in the different parts.
Then, too, I had to play very softly and soothing, so as to let the
guitar's sound protrude over the drum. I had to think all the time
what to put in, and what not to put in. But it was a great experience
and helped make me both versatile and light-handed. Even Gene
Krupa couldn't see how I did it. He was playing at the Chicago
Theatre and he came over.

" 'Well, Baby,' he said to me, 'I heard about this but I didn't
believe it. I came to see it. I don't see how you do it. Don't you use
brushes?' I told him, no, indeed, when you have to do something, you
just learn how to do it, and that is all there is to that. And he would
stand there and look at me and just shake his head."

On many of the jobs with Johnny in the 'thirties, Natty Dominique was the trumpet player. The jobs were sometimes difficult. At
one place, in addition to playing music for dancing, there was a
show and the then quartet had to play pieces like selections from
Faust and the *Hungarian Rhapsody*. And at times the jobs were
very scarce. "There weren't many jobs around but my brother was
a hustler and I worried about nothing. He used to get dates to
play in little taverns or saloons around town, usually on Friday and

Saturday nights. There wasn't much money attached to it but still it kept the wolf away from the door. . . . We managed to get along all right although we never did have any other trade like so many musicians did."

The brothers did have outside investments. John owned an apartment house, and for some twenty years, Baby was in the cab business with his oldest brother, Bill.

During these Chicago days, the brothers often showed up at rent parties, and sometimes worked with several white jazzmen at sessions handled by Paul Mares, formerly trumpet player and leader of the New Orleans Rhythm Kings.

"That was quite an experience too," Dodds told Gara, "because when I was just starting to play jazz music in New Orleans the white people weren't interested in it. They would laugh and poke fun at it and say it sounded crazy to them. It was music they thought was played only by illiterate Negroes."

Among the musicians who played at the Mares sessions with the Dodds brothers as "the specials" were Boyce Brown, Floyd O'Brien, George Brunies, Jack Teagarden, Bob Haggart, Bob Zurke, Nappy Lamare, Billy Butterfield, Yank Lawson, Tough, Krupa, Wettling, Eddie Condon, Jimmy McPartland, Wild Bill Davison, Bud Freeman, Pee Wee Russell, Art Hodes, Mezz Mezzrow, Jess Stacy. "A lot of the fellows who later hit big money in the swing music era learned from us oldtimers. And much of it was obtained at these Chicago sessions. . . . A lot of white musicians got ideas and pointers from me but I never really taught anyone how to drum."

During these years, Baby also free-lanced considerably and worked in several bands without his brother. "I had a tremendous variety of experiences playing in Chicago but the only time I had the contract for an outfit was on John's last job." John had had a stroke the year before, and because he was ill, was hired to play just Saturdays and Sundays.

"I was very proud to have him there. I'd seen the time when I first started that he wouldn't even let me sit in the band with him. And after working for him for thirty years, I was able to hire him in an outfit. It was one of the biggest thrills of my musical life."

John died of another stroke in August, 1940. "It was a terrible loss to all of us. We were very close as brothers and as musicians. And, as far as I'm concerned, there never was a clarinet player like my brother played. There just couldn't be another Johnny Dodds or anyone to take his place. And his passing on made a big difference in my life. I had been connected with him for many years and from then on I had to be wholly on my own."

In 1941, Baby worked in Jimmie Noone's quartet. "I never worried," says Baby, "about the instrumentation of any outfit but thought rather of who was in it and what they were doing. You worry about the harmony in the group."

When Bill Russell, the jazz historian, was setting up a band for the resurrected Bunk Johnson in 1944, he asked Baby to record with Bunk in New Orleans. At the time, Baby's health was failing. He had high blood pressure and carried too much weight for his small frame. Baby traveled between Chicago and New Orleans for the recordings, and finally went to New York with Bunk's band to play at the Stuyvesant Casino. It was his first trip to the city, and "I loved it very much."

One phenomenon puzzled him. "When I first went to New York it seemed very strange to have people sitting around and listening rather than dancing. In a way it was peculiar for me because I always felt as though I was doing something for the people if they danced to the music. It never seemed the same when they just sat around and listened. We played for dancing and quite naturally we expected people to dance."

Despite his age and his health, Baby continued to look for more challenging ways of self-expression. "In New York," he told Gara, "I tried different things with my drums that I had wanted to work out for a long time before. I varied my drumming from time to time. One night I would drum one way and the next night a different way. Sometimes I would use the wood block more, and again some nights I would beat more on the cymbal. Some nights I would use the rims and at other times I would put more work on the snare drums. I'd just change it around from time to time. But with my bass drum I always used what Natty Dominique calls my forty-five beat. That is, I always drew up my ankle to about a forty-five-degree slant when I hit the bass drum foot pedal. Some drummers don't bring their feet up high enough and instead of a distinct clear beat they get a rumble effect. But I always wanted a sharp beat whenever I hit that bass drum. And this I did with all the outfits in which I played throughout my whole career."

During the first half of the 'forties, Baby made some recordings with Sidney Bechet (including *Blues for Johnny* on Victor), Bechet-Mezzrow, pianist Tut Soper, Freddie Shayne, Chippie Hill; and in

1945, a session under his own name for Blue Note with Albert Nicholas, Art Hodes and Wellman Braud. "Of course, as leader I felt that it was my place to let everybody else have a showing. By the time my chance came it was all over and the recording was finished. But I didn't care about that. I was interested in being the leader and having my name on the records."

While in New York with Bunk, Baby recorded with the Johnson band for Victor and Decca. He had made some sides in New Orleans before for Rudi Blesh's Circle label, and he again recorded for Circle in New York. During a year with Bunk in New York in 1945, Baby sat in at Nick's and Condon's despite Bunk's instructions that his men not jam with other groups. After that year, Baby returned to Chicago for six months, and then returned to New York.

In 1947, he appeared on Rudi Blesh's Mutual radio "This Is Jazz Series," and made other records. His recording activity in these years, since it often involved New Orleans musicians and songs of his childhood, often pleased Baby greatly. He was not in good health; he was nonetheless drinking; and music was the main fulfillment he had left that couldn't hurt him too much. His quick flexibility and musical intelligence remained. When experimentalist dancer Merce Cunningham asked Baby to play for a dance recital of his during this period, Baby fulfilled his needs successfully. "It was just like playing a show; when you've played one show you've played them all."

Baby worked at Jimmy Ryan's for a while, went to France as part of a group led by Mezz Mezzrow in 1948, later that year worked with the Art Hodes trio, then to Chicago with Miff Mole. Back in New York in April, 1949, Baby had his first stroke. He couldn't play for a long time, but gradually returned to work in New York with the encouragement of Conrad Janis. His second stroke came in 1950.

"Of course, as soon as I got well enough, I wanted to play again." He did a series of concerts with Natty Dominique in Chicago in 1951 but couldn't drum for the whole evening. To help Baby, Natty billed the band as one that played "Slow drag" music so that there would be plenty of slow numbers for Baby to play.

He had a third stroke in December, 1953. He had been so anxious to play that when the Dixieland Rhythm Kings, a young revivalist band, called him for a job late one night, he went and worked throughout the night. Nervous, he had about a half-dozen drinks, and the stroke hit the next day.

The indomitable Baby has been sitting in whenever he could in recent years—in 1953 in Chicago with Natty Dominique, George Lewis and Lee Collins. As of the beginning of 1957, he was back in Chicago hoping to start a band again.

"I still live for my drums and feel that someday I will come back and play even better than before.

"Lots of ideas have come to me," he ended his dictation to Gara in 1953, "even though I haven't been able to execute them. One of my pet ideas is to write and work out a drum symphony, which would involve five or six drummers all carrying out the ideas of one lead drummer. I've done this with one other drummer and I don't see why a group couldn't do the same thing."

The color and irrepressible vitality of Baby's personality has, of course, been continually projected in his playing. Wrote Bill Russell in *Jazzmen:* "For subtlety of nuances, Baby has never been surpassed, and for obtaining the greatest variety of color and effects from the smallest drum set, he has no equal. In the Hot Seven days, recording engineers put a damper on dynamic drumming; hence we do not get the entire picture of Baby's enormous vitality." Actually the drummer in the 'twenties was usually banished to the far end of the studio, wasn't allowed to use his bass drum, and as a result, often kept on woodblocks to be heard.

It was during the 'twenties that Baby recorded frequently with the Oliver band, with his brother and with Jimmy Blythe, with Louis' Hot Seven, and Jelly Roll Morton's Red Hot Peppers. While it is true, as Russell said, that the extensive recording inadequacies of the 'twenties have left only a dim impression of Baby's variegated strength, feeling for dynamics and sensitivity behind each soloist, it is still possible to hear and feel the pulsation he set and kept going for these groups.

Fortunately he did some recordings in the 'forties, though not always with optimum engineering, even for the time. Two of his most important sessions were his first collection of solos, an idea of Fred Ramsey. He did a set for Disc and one for Circle, both in 1946.

Disc issued with its album a transcript of Baby's conversation on the talking tracks. In Ramsey's prefatory notes, he mentions that Baby "remembers that his grandfather drummed in Congo Square, in the days before any jazz bands had been formed." And Rudi Blesh, in his *Shining Trumpets,* footnoted that Baby said "his maternal great-grandfather played 'African drums' in New Orleans.

This would have been in the mid-nineteenth century. 'He talked on them,' Baby says, and then demonstrates the drum code as it was traditionally preserved in his family."

And a Gara footnote reads: "Baby once heard some records of Haitian drummers and at various times he experimented with African drums. He never considered using such an instrument, beaten with the hands, because he felt that he did not know enough about it. Baby believes his Indian background just as important a factor in his drumming as his Negro background. When asked where he got his idea for the tom-tom solo, he said: 'I believe some of it is in me from my Indian foreparents.' "

But Baby has always thought of himself as a "modern" drummer in that while he recognizes the possible influence of elements in his heritage, he has always been much more concerned with the musical demands of the particular job at the particular time and with his own individual growth as a developer of the language of jazz drums.

In the notes to the Disc solo album, later reissued on Folkways LP, Ramsey wrote: "In equipment as everything else, Baby is individual. His set is chosen for exactly the effects he wants, and there's no other set like it. One example only: he prefers two cymbals, separately mounted on his bass drum, to all mechanical devices, such as the foot-operated cymbal."

On the day of the recording, Baby used:

"One bass drum, originally used by Ben Pollack and presented to Baby in 1938 by Ray Bauduc; one snare drum, with Baby since 1921, and with angora goatskin in the head; three tom-toms: quarter-tone, half-tone, and whole-tone; two cymbals, one large, one small, the large one cost $75 in 1919; one speed pedal; one woodblock; one cowbell quartet that have been with Baby since 1916; one ratchet; one tim-tim; one part 4A drumsticks; one pair padded mauls."

For the session, Baby described a press roll of which he is a master: "It's made up in halves of rolls, two to the measure, and each ties over to the next, and so on. You got to make the left hand make 32 counts, and the right hand 32 counts too. They join in, to fill in the measure. It's a double-up of the four beats to a measure, so fast it joins up as a roll, although actually divided."

And Fred Ramsey described Baby: "When Dodds goes to work on the drum set, his whole body moves into action. His arms cross and uncross, rise and fall as he nicks a cymbal, or woodblock, then taps at the rim or strikes the tom-toms. They change positions as he varies the angle at which the sticks are held, to produce corresponding variations in tone. For the shimmy beat, his loosely hinged stomach wobbles up and down in perfect time while his arms flail at the drumheads. Throughout, a steady beat from his foot sets the tempo. It's a tempo that has worn out half a dozen foot pedals in the past twenty years."

The solos on the 1946 solo sets are consistently absorbing. An equally important collection of Baby Dodds records was made for Bill Russell's American Music label in the nineteen fifties. He demonstrated aspects of his technique and was heard in various instrumental combinations. On *Baby Dodds No. 3,* he talked to Russell about "playing for the benefit of the band":

"Each man has solo, I give him a different beat. It may sound to someone that's listening close by the same, but it's not. I would say it's a different *sound* to it, because I give every man a chance of his opening.

"In other words, like a guy is going to come in, I give him something for him to come in on, and it makes it different from the fellow that's got through. . . . Even if it's piano or trumpet or clarinet, I give some kind of indication that something is coming, and *that* a lot of drummers don't do, because you've got to *think,* and while you're thinking, you have to work with your companion, or work with your band or work with your outfit . . . you got to be thinking all the time.

"When they're thinking about doing something, you got to be thinking something too . . . and I try to make a distinction of some sort into the change so that you know even if the guy don't come in, you know that something come in there . . . and that's the way I play. I play for the benefit of the band."

(To Gara he had said: ". . . the way I tried to drum required a good thinking brain and a sharp ear. And it was always necessary to keep a sense of humor, for God's sake, so that if something didn't sound right I could always change it quickly or insert something else in its place.")

On the American Music record, Baby continued:

"And when I change like that, something else is coming, something different. It's got to be different because I've changed it. And you can feel a change. Even if you don't hear it, you can feel it. It's up to me to make the changes. Those who blow an instrument, they make a change, but it's up to me to give an indication of that. . . . If you just go along and beat, beat, beat right straight on, there's no *indication,* and it don't give you nothing to look forward to . . . it makes it very, very distinct where I do it, and it makes it very lovely for a band . . . but that's what you got to be thinking all the time, what the next person's going to do, who's coming in next. . . .

"It don't mean for you to be louder than the solo; it mean for you to keep down . . . if it's clarinet, you must keep low. A piano, you must keep lower. So these things fellows don't think about. They beat the same way for a clarinet playing or a piano playing. That don't make sense.

"Drums is essential in a band. They're very essential. You got to drum as though they *are* essential. Now that's a study I had to pick up *myself.* No one told me that. No one showed me how. That was just what I had to do, because I do work all the time for my fellow man, I want to see *him* happy same as I. Even if I'm not happy . . . I *want* to see him happy.

"Then when you do that and in conjunction with your band, your people dancing or sitting and listening, they will have a different reaction. Without someone that's drumming thinking about these things, it's no good. They don't want the same beat all the time, and then the band's not got no pep that way.

"And going along with a man blowing an instrument or piano you must follow the phrases and that's why I want to know each time a band starts to playing . . . what they're going to play. That way, if it's a number I don't know, I follow very closely, pay strict attention . . . if it's one I know, well, I know where the phrases come. That's the way I can keep up. A lot of fellows don't think about that.

"A lot of fellows call me old-fashioned because they don't know what I'm doing and if they was good drummers, they wouldn't say I was old-fashioned. They would say that was more up to date than what they're doing today.

"I feel them all out. I work with all of them—guitar, banjo, bass—I work with all of them because they all belong to me. I feel I'm the key man in that band. It's up to me to make all of them feel like playing. Even if it's no more than joking with them. You can joke along with a band and you have some with a grin on their face and still they're blowing and you can pass the word along and somebody will feel good. All that puts spirit.

"In drumming, you have got to pay attention to each, everyone. You must *hear* that person distinctly, and hear what he wants. You got to give it to him. And if he don't like that, give him something else. And that way you keep your band smooth jumping and keep your band lively. . . . You must study a guy's human nature, study about what he will take, or see about what he will go for. All that's in a drum, and that why all guys are not drummers that's drumming. For a fact you got to use diplomacy . . . you got to study up something that will make them work.

"You can't holler at a man. You can't dog him. You can't do that—not in music. It's up to me to keep all that lively. That's *my* job. There's more beside drumming than just drumming. There's more besides drumming than just beating. And it's my job to know what that part is. I got to find it and when I sit down in a band, that is what I hunts for.

"A band is playing in an ensemble, I find the kick to send them off. I find something. Now, unless a drummer can find those things, well, he don't even talk to me as a drummer, because I know he's none. . . . If a band's dead, a drummer can liven up everybody, make everybody have a different spirit. And he can make everybody pretty angry too. And he can have them so they'll be so angry with him but they have to play. So all these things . . . all in all, a drummer's a big factor in a band.

"There's lots of things I've learned, even sitting down, just thinking. . . . I do believe when I ever get back to my drumming, I think I'll be a different drummer than I used to be, because I have a deeper study in mind. Even a spirit study. Now, I know that sounds very funny to a drummer to hear me say spirit. But *drumming is spirit*. You got to have that in your body. In your soul. You got to have it even in your drumming. To go along, you got to have that spirit. And it can't be an evil spirit. It's got to be a good spirit . . . because music is no good if you're evil.

"If you're evil, you're going to drum evil, and when you drum evil, you're going to put evil in somebody else's mind. What kind of band have you got? Nothing but an evil-spirit band.

"Now if the spirit is good, any good spirit will dwell with good spirits. And God help a bad spirit band. They're subject to do anything. They're liable to step on each other's instrument. Anything. Might put limburger cheese on a man's piano. Anything.

"That's what the spirit is that you have to keep up. Well, I worked that so *many* times, Bill, until I just couldn't do anything different now. Of course, I haven't got the spirit of liveliness that I used to have because I'm getting older. But I still have a little bit left.

"So you've got to keep a spirit up. And it's the drummer's job because he's not playing nothing. He hasn't got nothing in his mouth. His job is to keep everybody in good spirits, keep everybody joyful, keep everybody playing, keep everybody's mind on what they're doing. And the changes is still up to you. If you want to make a band play loud, you can make it play loud. You want to make a band play medium soft, you can make it play medium soft. You want to make a band play piano, very soft, you can do that. No band's not going to play and the drum's not doing nothing. They're going to feel there's something wrong. . . .

"If the drummer is beating his head off, he (the musician) is going to blow louder, but if he feels that the drums are soft, he's going to come down too. I think the average young drummer today should feel that his part is to help the other fellow, not make him play himself to death, and not make him play something that he don't want to play. His place is to *help* him, and without help, there's no band. Without a drummer that knows how to help, there's no band."

(Said Sidney Finkelstein in *Jazz: A People's Music:* "The jazz drum, finally, is a social instrument. It has its own role and is, at the same time, part of a group, interplaying with and supporting the other instruments, subtly adjusting its timbres to back and fill out the solos, marking the end of one and introducing another, accenting a climax.")

For Larry Gara, Baby condensed his conception of the drummer's role into one sentence: "In my estimation drums should play according to the melody and still keep time."

In a conversation in New York at the end of 1956, Baby Dodds talked of the drummers he liked: "There was a fellow used to work with Clyde McCoy, I think it was, during the 'thirties. Down Downey. I think he was living in Evanston. He was a great drummer. He could give you some jazz beats and some straight beats. Don't leave Gene Krupa out. He's one of the best, especially way back in 1935. With Goodman he turned commercial and that I didn't appreciate. Don't ever forget Dave Tough and George Wettling. Tough was like a clock. Stick him under a band and he'd make everybody play. Wally Bishop, now in Europe and formerly with Earl Hines, is very good, more of the modernistic style.

"And Chick Webb. I didn't see him very much but he was a steady drummer and he could make an outfit work. Kaiser Marshall for the way he developed the cymbal beat. He would catch them, choke them off and make them ring. A marvelous fellow! He could almost beat a tune on the cymbal and that's not easy to do. Sid Catlett was a very fine drummer. We worked in Nice on the same stand in 1948. He was there with Louis. A very brilliant, lively drummer.

"When I played with Louis, I had to beat much more closed drums. Sid played open. I kept holes closed; he'd keep them open. Another drummer would say he could put a beat in or do something in those holes.

"I had my own style. Now they call me old-style. I remember that *Herald Tribune* concert where we played opposite the modern group. I remember Max Roach because he paid attention. A lot of drummers don't realize what I do. They don't pay attention. They think I do nothing but a press roll. But, for one thing, even a press roll has so many different outlets to it.

"About the need for drumming *for* the band," Baby added. "That applies even while you're taking a solo. So they'll all feel good. And whenever you're drumming, you've got to make something come out of it. You don't want to just drum because there are two sticks in your hand. You have to cue yourself in and cue yourself out.

"Drumming is not easy. I've lost some of my co-ordination. I just can't do the things I used to do. I used to be able to drum all night and all day and felt good about it.

"I remember the exercises I made for myself. I'd try to raise my hands and make them as light as possible; then I'd lower them and make them as heavy as possible. I practiced for years to get my ankle to swing a forty-five-degree angle. My foot was never down. I kept it at an angle all the time, never flat. The strain was on the ankle all the time. It's a life study. Everybody couldn't do it. I used to even beat from my toe when I wanted to beat heavy."

Baby is concerned at what seems to him the growing volume in jazz drumming. "In New Orleans, you could hear each and every instrument. The band would come down so low, you would think it was one man. Even in the street. The sweet part of it is when it is so low. What youngster now is going to play so low you hear it just above a whisper?

"Jazz is played to be loved—like opera. It shouldn't be loud all the way. But a lot of guys have gone commercial. They're not thinking about jazz music. They're thinking about money. We used to play jazz music just because we loved it. We didn't get paid sometimes. In that time, they said it was just Negro music, that there was nothing to it. Now the whole world's on jazz. I guess they found there's something to it."

Baby these days sounds rather negative concerning modern jazz. Part of this may be due to his feeling that too many of the youngsters have either forgotten him or regard him as old-fashioned. But Barry Ulanov in *A History of Jazz in America* remembers a more graphic proof than words of Baby's continuing interest in any jazz that strikes him as honest and imaginative.

"In 1947," writes Ulanov, "as a member of Rudi Blesh's broadcasting band, Baby played in a two-part radio battle of bands opposite a group that I organized. He listened with interest when he wasn't playing, and asked serious and probing questions of the finest of bebop drummers, Max Roach. He complimented not only Max but Charlie Parker, Dizzy Gillespie, Lennie Tristano and Billy Bauer. Much of the time that the modern musicians were playing he just looked up and across the studio at them with a smile on his face and a warm expression in his eyes, as if to say what he later almost put into words, that he was proud to be a musician in the same music, that there was no terrifying differences between the old and the new, that good jazz was good jazz."

Another witness is Jo Jones: "Baby *knows* what drums are supposed to be. And he himself was a pretty fast liver. He never relinquished the idea of living. He did the alphabet of living. The last time I saw him, after his stroke, he said: 'Well, I don't drink as much and naturally, I don't have as many chicks, but I'm still here! Actually, physically, he's about 95. He did more living than three men."

And Mezz Mezzrow, writing in the Sinclair Traill collection, *Concerning Jazz,* published in England: "Baby Dodds, our drummer in Nice in 1948, is a wonderful person, but in his younger days he was a real hellion, and would fight at the drop of a hat. Since he has stopped drumming he has turned into a kind and gentle soul—matured with age I guess. I have no kick against Baby, for on my tour—excepting for the time he threw his suitcase at Sammy Price's head in a hotel lobby—he behaved like a perfect gentleman. . . .

"I have never since, and probably never will again, hear any music more authentically in the real New Orleans jazz idiom than I heard played by that orchestra. Pops Foster and Baby Dodds would take several choruses together, just the bass and drums, and you never saw such a 'carryin' on' in your life. Pops would begin to slap his bass and Baby would start a rhythm going, running his sticks from the wood block to the rim of the bass drum. The swing these two engendered was truly phenomenal! . . . The nuances between the bass and and drumsticks beating from wood blocks to the rims of the drum were amazingly subtle and the syncopations they worked out made you feel good all over. They would begin softly, then work it up to an exciting pitch and come down to steady rhythm, finishing with a lead for the rest of the band to join in. By that time they had all of us waiting with anxiety to join in and play, and that is how it should be."

Another Nice eyewitness, British drummer Eric Delaney, noted with respect that "when that great traditional drummer Baby Dodds was at the Nice Jazz Festival he used to spend at least half an hour before each show tuning his drums to the piano which was being used."

And Natty Dominique, who has played with Baby often, told Larry Gara: "He reads and plays any kind of music . . . with all kinds of music which were handed to us, Baby read and played his part perfectly. . . . There are parts I've had to play on the trumpet that correspond to Baby's part on the snare drum. And more than once Baby Dodds has contradicted me and told me I didn't play a part correctly. And when I ran over it, I saw that he was right, even though I'm a musician myself. I've also seen Baby correct the piano player and other members of the band. . . .

"One night at Burt Kelly's Stables I was amazed to find out how softly Baby could drum. The outfit was off the bandstand and a great violinist named Joe Venuti was on the stand. I came upstairs and found that only the violin and drums were playing and the people were dancing, and liked it. And Baby was playing under the violin. The softer the violin would get, the softer Baby would get, and the rhythm was still there. I'll never forget hearing that as long as I live. . . .

"Baby was always giving the right kind of beat . . . and furthermore Baby Dodds has a rhythm of his own."

An indirect but illuminating tribute to Baby was paid by British jazzman-critic Humphrey Lyttelton during a recent visit of an Eddie Condon unit to Britain: "Listening to George Wettling, who reminds me very much of Baby Dodds when I heard him at Nice, you hear not only an over-all variation in volume from chorus to chorus, but a constant fluctuation in volume, from bar to bar, of each component part—snare drum, cymbal and bass drum."

George Wettling reports finally: "The last time I saw Baby was in the winter of 1956–57 at Condon's after hours. He could hardly hold a pair of sticks. Yet he looked fine. And he was in great spirits."

SELECTED DISCOGRAPHY—BABY DODDS

King Oliver, Epic 12″ LP LN 3208(1923).

Louis Armstrong and his Hot Seven, Columbia 12″ LP ML 54384 (also CL-852) (1927).

Johnny Dodds and Kid Ory, Epic 12″ LP LN 3207. Baby is on the six Johnny Dodds numbers (1926).

Johnny Dodds, Riverside 12″ LP RLP 12-104. Baby Dodds is on two numbers (1927).

Johnny Dodds' Washboard Band, Label "X" 10″ LP LX-3006. Baby Dodds is on four numbers (1929).

Jelly Roll Morton and Johnny Dodds: The Early Jazz Greats No. 2, Jazztone Society 12″ LP J1252 (1926–29).

Jelly Roll Morton's Red Hot Peppers, Vol. 2, Label "X" 10″ LP LVA-3028. Baby Dodds is on five numbers, including two trio tracks, one of which is heard in two different takes (1927).

New Orleans Jazz, Decca 12″ LP DL 8283. Baby Dodds is on two tracks under Johnny Dodds' name (1940).

American Music by George with Kid Shots, American Music 10″ LP 645 (1944).

New Orleans Revival: Bunk Johnson and Kid Ory, Riverside 10″ LP RLP 1047. Baby Dodds is on the four Bunk Johnson numbers (1945).

Echoes of New Orleans, Blue Note 10″ LP 7013. Contains one number, *Winin' Boy Blues,* recorded originally under Baby Dodds' name with Albert Nicholas, Art Hodes and Wellman Braud (1945).

Out of the Back Room, Blue Note 10″ LP 7021. Contains two numbers with the same personnel, *Careless Love* and *Feelin' at Ease* (1945).

American Music by Bunk Johnson: Blues and Spirituals, American Music 10″ LP 638 (1946).

This Is Jazz: The All-Star Stompers, Circle 10″ LP L 402 (label now extinct) (1947).

Wild Bill Davison with All-Star Stompers, Riverside 10″ LP RLP 2514, 1947. Baby Dodds is also on five numbers of *Wild Bill Davison,* Riverside 12″ RLP 12-211 (1947).

Baby Dodds: Talking and Drum Solos, Folkways 10″ LP FP 30 (1946).

Baby Dodds No. 1, American Music 10" LP. Baby Dodds "demonstrates the tone qualities of his set . . . further illustrations with Bunk Johnson 1945 New Orleans Band." Baby talks about New Orleans parades and plays snare drum with Bunk's nine-piece brass band. "Then Baby describes 'funeral processions' with further illustrations."

Baby Dodds No. 2, American Music 10" LP. Tom-tom solo from the early 40s; Art Hodes trio; and Natty Dominique's Creole Band (1953).

Baby Dodds No. 3, American Music 10" LP. Baby Dodds talks about "playing for the benefit of the band" (much of which is quoted in the chapter); "demonstration of cymbals, tim-tim, cowbells, ratchet"; Baby Dodds sings the blues with Bunk Johnson's 1945 band; *My Maryland, New Orleans March* (1944).

Natty Dominique and his New Orleans Hot Six, Windin' Ball Recordings 10" LP 104 (1954).

NOTE: American Music LPs can be obtained from Paul Steiner, 1637 N. Ashland Avenue, Chicago 22, Illinois. Windin' Ball Recordings: 5207 South Kimbark Avenue, Chicago 15, Illinois.

Louis Armstrong

* * * *

By George Avakian

It is entirely possible that the encyclopedias of the future will identify jazz simply as a semi-improvised music of the twentieth century, developed and popularized by American musicians, and perhaps they will say that in both respects the most noteworthy contributor and exponent was Louis Armstrong.

Similar telescopings and oversimplifications have taken place in the histories of other minor arts. Despite the expansions of jazz in the past fifteen years, Armstrong remains the most outstanding figure in its over-all development, and on a world-wide basis he is the most popular personality the field has ever known.

The scope of Armstrong's accomplishments is such that one chapter in this anthology cannot cover it properly. But a brief review of his contributions to jazz can serve as a reference, assessing the present position of this man, who, in his fifty-seventh year, has become the strongest single international symbol of jazz.

Louis Armstrong was born in the right time and place: in 1900 in the tough uptown Negro section of New Orleans. In his childhood years he heard the musicians who were the first to play what our ears would recognize as the origins of jazz. Louis's friendly, outgoing personality as well as his semi-tutored playing brought him to a favored position under the wing of Joe "King" Oliver, greatest of the New Orleans cornetists of the World War I period. Poppa Joe eventually brought Louis to Chicago where, at the age of twenty-two, Armstrong embarked on the most fabulous career that any American musician has ever known.

Within two years, Louis was playing the most exciting, powerful and original solo style of jazz improvisation yet to be heard. His fellow musicians quickly recognized his ability, and even the public, in a limited way, realized that this was an extraordinary talent. Louis's audience was confined at first to the Negro record public,

49

primarily in the Northern cities (although he also enjoyed good sales in the South, but again mostly in the urban areas), and the habitués of the clubs where he worked in his first jobs. There was no other means of reaching and developing a following in those days.

On records, Armstrong produced between 1925 and 1932 a body of work which was a primer to a whole generation of musicians. In person, he emerged as the first band leader to be a complete artistic personality as well; he played, sang, and took an active part in floor and stage shows wherever he appeared.

He was the most daring, skillful and impassioned of all improvisers. They didn't use the expression then, but he "swung" more than anyone else; again and again an otherwise dull performance would flash to life when Louis blew a solo, even if for only eight bars.

As an innovator, he tossed off fresh ideas which—spread by his recordings—became *the* clichés; out of them grew still other bits of good music (often by Louis himself), which in turn again became familiar to everyone in jazz. Eventually the popular music business came to know the ideas that Louis had thought of first, although often without recognizing the source.

Louis developed a whole school of jazz singing, based on a literal interpretation of the folk and blues singers' approach to the voice as an instrument. Louis showed that the emotional meaning of a lyric can be expressed through vocal inflections and improvisations of a purely instrumental quality just as effectively—more so, in fact—as through words. This line of development paralleled the growth of his instrumental influence. It still embraces every jazz and popular singer today.

Sometimes the line is sharply, though incongruously, clear. About a year ago, a veteran Miami club singer who had achieved no particular success suddenly skyrocketed to a short-lived but intense television and nightery fame on the strength of a close (though twistedly exaggerated) imitation of the vocal of Louis's twenty-five-year-old recording of *Lazy River*. Even Elvis Presley fans might find it rewarding to compare their hero's *Hound Dog* to the way Louis sang *Hobo, You Can't Ride This Train* on a record of similar vintage.

Louis has never stopped working before the public since he left New Orleans, but his career has had its ups and downs, mostly as the music business itself has gone through various stages that have affected jazz musicians as a class. By the nineteen thirties, he had achieved a limited success in his own country—limited both by the boundaries of the jazz field and the prejudice against Negro performers which has always kept them out of the biggest and most lucrative jobs. His reputation in Europe, however, approached the phenomenal.

Phonograph records were responsible. The American companies had exchange agreements with European labels. However, except in England, the pop songs which formed the bulk of the American catalogues were almost worthless because of the language barrier. Louis, as a trumpet player of striking qualities and a singer who barely used language at all, was highly importable—all the more so because post World War I Europe welcomed things that were basic and things that were different. Jazz was certainly both, and it was also American, which made it admirable in the special, mixed way that America fascinated intellectual Europe in those years.

It was the European press that first took American jazz seriously, although some of the early appreciations were more enthusiastic than discerning. Unfettered by the heavy chaff of radio and the popular music business, Europeans heard the best of jazz through the releases of a record industry that chose its American-made releases with an ear for exciting instrumental music rather than the most popular songs. When Louis went to Europe for the first time in 1932, he found the most wildly enthusiastic acceptance that any American performer had ever experienced.

Yet in this same period, Louis found his American career sharply limited to a few pointedly "black and tan" night clubs, theatres (usually in the Negro districts of large cities), and one-night stands—mostly through the South. He had the first network radio show ever given to a Negro artist, but lack of sponsorship killed it quickly. It was apparent that all the commercial radio shows, as with all the best "location" jobs in hotels and top night clubs, would go to white artists. This is as basically true in 1957 as it was a generation ago, although the edges have been chipped in many places by singers like Nat Cole, Lena Horne and Harry Belafonte.

The rising cost of "road" travel often trimmed Louis's accompanying band from thirteen to five in the early 'forties, but this proved ultimately to be the foundation of his greatest success. He went back to his roots and played in a sort of neo-Hot Five style, dusting off much of the old repertoire in the process. The quality of the sextet which he has since featured has varied greatly through the years, but his own playing and singing has maintained a high level, and the innate showmanship which developed gradually from his Chicago days blossomed to full proportion in the 'forties. Honed by an occasional appearance in a Hollywood musical, Louis soon became an entertainer who could have laid down his trumpet for keeps and still have made a good living. He is, within the limitations of his field, a great comedian, and he probably could have been a great actor. As it is, he plays in public a part which is based on his true personality, that of an enthusiastic, happy and elemental jolly-good-fellow, and he does it very well indeed.

Until recently, the American public has not given to Louis the idolatry that it has bestowed on others in the field of popular jazz. Actually, only two musicians before Louis have sustained an extremely high level of popularity for any length of time; both were white dance-band leaders, and one of them had so little to do with jazz that it is only politeness and the desire to set up a measuring stick that persuades one to mention him at all. (That, of course, is Glenn Miller, who was popular enough before he died, but whose posthumous fame was a unique phenomenon until James Dean piled up his sports car.) The other, Benny Goodman, never abandoned jazz, although sometimes the percentage of pay dirt dropped rather low.

Musicians recognized Louis as the master almost from the start; his coming to New York in 1924 to join Fletcher Henderson at the Roseland Ballroom was the real beginning of his influence on his compatriots. When he finally began to make an impression on the great bulk of the American public, it was not so much as the most important single figure jazz has ever known; it was much more as the most lovable and amusing personality the field has produced. This did not, of course, prevent the people who presented him in the latter capacity from cloaking themselves in the role of honoring Armstrong the musician while cashing in on Armstrong the entertainer. Nor should we scorn those who have done this; one has become part of the other, and Armstrong himself scarcely separates them.

In the period when "swing" became a household word, and Benny Goodman was catapulted to fame by leading a band which might have been described as "every man playing in the Armstrong style," Louis chugged along as he had before, leading a large band (usually on the road). The swing era touched Armstrong—the one person who had contributed most to what the public went for—

only in that bookings were easier and better because of the increase of interest in his kind of music. The emphasis on his personality had not yet begun; Louis was far better known for his pyrotechnical skill as a trumpeter than for his singing, mugging and emceeing.

His development as a public personality did not actually start on a large scale until the 'forties. His motion-picture appearances presaged his acceptance by a wide public, and obviously it was the rubbery, chop-shaking comedy that had the greatest appeal to John Q. So it was that Louis was sharpening his God-given gift for reaching out to every last person in the house when suddenly the jazz revolution exploded, giving birth to bop and creating a cleavage that all but cut off the influence Armstrong had exerted since the middle 'twenties on every jazz musician who thereafter drew breath. The two events were not related, however. In fact, in retrospect it seems surpising that Armstrong was so far removed from the thoughts of the revolutionaries who were, without realizing it, overthrowing his teachings of two decades. Perhaps it was because Louis was so much in the background of the swing era; he was acknowledged as the source of it all (if any one man could be called that), but otherwise he was little more than the leader of a second-flight band, getting along and occasionally being given a chance to work up his show-business personality in a movie or on an out-and-out commercial recording. (There was always some great trumpet blowing and fine singing on those records, nonetheless).

When Louis gave up his big band once and for all in 1947, he returned to the New Orleans format of three horns and three rhythm. This meant that he played more than before, but he also turned on the charm and built up the comic aspect of his personality. His vocal duets with Velma Middleton on *That's My Desire* and *Baby, It's Cold Outside* gave him a greater opportunity to expand his gift of comedy than he had ever enjoyed in the past, even with Bing Crosby on the Paramount lot. He had become a top concert and club attraction by the time he made his real bid for world fame in 1955.

The way was paved a year earlier by the proof that the Old Man was still the greatest when he recorded the "Armstrong Plays Handy" album. This was a miraculous blending of material and performer in which everything came out perfectly; it demonstrated for the first time in many years what a warm, ingratiating and communicative artist Louis was when he was presented in the proper way. It was a sensation among the American jazz fans, but in Europe it was a sensation with a still larger public; as in the pre-war period, the European companies were again releasing jazz as a sort of international currency, and the percentage of jazz sales in the total European record market had risen to new heights.

On the wings of this success on records, Armstrong went to Europe in the fall of 1955, just as he had done several times since his first triumphal trip, but this time a new excitement was in the air. Armstrong had finally become a major personality in Europe; an artist who did not have to be identified as the greatest jazz musician any more; he was known instantly by name in every level of European society. His triumph was complete when Felix Belair, a *New York Times* correspondent covering the four-power conference at Geneva that October, wrote a story about how much more Louis was accomplishing for world understanding (and sympathy to the United States) with his trumpet and gravel voice than all our diplomats put together. It landed on the front page of the Sunday *Times*. At the same time, Ed Murrow was filming the tour for a special report on CBS television; it was shown in December, 1955, and Louis was made as a top commercial attraction in his homeland at last. (That TV film has since been expanded into a feature for theatres, and the expectation is that it will be the most internationally popular documentary ever made).

As always, there are bad things with the good when an artist gets into the big chips. Louis has long been content to sit in a comfortable groove. Musically, he has fallen into the easy way of repetition and has resisted changes in his repertoire to such a degree that except for *Mack the Knife,* which Turk Murphy generously arranged for him, Louis is playing the same program which has served him for at least five years. His solos have become rather fixed in content. Novelty instrumentals and vocals have become the basic keynote of Louis's show—and it has, indeed, come to be a routined show that the public sees wherever Louis performs.

The result has been a slick stage presentation which has won incredible acclaim for Louis throughout the world. A new debate has arisen as a result; is it a good thing or bad that people everywhere are being won over to the idea of "spontaneous American jazz," with all its beauties and excitement, through performances of a repetitive, set nature, freely laced with comedy?

I don't profess to know the answer, but the winning over seems to be impossible to achieve on such a large scale in any other way. Jazz of a more representative nature—in spirit as well as content

—would certainly be far less successful than Louis has been in winning friends for the whole of American jazz. The more recent forays into the East by the big bands of Dizzy Gillespie and Benny Goodman could scarcely be said to be more typical of jazz than Louis's group. The small ensemble alone is an argument in Louis's favor; reports indicate that Dizzy's tour show was, if anything, even more gimmicked than Louis's comic routines; Benny and his band are even more limited in scope than Louis and Dizzy. Jazz is a big subject. A troupe of four contrasting groups would be able to cover most of its spectrum acceptably, but even the best possible one-night show would not do the job with anything near completeness, and it would have much less impact and success than Louis can accomplish by sheer force of personality and brilliance of showmanship. Uninitiated audiences—domestic as well as foreign—find it easier to attach to one person, and have proven to be quite capable as well as eager to equate Louis with jazz; which is another way of saying that, like it or not, Louis Armstrong remains our best musical ambassador to the world. And I would go so far as to say, with Mr. Belair, that he is the best ambassador this country has ever had, Benjamin Franklin's celebrated success notwithstanding.

But let us look, for a moment, at the musical objections that have been raised as Louis achieved the most dangerous thing (in the eyes of some of his fellows) that anyone can achieve—success. On the subject of repetition, both as to repertoire and as to the content of his solos within that rather rigid repertoire, one must confess that this has become a standard practice in the jazz field. George Wein, proprietor of the Storyville night club in Boston and producer of the Newport Jazz Festival, sounded off with courageous clarity on this very point during one of the 1956 Festival panel discussions.

"It's far more prevalent than the public—and even musicians —realize," he said, "but as a night-club operator I know at first hand how many bands do exactly the same thing every night, down to the solos." Referring specifically to Dizzy Gillespie's recent engagement, Wein said, "If you heard his solos the first time, you'd have sworn they were completely spontaneous. But they were all worked out and repeated every night, down to the last little turn. I could tell without looking at my watch what time it was, because every night the tunes were played in the same order on every set."

Wein did point out, however, that there are some things which have become accepted standards in jazz, such as the King Oliver solo of three choruses in a row on *Dippermouth Blues,* or the still older Picou solo on *High Society*. Each is a model solo which has yet to be improved upon, so that from the point of view of quality as well as tradition, neither should be appreciably altered. The fine British trumpet player, Humphrey Lyttelton, concluded that "When Armstrong has achieved such perfectly constructed and powerfully expressive variation on *Indiana* and *The Gypsy* as those we heard at his concerts" (Lyttelton became keenly interested in this question of improvisation in the course of hearing twenty-two Armstrong concerts during Louis's 1956 tour—more hours of Louis on-stage than most of us have taken in a lifetime) "only a lunatic would suggest that, having achieved perfection, he should rub out and start again."

Another aspect of this matter, as Lyttelton also points out, is that of showmanship. Louis maintains—as do Gillespie and many other jazzmen—a rigorous standard for himself. He'll get up there for the high one in his patterned routine every time, no matter how beat the chops may be, rather than fake a chorus without it which also has a chance of being of lesser quality. "I'll bet," Lyttelton concludes, "that the lesson was learnt, not from any agent or manager, but from Joe Oliver and the other New Orleans masters."

There is a definite implication here that Louis has a primary interest in pleasing his audiences. No artist can make a living without doing that, but there are ways and other ways of accomplishing this necessary end. Certainly it would seem that after a few years of performing essentially the same program, Louis would feel that his fans would like to hear something else. Why, then, is it that year after year, his programs almost never change (including the solos, in many instances)—and yet his audiences increase?

The answer is so simple that few people seem to realize what it is. Louis just keeps reaching out to more people all the time. And unfortunately, most of the new fans are ignorant and undiscriminating.

Speaking for many of Louis's staunchest fans as well as myself, I would like to hear Louis do more "fresh" repertoire like *Mack the Knife* and *West End Blues,* both of which are becoming staples in his present concert repertoire, but were definitely not until the beginning of 1956. (The latter revival still appears only occasionally.) But until Louis feels a need to change repertoire, there is little reason to expect that this will happen. On the artistic level, Louis obviously prefers the comfortable, old-slippers feel of running through the same routines to having to work on new tunes. How long he can feel he is sharpening his talent "in depth" is something only he can answer. Meanwhile only a small minority of his older fans and a few members of the trade press seem to be aware that the Old Master is opening every show with two full choruses of *When It's Sleepy Time Down South,* followed by *Indiana, The Gypsy,* and so on through *Tin Roof Blues, Bucket's Got a Hole in It,* and the various solo specialty numbers, including the inevitable same four songs with Velma Middleton. Only clarinetist Edmond Hall, a relatively recent entrant in the band, has shown real effort to vary his choruses, while Trummy Young and especially Billy Kyle continue to take the easy path behind Louis.

The changes will take place only when the cash customers stop turning out in droves to hear this same show. It is not likely to happen in Louis's lifetime. Meanwhile, jazz has benefited by this paradoxical situation, so it would seem best to accept anything Louis and anyone else can get for jazz in the way of broader appreciation, and if, along the way, greater sympathy to the country of its origin is generated, we are all the luckier and should be that much more grateful. It probably will be a long time before the United States will again have a Secretary of State of the intelligence and integrity of Dean Acheson, so it behooves us all to take delight in the accomplishments of Ambassador Satch.

In the long view of jazz history (if a history so brief can be termed long in any way), it would seem clear that any spread in the appreciation and even understanding of jazz has been on the basis of compromise. Today, everyone speaks of Benny Goodman as a potent force in popularizing jazz in the 'thirties. Yet I remember with uncomfortable clarity that in those years the jazz fans like myself—and certainly the public—regarded Benny primarily as a dance-band leader. True, he played "swing," and was considered acceptable on the fringe of the inner circle, but it was not merely semantics that persuaded us to reserve the word "jazz" for Duke Ellington and Muggsy Spanier and Sidney Bechet and Louis Armstrong—especially the out-of-print Armstrong on records.

But no matter. Every time the cause of jazz is advanced, in whatever guise, another deserving jazz musician gets a week's work. That's enough to satisfy this observer that Louis has done his job in making the world jazz-conscious, late in a career which has also included the almost-forgotten detail of having been the greatest internal influence for its own healthy development that jazz has ever known. Let audiences all over the world applaud Louis the great showman; our tight little crowd will be grateful that, whether they know it or not, they also honor Louis the great pioneer, Louis the great teacher, and Louis the great artist.

SELECTED DISCOGRAPHY—LOUIS ARMSTRONG

Young Louis Armstrong, Riverside 12-101
The Louis Armstrong Story, Vols. 1-4, Columbia CL 851-854
Louis Armstrong Plays W.C. Handy, Columbia CL 591
Louis Armstrong Sings the Blues, Victor LJM 10005

Jack
Teagarden

* * * *

By Charles Edward Smith

"I started up to see Bud Freeman, but I lost my way
An' I thought for a minute I was on the road for M C A."
—*Jack Hits The Road,* Columbia CL 6107

Jack Teagarden has been hitting the road since about the age of seven when he walked out on some of his old man's bad notes. He didn't get far, only to the next room, but you might say that that was the beginning of an odyssey. Another significant incident occurred when he was a youngster, studying music. He had heard blues and spirituals and was going off in a way all his own when his music teacher admonished him with creditable severity, to return to the beaten track. That was the hardest thing in the world for him to do and, fortunately for us, he didn't.

He is a big man, generally amiable and occasionally moody, with dark eyes and a lazy smile. The laziness is completely disingenuous, reminding one of the friendly panther who, in the interests of a high-protein diet, had just swallowed the Cheshire cat.[1] He doesn't flaunt his background, and perhaps that's what makes him a real Texan, blood brother to the hard-drinking, hard-living pioneers.

Weldon John Teagarden was born August 20, 1905, in Vernon, not far from the Red River Valley where the oxcart wagon trains of the early settlers came in from the east and only a matter of miles from the famous Red River crossing on the Chisholm Trail. But that most famous of the dozen or so cattle trails that snaked north out of Texas was marked, if at all, only by a thinner growth of grass and bush by the time Jack was growing up and the family had moved to Oklahoma. By then the oil fields were roaring with

[1] Who had just swallowed the canary trained at great expense to sing *The Eyes of Texas.*

59

life and he spent some time working around them. He was fascinated
with tools and machinery and before long he had a lifetime avoca-
tion, an unflagging interest in things mechanical, from power tools
to Stanley steamers.

But not a career. That was laid out for him when his mother,
who was of Pennsylvania Dutch background, gave him piano lessons at age five and when, at seven, his father presented him at
Christmas with his first trombone. By the time he was sixteen he
was with Peck Kelly's Bad Boys, and in 1924, when he worked in
Mexico with R. J. Marin's Original Southern Trumpeters, he was
billed as "The South's Greatest Trombone Wonder." He has always
been close in feeling to New Orleans musicians, who took their
pet name from an alligator named Al (who, when he smoked his
foul pipe—probably thrown overboard by Sam Clemens—blew up
a fog on the Mississippi). They got to call Jack *Mr. T.,* and *Jackson,*
and sometimes they called him *Big Gate,* after old Al.

With the Teagardens, you might say that the whole family was
musical, even though Dad was a trifle on the square side. Not too
long ago, out on the Coast, there was a musical reunion with Jack's
mother and his sister Norma both playing pianos, Charlie ("Little
Gate") on trumpet and Clois on drums. When Jack was a kid, his
father played trumpet and baritone horn but, says George Hoefer,
Jr.—that knowledgeable man about records and jazz personalities
—"with so many clinkers that two months after Jack got his Christmas trombone he refused to play duets with the old man but instead ran into the next room covering his ears with his hands and
shouting, 'first valve, first valve!' " [2]

While still in grammar school he was allowed to join the high-
school orchestra. The first thing he learned on the road to fame
and fortune was that his horn was pitched too high and that he had
to start all over. George Hoefer snatched for posterity a teacher's
ambiguous comment from its fast flight to oblivion. "I can't teach
that lad anything," was what she said.

"He used to sit on a fence," wrote George, "listening to the
music of the Negroes at Holy Roller meetings. Their spirituals and
blues fascinated him, and he began to apply the blues phrases to
his trombone playing." No doubt he also heard many an early
jazz trombone, born to blow unrecorded, during those early years
when (to quote myself) "he barnstormed around Texas, often without a barn to call his own." At any rate, by the time he got to work

[2] *Down Beat,* March 9, 1951.

with Peck Kelly, from all accounts, he sang and played horn with a Western drawl and a fast, Western draw. At one time during those early years he was romancing a switchboard sweetie. The long-lines operators co-operated in conveying messages and, for themselves, maintained a lively interest in developments. Once they were reduced to biting their fingernails when Jack failed to keep in touch. On that occasion, he'd got lost in the wide open spaces, no Texas rangers or telephones in sight and not even the smell of oil to guide him back to civilization.

At the age of fifteen he was working the roadhouse, honky-tonk circuit with a four-piece unit, which gives you a fair idea of where and why his schooling terminated. He was at the Horn Palace in San Antonio (the band had Terry Shand on piano) when three toughs, who hadn't been told that the days of Sam Bass were long gone, shot up the joint and the boss "who got seven slugs." [3] They were told to stick around and testify but, happily for them, a flood inundated the courthouse; the legal papers in the case got lost and the boys did likewise, fast.

Jack made his way to Galveston where he joined Peck Kelly's Bad Boys. "Peck Kelly played better piano than anyone I'd heard," Jack told Len Guttridge.[4] In later years Peck seemed to be a hard man to pin down. One critic may have antagonized him—at a time when *Jack* was recognized as a top jazz trombonist—by writing that *Peck* was playing typical cocktail lounge music at a place in Houston. Len Guttridge wanted to interview him but, unfortunately, was himself ill on his day in Houston, though he'd been assured that Peck would see him. Said Len, "His phone remains disconnected and he won't answer mail. Last I heard, his sight had just about gone."

"By now," wrote Len Guttridge, "Teagarden had discovered the strange blues flavor which the combination of trombone and water glass could produce. The sound became forever associated with him." [5] In his early years, and on such recordings as *Makin' Friends,* he simply took his horn apart and used an ordinary water glass as a mute on the unattached end of the mouthpiece half of his horn. Recently he has used a professional-looking cup-shaped job that he probably made himself.

While with Peck Kelly during 1921–1922, Jack made a trip to

[3] Hoefer.
[4] *Melody Maker,* London, December 1, 1956.
[5] *Op. cit.*

New Orleans to find a clarinet player for the band. Hoefer reveals that it was on this occasion that he first heard Louis Armstrong—the man who has had the greatest influence in the history of jazz—playing on the upper deck of a river boat off Canal Street. They met then and there, in the home city of jazz, and have matched horns in marvelous music, off and on, ever since, in jam sessions, on records, and finally, in 1947 and until 1951, on road tours here and abroad, with Louis Armstrong's All-Stars.

With Peck Kelly at that time were three jazzmen—Pee Wee Russell, Rappolo and Teagarden—who were to contribute to developments in jazz that, while related to Dixieland, and often interestingly so, were even more significant as establishing once more, vital and living contacts with the bloodline of jazz (Armstrong, Oliver, Keppard, Bunk, Bolden), which was, after all, what the Dixieland musicians had done in the days when they worked with Jack Laine before they branched out on their own. In some bands of well-intentioned young musicians during the revival of early styles in the 1940's, a too-faithful hewing to the Original Dixieland Jazz Band line achieved neither the interesting angularity of that group (which, on some numbers, was more staccato than swing) nor the rhythmic thrust of King Oliver.

In jazz, to borrow a distinction made in another field by the talented American designer, Elizabeth Hawes ("Fashion Is Spinach"), there is style and, since it is related to both folk and popular music, there is fashion. The essence of jazz is not in the blue notes—these often, but not always, indicate the presence of jazz or blues—nor in fact in anything that can be written down and played by rote. When one says that it is, in effect, an improvised music, the conclusion might sensibly be that this refers to the melody alone, or the melodic line in relation to the chords on which it is based. However, in jazz, improvisation begins—for the blowing instruments—with the breath, the vibrato; and breath and blowing combine to manipulate—always sensitive to certain canons of unwritten tradition—the tone itself, the rhythm and the instrumental timbre. Some jazzmen have been so from their earliest beginnings, and among them Jack Teagarden is outstanding.

When popular bands imitated jazz, particularly in the nineteen twenties, they pounced upon its most familiar and least unique aspects. The hot musicians called them "ricky-tick," for their plodding ploppity-plop rhythms and cornball tricks of intonation (which escaped jazz intonation by a narrow, bridgeless chasm). Yet, because of the close relationship of rhythmic conventions to dance steps, the hot musicians, masters of style though they were, shared with the Mickey Mouse artists something of this pandering to rhythmic and melodic fashion. All the more so because hot jazz furnished the root music for the bona fide dance steps, close to folk art, that in turn inspired ballroom conventions—from the Bolden band playing for the *free steps* and the cakewalk in the Quadrille to Cootie Williams playing for Rock and Roll at Harlem's Savoy ballroom. (In Chicago, that toddlin' town, they toddled, the lucky ones did, to King Oliver and Louis, to the Rhythm Kings and Rappolo; in St. Louis, as elsewhere noted, they did the Charleston to Bix and Pee Wee; at Roseland in New York, they danced *cake*—tight and cool style—or *collegiate*—real gone rococo—to Fletcher, Red Nichols, Mr. T.; and all over the map and to any number of jazz bands, they did the Lindy Hop.) This is why, when you listen to old jazz records, you often listen to the fashion of the times, the then-popular treatment of tone and rhythm, as well as the style (that worships the beat and wrestles with it at the same time). Some benighted souls have only an ear and a memory for the musical spinach. In Hollywood they seldom show a proper appreciation of either. And though nowadays thousands of musicians have a working knowledge of jazz, surprisingly few, considering the many who play it, have a deeply ingrained sense of style. And no arrangements, no assortment of well-learned *licks,* can substitute for a sound, blues-oriented jazz technique.

Jack has been chided sometimes by critics for a sentimental streak, as well as a sort of maverick genius on trombone. This is liable to show, perhaps, when he does not work too hard on a number, when he is, as they say, coasting, making an honest buck, come what may. No one is always at his best and, with Jack, the soft spot of sentiment is part of his mental make-up; without it, the vocal masterpieces, which are the opposite of *schmaltz,* just wouldn't come through. Though some of the more cynically disposed may not like it that way, jazz—as Nick LaRocca and many other musicians have remarked—is from the heart. The great danger to a present-day vocalist is that he might be ill-advisedly "packaged" out of his métier and learn the hard way about square pegs and round holes. One suspects that Jack's good sense would prevent such a catastrophe. Remembering such lighthearted foolishness as *The*

Waiter and the Porter and the Maid Upstairs [6] with Mary Martin
and Bing Crosby, the odd thing is that more use hasn't been made of
Jack's real and very versatile talents. As Hoagy Carmichael remarked, "He is one of the best things that has ever appeared on the
popular music scene. A warm and honest talent like Jack's is a rare
thing indeed."

When a concert pianist is influenced by commercial considerations—which influence us all—that nasty word is seldom used. Instead we learn that he has an unusual flair for *bravura* pieces or
that he is especially adept at resurrecting the soul of Schumann. Also,
to be commercial in the classics is, generally speaking, more in line
with one's esthetic aims (which are colored by nonesthetic needs
anyway) and implies not so much a misuse of musical gifts as an
adroit exploitation of them.

The *hot* musician is in a slightly more difficult predicament.
Not only must he stand in some relationship to what is currently
popular (which may or may not coincide with his personal taste),
he is often asked to play or record numbers about which, to put it
bluntly, he couldn't care less. Few jukeboxes are serviced by the
actual tastes of a locality, except in a most general and haphazard
fashion. Radio disc jockeys have one eye on *Cash Box* record rat-
ings, are harassed and flattered and sometimes flummoxed by pro-
moters of this or that band or singer, and often disdain pieces
of more than two or three minutes' duration. (Oftentimes the bartender or the candy-store owner leaves it to the jukebox serviceman
to fill the slots; this contributes to a sort of mass-media approach
to popular taste—reported, it must be said, quite honestly, in a
statistical fashion, by *Cash Box*—and reflected in the tendency of
most disc jockeys to play only a pittance of the many really fine jazz
records issued month after month.) There are exceptions, happily,
but as Jack expressed it in an interview with John Tynan [7]
". . . they could do a lot to help jazz—all kinds—if once in a
while they played a good jazz record.

"For me, especially, this would be important," he went on.
"I'm bending over backwards these days trying to please the peo-
ple with my kind of music, but I don't know if I'm reaching them.
It's frustrating trying to fit yourself into this new world of music.
You feel so insecure in what you're playing."

[6] Decca: from a movie sound track.
[7] *Down Beat*, March 6, 1957.

Long before coming to New York, Jack made it out to the West Coast with Doc Ross and His Cowboy Band. They were supposed to make a grand entry into San Diego. Saddle horses were waiting for them when they got off the train. The musical cowhands weren't too happy about that, being more accustomed to barstools than saddles, but they managed to mount and, luckily for them, no riders of the range were around to give them the horselaugh. As for the horses themselves, they were as nervous as Boppists at a Dixieland jam session. When the band let out a blast of Texas music, the horses promptly dumped the band members, one horse neatly tossing the drummer into his bass drum.

Carson Robison is a good friend of Jack's, and has been for more than thirty years, though possibly the only jazz record Carson is listed as working on is the Hoagy Carmichael disc [8] on which Bix played cornet and Jack and Hoagy sang *Rockin' Chair*. (Probably that should be revised to read: *the only one listed in Discography;* it seems to me I've heard him with some small recording groups of the nineteen twenties.) Be that as it may, Jack looks back upon the days with Robison as a happy period, and one that seasoned his style. Frankie Trumbauer had planned to have Jack in his outfit in St. Louis (1926) but local union rules prevented it and, after staying with his friend Pee Wee Russell over night, he left the next day for Indiana.

Working in a band that had Wingy Mannone on trumpet during that Southwest period, Jack found himself in the company of a New Orleanian who could, when he wanted to, toss off a whacky vocal; who was, like himself, an admirer of Louis, and who was also an entertaining guy to have around. Jack had begun to tote Louis's records in his trombone case. He listened to Louis by the hour and tried to match his ease of phrasing.

George Hoefer notes that, although not a bop musician, Jack made bop possible for trombone, handling the quick changes with the ease of a skilled trumpet player (a fact testified to by top modern trombonists as well, *e.g.*, Kai Winding). And this came, above all, from listening and learning from Louis on *Cornet Chop Suey, Muskrat Ramble* and other records, most of them now in the Columbia LP series, *The Louis Armstrong Story*. Said Hoefer: [9] "He and Wingy revered *Oriental Strut* to such an extent they took

[8] Victor.
[9] *Op. cit.*

it out on the desert and buried it." Wingy had heard that, thus
interred, it would become petrified and forever preserved!

Jack blew into New York with Wingy Mannone and promptly
decided that he'd—

". . . rather drink muddy water, Lord, sleep in a hollow log,
Than to be up here in New York, treated like a dirty dog . . ."

Not that there wasn't work. There were records dates and society dates or gigs. "They would not play jazz at those social func-
tions, of course," commented Tony Parenti (*Hear Me Talkin'
to Ya*) "but they did want a man with them who could play a
couple of solo choruses on the up-tempo things." In his first book,
We Called It Music, Eddie Condon referred to this situation and,
bemoaning the loss of hot men to name bands, compared it to a jigger
of whiskey in a quart of milk. You couldn't even taste it.

"I was having a couple of drinks with Bud Freeman and Pee
Wee Russell one evening in a little speakeasy on Fifty-first Street,"
said Jimmy McPartland (*Hear Me Talkin' to Ya*), "when Pee
Wee began talking about a trombone player, the greatest thing he
had heard in this life.

"We said we would like to hear the guy, and Pee Wee said,
right, he'd just pop over and get him. Two drinks later, Pee Wee was
back with the guy, who was wearing a horrible-looking cap and
overcoat and carrying a trombone in a case under his arm.

"Pee Wee introduced us. He was Jack Teagarden, from Texas,
and looked it. 'Fine,' we said. 'We've been hearing a lot about you,
would sure like to hear you play.'

"The guy says, 'All right,' gets his horn out, puts it together,
blows a couple of warm-up notes and starts to play *Diane*. No accompanist, just neat; he played it solo, and I'm telling you he
knocked us out. He really blew it. And when he'd done with that,
he started on the blues, still by himself. We had to agree with Pee
Wee, we'd never heard anyone play trombone like that. We were
flabbergasted."

Jack once sang that he was born in Texas, raised in Tennessee,
and this is only partly true, the Texas part. Much to his amazement, some writers took him seriously and had him learning his
licks in the Great Smokies! There are many anecdotes about Jack
that also verge on folklore, like the countless scenes in which he's

wearing a horrible cap. Now that caps are once again in vogue, someone truly enterprising should locate the Teagarden model. Who knows? It might replace the beard and beret.

There is one story, heard in slightly different versions, that appears to be reasonably accurate. In this, a musician knocks on Jack's hotel door. Jack mumbles sleepily. The musician comes into the room. Jack appears to be asleep but, having a wide experience of jazz musicians, the visitor speaks in a normal voice, not bothering to raise it, and says, "How'd you like to work in my band?" Jack grunts, in effect, "Go away and let me sleep." The visitor does not act offended as this response is normal for a jazz musician at high noon. "Well," says the visitor, looking dubiously at the drowsiest Texan he'd ever seen, "if you change your mind, just come over to the Park Central. Ask for Ben Pollack." Jack sits up, suddenly less sleepy and even beginning to tingle with interest. "Who are *you?*" he asks his visitor. "I'm Ben Pollack," says Ben Pollack.

Jack recorded with The Whoopee Makers, a pick-up band, in the summer of 1928, and made his first records with the Ben Pollack Orchestra that fall. At a guess, Eddie Condon may have been the first to record a Teagarden vocal. However, the tune recorded by a Condon group, *Makin' Friends,* was recorded more than once, with differing personnel, and while at least one excellent discography of Teagarden has been published in *Down Beat,* there seem to be some areas where further research is indicated. (The Whoopee Makers' *Makin' Friends* was issued on various labels under a variety of pseudonyms, among them such unlikely groups as The Kentucky Grasshoppers and the Carolina Collegians. I bought Eddie's record and The Whoopee Makers' version shortly after they were issued, thought that his vocal was excellent on both and that on the latter his muted chorus—the water-glass trick—was very plaintive, a really lost, sad sound.)

Possibly the next mixed date after that of the New Orleans Rhythm Kings with Jelly Roll Morton on piano, was one Eddie Condon dreamed up when he heard the phenomenal drummer, George Stafford, playing in Charlie Johnson's band at Small's Paradise in Harlem. With Joe Sullivan, piano, Happy Cauldwell, tenor sax, Jack Teagarden and others, they made two sides on February 5, 1929, both with vigorous, rocking vocals by Jack, *I'm Gonna Stomp, Mr. Henry Lee* and *That's a Serious Thing.* Ralph Peer of Southern Music Company, then a subsidiary of Victor, remarked to Eddie that the music was excellent, and added, "All in all, this has been an interesting experiment." [10]

The following month Condon suggested a similar "interesting experiment" to Tommy Rockwell, Louis Armstrong's adviser. After a bit of palaver, Tommy changed a Luis Russell date to the afternoon (Armstrong's great disc of *Mahogany Hall Stomp*) and in the morning—with Happy, Jack and Joe in the band and with Eddie Lang on guitar—they made *Knockin' a Jug,* an on-the-spot number named for the jug of whiskey some of the boys had brought along to help them keep awake.

Not long after coming to New York, Jack Teagarden worked with Billy Lustig's band at Roseland. On the opposite stand was the band of Fletcher Henderson, with an incomparable brass team that included Jimmy Harrison on trombone, and thereby hangs the clue to a myth, or rather, clues to two of them, both closely related.

The first myth is that Jack was the first person to effectively use the trombone as a solo instrument in jazz. This is a rather careless brush-off of the many fine trombonists who preceded him. One doubts if any knowledgeable jazz collector would agree or that Jack himself would so lightly dismiss his predecessors. To do so would bypass, for example, the great technical facility and far from negligible solo work of Miff Mole, about whom Otis Ferguson wrote in 1939: [11] "He played jazz when jazz was pretty crude; he played on the beat and on the chord and he played with a certain easy bounding zest. . . . He is still so much more interesting in any stretch than all but Jimmy Harrison and Teagarden that I would not guarantee what might now be said of him if he had died ten years ago in rather horrible circumstances."

What distinguished Jack Teagarden in jazz (apart from his scat-singing and vocals) was not that he was the first to employ the trombone creatively in solos, but that he did this in an easy swing with very blue intonation, in a panther style, lazy and lightning-quick. He played with remarkable facility and with no unintentional smearing of notes. His first loyalty was to *hot* intonation and phrasing and to the basic, beat-contending rhythm of jazz.

In *Jazz-Tango Dancing,* a predecessor to *Jazz Hot,* Paris, October, 1933, Joost van Praag contributed an allegorical description of *swing* that is particularly apropos in relation to Jack's trombone

[10] *We All Played Music.*
[11] "The Five Pennies," *Jazzmen.*

style.[12] "Imagine a man who is going to catch a train," says van Praag. "He enters the station very calmly, moves toward the train without hurrying and, on reaching his car, enters it sedately with perfect tranquillity. At the moment the train leaves, he closes the door. Anyone else would already have been in his place for a moment or two, or would at least had the door closed before the train started. But our gentleman is in the habit of getting on the train at the latest possible second, without hurrying himself a bit—in brief, with the greatest of ease."

Where others' preoccupation with Dixieland angularity lent their work the awkwardness of music on stilts, with Jack—as with Pee Wee Russell—it was assimilated, to give style yet another dimension. You can *hear* this in choruses of both men today—Jack in his recent album, *This Is Teagarden*. Weighing all the ponderables and imponderables, the quantitative and qualitative, the measurable and immeasurable, Bill Russo—whose work in jazz and on trombone is rated highly—concluded that Jack *"is* the best trombonist." Explaining further, he says, "He has an unequaled mastery of his instrument which is evident in the simple perfection of his performance, not in sensational displays; the content of his playing illustrates a deep understanding of compositional principles—and this is the true though unspoken ultimate of the jazz improviser."

The fact is, Jimmy Harrison probably blew solos on trombone in New York at about the time Jack was blowing them in the Southwest. That brings us to the other myth, which has some basis in fact. It is that Jimmy influenced T.'s style. And this is a half-truth. The other half is that Jack influenced Jimmy. When Pee Wee Russell says that all the essentials of Jack's way of playing were in evidence back there when the Big Gate was a teen-aged trombone wonder, this writer, for one, will take Pee Wee's word for it. As one might expect, it developed considerably and became stronger and surer of itself. (I have yet to hear Jack freshly, after an absence, without realizing that he always has something new and pretty wonderful to listen to.)

The truth is better than the myth or the half-truth. When Jack and Jimmy heard each other play, they were really knocked out, which was not so surprising, seeing how much they had in common. However, they were anything but trombone twins. In some ways, J. J. Johnson seems closer to Jimmy than does Jack. But that's begging the point—what Jimmy and Jack did have in common was a

[12] Quoted in *Hot Jazz* by Hughes Panassié, Witmark, 1934.

solid, blues-based approach, great technical facility that never ob-
truded and above all, an appreciation of how much any jazzmen,
playing any instrument, could learn from Louis Armstrong.

You can trace the coincidental line of development—and a
lot more of interest that we haven't room for here—by consulting
the index of *Hear Me Talkin' to Ya* (a most valuable book for
home work as well as entertainment)—with the added suggestion
that you also listen with unjaded ears to *Mandy Lee Blues* and
Snake Rag on Riverside's "Louis Armstrong; 1923: With King
Oliver's Creole Jazz Band" (12-122). On the records you'll refresh
your memory as to how the greatest cornet team in jazz sounded
—assuming that you once heard the Gennetts of which these are
reissues. And in the book you'll learn that June Clark and Jimmy
Harrison "were known as the greatest brass team of that (wonderful) period," (in Harlem jazz, c. 1923–24) and the interesting side-
light that Fletcher Henderson sent Jimmy home to bone up on his
reading ability! The latter was admittedly a technical asset but not
at all what the Fletcher Henderson Orchestra was famous for.

Kaiser Marshall, the drummer, said of Jimmy: "He liked Jack
Teagarden, who used to come to our house often, sometimes staying
all night, and we would have a slight jam session with Hawkins,
who lived only a few doors from us. So Jack would play the piano,
Jimmy trombone, Hawkins tenor, and myself on my rubber-pad I
kept at home. Then Hawkins would play piano, Jack and Jimmy
trombone. My, what fun we had! Of course, we brought home, in
my car, twelve bottles of beer, some wine, whiskey, ice cream, cake,
barbecue ribs, and chitlin's, to make our morning complete." [13]

Jam sessions were the life line of jazz in the 'twenties and
early 'thirties and had an intimacy oftentimes (but not always) lacking in the more or less public sessions of later years. Even the ones
open to the public in a limited way provided a different environment for the musician since, among the small number of jazz fans
likely to be present, there were fewer "tourists"—only an occasional
slumming party that got an earful and left. So Jack brought his
trombone along to Small's and other places uptown and downtown,
and in those places it seemed like home was where you blew your
horn.

It was so in Kansas City a few years later, where Mary Lou
Williams (talented arranger and first lady of jazz piano) with her
sisters made the rounds of the clubs. "One night," she recalled,

[13] *Hear Me Talkin' to Ya.*

"we ran into a place where Ben Pollack had a combo, which in-cluded Jack Teagarden and, I think, Benny Goodman. The girls introduced me to the Texan trombonist, and right away we felt like friends. After work, he and a couple of musicians asked us to go out, and we visited some of the speaks downtown. One I remember particularly, because it was decorated to resemble the inside of a penitentiary, with bars on the windows and waiters in striped uni-forms like down-South convicts. In these weird surroundings, I played for the boys and Jack got up and sang some blues. I thought he was more than wonderful. While they stayed in Kaycee, Jack and some of Pollack's men came round every night, and I was very happy to see them." [14]

Otis Ferguson wrote [15] ". . . there had blown into town a man from Texas with a trombone under his arm and a fine blues timbre in his voice; a Mr. Jackson, a Mr. T., otherwise Jack Tea-garden. Pollack's boys spotted him (playing with a band called Dexter's, I believe); and when they left for Atlantic City, to which Glenn Miller quite understandably did not wish to go, they took him in the band. Later when Pollack decided to stand in front in-stead of behind the drums, Teagarden got a man still pretty hot from New Orleans in the band: Ray Bauduc."

George Hoefer noted that when Jack first took a chorus with the Pollack band, the boys were still and silent. He thought they were being unfriendly to a Texas trombone, but soon learned that the silence was because they liked him and liked what they heard. Later, as older members quit, the band style came to be built around Jack and he, wrote Hoefer,[16] "brought most of the New Orleans boys into the organization."

While with Pollack, he cut his first, still-famous record of *Basin Street Blues,* in February, 1931.[17] The evening before the record date, Glenn Miller, who was to do the arrangement, phoned from his apartment in Jackson Heights. "I think we could do a better job," he told Jack, "if we could put together some lyrics and you could sing it. Want to come over and see what we can do? My wife will fix us some supper." [18]

[14] *Op. cit.*
[15] "The Five Pennies," *Jazzmen.*
[16] *Op. cit.*
[17] *Benny Goodman and The Charleston Chasers,* reissued in *The Vintage Goodman,* Columbia CL 821.
[18] *Hear Me Talkin' to Ya.*

"After we had worked out a first draft of verse and chorus,"
Jack recalled, "Glenn sat on the piano bench and I leaned over his
shoulder. We each had a pencil, and as he played, we'd each cross
out words and phrases here and there, putting in new ones. . . .
Next day we cut the record. . . . The lyrics were later included in
the sheet music, but never carried our names."

In 1933 Jack worked at ninety dollars a week in a band with
Sterling Boze at Chicago's Centenary of Progress. "Right outside
the 23rd Street entrance," wrote Hoefer, "Wingy Mannone, Joe
Marsala, Charlie LaVere and Jim Barnes were playing at a roof-
garden beer joint. T. walked in one night and asked the boys to
make room, and was again playing for $60 a week and gin." [19]

In the fall he was back in New York and on October sixteenth,
made four sides with a group led by Benny Goodman, two with
Joe Sullivan on piano and two with Frank Froeba. In sequence, these
were: *I Gotta Right To Sing the Blues, Ain't Cha Glad, Dr. Heckle
and Mr. Jibe,* and *Texas Tea Party,* the last a two-way pun.[20] John
Hammond had suggested these sides for Columbia's English label.

In those days pop tunes were usually recorded with stock arrangements but, observes Marshall W. Stearns in *The Story Of Jazz,*
"Hammond had insisted on special arrangements, and Goodman's
first record for the English Gramaphone Company . . . was a notable success in England. When the American record executives woke
up and decided to issue it in the United States, only Hammond's violent objections kept them from coupling each side with a commercial
number by Clyde McCoy or Harry Reser 'to insure the recording's
success.' "

Even though it didn't make much of a splash, state-side, at the
time, this was one of the most exuberant recording sessions of that
period. The rhythm was very much alive (Joe Sullivan, Dick Mc-
Donough, Artie Bernstein, Gene Krupa) and the music had a happy
sound. Taken at an easy jump tempo, Jack's vocal on *Ain't Cha Glad*
is infectiously joyous and his classical vocal and trombone work on
I Gotta Right To Sing the Blues, a superb performance, is in most
jazz collections worthy of the name. All four numbers are played
in a relaxed manner, to which Jack's trombone contributes an easy,
seemingly effortless, swing. Moreover, a sense of humor is discernible in these and, indeed, in many Teagarden performances.
Not the brash humor of Wingy nor the sly spoofing of Fats—rather,

[19] *Op. cit.*
[20] Reissued on Columbia B-1806, *Benny Goodman.*

a casual whimsicality that, oftentimes, could be expressed more deftly with a slur and a slide or an insouciant arabesque on horn than with the voice. T. was one of the few jazzmen who could articulate a coda, in two to four bars, without putting pen to paper.

Beginning in 1928 (as nearly as we can establish the date), Jack took part in numerous recording sessions, so many, in fact, that they would merit a detailed study in themselves. Among the earlier ones was *Loveless Love* (a Hot Record Society reissue). In the same year were released four wonderfully rhythmic sides with the Venuti-Lang All-Star Orchestra, on Vocalion: *Beale Street Blues, After You've Gone, Farewell Blues* and *Someday Sweetheart.* On the first two, Jack's vocals are explosive and exhilarating, and that goes for his trombone on all four. The team of Eddie Lang and "Four-string" Joe Venuti were in top form on this date (guitar and violin).[21]

He recorded *Stars Fell on Alabama,* a ballad to which he took a fancy, in 1934 with Caspar Reardon on harp,[22] with a recording band in 1943 [23] and in 1954 with Ruby Braff on trumpet.[24] Commodore has wrapped up some of its best Teagarden sides in a noteworthy long-play package called "Big T," in a variety of appropriate musical settings (Hackett, Condon, Pee Wee, Jess Stacy, etc.): *Serenade to a Shylock, Rockin' Chair, Pitchin' a Bit Short, Meet Me Tonight in Dreamland, Diane, Big T Blues, Chinatown, My Chinatown.*[25] Along with Chu Berry, Frankie Newton and others, he was on Bessie Smith's last recording date; these four historic sides are included in Columbia's *The Bessie Smith Story, Vol. 2: Blues to Barrelhouse,* ML 4808. One should also mention with these examples of Jack's extensive output, three memorable Victor sides with Hoagy Carmichael and His Orchestra when both Jack and Pee Wee Russell were on the job on what seems to have been Bix's last recording date.

Although the album belongs a bit later chronologically, when the Jack Teagarden Orchestra was already organized (1940), it might well be mentioned here. This Bud Freeman album, now on long-play,[26] is something special. Max Kaminsky, Pee Wee Russell, Bud—in fact, all the men—are in good form and the entire job

[21] Brunswick.
[22] Brunswick.
[23] Capitol.
[24] Urania.
[25] Commodore 20015.
[26] Harmony HL 7046.

represents jazz just swinging along, without pretensions. Jack's humorous trombone solo on *Muskat* (a vintage piece with a title clouded in obscurity) is followed by a witty and squeaky one by Pee Wee. On *Forty-Seventh and State* Dave Tough's drumming is magnificent, his use of cymbals sensitive and wonderful to hear. As the blues verses of *Jack Hits the Road* imply, the South's great trombone wonder was a bit late in arriving. The Music Corporation of America handled bookings for Jack's big band, and you have only to read further to find that reference completely explicable.

Jack was with Mal Hallett for a short time in the New England (Boston) area, and Toots Mondello, Frankie Carle and Gene Krupa were among his fellow sidemen. But with no reflection on Mal Hallett or his music, Jack did not seem especially happy in that particular name band. For it was a name band and not a gathering of the clan, as Pollack's outfit had seemed at times. Also, in Pollack's band there was, now and again, the excitement of creation and discovery. Corny as some of the stuff sounds today, you can still pick out spots on Pollack's records that showed how the discoveries of little-band, New Orleans jazz were being applied to the then emerging big-band style.

Just as the bands of the 'thirties learned some lessons from Pollack, Paul Whiteman, in the 'twenties, appeared not only to have taken the best *hot* men from Goldkette's historic band but took a few pointers from the way Goldkette had used *hot* men. One got the impression that Jack—while not completely happy (what *hot* man could be?)—was at least happier than he had been with Hallett, and more with it, as they say. And this may have been partly due to Paul's determination not to use *hot* men to salt the *schmaltz* (as a gold-brick promoter salts a mine) but to present them in something approaching a congenial musical atmosphere, even though this was a popular—for some years *the most popular*—name band, using for the most part popular arrangements.

It wasn't that Paul's arrangers exactly burned up the bandstand—the Whiteman book would hardly be compared to orchestrations by Edgar Sampson, Jimmy Mundy, Sy Oliver, Mary Lou Williams and Fletcher Henderson that gave the bands of Tommy Dorsey and Benny Goodman something to sink their chops in during that decade that saw the great boom of commercial swing.[27]

[27] *Commercial swing* was a term used by musicians to distinguish corny imitations from the real article that B.G. and T.D. played often enough to

But though the arrangements were not truly *hot*—Whiteman's, that is—neither were they always hopelessly sweet. Once in a while, for a Bix or a Mr. T., they came out clean and uncluttered. And with both Big Gate and Little Gate in there, did the brasses sometimes bite? They did, indeed. It was a wonderful thawing out of the spirit, after a particularly *schmaltzy* number, to listen to the brothers Teagarden set the pace for the brasses. You wanted to get up and shout to the saxophones: *They went thataway!*

On January 5, 1939, Jack Teagarden, as an orchestra leader in his own right, "embarked on seven years of bad luck." [28] He had experience and ideas, but somehow the group seldom shaped up to the stature of its leader. "The first band put him in bankruptcy," George explained. "By the end of the first year he owed $46,000. His second, less expensive orchestra, got gone with the draft, losing seventeen sidemen in four months. His health broke on him several times, his managers got his income tax messed up and his domestic life got tangled up." It was in the early part of this unhappy period that a *Down Beat* interview carried the plaintive headline : "There's No Back-Biting in My Band." There were also an untoward number of auto accidents, hotel fires and other calamities that fall to the lot of jazzmen on the unglamorous grind of one-night stands.

The big Texan had broad shoulders and that was fortunate; the load they had to carry would have broken most. Even when bad luck haunted him like a zombie looking for blood, Jack kept his sense of humor. He could smile wryly at his own misfortunes, and without even thinking about it, you knew the smile was sincere.

In his spare moments Jack reconditioned a museum piece on wheels and thanks to what is known in this line of country as old American know-how (in New Delhi it's probably called old Indian ingenuity) he was the only jazzman of distinction to drive to the job in a Stanley steamer. With or without the vintage chariot, he didn't always make it. Take the time the band arrived, as per schedule, for a booking at Greenville, N.C.—Jack showed up all right—but at Greenville, Carolina South! Once, at a society wingding for charity in South Bend, Indiana, the boys waited on the stand for the maestro, no mere jazz band but a symphony in black and white. Our boy Jackson showed up in street clothes. The next date

---

merit mention and that Bill Basie from Red Bank played almost always. *Commercial,* in musicians' slang, has many shades of meaning, however, not all of them altogether derogatory.

[28] *Op. cit.*

was in Hoagy's old alma mater town, Bloomington, and Jack wasn't
going to be caught in his expensive old gabardines this time—he
rented a tux. It is well known by thousands of women in these United
States that Mr. T. cuts a handsome figure in dinner clothes. There
was only one thing wrong on this occasion. The boys were in mufti.

In 1947 all that Jack had left was the band bus, which his
manager proceeded to take off his hands. He opened at a West
Coast club, the Suzy Q, and Local 47, American Federation of Musicians (Los Angeles area) pulled him off the job for some four
hundred dollars arrears in traveling band taxes. His friend Bing
Crosby, with whom Jack had appeared in the movie, "Birth of the
Blues," in 1941, suggested he build up his name as a single. Writes
George Hoefer, "A disgusted Jackson flew into Chicago with his
only possession, a new trombone in an old case . . . moaning, 'I
wouldn't like California even if the weather was good.' " Yes, that's
what the man said. But while on the road the next few years he often
spoke with genuine nostalgia of a place where one could settle down
and relax—home—California. He now lives in a comfortable house
on a cliff in the hills above Hollywood, with his fourth wife, Addie,
and a son, Joe, now aged five.

Jack was with Louis Armstrong's All Stars from 1947 until
1951. The All Stars didn't always light up the galaxy but when they
did it was extra-terrestrial. They were that way when they played
the Apollo, in Harlem, and when they played at Symphony Hall,
Boston. Nor do you have to take anyone's word for the latter performance; it's ready and waiting on Decca DL 8037 and 8038.
Forty-eight inches, all told, of the best.

Once a woman remarked of Jack, "He's profound, isn't he?"
No doubt Jack would have been surprised, had he known of this
reaction. However, she didn't mean anything complicated or ab-
strusely intellectual. She only meant that he didn't live on surfaces.
But, however deep Jack's thoughts may be, they are voiced in
everyday speech, never show-cased.

While he likes to talk about sports and the kind of mechanical,
modestly scientific stuff that intrigued Ben Franklin all his life—
and of course, music—he is also an excellent yarn-spinner when
he's in the right mood. (Some years ago Leo R. Herschman, to
whom I had been introduced by Dean Shaffner—a friend of mine
and a discerning jazz collector, who is with the ABC network—
supplied the long-play equipment for a documentary experiment.

My typewriter being allergic to ghosts, I wanted to see how much of Jack would come through, if he was allowed to speak, in his own words. Quite a lot did, although the project has not yet been completed. I am East and Jack is West and we haven't met in one hell of a long five years or so. On that occasion, for a few evenings, we sat around a microphone and Jack talked. Once when he stopped for a break, the minutes dragged on and on and Jack didn't return. Finally we went to look for him. He was down in the big basement workshop, having a ball with power tools.)

"There isn't a more musically forward-thinking man in jazz," observed George Hoefer. "He is constantly dreaming of progress. This writer heard him rehearse a French horn, a trumpet, and a couple of saxes, around a table in the kitchen back of the old Panther Room of the Hotel Sherman, after the job. . . ." [29] He has an understandable admiration for men who are highly rated (that is, if they are deserving of it) and this may be one out of several reasons for the losses sustained when he first got into the big-band business.[30] "Unless I've got good men around me," Jack confessed to John Tynan, "I'm no good. Guess you could call me strictly an inspiration man. Louis is that way, too. He's gotta be in good company. The better the company, the better Pops will blow." [31]

An inspired companion volume to *This Is Teagarden,* previously mentioned, is *Swing Low, Sweet Spiritual.*[32] In the former, he displays his mastery of the jazz vocal and the jazz trombone in a collection of Teagarden favorites; his compositional ideas fully confirm Bill Russo's remarks. And in the second album, he recalls early influences not so widely known to his followers. Before it had been released he was already talking about future albums, perhaps of show tunes, but not the usual run-of-the-mill stuff, and pop tunes that fit his style and moods. In the Tynan interview he noted that

[29] *Op. cit.*
[30] Most agency people would appear to be more at home in the popular promotional slant, rather than in the jazz department. The great big-band successes are men who were not only able to think orchestrally but who were also able to take charge of the entire operation and see that jazz was not slighted, from the lowliest band boy to the highest paid arranger. Despite his easygoing ways, Jack has very definite orchestral ideas and is by no means —despite his failures—limited to a one-man or combo field.
[31] *Op. cit.*
[32] Capitol T-820.

many old tunes had been done to death. On the other hand, many haven't—such as Tony Jackson's *Pretty Baby* that might have been written to be sung and swung by the *Big Gate,* medium drag tempo.

(As you may have surmised, Jack never gets very far away from music. Once I phoned him at a Brooklyn hospital where he was getting over a repeat performance of pneumonia—the first had caught him when he was with Whiteman—and asked if there was anything he needed. [Jack was in a private room, with paperbacks, a portable television set, a friendly hospital staff, and visitors as and when allowed.] He started to say no and then changed it to, yes, there was. He asked if I'd stop at the Hotel Markwell and pick up his trombone. I did that, and brought it along. Almost the first thing Jack did after thanking me was to take the personally machined mouthpiece and rub its edges on the floor. I was reminded of Louis's cornet mouthpiece that I'd seen at the Milne Municipal Boys' Home in New Orleans, which he'd filed with crosshatches to assure himself a firm mouth-grip, or *embouchure*. Well, Jackson played, not very loud because he wasn't supposed to give his lungs too heavy a workout just yet, and some nurses and an intern paused at the doorway—I thought, to protest, but that wasn't it at all; Jack had already built up a loyal following in Brooklyn!)

"This twenty percent tax is murder," Jack told John Tynan. "Where we're working now, at Astor's in the Valley, I can't sing a note because of the tax. It isn't only that I like to sing, but people come to the stand, wanting me to sing particular tunes. It keeps me busy explaining why I can't." [33]

That should have been a good excuse for a headache, but Jack only has moods, not migraines. Queried on this by Tynan, he laughed and explained, "It goes back to our Whiteman days. On the bandstand Johnny (Mercer) used to sit right above the trombone section. He was, and I guess still is, a chronic sinus sufferer, and always had a headache, it seemed. He'd look down at me and ask, 'How ya feel tonight, Jack?' I'd say, 'Why, just fine, Johnny. How you?' Then he'd moan, 'Man, my head is killing me. Don't you ever have a headache?' And the truth is, I never have."

"Guess I'll be off to Europe in March," he said, "Joe Glaser's setting it up." And though he was no longer in the San Fernando Valley in April, 1957, neither was he in Europe. He was at a place on the Strip in Las Vegas. But at least he could sing.

[33] *Op cit.*

SELECTED DISCOGRAPHY—JACK TEAGARDEN

The following long-play sets all feature Jack on either vocals or trombone, or both, and furnish a variety of examples of his recorded work through the years:

Comes Jazz, Harmony HL 7046

The Louis Armstrong Story, Vol. 4: Louis Armstrong Favorites, Columbia ML 54386

This Is Teagarden, Capitol T 721

Folkways Jazz Series, Vol. 7: New York (1922–1934), Folkways FP 67

The Vintage Goodman, Columbia CL 821

Benny Goodman Presents Jack Teagarden, Columbia B-1806

Big T, Commodore 20015

The Bessie Smith Story, Vol. 2: Blues to Barrelhouse, Columbia ML 4808

Satchmo at Symphony Hall, Vols. 1 and 2, Decca DL 8037, DL 8038

Swing Low, Sweet Spiritual, Capitol T-820

Earl
Hines

* * * *

By John S. Wilson

The factual mistiness surrounding the early days of jazz has left in some doubt the identification of the errant geniuses who first gave a positive jazz voice to most of the basic instruments used today. Two instruments were brought into jazz focus late enough in the game, however, so that the act was performed before an admiring audience which has left no doubt where the credit should lie. Both events happened at approximately the same time —the middle 'twenties. That was when Coleman Hawkins gave the tenor saxophone its first real jazz voice and Earl Hines changed the piano from a sort of solo-centered fellow traveler of jazz to a full-fledged member of the jazz ensemble with all the rights, privileges and responsibilities that this implies.

Hines found the piano working its way out of the ragtime phase. Before he came along, only two pianists had managed to make a strong and lasting impression in the gestating jazz world. One was James P. Johnson, a ragtime man with aspirations as a serious pianist and composer whose feeling for jazz helped him to bring the stride piano style to its peak. But his ragtime roots remained strong and continually colored his work.

The other pre-Hines master was the illustrious Jelly Roll Morton. Like Johnson, Morton also came out of ragtime but its effect on his playing was less lasting. The bouillabaisse of musical sounds that billowed out of New Orleans at the beginning of the twentieth century streamed through Morton. All of these sounds, including ragtime, were strained through Morton's often dogmatic personal notions to become his style. Both Johnson and Morton, like any pianist of solo pretensions in the first quarter of this century, worked largely on their own. Johnson was the dominant figure in the Harlem rent party picture, strictly a solo situation, while Morton for most of his life was an itinerant (*i.e.,* moving from place to place without benefit of booking agency) musician who worked alone as a matter of convenience.

There is a line that flows from each of these men to Hines, but the one connecting him with Morton is by far the stronger. Hines grew up in the ragtime era and acquired some of its feeling, which quickly faded as he found his own musical personality. However, the often stark, solid, beat-conscious and quirkful playing of Jelly Roll Morton glows warmly in the work of even the mature Hines.

Hines made a place for the piano in the jazz ensemble by turning his back on one of the primary concepts of these earlier pianists—the idea, natural in a performer playing alone, that the piano had to be used as though it were a full orchestra, constantly creating an ensemble sound. This served a purpose when the pianist was playing alone, but it was of little help when the piano was already surrounded by an ensemble. Piano solos played within an ensemble in this style (Lil Armstrong's with Louis's Hot Five, for instance) are pale and diffuse in comparison to the other solo instruments.

By phrasing in the manner of the horns with which he had to compete in a band, Hines created a new approach to the jazz piano. He was, as the saying now has it, "phrasing like a horn" but, unlike more recent pianists who phrase so much like horns that they seem to forget the piano has potentialities a horn lacks, Hines has always been a two-handed pianist. His left hand has never been anything that could be taken for granted—suddenly breaking up the rhythm, roaring into a turbulent bass passage while the melodic line is momentarily suspended or impulsively reversing the roles of the two hands. His tone—bright, brassy and fully formed—has a compelling quality in solos and slices keenly through full band ensemble.

The handy appellation for Hines's playing has always been "trumpet style." It fits neatly because there is a trumpet quality about his best work, and he first came to attention during his association with one of jazz's greatest trumpets, Louis Armstrong. Many of Hines's solos have been described as virtually piano transcriptions of what Armstrong might have done.

Actually, the trumpetlike parallel of Hines's playing probably has a much more natural origin. His father was a trumpeter in the Eureka Brass Band in Pittsburgh and Hines's first interest was the trumpet.

"But I had no system and my father couldn't teach me," Hines has said. "I didn't know those systems of breath control they have now, so I blew wrong and it used to hurt behind the ears. I'd get lumps back there and so I put the horn down. Then I decided to use the same ideas on piano—that was the reason for my 'trumpet style.' The ideas I had wanted heard through the band could only be done like that."

Hines's transfer to the piano was helped along by his mother, an organist and pianist, who preferred to see her son playing piano rather than trumpet. He was born in Duquesne, Pennsylvania, a suburb of Pittsburgh, on December 28, 1905, but the family soon moved into Pittsburgh and when Earl was nine he was started on piano lessons. He moved along so fast with his first teacher that she gave him up and he was transferred to a German, who put him to work on the Czerny books of piano exercises. These exercises, Hines feels, formed the foundation of his technique.

The first influences in forming his jazz style came from a pair of Pittsburgh pianists, Jim Fellman and Johnny Watters. Hines admired Fellman's left hand and Watters's right, and he tried to make use of what he considered the best features of both. When he fell under the spell of Fellman and Watters, he had just quit high school and was on his first job at the Liederhouse, playing with Lois Deppe and making fifteen dollars a week. Besides trying to live on this munificent sum, Hines used part of it as informal payment for his equally informal lessons from Fellman and Watters.

"They both liked different types of drink and tobacco," he has recalled. "Fellman liked chewing tobacco and beer and Watters liked gin and Camel cigarettes. So out of my fifteen dollars a week I had to buy for both of them. I'd get them up in a hotel room, one every other day, buy them what they liked and have them show me how to do it."

Deppe moved on to Chicago and when he got set there in 1923, he sent for the eighteen-year-old Hines. Hines's first job was at the Club Elite, No. 2, one of a chain of Elite night clubs. During the year that he worked there, the basic inspiration offered by Fellman and Watters was implemented by a new idol, Teddy Weatherford. Weatherford was the twenty-year-old piano sensation of the day in Chicago. He was playing then at the Red Mill Café in a six-piece band that also included Tommy Ladnier on trumpet and Roy Palmer on trombone. His powerful left hand and generally straight-forward style were being copied assiduously by the young pianists in Chicago when Hines got there and he enthusiastically followed suit. Weatherford subsequently had one of the most exotic careers in jazz. He left Chicago in 1926 and settled in Asia. Except for a brief visit to Europe in 1937, he spent the rest of his life playing in China, Japan, India and the East Indies. He died in Calcutta in 1945.

Hines's next stop after the Elite was the Entertainers' Cabaret where he played a miniature piano on wheels and evolved a trick of winding up a chorus with an involved break, giving the piano a shove to the next table and picking up where he had left off. Carroll Dickerson's orchestra was also playing at the Entertainers' and Hines joined the band on a forty-two-week tour of the Pantages vaudeville circuit which took them to California and back.

The band returned to Chicago in the spring of 1926 and went into the Sunset Café, right across Thirty-fifth Street from the Plantation Café where King Oliver was playing. Louis Armstrong joined the Dickerson band then and, with Hines on piano, Darnell Howard on clarinet and alto, Honoré Dutrey on trombone and Tubby Hall drumming, it won quick recognition as the best band in Chicago.

Dickerson bowed out as leader in 1927 and Armstrong took over, installing Hines as musical director. This was the band that the young Chicagoans who were about to launch "Chicago style" jazz came to worship admiringly and to sit in with whenever they had the slightest opportunity. Jess Stacy, whose playing is strongly marked by the Hines influence, was allowed to fill in for Hines whenever Earl wanted a rest. Muggsy Spanier, Frank Teschemacher and George Wettling rushed over to the Sunset regularly whenever their night's work was done.

While Armstrong's band was playing at the Sunset, he started using Hines on his small-group recording sessions. Hines made his first appearance with them on a Johnny Dodds's Black Bottom Stompers date for Vocalion in April, 1927, a session which produced *Wild Man Blues* and *Melancholy*. A month later he made a single side with Armstrong's Hot Seven, *Chicago Breakdown*. Except for some 1924 Gennett sides as accompanist to Lois Deppe, these were Hines's first records.

A new spot, the Savoy Ballroom, opened in Chicago on Thanksgiving night, 1927, and Armstrong, Hines and drummer Zutty Singleton, who had become something of a musical triumvirate and were unashamedly impressed with themselves, decided to go into business on their own with the immediate objective of knocking off the Savoy. They rented Warwick Hall on Forty-seventh Street and opened up in December with Louis Armstrong's Hot Six. The triumvirate had become accustomed to the admiring crowds at the Sunset. But the crowds didn't follow them to the Warwick and, after a hungry winter, the three operator-musicians threw in the towel.

Armstrong and Singleton caught on with Carroll Dickerson once again. Dickerson, ironically, was playing at the Savoy. Hines went back to Thirty-fifth Street to an after-hours musicians' hangout across the street from the Sunset, which had once been called The Nest but was now known as the Apex Club. Hines took the piano chair in Jimmie Noone's band there and during his ninemonth stay the Noone band cut a dozen sides which remain among the most exhilarating small group works on disks. At the same time, Armstrong began using Hines again in his own small-group records which were released under a variety of titles—Louis Armstrong and His Hot Seven, Louis Armstrong and His Savoy Ballroom Five and Louis Armstrong and His Orchestra. This series produced disks that are unquestioned classics of their type—the gloriously full-toned *West End Blues* and the brooding *Muggles* are among the best—but the only really unique performance was a duet between Armstrong and Hines on the King Oliver tune, *Weather Bird Rag,* a kaleidoscopic display by two masterful musicians in close rapport.

Hines eventually tired of the hours and the work with Noone, so he quit and started rehearsing a small group at his hotel. They had worked out twenty-five or thirty numbers when the QRS Piano Roll Company asked him to go to New York to record some piano solos. QRS, astutely observing the way the wind was blowing in the matter of reproduced music, had decided to hedge on its piano rolls by going into the record business. Unfortunately, aside from recognizing the latent possibilities for records of a talent like Hines's, QRS was neither informed nor instinctive about the operation of a record business. After Hines had cut eight solos, all his own compositions, QRS threw them all on the market in a solid batch on the same day—tantamount to throwing them away.

"Oh, it was a panic!" Earl recalls. The disks quickly shriveled and died. QRS promptly followed suit and the Hines solos became collectors' items almost as soon as they were issued. (They are now readily available on LP on Atlantic 120, thereby proving that watchful waiting can even be a good policy for a record collector.)

While Hines was in New York, Lucky Millinder, who had not

yet achieved his later status of band leader, was desperately trying to organize a show to open a new Chicago night club, the Grand Terrace. He needed a band with plenty of name and plenty of talent, but he hadn't been able to get one. He wired Hines, asking if he could come back to Chicago and put together a band. Hines wired back that he already had a band, a not unreasonably exaggerated reference to his little rehearsal group. However, by the time the Grand Terrace opened—on December 28, 1928, Hines's twenty-third birthday—he really had a full band.

The band had been signed for the opening production only. But it stayed on and stayed on for more than a decade. During these years, the nightly broadcasts from the Terrace, introduced by the pulsingly exotic *Deep Forest* and shouts of "Father Hines! Father Hines!", gave the pianist a nationwide reputation. It was on one of these broadcasts that Hines acquired his paternal title. Ralph J. Gleason of *Down Beat* got the details from Hines:

"One night an announcer—let his name be forgotten, Earl says—was given a fatherly talking to by Hines. He'd been drinking too much on the job and Hines was asked to talk to him and did. Later that night he opened the show, sprawling on the table and leaning over the mike lushed to the gills. He said, 'Here comes Father Hines through the deep forest with his children.' And the tag stuck."

The Grand Terrace was controlled by the Capone mob, but Hines found that working for gangsters could sometimes have its points. During one of his Southern tours, Hines heard a singer named Arthur Lee Simpkins in Atlanta and invited him to come to Chicago. Simpkins was working as a handyman in a white bank at the time. After the Hines band got back to the Grand Terrace, Simpkins turned up one night, asking for a chance with the band. He auditioned and was given a job. A little later Simpkins's ex-boss arrived from Atlanta to demand that his "colored boy" be returned. When Hines warned the Grand Terrace's owners that they were about to lose their popular new tenor, a couple of tough bouncers were assigned to get the banker started on a fast trip back to Georgia.

Several years later Hines was impressed by the singing of a thirty-five-dollar-a-week crooner at the Club DeLisa and asked him to join the band. The singer was Billy Eckstine. When Eckstine opened with Hines at the Grand Terrace, the DeLisa sent over some emissaries armed with badly concealed revolvers to bring

Eckstine back. The Terrace's bravos had their own ideas, however, and after a discussion of comparative arsenals, the DeLisa's representatives went home and Eckstine stayed with Hines.

Along with Simpkins and Eckstine, Hines also unearthed Herb Jeffries while Hines was leading his band at the Grand Terrace. His first band there included George Mitchell and Shirley Clay on trumpets and Hayes Alvis on bass. In 1932 he picked up three men who were to be his mainstays for many years—clarinetists Darnell Howard (six years) and Omer Simeon (seven years) and trumpeter-vocalist Walter Fuller (eight years). The next year Trummy Young was added to the Hines trombone section, and Jimmy Mundy arrived to play tenor saxophone and write arrangements. Budd Johnson, Hines's right-hand man for ten years, came in 1934 and in 1938 Ray Nance, now a long-time veteran of the Ellington band, had a brief fling with Hines as a trumpet man and singer.

The Hines band made its first records for Victor in 1929—nine none-too-remarkable sides. However, the series of disks it turned out for Brunswick between 1932 and 1934 represents one of the high points of Hines's recording career. It includes *Harlem Laments, Blue Drag, Cavernism, Rosetta* and *Madhouse.* Subsequently the Hines band recorded for Decca and Vocalion, but on neither label did it generate the gutty, swinging drive that came through on the Brunswicks.

As a band leader, Hines was able to dramatize his playing in a way that could only be suggested when he was working as a single (the rolling piano bit, for instance) and was practically out of the question in a sideman. For stage presentations, a baby spotlight played on his right hand as the curtains parted, and his purposely large and multi-faceted ring gleamed and glistened as his fingers roved caressingly over the keys. He liked to wind up a solo by lifting his hands slowly and dramatically from the keyboard as he turned to the audience with a gleaming and assured smile. He was an imposing figure at the piano, erect, solid, his hands seemingly covering most of the keyboard.

For many years a story circulated that Hines was able to play as he did because he had had the webbing between his fingers cut to give his hands a wider stretch. Hines dismisses this as nonsense.

"My normal reach is a tenth," he says, "though I can make elevenths and sometimes twelfths. But I really have to slip over them. The way I invert the chords makes them sound bigger."

Hines worked steadily during the years when he was centered

at the Grand Terrace, but for a successful band leader he made remarkably little money—at times he was getting $150 a week. He was under contract all through this period to Ed Fox who managed the Grand Terrace. Toward the end of the 'thirties, Hines began to find it tough going. New bands had come up since he had started —Jimmy Lunceford, Benny Goodman, Count Basie—and they were getting all the play while he seemed to be getting none. After a particularly disastrous tour to Los Angeles and back to Chicago, Hines found himself laying off with no work in sight.

In October, 1940, Benny Goodman offered Earl a job with his band. Hines was tempted to accept although he hated to backtrack from his status as a leader to become a sideman again. While he was thinking about Goodman's offer, he took his contract with Fox to the Musicians Union to find out if he had really been getting all the money he should have. The union looked over the contract, told Hines it was unfair and illegal and Hines suddenly and unexpectedly found himself freed of Fox's management.

That was all the stimulant he needed to turn down Goodman's offer. Budd Johnson started revitalizing the Hines band, bringing in new men and whipping them into shape. Hines signed with the William Morris office and made Charlie Carpenter, his onetime valet, his manager. Soon the new Hines band was booked solid for five months ahead. It was recording for Victor's Bluebird label and had a strong hit in *Boogie Woogie on the St. Louis Blues*.

During 1941 and 1942, the Hines band began to show the first signs of the pre-bop incubator that it was about to become. Billy Eckstine was already with the band by then, singing and playing a little trumpet. Little Benny Harris came in on trumpet in April, 1941, and Freddy Webster recorded with the band the following August. The next year Dizzy Gillespie and trombonist Benny Green joined up. Charlie Parker replaced Budd Johnson, playing tenor (Parker, of course, was an alto player, so Hines bought a tenor for him). Shadow Wilson took over on drums. At the Apollo Theatre in Harlem, Hines heard one of the Apollo's Amateur Night winners, Sarah Vaughan, and immediately took her on as second pianist and vocalist.

This was a band that holds a unique transitional place in jazz history, almost documenting within itself the shift from swing to bop. But although it stayed together at its peak for almost a year, it left no records behind. Its entire existence coincided with the Musicians Union ban on recording that lasted from 1942 until

1944. Long before the ban had been lifted, the band was falling apart. It had been booked on a long series of unprofitable and dispiriting Army camp shows and, without disks to back it up, it remained virtually unknown. One by one the potential stars that Hines had assembled dropped out. The biggest blow came when Eckstine decided to build a big band of his own in 1944, using the heart of the Hines band—Gillespie, Parker, Sarah Vaughan, Shorty McConnell and Gail Brockman.

Undaunted, Hines kept on going. In 1945 he had Wardell Gray on tenor, but he was moving toward an odd goal.

"I've always had a funny ambition to do something like Waring and Whiteman along jazz lines," he once said. "Groups of singers, large bands, every kind of instrumentation and scoring possible."

Soon he had just that kind of band, a band with French horns and eight girls sawing away in a string section ("Man, those women like to run me crazy!") This unlikely gambit, combined with the trend of the times against big bands, foreshadowed the end of the Hines band. In 1948, Earl gave up as a band leader and joined Louis Armstrong's small group which, briefly, was an amazing collection of jazz masters while Jack Teagarden, Cozy Cole, Hines and Armstrong were all working together. But Hines chafed under the tedious and repetitious musical strait jacket within which Armstrong has sheltered himself in the past decade, and he dropped out of the group in 1951. Since then he has spent most of his time on the West Coast and, in 1956, settled in San Francisco.

Today Hines's once hard and brilliant manner has softened noticeably. The strutting, dazzling displays which have been characterized (by Hugues Panassie) as "the best example of the errant, audacious, inventive genius, as opposed to the comfortable, solid style of someone like Fats Waller or James P. Johnson," have become, on the evidence of his most recent recordings (Fantasy 3217), rather comfortable and solid themselves. The daring innovator of the late 'twenties is now, quite understandably, a viewer-with-alarm.

"The modern piano has just about changed the whole system as far as the public is concerned," the man who changed the whole system thirty years ago said recently. "They're getting to the place where they're disinterested . . . it's getting so farfetched that the general public actually doesn't know what's happening when it comes to playing a tune that they're used to listening to for some time, such as *Body and Soul*. The way some of the fellows are playing it now, after the first four bars you don't know what it is. So the average pianist nowadays I think is just getting too far out and is not actually playing from the heart. Looks like it's a challenge now . . . every new guy is trying to find a new sound and is just getting completely away from the good feeling."

This point of view neatly fills out a jazz piano cycle. For when young Earl Hines started breaking up the rhythm, interpolating sudden fantastic passages and going out on venturesome limbs which seemed to have no relationship to the basic tune and tempo, he was accused by the conservatives of the 'twenties of "getting too far out," of "not actually playing from the heart." It is probably one of the most meaningful compliments that modern jazz pianists could receive, coming—as it does—from the man who is, at the very least, the stylistic and philosophical father of them all.

SELECTED DISCOGRAPHY—EARL HINES

PIANO SOLOS:

Earl Hines, Atlantic 120 (the original QRS solos).

The Art of Jazz Piano, Epic LN 3295 (with Art Tatum, James P. Johnson, Joe Sullivan).

Earl Hines, Piano Solos, "X" LVA-3023.

Fats Waller Songs, Brunswick BL 58034 (with Nat Jaffe).

"Fatha" Plays "Fats," Fantasy 3217.

LOUIS ARMSTRONG SMALL GROUPS:

The Louis Armstrong Story, Vol. 3, Columbia CL 853.

Satchmo on Stage, Decca 8330.

New Orleans Days, Decca 5279.

OTHER SMALL GROUPS:

Jazz Royalty, EmArcy 26023 (with Count Basie).

Earl "Fatha" Hines and His New Sounds, Nocturne 5.

BIG BAND:

Oh, Father!, Epic LN 3223.

Bix
Beiderbecke

*   *   *   *

By George Hoefer

Except for his immediate family and a few fellow musicians, no one paid much attention to Bix Beiderbecke while he was alive. Then, suddenly, five years after his death, everyone in jazz had roomed with him and had his own "Bix story" to tell. How come?

It was because America's jazz world found itself being taken seriously and needed a hero, preferably of the martyr type, to build a romantic legend for a new American art form.

Bix was perfect for the role. He died young, at twenty-eight, and what's more he died "in the saddle" they said. He had forced himself up out of a sick bed and journeyed to Princeton to play a fraternity prom in a blizzard. When he got back to New York City, he expired in two days from double pneumonia. This sacrifice was made by our "young man with a golden horn" because the good Princeton brothers had informed the New York agency that they would not accept the band unless Bix was playing cornet.

Bix died in August, 1931. The legend thrived for over twenty years before anyone began wondering in print what the hell Princeton was doing having a frat dance in a blizzard during the month of August!

Yes, everyone wanted in the act back there in the middle 'thirties, when a surge of interest in jazz and its historical backgrounds hit the unsuspecting musicians. Fond remembrances of Bix were published in quantity. Music journals and trade papers brought out "Bix editions" in which every column was a tribute.

All who had heard or played with Bix got misty-eyed and took on an air of superior intelligence with, "Oh, you should have heard that horn." Hoagy Carmichael reported that hearing four notes on Bix's cornet made him collapse exhausted onto a davenport. Paul Whiteman said that Bix could play more in three notes than most men could in an entire chorus. The late Frankie Trumbauer compared the work of Bix with the beauty of flowers, clouds and autumn leaves.

The recitals of Bixian antics poured out until the point of saturation was reached and contradictions became rife. Bix was the "roaring 'twenties" personified and a product of the Prohibition era of flagpole sitters, channel swimmers, the Lone Eagle and bathtub gin.

It was pure romanticism and helped to counteract the depression blues; but all the braggartism, superabundance of praise, and sentimentality began to wear mighty thin. Reaction set in.

Jazz students and writers began to have opinions of their own and the legends began to rankle, especially, when syrupy novels and movie scenarios began to crop up.

Critics then began evaluating Beiderbecke out of context. The examination of jazz history and origins had progressed considerably, and become concentrated in the study of the small bands of the New Orleans Negroes. Any musician who had anything to do with saxophones or big bands didn't deserve to be called a *jazz musician*. This curious coterie of critics even managed to disown Duke Ellington and his band.

Rudi Blesh in *Shining Trumpets* stated, "Bix's playing is weak. He just pretended to be a jazz musician because his weakness permitted him to play in the commercial orchestras of Paul Whiteman and Jean Goldkette. Bix was neither a tragic nor a heroic character; he was a figure of pathos."

So, we have Bix Beiderbecke, an unappreciated artist while still alive, going through a complete cycle of favor and disfavor in the short space of twenty years: from the greatly exaggerated, "He was the greatest," to the "He was grossly overrated" schools of thought.

A re-assessment of Bix is long overdue. And this time more attention should be given to the music itself as it exists on available records. Furthermore, an evaluation of Beiderbecke should be predicated on the realization that he was an enigmatic individual and a man apart, who received very little understanding from the world around him. He had the restless creativity that constantly required striving towards an inaccessible goal. This inner burning could never be satisfied, but could be quieted and transformed into passive satisfaction by pouring liquor on the flames.

An unprejudiced review of some of the authenticated facts of

Bix's life is necessary to bring the picture into proper focus. It must be remembered the legend was formulated, as legends usually are, with the hero being exactly what the creator wants him to be. Many of the musicians who helped build the legend will today admit they really didn't know Bix. No one really did; he was a strange guy.

It also must be recognized that many of the legendary stories were true in fact. What made the legend untenable was the interpretation of the facts.

Leon Bismarck Beiderbecke was born on March 10, 1903, in Davenport, Iowa. His birthplace was not what one would call a typical Midwestern town. It was a river town; and a half century before, the big, muddy, rambling Mississippi had been alive with traffic going up and down the "Father of Waters." This activity meant river towns were infiltrated with strangers from glamourous New Orleans, Memphis and St. Louis.

Davenport's busy levee was visited by the show world as well as by commerce. Showboats, large floating palacelike theatres, were towed and pushed up and down the river by auxiliary craft, and spent long intervals tied to Davenport's docks. There are two Illinois towns directly across the river from Davenport—Rock Island and Moline—which gave the area the importance of one large city.

Similarly, the Tri-Cities attracted steam-driven excursion boats which offered "Moonlight Cruises," with dancing to a five-piece band, as they plied the river from place to place.

There is a certain beauty belonging to the town itself, built on the slope of a bluff commanding an extensive view of the landscape and the river scenery.

Colonel George Davenport founded the town in 1835 and among the early settlers was a German family named Beiderbecke. They became bulwarks of the community's business life. The men were bank officers, merchants and pillars of the Lutheran Church. Bix's grandfather was the leader of the Mannerchoir, which sang every Sunday in church, as well as at social affairs.

The boys newly born into the Beiderbecke clan seemed always to inherit the nickname "Bix," derived from Bismarck. Leon's father was named Herman Bismarck Beiderbecke and he and his wife Agatha had three children, Charles, Mary Louise and Leon Bismarck.

At the time of the birth of their third child, Mr. Beiderbecke was the owner of a coal and lumber business, and the family lived in a large frame house in a quiet residential neighborhood. It was a

German home, with a Victorian aura about it, and it was furnished in the mode of that age of gilded opulence.

The stolid Beiderbeckes were not so austere that they didn't like some gay music from time to time. The parlor organ frequently resounded with the likes of *Old Black Joe*. Mr. Beiderbecke was said to have played a zither, and Mrs. Beiderbecke was quite adept on the organ and piano.

When Leon was born, the nickname Bix had already been assigned to his older brother Charles Burnette, and so he was designated "little Bickie." Even as a very young child, with bangs and clad in dresses, he began to show signs of an unusual aptitude for and interest in music. He had a wonderful ear and his mother has said that at the early age of three he would stand at the piano reaching one hand up to the keys and pick out with one finger the melody of Liszt's *Hungarian Rhapsody No. 2*. Later, when he would get tired and out of sorts, his mother would suggest he go to the piano and play something. This always seemed to work and when they saw him playing, he never looked at the keys or watched his hands, but set his gaze off into space.

The Beiderbeckes were quite pleased and envisioned their third-born becoming a concert pianist. Some quirk that affected Bickie emotionally may have happened during this early period. He became quite shy about playing with other people in the parlor. Frequent mention has been made of how Bix loved to sit alone at the piano and play for himself throughout his lifetime.

Bix's musical fame became known to Davenport as early as 1910, when the local paper ran a piece about the little seven-year-old musical wonder, who could play any selection he heard. It went on to report that the child had never had a music lesson and didn't know one note from the other.

It was about this time that the Beiderbeckes decided that Bix should have some formal instruction. He tried it for about a year until the teacher gave up, realizing he couldn't teach the boy anything and that the talent was one that lay deep within. And here is the enigma that was Bix; all through his life he ignored the mechanics of music, although he was constantly pent up with a driving passion for new sounds and new forms. His teacher noted his ability to play perfectly by ear anything that he heard and his lack of inclination to learn to read music.

Available information indicates that Bix was introduced to jazz music and the cornet at about the same time, in 1918, when his brother Charles had been discharged from the army. Big Bix celebrated the occasion by buying a victrola with a stack of records thrown in free. One or more of the records were by the Original Dixieland Jazz Band featuring Nick La Rocca's cornet. Bickie was hooked.

During this same year, young Beiderbecke was reported to have acquired a secondhand cornet, much to the consternation of a family that still dreamed of having a concert pianist in its bosom. His uncle, Art Peterson, a Davenport bandmaster, was more than a little perturbed. When Bix came to him for lessons on the cornet, he refused to go along. Bix never asked again.

Bix learned by playing along with the records that came with the victrola. His method of holding and manipulating the instrument was completely unorthodox, and was probably due to the simple fact that he taught himself to play that way for lack of knowing any other method. The usual fingering technique employs the first two valves much more than the third valve. Bix relied heavily on the third valve, and this peculiar fingering method was to stay with him throughout his career. Some of his unique effects and his individual style have been attributed to this "wrong" way of handling a horn.

Bix's impeccable good taste was being formed during this stage of his development. Tricks like "triple tonguing," and the use of growl and wa-wa mutes didn't appeal to him, ever. He kept one straight mute for occasional use and sometimes played a short chorus with the bell of his horn in a derby.

He was destined never to forsake the cornet for the more brilliant-sounding trumpet. He was to always prefer the mellower tones of the shorter horn with the bigger bore.

There is good reason to believe that Bix derived some of his preference for the cornet from Emmet Hardy, a legendary horn player from New Orleans, who died in 1925 without ever making any records. There is not much doubt that Hardy played in Davenport in 1919 with either Carlisle Evans's Jazz Band or Bee Palmer's vaudeville act. Many of the New Orleans musicians insist that Hardy, who also preferred cornet, taught Bix how to use the third valve of his horn for quick passages, and also showed him the value of slurring his notes. Evidence that Bix thought a great deal of Hardy is borne out by the fact Bix wrote Hardy's mother in 1925, after Emmet's death, "Emmet was the greatest musician I have ever heard. If ever I can come near your son's greatness, I'll die happy."

His family has recalled that Bix would sit cross-legged on the floor by the victrola and play along with the records. His technique was to feel for notes as he went along, and when he learned the tune in one key he would speed up the phonograph and play the same number in another key. One of his fellow musicians during the early days has said Bix had a highly developed sense of tonality, which was entirely intuitive.

Bix spent two and a half years at Davenport High. People were already beginning to think him a little strange because of his constant preoccupation with music. Yet, he was a "typical American Boy" in many ways. He was full of jokes and seemed to possess considerable athletic prowess. He liked baseball and managed to win the Tri-Cities championship in tennis for his age group. But he had a way of sauntering down the streets of Davenport totally oblivious of his surroundings, with his cornet under his arm wrapped in a newspaper. This method of transporting his horn assumed quite a bit of emphasis in the legend. The screwy musician with his horn in a paper bag figured in all of the stories. Bix didn't get a case with his first horn. It had been bought secondhand. In later years he always used a blue corduroy drawstring bag which he could hang on hat racks in bars and restaurants. He always seemed to be leaving his horn on chairs in those places.

The pattern of his future life was forming during this early period. He was absent-minded. Once, in later years, he packed his trunk and sent it out to be shipped to the next town without leaving himself anything to wear.

He heard whatever music there was to be listened to around Davenport, which was probably quite a bit. There were river boats, roadhouses and dance halls galore in the Tri-City area. Louis Armstrong was with Fate Marable's band on the *Dixie Belle* in 1920 when it stopped in Davenport. Bix could have easily heard him without knowing his name. He frequently heard Tony Catalano playing trumpet with his Iowans at the Terrace Gardens. But who heard whom is not too important. The influences of value on any worth-while artist are the sum of many exposures.

Bix wanted to create true Dixieland jazz as he heard it on the ODJB records. This was to be his main interest for the first few years, and he was to find it difficult to get musicians to play with who could keep up with him. Bix's early repertoire consisted of *Fidgety Feet, Ostrich Walk,* and *Tiger Rag.* A musician noted many years later that on Dixieland numbers in jam sessions Bix was still using La Rocca's endings note for note.

Illustrative of the musical growth that Bix underwent through the years is the following story told by a local Davenport musician. In the early days, *Tiger Rag* was Bix's favorite tune. His mother has said he would sit for hours practicing along with the record. Years later when Bix returned home on sick leave from the Whiteman band, he would occasionally sit in with Bud Davis's orchestra at the Blackhawk Watchtower in Milan, Illinois. He was usually quiet and withdrawn and would smoke his pipe on the stand until he felt like playing. On one particular night, Davis, hoping to cheer Bix up, called for *Tiger Rag*. Bix looked up and said, "Oh, my God, NO!"

During this period of learning, Bix would want to sit in with the dance bands around town. As a rule, they had their regular arrangements, and Bix made a nuisance of himself trying to sit in when he wasn't wanted. The same thing happened a couple of years later when Bix started to hang around the New Orleans Rhythm Kings at the Friar's Inn in Chicago. Paul Mares, the NORK trumpeter, and Elmer Schoebel, the pianist, tell the story about Bix begging them to let him sit in when he knew only one number of theirs. They said they just couldn't play that same number over and over again. Evidence from many musicians involved with Bix's sitting-in adventures indicates that Bix wasn't considered much of a musician. One remarked that Bix seemed to know what he wanted to do on his instrument, but couldn't seem to get the notes out.

By 1921, the family was really worried about Bix and his music, and decided that he should either be a concert pianist or join his father at the East Davenport Fuel and Lumber Company. In the middle of his high-school career, they decided that Davenport was bad for him and that his place was in a school where he might forget jazz. They innocently selected Lake Forest Academy, just north of Chicago, and unknowingly dispatched him to as jumping an incubator of hot music as could be found in the Midwest.

Bix began his career at Lake Forest in September, 1921. He gravitated into the student band and the concert orchestra, and played on the baseball team. At least he posed in uniform for the baseball picture in the Lake Forest Year Book.

With Walter "Cy" Welge of Evanston, Bix organized a small dance band known as the CY-BIX Orchestra. They jobbed around at parties on the North Shore and picked up loose change which they began spending downtown in Chicago at the all-night Friar's Inn. Bix's acquaintanceship with musicians began to widen considerably. He soon lost interest in classes and sometimes was off campus for days at a time. He was eventually dropped from the class rolls.

Bix must have known by this time that he would be making music his life work. He had tried to join the Musicians Union back in Davenport while playing with Buckley's Novelty Orchestra at the Terrace Gardens. The entire band had to join up in order to hold the job. Bix memorized several tunes to play, but on the day of the test, they placed a sheet in front of him that he hadn't learned. He didn't make it, and the band lost the job.

Later when he came back from Lake Forest, Mrs. Beiderbecke called Uncle Art Peterson, who was on the examining board of the Davenport local at that time. Uncle Art gave the board a pep talk about Bix and his cornet saying, "He may be a little light on reading, but since he has some talent as jazzer, it would be a shame to turn him down." Bix came in on the appointed day and the board asked him where his cornet was. He had arrived empty-handed. Bix answered, "I'm taking the exam on the piano this time." He played several semi-classical numbers and passed.

Although Bix began life as a professional musician in 1922, there was to be one short deviation later on. This was in 1925 after he had left the Wolverines in New York. Les Zacheis of Cedar Rapids, Iowa, did some research at the University of Iowa, and came up with proof that Bix entered school at Iowa City as an unclassified student in February, 1925. He was registered for English, Religion and Ethics, Music Theory, Piano lessons, and Music History. He lived at the Beta House and the following is his complete matriculation record: On February sixteenth he had the usual interview with his Freshman Counselor. Bix asked if he could drop Religion so that he could take more music. The counselor's answer was, "I note you didn't register for Military Training, Physical Education and Freshman Lectures. Do so immediately." The next entry —February twentieth—"Dropped from the University."

Throughout Bix's life there was an everlasting seeking; and terrible, sometimes frantic frustration. According to the legend, Bix must have composed or revised *In a Mist* on the piano of every dance hall, bandstand, back room and hotel room in the country. His relaxation was playing the piano and he was constantly experimenting between band sets. But he never seemed to find what he was looking for.

Wilbur Hatch, an arranger and prominent music director, noticed Bix's interest in new harmony ideas as early as the summer

of 1922. Hatch, then a student at the University of Chicago, organized a four-piece combo to play at Delavan Lake, Wisconsin, and
Bix was hired for the date. During intermissions, Bix would park on
the piano bench and improvise, much to the consternation of the
other musicians, who thought he was playing nothing but progressions of discords. Hatch points out that he was playing sixth, ninth
and thirteenth chords, which became common in modern dance arrangements. In those days, dance numbers were played with only the
simplest harmonies.

All of Bix's compositions with the exception of *Davenport
Blues* came forth as a result of his constant noodling at the piano.
Another musician, who heard Bix's pianistic excursion between numbers, noted that his dominant ninth and eleventh progressions and
false modulations were way ahead of time. Through the years Bix
became much more interested in the modern impressionistic composers than he was in Dixieland jazz.

His musical life was progressive. We have seen how he was
taken by the Original Dixieland Band back at the beginning. Then,
when he started to work around Chicago he discovered Louis, King
Oliver, Bessie Smith and Jimmie Noone. These musicians had a tremendous influence on him, for he felt that this was the real jazz, and
the ODJB had developed its style by using the real stuff as a base
and combining it with ragtime.

Bix was the Wolverines. Without him there was no band. The
Wolverines have been credited with being the first white band to play
the genuine Negro style of jazz. It was Bix who inculcated the group
with both ideas and guts, and some of the Wolverines themselves
have admitted that Bix left the band before the end of the Cinderella
Dance Palace run on Broadway because he felt they were too far
behind him musically. Here again he was restless and felt he had
gone as far as he could go with a particular "sound."

That was when Bix went back to Chicago, even back to school;
and while playing with Charlie Straight, he ran around with the
Chicagoans. Some critics have bemoaned the fact that Bix didn't
stay with the Austin High Gang and make records with them. But
Bix was restless and soon took off for St. Louis. He had met Frankie
Trumbauer in New York while with the Wolverines. They had exchanged musical ideas and become friends. When Bix went to St.
Louis to join Trumbauer at the Arcadia Ballroom, a musical partnership was formed. It bore fruit later in the famed Bix-Tram chase

choruses. They worked well together, and when Jean Goldkette offered Tram the leadership of his unit at Hudson Lake, he accepted only on the condition that Bix be included in the deal.

Then came the Goldkette band of 1927, perhaps the greatest white jazz band before Goodman's. Only those who heard or played in that band can substantiate that, because the records, with one or two exceptions were poor, although the musical power is discernible.

It has been said that Bix sold out to commercialism by joining Goldkette and Whiteman. As George Avakian aptly put it, "No one had a gun at Bix's back when he joined the big bands." Bix could have gotten plenty of work elsewhere in those days. No, Bix joined those bands because he wanted to be in them, despite the fact that his reading deficiencies were against him. Distinguishing the Goldkette band from its ricky-tick contemporaries during Bix's time were its advanced arrangements. The Bill Challis book was skillful and progressive—and in becoming a member of the band, Bix probably felt that he was taking a step forward musically. This might also explain his subsequent move into the most important commercial band in the world—Paul Whiteman's. There were things going on. Things that meant more to Bix than the three-hundred-dollar weekly check. Bix was fascinated by the work of Challis and Grofe. Challis had moved to P.W. with Bix and Tram in late 1927 after the fabulous Goldkette band had to break up because the group was unable to perform the necessary "hokum" to pay the freight.

George Avakian has offered the thought that Bix may have been schizophrenic about the Whiteman band. Hating it on the one hand, loving it on the other. There is no doubt that there were many things about the band that would have made Bix cringe. In New Orleans the local musicians had to plead with Whiteman to let Bix play during the band's appearance at a theatre. In that particular case, Whiteman did alter the show so that a hot group descended from the pyramid formation on stage and played a few numbers with Bix. The maestro walked off into the wings. But in 1938, when jazz was paying off, Whiteman wasn't quite so indifferent and wrote warmly of Bix in an article in *Collier's*.

Bix undoubtedly received a certain amount of genuine musical satisfaction out of playing in the big "concert" orchestra. We know, for example, that he was thrilled about joining the band. On the way to Indianapolis to join Whiteman he wrote to his mother about how frightened he was at the prospect of being in such a famous or-

ganization. One of the happiest interludes in his musical career was
having his mother stay with him at the Edgewater Beach Hotel
when the Whiteman orchestra played an engagement in Chicago.

When Bix returned to New York City, following his sick leave
in 1930, during which Whiteman had paid him his regular salary
and the band had left an empty chair on the stand for him, he wanted
very much to rejoin the orchestra. By this time though, his health
was just about gone and he just couldn't make it. It was a bitter disappointment and contributed a great deal to his poor mental and
physical condition during the last year of his life.

Another curious part of the Bix legend has to do with his supposed indifference to women. There's no doubt that music came first,
and more than a few musicians have sworn that they never saw Bix
in the company of a girl. It is true that he was shy and not the usual
musician type of "lady killer." Pee Wee Russell has the impression
that while Bix didn't do much running after women, they went for
him, and he occasionally had a time beating them off.

There is considerable evidence that girls *were* attracted to Bix.
There is also reliable proof that Bix had more than one love affair.
His mildness and good manners were in contrast to the aggressive
"on-the-make" traveling bandsman. Bix disliked the playgirls who
hung around the dance halls and resort ballrooms. His standards
were rather high for the kind of environment in which he spent a good
part of his time. He always held his mother in great regard and may
have been afflicted with a slight case of "Momism."

In his chapter on Bix in *Jazzmen,* Ed Nichols mentions a girl
who was following Bix around during the days of the Wolverines.
He also mentions two women in St. Louis who were supposed to have
been still in love with Bix in 1938 when the book was written.
Avakian, in writing the notes for *The Bix Beiderbecke Story* (series
of albums) mentions that the only girl who seemed to mean anything
to Bix was a cheerleader at Indiana University. She played good
piano and it was supposed to have been Bix's music that attracted
her. She lived in Hammond, Indiana, and things were said to have
gotten serious for a while. Sixteen years later Ed Nichols found this
girl singing in a gin mill and she refused to talk about Bix or anything else.

Mezz Mezzrow mentions a big blonde who "dropped everything" in order to follow Bix around for several days. And someone
in Davenport has written about a woman who has been seen visiting Bix's grave on various occasions.

And finally, Hoagy Carmichael, in *The Stardust Road,* tells about the mysterious girl Bix met a few weeks before his death who was going to get him settled in a flat on Long Island.

There is definite proof that Bix was in love with or very fond of a girl who lived in Indiana. The relationship was in force during the time he was playing with Charlie Straight at the Rendezvous Café in Chicago. The Indiana girl made several trips to Chicago to see Bix. On one Sunday morning after he met her at the railroad station, he asked her what she wanted to do. She said she was agreeable to anything he wanted to do. He took her to church. Bix had felt serious enough about her to visit her family home and play the piano for her mother. He left two Wolverine records with the girl, and she still has them along with a picture signed L. B. Beiderbecke.

The affair broke off when Bix went to St. Louis. The girl married another musician; and some years later when Paul Whiteman played an Indiana theatre, she thought about going to see Bix. She didn't, however, because she felt insufficiently beauty-parlored for the occasion; and besides, her husband was playing in the theatre pit band.

A very significant factor in Bix's musical development is his lifetime interest in impressionistic composers. Late in his jazz career he was heard to say rather cryptically, "Jazz isn't written music but just lip technique." Some of Bix's favorite music included Debussy's *Afternoon of a Faun* and *Clair De Lune;* Stravinsky's *Firebird* and *Petrouchka;* MacDowell's *Epilogue* and *To a Water Lily;* Eastwood Lane's *Adirondack Sketches;* Schoenberg; and Ravel. He also was fond of Gustav Holst's *The Planets.* His favorite section of the *Adirondack Sketches* was called *Dirge for Indian Joe.* Jim Moynahan has often spoken of the night he went downtown with Bix to a Hungarian restaurant to hear the orchestra. Bix was completely knocked out by the cymbalon player. The evening wound up with Bix playing Eastwood Lane's *Land of the Loon* for the Hungarian Orchestra.

Itzey Riskin, who played piano with the Goldkette orchestra, said Bix was the first one to introduce the whole-tone scale into dance music. This assertion is based on the fact that one lick in Bix's *Davenport Blues* was based on Debussy's scale.

Bix frequently attended the Symphony concerts in St. Louis, Chicago and New York. Other musicians considered him an authority on symphonic music.

The last year of Bix's life was hard. It was depression time and he didn't seem to have any interest in anything. He could be found frequently in Plunkett's speakeasy on Fifty-third Street, and was often broke. What musical interest he had left had been directed towards classical music. In 1930 he had spent a lot of time in Bill Challis's apartment playing the piano and working on his compositions. These were his piano pieces *In a Mist, Flashes, In the Dark,* and *Candlelights.*

His last year was spent in a bare hotel room. The late Josh Billings used to tell how he often visited Bix and how they filled the bathtub with prohibition gin. There was a piano in the room and Bix would play for hours. When his tumbler was empty, he would tell Josh to "scoop him up some gin." They had a big dipper to use for filling the glasses.

The girl mentioned by Carmichael made good her promise at this time to get Bix out of the crowded city to an apartment on Long Island. His last weeks were spent in the apartment of a bass player named George Kraslow, out in Sunnyside, Queens.

Kraslow recalls that many times through that period Bix would pick up his cornet, no matter what time it was, and play for himself. The tenants in the building would mention to Kraslow that they had been awakened at two or three in the morning by the lovely music emanating from his apartment. They would also make a point to add, "Please don't mention we said anything as we don't want him reprimanded and would hate for him to stop."

Bix collapsed in Kraslow's apartment on August 6, 1931. He died at nine thirty P.M. of lobar pneumonia and edema of the brain. His funeral was held at Oak Dale Cemetery, Davenport, Iowa, on August eighth.

Bix's unique cornet style has been copied and quasi-reproduced by many musicians, but no one has ever quite reached the consistency of lyrical clarity that had been most characteristic of Bix. Nor has anyone ever possessed Bix's odd, disturbing combination of the lost and the ingenuously found.

SELECTED DISCOGRAPHY—BIX BEIDERBECKE

The Bix Beiderbecke Story—Volumes I, II, III. 12″ Columbia ML 4811, 4812, 4813.

Bix and The Wolverines—Volumes I & II. 10″ Riverside 1023, 1050.

Beiderbecke Suite (Piano) by Ralph Sutton. 12″ Commodore 300001.

Pee Wee Russell

*   *   *   *

By Charles Edward Smith

Pee Wee Russell, christened Charles Ellsworth, lives with his wife, Mary, in an apartment in lower Greenwich Village, New York City. Mary has decorated the walls with photographs illustrative of the life and times of Pee Wee. One photograph shows him at the thumb-sucking stage, busily working up an embouchure. Another shows him with the family's pet pooch, both of them looking anxiously out at life. In a third, he looks like a World War I rookie; this was taken when he was at military school, where he was forced to practice clarinet an hour a day and was known simply as "Russell." In still another he holds a saxophone in a *port arms* position. A recent one by Richard Avedon [1] is a character study that takes in the sadness and the smile and suggests something of the febrile nervousness with which he appears to approach each chorus (not a tic but a technique); one might describe it as a portrait, in detail and in depth, of a man and his clarinet. Sharing the apartment is a miniature schnauzer named Wink, a pepper-and-salt bundle of fire who might take offense if she were not mentioned.

Recently, as is often their custom, the Russells dined at a nearby restaurant. They were eating quietly and minding their own business when a woman, younger-looking than her memories, came to their table. She appraised Pee Wee with a glance and, without preamble, said, "Weren't you one of the Arcadians?"

"Oh, no!" Pee Wee expostulated, scared to death. Ghosts should at least wear shrouds. This one walked and talked and was in blooming good health.

Actually, Pee Wee had worked in the *relief band* at the Arcadia in St. Louis, at a time when this woman, then a girl, was often dated by Bud Hassler, who played tenor sax and did arrangements for Sunday-afternoon sessions, sometimes in whole-tone parlance. Pee

[1] *Harper's Bazaar,* July, 1955.

Wee, remembering, could almost hear someone (flushed from a Charleston) say admiringly, "Play those awful things!" There may not have been a big jazz following back there in the early 'twenties but it knew what it wanted.

Pee Wee was born in Maple Wood, Missouri, though his birthplace is sometimes given as Webster Groves, which is right next door. Both are considered part of St. Louis. Pee Wee's ancestors lived in border states—Missouri, Maryland—and though one was a colonel and one of the first, if not the first, officers to die in the Civil War (according to family oral history), Pee Wee does not know what side he was on. Pee Wee was named after him, as was his father. He is probably part Southern and certainly part Cherokee, which clinches it. This was one of the great Iroquoian tribes known as "The Five Intelligent Nations." A famous member of this tribe, Sequoyah, for whom some tall timber in the Sierras was named, invented the Cherokee alphabet. Pee Wee is one of the five or so intelligent men on jazz clarinet and invented an alphabet and a calligraphy for it peculiarly his own. One of his clarinet choruses, *I Ain't Gonna Give Nobody None of My Jelly Roll*,[2] is in the Library of Congress, where you'll probably find Sequoyah's alphabet as well.

Even when Pee Wee was small enough to be called that, he had the long bony fingers that today, when he is blowing, seem an extension of his personality. An Uncle Brouton, a surgeon, thought they were the hands of a surgeon; had he been musically minded, he might have thought them the hands of a pianist or a Paganini. The Russells had moved to Muskogee, Oklahoma, when Pee Wee was very young. They were reasonably well off, by no means wealthy. In the parlor was a Kimball piano, not an upright but one of those rectangular-shaped affairs that one used to see in moderately affluent surroundings, for which they had a pianola. Since Pee Wee played both but, in retrospect, seems to have had some slight affection for the latter in his musical memories (every kid's dream, piano without practice!), the following description, from *Music Lovers' Encyclopedia,*[3] may be of interest:

> *pianola.* A detachable pneumatic attachment by which a piano may be played mechanically, the performer controlling the speed, the force, and, in a remarkable degree, also the expres-

[2] Condon: CMS 531.
[3] Garden City Books, 1950.

sion; inv. by E. S. Votey of New York, in 1897. It has 65 felt-covered fingers brought into play by air-power forced through perforated music by treadle action.

In the Russell home, the perforated rolls were mostly standard piano pieces, but there were a few things that especially interested Pee Wee—popular tunes and piano rags. Another nineteenth-century invention of great interest to him, as to all *hot* musicians in those days, was the phonograph, the growth and development of which coincided with that of jazz itself and ensured the preservation of improvised, unwritten compositions. It was by way of the phonograph that Pee Wee heard much early jazz beyond the reach of his hitch-hiking feet or a car. It was thus he heard Larry Shields, of the Original Dixieland Jazz Band, for whom he had and has, sincere admiration. On a visit to New Orleans decades later, he asked Larry to sign his name to a menu card at a club on Lake Pontchartrain. Said Pee Wee, "That was the only time I asked anyone for his autograph."

If any proof were needed that Pee Wee was cut out for music, it must be apparent in the tenacity with which he stuck to it, though he had the normal child's impatience with practice. And though his parents encouraged him to the extent of paying for the instruments and lessons, probably the greatest encouragement his father gave him was when he would sneak him into the Elks Club, when they held a dance, leaving him back near the bandstand (out of sight) so that he could listen to a man who was—though Pee Wee was not then aware of it—one of the veterans of jazz, Alcide "Yellow" Nunez, clarinetist. That, and listening to a clarinetist in a pit band, Charlie Merrill, brought Pee Wee and the clarinet into focus, and they've been that way, now, for almost forty years.

The chronology of Pee Wee and his clarinet is not easy to establish, particularly as he is sometimes modest, or reticent, concerning episodes the telling of which might throw light on his personality, whether it be winning a musicians' popularity poll—in 1943 he won the *Down Beat* trophy for clarinet with 1,632 more votes than his nearest competitor—or paying a visit to old friend Leon Rappolo when the latter was in the Louisiana State Hospital. Like many top-ranking *hot* musicians, he is conscious of and conscientious about his art but doesn't beat any drums and doesn't talk about it in abstruse technical or intellectual jargon. If he appears to talk *of himself* in a garbled voice at times, it is certainly not because he lacks a lucid mind but because he prefers to play it rather than promote it.

As a youngster, Pee Wee had a sensitive ear to which the sounds that came forth from his early instruments were not exactly music. "The violin came first," he recalled, and added abruptly, "I couldn't get along with it." At music school, "There were sixteen pupils and I was number sixteen on the list. I was about nine then. So that was all right. Once a month the proud parents came to hear us. Then there was this big concert. I was so nervous I had the shakes and broke a string. I had to stand there, with everyone waiting, and change the string. *That* stopped as of then! The violin was not for me!"

He shifted to piano, with a lady teacher, and still recalls with a shudder the scales and chords in the exercise book. Next came drum lessons (traps: bass, snare, xylophone, bells, triangle, bird whistles—the works). And more exercises. Sometimes a friend would manipulate the pianola to help along a good cause.

It was about this time he got to hear Nunez. No children were allowed in the ballroom but Pee Wee, wearing knickers, was allowed back of the bandstand (thanks to his father) where he could let it soak in. Alcide "Yellow" Nunez had played with Jack "Papa" Laine (grandfather of Dixieland jazz) probably before 1905. In 1915, asked to bring a band north to Chicago—where Tom Brown was already at Lamb's Café with Shields—Nunez got Ragas (piano), La Rocca (cornet), Edwards (trombone), and Sparbaro (Spargo) (drums). This became the Original Dixieland Jazz Band, with Shields replacing Nunez before they recorded. On a postcard headed "Dixie Land Jass Band" and addressed to Jack Laine, Nunez wrote, "This is the band that clean up Chi. Ill. . . . Jack, you no that, what the use of bringing up again. And when we come back home this band will be Jack Laine's Band, that what all us boys said to each other. . . ."

As we said, Pee Wee knew none of this when he heard Nunez at the Elks Club; but he got the message. Nunez had a four-piece outfit (clarinet, piano, bass, drums, sometimes trombone added) at the Elks Club and at Seiver's Hotel. This was clearly a different kind of music, with a different approach and technique than that of his teachers. "Yellow Nunez played the melody, then got hot and played jazz. That was something. *How did he know where he was or where he was going?*"

These remarks—one feels redundant in saying so—express

succinctly the appeal of jazz to young, aspiring musicians in the very early 'twenties, when there was only the phonograph to hear it on, if one did not hear it live (radio was at the crystal set stage). All other music with the exception of folk music (which was very barefoot in that decade) seemed cut and dried by comparison. It might be worth listening to—most young jazzmen listened to and liked concert music—but very seldom did it encourage innovation or originality, even in performance. In jazz there was room for the creative thrust, from the way in which the instrument was played to the completed structure of a chorus (or piece). Jazz, in short, was accessible and exciting. Jazzmen slowly began to be added to name bands, to flavor the schmaltz with a *soupçon* of real old, down-home gumbo. But only a flavor. The majority of young jazzmen kept on playing gigs, tea dances, etc. As Benny Goodman once remarked,[4] "The whole spirit of jazz was astonishingly different. Believe it or not, we had only a small audience, so there was practically no temptation to commercialism."

At the Broadway in Muskogee, a theatre on the Junior Orpheum Circuit, the pit band included eight or nine men. This was, of course, no jazz band. But the clarinetist had style, and played with feeling. Pee Wee finally got up the courage to go backstage to meet him. He found out his name was Charlie Merrill. Pee Wee asked him if he would give lessons. Sure thing, was Charlie's answer, if Pee Wee could get a clarinet. Sensing that his enthusiasm for clarinet was the real thing, his father agreed to the project, and Pee Wee bought his first clarinet (Albert system) at the local music store.

He has an affectionate memory for those first lessons with Charlie Merrill. They came at $1. or $1.50 for half-hour periods. "I'd go to his house," Pee Wee recalled. "He'd say, 'Excuse me a minute, Mr. Ellsworth.'" (Pee Wee was then barely of high school age and the "Mr. Ellsworth" stuck in his mind.) "He'd go out to the kitchen, pour himself a hooker of corn whiskey—he didn't know at first that I caught on to that—and after two or three lessons we'd go overtime one, sometimes two, hours. It got so I was ahead of him on the lessons."

"This was for me," Pee Wee said. "I could play loud. I could play soft. . . . Then you'd get on with the fingering and get a little lip, some kind of embouchure, and you felt good when teacher praised you."

[4] Quoted by Charles Edward Smith, *High Fidelity*, July, 1956.

Pee Wee got his famous name when he was a sawed-off shrimp working band dates with big bruisers. School studies were neglected in ratio to his increasing absorption in music. But the latter was by no means all-consuming; he didn't need that excuse to skip classes. At what would be the equivalent of junior-high-school age, he sometimes drove his father to work, reported to school for maybe one class, then (usually with a fellow flaunter of authority) would devote the day to girls, good times and devilment, after which he'd call for his father and they'd drive sedately home.

This deviousness did not long remain hidden but what really blew the lid off was his insatiable zeal for after-hours blowing. At first his gigging around was on the up and up. Oddly enough, this is where Pee Wee's path first crossed that of Red Nichols. Red played at one time at the Playmore, in Kansas City, and Gene Perkins, cornet, was in the house band. Gene's brother Fred played piano and they had a summer job set for a lakeside pavilion near Agency Hill, not far from Muskogee. Their father was manager of a Muskogee department store and through him Pee Wee got his first vacation-time job, with the Perkins brothers. He worked from twelve noon to eleven at night for three dollars. Commented Pee Wee: "It strengthened my lip."

It was after this that Pee Wee played his first river-boat date. He should remember it. That was the night the lid blew off. He even recalled two of the musicians, Boozy Weather (drums) and Cookie Tranthem (violin). There was also a piano. "I needed long pants for this job. I'd never worn them in my life. I hid them in the garage. I got a ladder up near my window—sneaked out, got the pants, met the boys and went on this moonlight cruise on an Arkansas River boat that went out from a little amusement park about twenty miles from Muskogee." Well, Mr. Russell was no fool. When he found that Pee Wee was missing he made one good guess and got on the trail. He caught up with Pee Wee but let him finish the job that night. Then he let him know what he thought of him, and the upshot of it was that this time Charles had gone too far. "And that," said Pee Wee, "started me on the way to Western."

Western Military Academy, an honor school at Alton, Illinois, was, like most such schools, somewhat strict. Discipline was the operative word. This was a regime calculated to chasten the callow importunities of youth. Where these were strongly motivated, it strengthened resilience. "It was either that or reform school," said Pee Wee, not meaning to exaggerate in the least.

So there he was again, with no Charlie Merrill to pat him on the back or sweeten the air with the bouquet of Missouri corn. At Western, as noted, he *had to* practice! He did it in his room, standing up or sitting down, facing a music stand and reading the exercise book with all the enthusiasm a thirteen-year-old would have for Gibbon's *Decline and Fall of the Roman Empire*. And the clarinet had better be blowing or there'd be someone around to monitor the silence! It should be a great comfort to his many admirers to learn that for three periods his grades in deportment were, respectively, 100, 89 and 98. There was a jazz band of sorts, but Pee Wee didn't play in it. He played in the brass band and in the school orchestra. "They may not have the best instructors in the world," he said, *"but they told me what I was doing wrong and set me right*. And the discipline was good. I *had* to learn. It took me a while—it seemed a long time—but finally I made it, up to first clarinet."

To break the monotony he and another "bad boy" went on an unauthorized trip to St. Louis, an impulse that anyone who has studied at a somewhat strict school will appreciate, and this straying off the reservation may have been the cause for his dismissal. In response to an inquiry, Colonel C. L. Persing, headmaster at Western Military Academy, wrote: "Our records indicate that he attended Western from September 15, 1920, to October 21, 1921. He came to us from Central High School, Muskogee, Oklahoma. His birth date is March 27, 1906. This indicates that he was a very young man during his tenure at Western." He was dismissed in October, 1921, and although Colonel Persing was good enough to search the records, no explanation was found. "The reason for his dismissal," he concluded, "is lost in the minds of the men who were his teachers at that time—men who were very tolerant of the changing interests of young men. It may be that when he returned in the fall term he was like another great Western man, Thomas Hart Benton, who after a brief tour of duty in a military school found it not in line with his artistic temperament. As far as we are concerned, on our records he was an exemplary cadet."

During his very brief stay at the University of Missouri, which was midway between Kansas and St. Louis (at Columbia), he tended to wander off in either direction, wherever a jazz band was playing. While at Western he'd been accepted for the university and pledged to a fraternity. Aside from the fact that he wasn't attentive to his studies, that Joan Crawford was once an undergraduate there and that Orville Knapp played for tea dances at fraternity and sorority houses, there isn't much to report of that interlude which, as stated, was brief.

You can put down Pee Wee as one of the river-boat jazzmen, not from that one Arkansas River caper but because he played on the Mississippi River boats, the *St. Paul* and the *J.S.*, both venerable names in jazz annals. With his usual frankness he admitted, "I worked afternoons; the 'name' bands worked nights. We'd go up to Keokuk and Davenport on the Strekfus Line boats. This was around the time I was at college." Also around this time he worked dates with Herbert Berger's St. Louis Club Orchestra, including some recordings for Okeh.

Pee Wee met Louis and heard him play when Louis worked the river boats (1918–19) in bands that sometimes included Baby Dodds, drums; Sam Dutrey, trombone; and Pops Foster, string bass. In St. Louis he heard Charlie Creath, playing cornet with a deep, rough tone, and heard the great jazz drummer, Zutty Singleton. He skipped classes (when he got to Columbia) to play jobs and just for kicks. This is the basis for the often-quoted remark, "I'd go away on a Saturday and turn up on a Tuesday in time for a Monday morning class." In those early St. Louis years (possibly a bit later than the college years) he studied clarinet for a while with Tony Sarlie of the St. Louis Symphony Orchestra, who bore down on him for playing rags. One of the high lights of early St. Louis days was playing a benefit, with Sonny Lee on trombone, at the Booker T. Washington Theatre, at which Zutty and others also played. This theatre was built in 1910 by Charlie Turpin, who had previously had a tent show at the site (Market near Twenty-third). (Charlie was the first Negro to be elected constable in the county and the brother of Tom Turpin, 250-pound, Stetson-hatted, diamond-stud-shirt-fronted dean of St. Louis ragtimers in the 1890's.)

The period around 1920 and a bit later would take months to sort out—from the time he first heard records by the Dixieland Band to the time he heard them, and later Bix, in person. Pee Wee had considerable respect for that band, as did Bix, and for both of them this meant respect for Shields. Between them, they knew every note and nuance of those Dixieland Victors. Pee Wee heard Johnny Dodds and many Chicago musicians or musicians working out of Chicago, such as Wayne King. He remembered Wayne King for his kindness and for an interesting remark he made about Pee Wee's clarinet style. Wayne had come into town with the Benson Orchestra (remember them, boys and girls?) and let Pee Wee sit in once or twice. Once Wayne said, not unkindly, "Why don't you play clarinet—instead of cornet on clarinet?" That remark stuck in Pee Wee's mind, too, because the answer to it helped to explain himself to himself. Well, Nunez, for one, sometimes played that way. Dodds, for another. He opined that Wayne King had hit it right on the button and added, "I'd heard clarinet playing leads and that has a lot to do with the way I play."

Something else is implied in Wayne King's question and in Pee Wee's explanation and it is this: that a new concept of music had come out of New Orleans: *Every Tub on Its Own Bottom,* as the old song title had it. The *hot* chorus may have evolved from simple *breaks* and the tendency in the small ensemble to rove around in a sort of loose polyphony (of course, it evolved from other things as well, which have been discussed in many books on jazz), a tendency which increasingly found its ultimate expression in the *hot* chorus. In the *popular* bands, with which Wayne King was familiar, each instrument knew its place and assayed no comeuppances. The lead function of cornet or violin was unassailable. In the early New Orleans bands, though the cornet has the lead, the *cantus firmus,* all instruments kick it around. Hence, these things work both ways. When he first recorded a solo of *Tiger Rag,* Bix based it upon Shields's clarinet part!

Pee Wee toured the Western lands—Kansas, the Dakotas, *et cetera*—with a tent show, going over the same territory later in bands playing vaudeville. The Allen Brothers show had an elephant, a steam calliope and a band that included Orville Knapp, by this time an old acquaintance. It wasn't much of a musical job, it wasn't money and, except to the elephant, it wasn't hay. When the show was playing Moulton, Iowa (population 985), Pee Wee got a wire from Herbert Berger saying that there was a job in Juarez, Mexico. Pee Wee wired that he was on his way.

It turned out that the job Berger had found for him was not with his own band at the Central Café but across the street, at the Big Kid's Palace, where clarinet, piano and drums were to hold forth. If they could! The joint was colorful, crowded and a maelstrom of noise. The Big Kid's was known as the longest bar on the border—and one of the toughest. "That bar was a block long, literally, and always packed. And, of course, in those days we played without amplification." Sousa's brass band might have made it, but Pee Wee, understandably, couldn't cope. After three days, to no one's surprise, they were kicked out.

Pee Wee went across the street, sat in with the band at the Central Café, and joined the El Paso local of the Musicians Union. After a while he was made a regular member of the band. James Cruze, the famous moving-picture director, was in town; they were doing location shots for "The Covered Wagon." Cruze came to the Central—it was the only civilized place along that stretch of the border—listened to the Russell clarinet, and said, "If you come to Hollywood, look us up; we'll do something for you," and meant it. This was not because he had observed that Pee Wee was sardonically photogenic—he has since become a favorite of photographers—but because the new glamour town on the Coast hadn't heard anything like that clarinet. For the clarinet, and for his likable personality (which was which, anyway?), the management liked him very much, didn't want him to go and urged him to return. Pee Wee never did, but Brad Gowans, valve trombonist and sports car enthusiast, breezed into the place, just by chance, not knowing any of this, many years later. He almost choked on his drink. Staring at him over the bar was a huge picture of Charles Ellsworth Russell, in bell-bottom trousers, *circa* 1923!

After almost a year with Berger, Pee Wee worked with Floyd Robinson's band at an El Paso hotel. Then he went to Tucson for a band job but the Local wouldn't let him work; he hadn't been in town long enough to be "local." This is the period, often mentioned, when he went on a peanuts-and-water diet. A friendly stationmaster let him sleep in the station, tipped him off when the cop made his rounds. Some nights he slept under a palm tree on the campus of the state school. When he'd had more than enough of this, he managed to get back to El Paso. There Berger got in touch with him and they played the state fair at Phoenix, then went on to Tucson, and this time, since Berger had a night-club job lined up, everything was all right with the Local. The Brown Brothers—famous saxophone act of vaudeville—was playing a local theatre and one of the brothers was under the weather. Pee Wee substituted. "Pee Wee Brown," said Mary, trying it on for size. Pee Wee shrugged and conscientiously tried to pin-point when he'd changed from Albert to Boehm system clarinet (b-flat). He gave it up for the moment, though he did recall one time when Jimmy Dorsey brought back from a European trip a clarinet that was real screwball, it combined *both* systems. "Try to play this," Jimmy said. Ted Lewis played an Albert, he remembered. Then he gave the whole thing up for the time being (we never got back to it) and said that he finally made it to the Coast with Berger.

The in-between and in-and-out jobs are the hardest for a musician to remember. For the most part this is just as well. Who'd want to read about a long series of weddings, country-club and society dates, countless gigs in beaten-up bistros with Sterling Boze and other old colleagues? Well, the last, possibly. Still, if you kept only to the high points, you might neglect to mention that an old friend, now Dr. Gerry Simon, played piano on such dates with Pee Wee when he was called "Ells," or that benefit, before mentioned, of a mixed roster of professionals at the Booker T., back there when *de-segregation* was a naughty word.

The interval in the Southwest with Peck Kelly's jazz-famous, never-recorded band was, of course, stand-out. Add Pee Wee as one more to vouch for Peck's piano and personality. Peck's Bad Boys included Louis Prima's brother Leon, who played some nice horn; Jack Teagarden, who was playing very good trombone, and in his unique style, even then. Leon Rappolo and Pee Wee doubled on alto saxes and clarinets; third man on sax was Billy Watts. Arnold "Joe" Loyocano, who had played with Jack "Papa" Laine and with the New Orleans Rhythm Kings, was on bass; Sammy Byrd on drums. At least three New Orleanians! In one way or another, the home city of jazz was well represented. After work at Sylvan Beach, between Galveston and Houston on the Bay, they'd take it easy on the beach. Sometimes they'd bring their instruments; more often Rappolo would bring his guitar, sit on a low wall and play it, sometimes singing back-room blues.

Had they recorded, Peck's Bad Boys would probably rate along with the Wolverines and the Rhythm Kings. The growth of jazz undoubtedly marks the first time that historical emphases in an art form have been markedly influenced by phonograph records. Considering the tremendous impact of records on musicians, it is no doubt justified, though sometimes this results in a distortion of *real* history. Probably the Goldkette unit that played at Hudson Lake, Indiana, a bit later on, was important in jazz history—the amount of words devoted to it would so indicate—yet they never recorded.

The Arcadia Ballroom period began in the late fall of 1925, when Bix came in from Detroit to join Frankie Trumbauer. In the band, in addition to Pee Wee, Bix and Frankie, were Sonny Lee, trombone, and others less known to jazzmen of today. But they were known then. The Arcadia, as Frankie Trumbauer put it, was "the stopping-off place for all musicians passing through." Pee Wee describes the Arcadia as it was in 1926: "I remember we used to have a Sunday afternoon thing at the Arcadia Ballroom. Ordinarily the band would complain about the extra work, but Bix would really look forward to it. He said he liked to see the kids dance. He liked to watch them do things like the Charleston. He said he liked it because the kids had a fine sense of rhythm. And, in their way, the kids knew what Bix was doing. They knew he was doing something different because he made them want to dance." [5]

In the summer of 1926 several of the men in Trumbauer's Arcadia Ballroom Orchestra joined a Goldkette unit, were fitted out in natty two-tone uniforms that didn't always stay that way, and were installed in a dime-a-dance place at Hudson Lake, not far from South Bend, Indiana, and only about eighty miles from Chicago, the hottest jazz city in the United States in the nineteen twenties, with New York nosing it out of first position towards the end of the decade. In addition to those mentioned above, the eleven-piece outfit included Ray Lustig, trumpet; Andy "Itsy" Riskin, piano; Dan Gabe, bass; Dee Orr, drums. Sometimes the group would alternate in five- and six-piece combinations, at which times Bix played cornet in one and piano in the other.

Many young jazzmen came down from Chicago to sample the local hooch and catch the band, and legion are the anecdotes of those days. "And," said Pee Wee, "we'd go to Chicago." But only as visiting firemen. Still, this helps to explain why Pee Wee is identified with developments related to Chicago jazz. He should be, for his influence was strong, but as he said, "I never had a full union card in Chicago."

In those days, said Pee Wee, "Benny Goodman was at the Southmore. Tesch (Frank Teschemacher) was at Marigold Gardens near the Lake. We'd pay off a cop and set up shop on the beach. Sometimes we'd play jazz, sometimes just sit around and drink and talk." Then to Thirty-fifth and Calumet to hear Louis, and maybe catch Noone at the Apex or Nest, whichever it was then, where he was with Earl Hines. ("I used to hear King Oliver at the Plantation Club.") And, of course, they would listen to the young jazzmen they knew, such as the group around Tesch (Austin High School gang). In 1939, in *Jazzmen,* this writer noted, "Goodman, on his early records, seemed to vacillate between Tesch's phrasing and

[5] Quoted in *Hear Me Talkin' to Ya,* p. 154.

Pee Wee's growl. Tesch, by his own admission, was an admirer of Pee Wee's style. Pee Wee was surprised that Tesch's opinion of him had survived. 'I learned plenty from Tesch,' he said. 'If he was alive, he would play more clarinet than anyone in the world.' "

Bix and Pee Wee used to visit a speakeasy in South Bend. It was a pleasant place and had a piano that Bix liked to play. But it was too expensive for the amount of liquor they were putting away, especially when it came to wrapping up bottles for the cottage they lived in out at the lake. The bartender, being sympathetic to musicians, as bartenders often are, told them of a place where they could get good homemade stuff, jugs of corn buried in the cornfield to elude the revenuers. That sounded fine. The bartender drew a map, without which they'd certainly have gotten lost. Then they were off, in Dan Gabe's Studebaker, following directions which, as it happened, took them past the Studebaker proving grounds. At last they came to a dirt road and driving down it, saw a faded brown house, barns equally nondescript, and were met by two yapping dogs whose eager menace reminded them of the bartender's warning: "When you get there"—the bartender had leaned confidentially across the mahogany —"don't go inside. Don't go up to the house. Don't even get out of the car. Just blow the horn and yell."

They blew the horn and yelled. What they saw at first gave little cause for alarm—three blowsy and barefooted old maids, waiting for *Esquire* to be published so that they could get into a cartoon! Then a fourth party—they soon learned he was a brother—emerged from the barn, holding a double-barreled shotgun. Pee Wee shook his head, thinking about it. "It was a cannon!"

"When he came up close we told him the bartender's name."

"Who else you know there?"

They told him.

"What d'yuh want?"

"We understand you've got some good whiskey here." Adding, as though in explanation, "We're musicians."

"Where are your horns?"

They explained that the instruments were out at the lake. Then Bix added helpfully, "I can play piano."

"That so?" Bix got a calculating look; then they were asked inside. It was neat and tidy inside the house, in contrast to its worn and weathered exterior. They were shown into a papered parlor with a pull-down kerosene lamp, a potbelly stove and, conspicuous to Bix and Pee Wee, the old-fashioned parlor organ that was to test their veracity. Bix took it in stride, playing something sweet and simple. This wasn't a time for cats and alligators. The barefoot boot-leggers simpered and began to look like three dear old ladies from Dubuque. The defender of home, hearth and hooch lowered his gun and gave them a taste of good corn whiskey. "It must have been 150 proof," said Pee Wee. Well, that's about the end of the story. They got to be real neighborly, with Bix playing the organ and the farmer—oh, yes, it was a real Indiana farm, with all the trimmings, cows, pigs and (if you'll pardon the repetition) cornfields—coming in from work to join them in cuts of meat and some of the best homemade pies either of the erstwhile Arcadians had ever tasted. "That'll be five dollars," the farmer said, on their first visit, and they took two gallons, so as not to run short. "Don't come 'round after nine," said jazz history's "Titus Moody"—"we got to be up with the cows."

Once when Pee Wee was with a group in St. Louis, Red Nichols came into town to play a theatre date with the Bennie Kreuger Orchestra. "We were in a house-broken place, a class hotel," Pee Wee said, "the Coronado." Joe Johnson, later NBC's musical di-rector in Chicago, led the band and played violin. Sonny Lee was on trombone. There was some after-hours fraternizing with the Nichols group. And when, some time later, Sonny had a job at the old Waldorf Astoria in New York, he wired Pee Wee that Nichols could use him for record dates. Pee Wee almost didn't get out of Chicago, got stalled in Allentown, Pennsylvania, where Sonny met him and brought him to New York. Once Pee Wee was installed at the Manger (now the Taft) he was introduced to a speakeasy below Roseland Dance Hall, where the Red Nichols crowd hung out be-tween sets—they often played upstairs on the stand opposite Fletcher Henderson. The Nichols men drifted in to join Pee Wee in drinks. Pee Wee needed the drinks—now that he was in the big town he felt panicky—but he tried not to hit it too hard. The recording date set for the next morning, was what he'd come to town for.

He got up to the Brunswick studios on Seventh Avenue (a block from the hotel), the same place where he recorded the Con-don *Treasury of Jazz* album (Columbia) in 1956, at eight in the morning. The date was set for nine A.M. He sat and fidgeted until nine A.M. when Miff Mole came in, looked at him through his spec-tacles, and said, "How do you feel?"

"Nervous," Pee Wee admitted.

Miff pulled out a flask and gave him a couple of jolts. (The flask was a big thing in those days.) After a while the men showed up and the session got under way. Between the jolt from the flask and the familiar clarinet in his hands, Pee Wee's jitters had all but evaporated. Pee Wee, who is modest but truthful, said, "I scared the band." He meant on *Ida,* the first tune he recorded in New York. It broke the band up and they crowded around him to tell him how good it was.

"You played a beautiful chorus," one of the musicians said.

"No," said Pee Wee, "it was just unusual."

It was so unusual that it's been reprinted on more than a dozen labels, including several in foreign countries, for Pee Wee is internationally famous.[6] Many years after the record was made a man —then a stranger to Pee Wee—phoned him from Local 802 to tell him that he had a check for him. But when Pee Wee put the receiver to his ear he heard no words—only someone whistling his clarinet *break* from *Ida.*

In the Garden of Eden depicted by Benny Goodman some paragraphs back there was, as you might have guessed, a money tree, and a whole flock of snakes, all disguised as "name band" leaders, leering at the Innocents. It wasn't, in short, quite as free from commercialism as one's memories might lead one to think, though Benny had the general picture right. (Take Benny, he practically got out of knee pants and into a band uniform to join Ben Pollack, but you couldn't call that an entirely commercial band, one has to admit.) No, the thing about the money tree is this. They (the young, *hot* musicians of St. Louis, Chicago and other towns) liked money. That's no crime. Most of us do. But they were frank about it. Money bought beautiful new instruments and hotel rooms and paid bar bills. But here is the quirk: they might get a little kick out of sitting in a brass section or a reed section, or wearing a Goldkette or Whiteman or Specht uniform for the first time, but it wasn't, for some musicians, the *big* kick. And in this, Benny G. was right. It came back to the vibrant, jazz-oriented enthusiasm without esthetics. This was their kick and, with some few out of many, still is. Others went into concert groups, business, radio, as befitted their aspirations. In the nineteen twenties, to be sure, jazzmen were frequently blow-

[6] *Discography* published a special Pee Wee Russell edition in February, 1944.

ing out their brains, figuratively speaking, *but usually in gin mills of their own choosing.* Some historians, the writer included, perhaps unduly stressed the "Who'll buy my violets?" motif and made jazz-men *hot* heroes of some nonexistent art-for-art's-sake crusade. If you think back to the Arcadia period and the artist-audience setup there, you'll come nearer to the true picture. And the name bands, such as Goldkette's, that exploited jazz commercially, needed men who, as they used to say, could double *hot* or *commercial* (*e.g., hot* or *sweet*).

In the 'twenties, before the long arm of inflation lowered the boom, there was plenty of work, one had only to be able to stand it. Name bands paid very good money for comparatively hard but uncerebral work (four and five shows a day, recordings, *et cetera*). Once when Pee Wee was rooming with photographer Charlie Peterson, who was then playing guitar with Rudy Vallee, he had offers of good-paying jobs with either Rudy or Paul Specht. He flipped a coin and it came out Specht. With the latter he was the clean-up man, playing variously bass clarinet, tenor, alto and soprano saxes, and b-flat clarinet. He was also one of the musicians who interested collectors on Cass Hagen records. And, of course, he was in and out of the Nichols crowd, in pit bands, recordings, all the odd jobs a musician falls heir to.

"They were boom years all along the line," observed Otis Ferguson in *Jazzmen,* "and any good music show could support a band in the pit; the radio was going great guns; records were being stamped out as fast as wheatcakes in Child's; and other boys came to town. People like Joe Sullivan and Frank Teschemacher and Pee Wee Russell and Gene Krupa began to show up on records made in New York. Louis Armstrong and Bix Beiderbecke kept setting an impossible pace on their Okeh recordings, and what with the mixing up of Bix and Lang, Teschemacher and Mole, Nichols and Goodman and Teagarden and all, the recording clique was completely resolved.

"The later 'twenties," he continued in his chapter, "The Five Pennies," "have been set down as the jazz doldrums. Certainly the honky-tonk tradition of a few men blasting it out to their hearts' content was going definitely underground then. But the days around 1927 and '28 were in another sense the golden days, with the first rise of the big-shot hot band carrying as many good men into New York to get together with other good men as the bands of 1920–23 brought in soloists from the outlands."

Once, when Pee Wee was playing gigs in the hinterlands of New England, he was lost track of, so far as his colleagues in New York were concerned. Somehow a rumor started that he had broken a leg or was dying and finally, as rumors will, this one had Pee Wee at death's door in no time at all. Around Plunkett's, the speakeasy under the 'El, listed in the phone book as the Trombone Club in honor of Tommy Dorsey's fine, upstanding bar bill, the boys were trying to think of all the nice things they'd forgotten to say when Pee Wee was around. Unaware of this morbid turn of events but, like Ulysses, having gone through a series of unforseen crises, Pee Wee walked into Plunkett's with an eye for the bar, and was caught up short by the expressions on his friends' faces. Everyone looked frightened and, for a split second, no one spoke. Then Pee Wee said, "What's wrong? What's going on here?"

"You're supposed to be dead!" There was shock and accusation in the tone of voice.

Then it all came out. How Pee Wee was ill or something and had passed away. All his friends had been pitching in to buy flowers. Well, that was that. They spent the money in Plunkett's instead.

Red McKenzie stood with the writer outside the Brunswick studios one day (he thought they should record a guy named Bunny Berigan; a laudable idea), and he pointed over in the general direction of the site of Plunkett's to a nondescript hotel. "One of the nicest guys in jazz lives over there," he said—"Eddie Condon."

Condon and Pee Wee have known each other since the St. Louis-Hudson Lake days; since the nineteen twenties they have recorded in the same bands (often led by Eddie), such as that Billy Banks' Rhythmakers date on which Pee Wee played gutty tenor. Another friend of the New York period, but dating back to Goldkette days, was Tommy Dorsey. They used to go out to Tommy's place on Long Island where (during Prohibition) he had all the works to turn out batches of home brew, even to a bottling machine. They drank the stuff before it was ready, then often played baseball. Recalling this, Pee Wee pondered that so many musicians often think of themselves as real outdoor men, though they are not,—Bix and Bunny, gossiping about golf, grown-up jazzmen playing baseball that would give the sandlot set a laugh. Well, at least they got a little exercise and fresh air.

At Tommy's funeral, his brother, Jimmy, took Pee Wee aside and gave him a picture of a dinner party at which they'd all been happy a few nights before—the last picture taken of Tommy. Tommy, especially, looked more relaxed than he had in a long time, in the company of Jimmy, Pee Wee and other old friends. When a writer for *Down Beat* asked Pee Wee to comment—they were doing a special T.D. memorial issue—Pee Wee only said, "I came up with Tommy in the music business more than thirty-five years ago. When you know a man like him for that many years, it really hurts when he leaves you."

Pee Wee helped to open up Fifty-second Street during Prohibition, when the Stork Club was a speakeasy a few blocks away (combining champagne with the jazz music of Condon's cacophonic rascals). On the street—this was long before it became an incubator for the new sounds—you could hear, if you hung around long enough, just about everyone from Teagarden to Tatum. Bessie Smith sang, and Bunny Berigan played behind her, at Sunday afternoon jam sessions. Joe Sullivan, one of the great piano men of jazz, often played at the Onyx and later opened up Café Society Downtown with one of the first mixed bands on a regular job. Pee Wee played at the Famous Door and later was featured at its namesake in Hollywood.

Pee Wee has made hundreds of records, some of them reprinted countless times, as new generations of jazz followers have come to maturity. He gets royalties from only one, the Storyville long-play set, *We're in the Money* (hereby recommended, musically and monetarily). Pee Wee has several tunes to his credit but, though he gets some piddling royalties on them from time to time, he gets nothing, for example, for his chorus on *Ida,* though such variations (like arrangements under copyright law) are undoubtedly compositions in their own right. On one date with a Condon group, Bing Crosby stipulated that the musicians were to share in the royalties; that, needless to say, was a rare exception.

The ridiculousness of this situation became clear in the 1930's when writers such as the author, or jazz collectors hot on the spoor of old masters, would harass Pee Wee and his friends about personnels of records long gone, for which they'd been paid "scale." This harassment was necessary, of course, if the men were to be given their proper stature. But as a trend, it stirred up mixed emotions. (Young jazzmen of any era will play for "scale" and like it, because they want to blow and want to become known. Other than that, it may be that a copyright question is involved; at any rate, it deserves study.)

Suitably encouraged, Milt Gabler of the Commodore Music

Shop (now with Decca) decided to *at least* give the often poor and seldom proud jazzmen a chance to record. This was doubly welcome, as it came during the nineteen thirties when thousands of musicians were unemployed in New York City alone. On the first Commodore date, as on the first date Pee Wee played in New York, he did something special. It was Eddie Condon's idea (and Milt's) to give the men elbow room and on that first Commodore record—except for some reissues on the United Hot Clubs of America label—the tune chosen was *Love Is Just Around the Corner.* After Pee Wee had wrapped it up in thirty-two bars Eddie gave him the signal to stay right in there, and Pee Wee did. It's quite a record, for Milt, for Pee Wee, for everyone on the date.

Another Commodore date was *Serenade to a Shylock* which, it is reported, got its title because it was made under duress—there was a creditor waiting outside the studio door! Some of his best choruses, like his interpretation of his own composition, Disc's *Muskogee Blue,* are out of print.[7] (Comparable in quality, and currently in print, is his *3-2-1 Blues,* in Condon's *Treasury of Jazz* set on Columbia.) On Brunswick with Louis Prima, Pee Wee used a small trumpet mute (*Basin Street*) and on a Disc record, *Take Me to That Land of Jazz,* he did the vocal which, to no one's surprise, followed the unpredictable but nevertheless recognizable pattern of his clarinet style.

Most of us who have written about Pee Wee have used all the adjectives in the book, not in an excess of praise—though he deserves plenty—but because of the adaptability of a style that, for all its variety, remains uniquely his own. Depending upon mood and material, he might employ a thin, limpid, harsh, growling, phlegmy, punching style of intonation and attack; a somewhat lyric, legato line or an almost angular one; fluid, many-noted passages in the low register or riding, driving tones in the upper ones. One cannot say Pee Wee *always* plays this way or that way; he's never type-cast himself in that narrow sense, yet, for all its complexity and variousness, as we've said, his style is readily recognizable. Listeners, especially new listeners, are fascinated by his tone which is utterly at home in that never-never land between exact tonality and flatness. They are intrigued and, if truly appreciative of jazz, hold their breaths in suspense as Pee Wee goes into a chorus, saying to

[7] Just as an indication that the reissue business is still thriving, if sometimes in a haphazard fashion, *Muskogee Blue* is once again available, this time on long-play—Folkways FJ 2810.

themselves, much as Pee Wee must have said when he first heard
"Yellow" Nunez: *he got into it all right but will he get out, will he
make it?*

He usually does, but not always, and, as he says, "If you get
lost, well, that's it, you get lost." (And this is why a goof, in jazz,
is just a goof, and not comparable to an error in reading by a concert musician.) "Each time you play it, you play something different; you get tired of playing the same thing night after night." When
Mary remarked that he'd once called himself a gambling musician,
he nodded. "If you miss, you miss. If you get lucky, you get lucky
—but *you take a chance.* Of course," he added, "you can play four
bars, and all of them correctly." He paused and smiled fleetingly,
a smile edged with irony. "You've got to get lost once in a while.
You get in and, if you're lucky, you get out. To get in a spot and get
out—you think in a split second. If you think of what change or
progression will get you out of it, you know it and every musician
in the band knows it." One was reminded of Wilder Hobson's remark, describing a Fifty-second Street jam session: [8] "And Benny
Goodman's face wryly following the unpredictable turns of Pee Wee
Russell's clarinet line—would he get out of this one all right or
wouldn't he? He usually did." But not always. "With it goes plenty
of mistakes," said Pee Wee, "but the more you try the luckier you
are."

The *3-2-1 Blues* previously mentioned is a good example of what
a clarinetist is up against. This gets its title from stop-time chords
of the ensemble. The first chorus is punctuated by three beats, the
second by two, the final by one. The first is taken in low register
and since less blowing is required, allows for fluid, lyrical, many-
noted passages in a somewhat forthright melodic delineation. The
middle register calls for more strength and fewer notes and, finally,
the upper register calls for more notes, more wind, harder blowing
and, through all this, spacing notes and tones intuitively (one reason
why *swing* is such an essential ingredient of good jazz), since there
isn't time to write yourself a memo on the subject. In the upper
register you "take a couple of deep breaths—from then on you
haven't time for more than a gasp; and you have to keep the wind
moving the same strength." (The blowing vibrates the reed, which
serves a purpose analogous to that of the membranous reed in the
human larynx.) The final chorus, which reminds one structurally of
his chorus on *Muskogee Blue,* breaks up the melody, as it were, and

[8] *Jazzmen.*

reassembles it so that, however moving a single phrase may be, compositional structure is resolved only when the final note is played.

Apparently befuddled by the first onslaught of Pee Wee's clarinet, a critic for *Orchestra World* some years ago dubbed him, "the Gertrude Stein of jazz." Carlton Brown once wrote [9] that "he does with musical phrases just about what Joyce did with words —he breaks them up, violently rearranges their structure and accustomed order, and puts them together into fascinating new patterns. Pee Wee Russell makes a clarinet sound like a unique and marvelous instrument that he invented for his own ruggedly individualistic purposes. He is by turns hilarious and tragic; he can express the heart of melancholy with overwhelming directness, or make surprising satirical comments composed of incredible dissonances and ornate embroideries."

Contrasting Pee Wee's style with that of Teschemacher, Wilder Hobson observed in *American Jazz Music* [10] that "Pee Wee Russell's clarinet playing was even more broken in line, full of both lyric sweetness and 'dirtiness,' highly vocalized." This perceptive statement emphasizes what Pee Wee himself said concerning the manner in which his style evolved. In a rather astonishing—Panassie can still astonish one with remarks made decades ago—glimpse of the musicianship underlying Pee Wee's unorthodox style, Hughes Panassie, in the first book on jazz published here [11] stated, "Among all hot clarinetists, Pee Wee Russell is undoubtedly the one who uses the soberest melodic style: short phrases of uncomplicated, clear contour played in an even, measured tone. . . . Another peculiarity of his is his 'dirty' tone, full of definite huskiness. Curiously enough, even though Pee Wee fills his playing with these effects, his tone keeps its finish and polish. . . . His intonations are very beautiful and vibrant, and his attack is exceptionally forceful." And, finally, this, by Edwin Hinchcliffe: [12] "High over the intermingled sonorities of a final free-for-all, fugitive wisps of clarinet phrases, floating in and out of the more aggressive brasses, swelling and falling, prick out a weird commentary on the tangled skein of collective improvisation."

Photographs of Pee Wee, taken by many photographers through the years, are of interest both in relation to jazz history and in rela-

[9] Quoted in *Current Biography.*
[10] W. W. Norton, 1939.
[11] *Hot Jazz,* Witmark, 1934.
[12] *Jazz Music,* London, Vol. 3, No. 1, 1946.

tion to the personality that is Pee Wee (or "Wee" as Jack Teagarden calls him, or "Charles," as Eddie Condon calls him, or "Mr. Russell," as one hears a fan say, now and again, very polite.) Sometimes, indeed, happily quite often, the photographers have been men who knew and appreciated his music, like his old friend Charlie Peterson, who did that *Life* shot of Pee Wee, like a bent reed, bending with the force of the music. This was taken at Nick Rongetti's, where Pee Wee played for many years, and there is a hilarious account of it in Eddie Condon's *We Called It Music* [13] (Nick, who was a friend of many musicians and some fortunate writers, such as the author, pioneered jazz music in the Village. In a little hole-in-the-wall he "looked the other way" while Larry Shields sat in with Sharkey Bonano. Larry, who hadn't been given permission to play locally yet, said to the writer, after having played a beautiful *Tiger,* "I just had to play one set!" Meade Lux Lewis played there, and when Nick moved across the street, you might find Jelly Roll Morton there on a Sunday afternoon, to instruct the young and edify the old, Sid Bechet sitting nearby, smiling in ironic benignity.) Photographers caught Pee Wee when he helped Eddie Condon break the classic sound barrier at Town Hall; Frederic Ramsey, Jr. caught him between sets at Stuyvesant Casino (even musicians get tired).

Pee Wee is gentle and friendly with children and photographs of him playing for kids at the Little Red Schoolhouse, for a block party on Bleecker Street (Skippy Adelman) or for moppets at the Walt Whitman School (Otto Hess) are particularly heart-warming, especially since so much writing about jazzmen (not accidentally, of course) has to do with guzzling, gin mills and gone gates. At the Walt Whitman school affair, Joe Sullivan was on piano and Louis Armstrong sang and played trumpet. It was wonderful to see those kids as Louis "cleaned up" for them, in lyrics improvised on the spur of the moment, some off-color blues, and Pee Wee played with a special kind of joyousness that matched the mood of Joe's piano and Zutty's drums, and seemed to twitch every tender little lobe in the place.

"A jazz patriarch at forty-four," *Life* noted in the issue of February 12, 1951, "Pee Wee since youth had studiously avoided the relatively healthy, more profitable life of a commercial bandsman to spend his nights (the sunlit hours were naturally for sleeping) in a long succession of smoky night clubs, blowing his heart out in choruses of *High Society* and *Sister Kate,* a bottle of gin and a rapt

[13] Henry Holt, 1947.

audience always at hand. It all caught up with him in San Francisco, where he collapsed of what appeared to be a fatal liver ailment. Friends came around to see him, making the supreme sacrifice of getting up early in the afternoon to do it, and straight away arranged a benefit. 'Tell the newspapers not to write any sad stories about me,' begged Pee Wee. At week's end it looked as if they would not have to. Following an operation, the doctors gave Pee Wee a good chance of recovery. All over the world people who knew Pee Wee only through his records felt good about that."

He was up and about and playing with a band of men, most of them in their twenties, at Storyville in Boston in 1952 (Ruby Braff, trumpet; Ephie Resnick, trombone; Red Richards, piano; Kenny John, drums). "The kiddies," he said, waving his clarinet for the audience to applaud, "the kiddies—they're the ones!" And when he got Christmas cards from Gerry Mulligan and other young musicians active in modern jazz, he felt as good as he did that day in a San Francisco hospital when his old friends, Jack Teagarden and Louis Armstrong, stopped by to wish him well.

The spring of 1957 found Pee Wee doing special concerts and filling in occasionally locally, particularly in the congenial atmosphere of Eddie Condon's night club. In January, George Wettling got together a group for a special concert with the Savannah [Georgia] Symphony Orchestra. Max Kaminsky (trumpet), Ray Deal (trombone), Dick Cary (piano), and Pee Wee were augmented by a couple of men from the symphony orchestra. The jazzmen didn't jazz up the classics. What they did was to take pop tunes adapted from numbers on the program—the classical originals being played by the concert group—and improvise on them. Thus, it was not a battle of music but an amicable sharing of the stand and the spotlight. After fulsome praise for the visiting firemen the critic for one of the Savannah papers noted with relief, ". . . the Savannah symphony held its own auspiciously last night."

Perhaps because of Pee Wee's willingness to talk about others, Bix, Louis, Jack, *et cetera,* interviewers have sometimes missed the point—that when Pee Wee talks about the reactions and attitudes of others he is often, indirectly, talking about his own. When he was written about, sometimes it would be only his discussion of a weird character, a contortionist of the clarinet, who drank buckets of gin and blew gutbuckets of choruses; with voice and speech as semantically unintelligible (to their ears) as the growl of his horn. This character existed only in the minds of the writers. Yet in its

own hyperbolic fashion it described a *familiar*—everybody's Pee
Wee and the Pee Wee nobody knows, all rolled up in one long lean
bundle—*and sometimes penetrated the outward appearance*—for
one cannot tell even the most outrageous fabrications without at the
same time hinting at the truth! Monetary success did not, when Pee
Wee was young, depend upon ability, nor does it today. It depends
upon luck and/or exploitation. From the agency point of view, perhaps it is as simple as that. Perhaps no one has properly assessed the
commercial possibilities in this man from Muskogee.

"What's jazz?" Pee Wee repeated an interviewer's question.[14]
"It's kind of tough to get into words. You could use ten-syllable
words, and it wouldn't mean a thing. If I say something in the way
of a definition, I'd probably retract it a second later. I'm not sure
that this will do it, but in a way it sums down to this—a certain
group of guys—I don't care where they come from—that have a
heart feeling and a rhythm in their systems that you couldn't budge,
a rhythm you couldn't take away from them even if they were in a
symphony organization. Regardless of what type of music they decided to play, they could feel a beat. They could feel the beat better
than someone who has memorized the book. These are men whose
way of playing you couldn't alter no matter where you put them or
what you tried to teach them."

To which we add George Frazier's remark: "His life and hard
times and the stuff he dreams up on his clarinet are in the true jazz
tradition. He *is* jazz, and the best, too."

SELECTED DISCOGRAPHY—PEE WEE RUSSELL

Jazz at Storyville, Vol. 1, Savoy 12034
We're in the Money, Storyville 909
Ivy League Jazz, Decca 8282
Treasury of Jazz, Columbia CL 881
Great Jazz Reeds, Camden 339
Comes Jazz, Columbia CL 6107
Jazz in the Forties, Folkways FJ 2810

[14] *Hear Me Talkin' to Ya*, p. 406.

Bessie Smith

*   *   *   *

By George Hoefer

Big Bill Broonzy began one of his blues: "Oh I feel like hollering but the town is too small."

Bessie Smith often felt the same way, but she hollered anyway. For Bessie, not only were the towns too small for the deep and free living she knew could be; but even her big body was too small for all the living and enjoying and drinking and hating and eating and loving that she wanted, needed to jam into one small lifetime.

Bessie sang the blues to make a living; but she also sang the blues to communicate who she was, who she wanted to be, and why. And basically, she told the blues as a Negro who grew up in the South with Jim Crow; who moved through the North but couldn't shake Jim Crow; and who, as some stories have it, may have died because Jim Crow ran a hospital that didn't take in colored, even when they were bleeding to death.

Her blues could be funny and boisterous and gentle and angry and bleak, but underneath all of them ran the raw bitterness of being a human being who had to think twice about which toilet she could use. You can't hear Bessie without hearing why Martin Luther King doesn't want to wait any more.

Bessie was born in blunt poverty in Chattanooga, Tennessee, around 1900. She grew up with no money and not much more hope. She bumped into an unlikely fairy godmother however, when Ma Rainey's Rabbit Foot Minstrels came through town. Ma, perhaps the first of the classic blues singers (although she may never have heard *that* said about herself) liked the way Bessie hollered and took the girl on the road with her.

Bessie sang her hungry blues through years of tent shows and carnivals that barnstormed all through the Southern states, as well as in the honky-tonks, gin mills, and small theatres of the larger ghettos like Atlanta, Savannah, Birmingham and Memphis.

Frank Walker, recording director for Columbia Records, heard Bessie, and he sent New Orleans pianist-composer Clarence Williams to find her. Walker had a feeling that Bessie could reach a lot of record buyers with the truth of their own lives. He was right.

Bessie Smith made her first session on February 17, 1923. Her stomping-record sales made her a "star," and she began to work regularly with her own show in New York, Chicago, Boston and Philadelphia, as well as in the large Southern cities. It must be remembered that during her period of wide acceptance between 1923 and 1930 she played almost always to Negroes. What she had to say was as naked and yet untranslatable as a Jewish cantor piercing his congregation with *Kol Nidrei*.

Bessie's legacy consists of 160 recorded sides and a two-reel motion picture short. Some of the records, especially those made after 1928, are quite rare, although they do exist in isolated hot-jazz record collections. This rarity is accounted for by the fact that her later recordings did not sell well. Around 1926–7, she had begun to change her repertoire and, in a way, she tried to sing her songs differently, sensing that tastes were changing. But it was hard for Bessie to change with them.

But before going into the twilight of Bessie's blues, there is much to be said about what happened before. She had three sisters —Viola, Tinnie and Lulu—and a brother, Clarence. After Bessie began to earn money, they all moved North and made their home in Philadelphia. Bessie had beaten being poor for a time, but she had picked up other demons that kept riding with her.

The years of barnstorming made Bessie tough, ribald and able to fight for herself. From all indications she seems, in her early years, to have been an extrovert and tended to accept things as they were. This was to change radically during her years of success. According to George Avakian, she became two diametrically opposed personalities. Her drinking, an emotional release, became progressively more compulsive through the years. She was basically an embittered woman who not only didn't know all the answers but found many of the questions unfamiliar. At the same time, Bessie was gentle, sentimental, and full of sympathy for the downtrodden among her people. When she had money, she was inclined to squander it, or let her favorite man throw it away. She has been said once to have bought a rooming house in New York so that a group of her friends could live together under one roof.

Bessie was married to a policeman named Jack Gee on April 5,

1922, in Philadelphia. He left the force and became her manager. His managerial abilities were such that the two of them are said to have gone through sixteen thousand dollars in six months' time. Some of Bessie's early blues compositions were registered in her husband's name. The couple separated in 1930 but continued friendly and close relations until the time of her death.

A poignant insight into the kind of woman Bessie wanted to be is revealed by an episode that occurred at the height of her success in 1926. Bessie, who thought her days of cleaning up after whites were long past, volunteered to be a maid. During a busy and professionally triumphant period, she cancelled her bookings. Frank Walker's child had suddenly become ill, and Bessie came to this man to whom she was grateful and offered to care for his child. Despite protests, she insisted on helping with even the most menial tasks and did not return to her tour until the child was well.

At other times, Bessie could be brutal and violent. Her addiction to gin took hold during her teens and, as she grew older, it kept pace with her added responsibilities, troubles and frustrations. Bessie, who as a child had been dominated by people and situations, acquired an insatiable desire to dominate people and situations. When thwarted, she was inclined to start drinking and was soon ready to take on the world. There were times when her recording dates and public appearances had to be cancelled because she was on a rampage. It was also during these bad periods that she made an exhibition of spending money.

Bessie Smith was always a very attractive woman. Pictures taken when she first came North reveal her as fairly slender and rather tall. In one famous early photograph, her sad eyes are open to love, and there is sensitivity in the way her hands rest. In another early picture, she is doing the Charleston and wearing her hair in bangs.

By the time Bessie became a headliner and the star of her own show, she had attained considerable stage presence. She always came on in the headline spot next to the closing act, a well-groomed formidable personality. Her black hair was combed close to the top of her head, and her large earrings sparkled in the spotlight. If she were playing a week in a theatre, she would usually save a particular white evening dress for the last show. According to drummer Zutty Singleton, who played in the pit orchestra for her whenever she appeared at the Lyric Theater in New Orleans, the audience was always awed when the colored spotlights shone on this white dress and the regal headdress that she wore with it. When Carl Van

Vechten heard Bessie for the first time in Newark on Thanksgiving night, 1925, she was wearing a crimson satin robe embroidered with multicolored sequins. He recalls her round, beautiful face, a deep, bronzelike shade of brown which matched her bare brown arms.

In her performance, Bessie would walk slowly to the footlights, accompanied by the pounding of the drum, augmented sometimes by muted brasses. It is interesting to note that Bessie had a strong antipathy to percussion and on her records used drums only once or twice. Onstage, she would sometimes remain in the spotlight singing a repertoire of her most popular tunes as she had recorded them, swaying slightly to the beat. Art Hodes, the jazz pianist, says that when he heard her in Chicago, she walked slowly around the stage, with her head somewhat bowed. Either way, her blues numbers were greeted with "amens" from the audience, whose attention she commanded completely, and after her final encore, the applause and shouting were deafening. Her people called her "The Queen of the Blues." It was the Columbia Record Company that labeled her "The Empress of the Blues," when she signed an exclusive contract with them in 1923, to distinguish her from other "comediennes" on their roster.

Bessie had a rich, full-toned contralto voice. It was as powerful as any voice that has ever been heard in jazz. When the microphone made its appearance on the stages of the country, Bessie pushed it away in disdain. The late Oran "Hot Lips" Page, who accompanied her on trumpet once, was greatly impressed by her powerful delivery. "Man," he said, "she could sing over and drown out the loudest swing band going."

Pictures of Bessie during her good days, 1923 through 1926, show her with a laughing face. She had a strong, earthy sense of humor. Milton Mezzrow has described his first meeting with Bessie at the old Paradise Gardens in Chicago. She came to his table and he asked her to sing *Cemetery Blues*. Bessie ruffled Mezz's curly hair and said, "Son, what you studying cemeteries for? You ought to be out in the park with some cute little chick."

Shots of Bessie taken during the late 'twenties and early 'thirties show the ravages of hard living and an insatiable thirst for tall glasses of gin. She was still beautiful but had aged considerably, and much of the luster in her eyes and expression was gone. She had become increasingly moody in those years, and it was plainly to be seen in her face.

Some time in 1929, Porter Grainger, one of her piano accompanists, took her to Carl Van Vechten's studio in midtown Manhattan. It was then towards the end of the so-called Negro Renaissance, a time when Negro performers were welcomed to intellectual parties and fawned over by Park Avenue.

Other guests on this occasion were the late composer, George Gershwin, actress Constance Collier, and opera singer Marguerite d'Alvarez. Bessie entered the room and immediately demanded a drink—not a cocktail, but a full tumbler of straight gin—which she downed in one lusty gulp. She then got down to business. With a lighted cigarette drooping from a corner of her mouth, she gave them the blues with Porter at the piano. Van Vechten has stated, "This was no actress, no imitator of woman's woes; there was no pretense. It was the real thing: a woman cutting her heart open with a knife until it was exposed for all to see. . . ."

It would be interesting to know what Bessie thought of the reaction to her performance. Would it have been a "my best friends are my enemies" sort of feeling? After all, Bessie had a need to *belong* as well as to be the main attraction. But if she couldn't belong, she could at least try to boss as many as she could of those who did. As far back as 1920, Bessie had attained enough stature as a leading blues singer to be able to dictate theatre policy to managers. She insisted that no other act or acts on the bill with her were to perform blues songs. This didn't always work.

Once Ethel Waters was on the same bill with Bessie at the 91 Theatre on Decatur Street in Atlanta. Ethel was advised to stay away from singing the blues. Before she had finished her first number, the audience was clamoring for her blues. The manager went to Bessie and said he would have to go back on his agreement and permit Ethel to give the crowd what they wanted. Miss Waters recalls overhearing a stormy battle in Bessie's dressing room, with Bessie yelling things about "these Northern bitches," who came down into her territory.

Some years later, after Bessie had won acclaim through the phenomenal sales of records to her own people, she was on a road tour with her show called "The Harlem Frolics." For one week in the summer of 1927 they were playing in the Grand Theater, a leading Negro house on the South Side of Chicago. That same week Ethel Waters was appearing before a white audience at the Palace Theater in Chicago's Loop and taking the town by storm. This sort of double-edged irony was to occur many times and undoubtedly made Bessie's inner life darker and more puzzled.

It is probably true that Bessie was shunned by the more urbane and sophisticated Negroes. There is evidence that even Negro show people were reluctant to welcome her into their homes. For instance, Mrs. James P. Johnson, wife of the late pianist, who was one of Bessie's favorite musicians, has been quoted as saying, "Bessie would come over to the house but, mind you, she wasn't my friend. She was very rough."

In accounts of activities and gatherings of Negro show people during the 'twenties and early 'thirties, Bessie Smith's name is conspicuous by its absence. For example, Ethel Waters is listed as an honorary pallbearer at Florence Mills' funeral, and everyone else with a name in show business seemed to be there to pay tribute to the beloved entertainer. But not Bessie.

No artist is without detractors, and the great blues singer has had many. When Bessie's blues touched a listener, he usually became a convert. On the other hand, there were, and are, many who do not appreciate her work. She was an artist whose work was either loved or hated with a vengeance.

Jazz is a highly individual art for both the performer and the listener. Bessie sang her life story, just as others have written autobiography. A good many music listeners, even jazz fans, are prone to allow an allegedly archaic style, or non-hi-fi archives, to cause them to close their ears to a message so throbbingly alive that it should become dated only when automation has replaced us all.

There is available today a fairly complete collection of Bessie Smith recordings. These sides embrace her career from the 1924 *Weeping Willow Blues* to the four sides she made on her last date in 1933.

Bessie signed an exclusive contract with the old Columbia Phonograph Company in 1923. Her recording activity with Columbia came to an end in November 1931 when the record market became almost nonexistent. John Hammond produced a Bessie Smith date in November, 1933, expressly for England. These sides were issued in this country on the Okeh label, which by that time was owned by the American Record Corporation interests, who also had Bessie's old Columbia company.

It has been reported that there were several other attempts to make Bessie Smith records. Before joining Columbia, she had been asked to make sides for the old Black Swan Record Company, owned by Harry Pace. The story goes that she was fired in the middle of her first side because she said, "Hold on a minute while I spit."

Ironically, Bessie went on, a few months later, to pull the Columbia company out of receivership, while Black Swan went bankrupt.

Sidney Bechet, the great pioneer New Orleans jazzman, remembers making a record with Bessie shortly after he returned from Europe in 1921. At this time he was about to join a show in which he was to play a Chinese character and was also to be featured playing a clarinet solo. He recalls that Bessie was slated to be the blues singer in the show. It never opened, but, during the rehearsal period, Clarence Williams made an audition record for the old Okeh company. Bessie sang *Sister Kate* accompanied by Clarence on piano, Bechet on clarinet, and the late Bubber Miley on trumpet. Okeh thought that Bessie's style was unorthodox and rejected her as having no sales potential. Williams gave the test record to Bessie, and that was the last that was ever seen of it. Clarence regrets that he doesn't have the side now, since he figures it would be worth several thousand dollars. Clarence has always had a strong commercial feeling for jazz—and his instincts have usually been right.

Record collectors are still perplexed by an advertisement in the *Chicago Defender* on February 12, 1921, which announced that Bessie Smith was making records with six jazz musicians for the Emerson Record Company. The first release was scheduled to be issued on March 10, 1921, but no one knows what happened to the test records or the masters—if they ever existed at all.

The first blues singing record, incidentally, had been made in 1920 by Mamie Smith (no relation) for Okeh. It was a success and caused Frank Walker of Columbia to eye future possibilities in the blues field. Walker had heard Bessie singing in a gin mill in Selma, Alabama, back in 1917, says one source, and was impressed. He inaugurated Columbia's "Race Record" Series, and one of the first artists to record was Bessie.

On her first record date in 1923, Bessie made four sides accompanied by Clarence Williams on piano. One of the tunes waxed, *Downhearted Blues,* had already been released by all the other companies, including a version on the Paramount label by the famous Alberta Hunter, who had written the lyrics. In spite of the lateness of Bessie's release, it outdistanced all the others and sold 780,000 copies. The success of Bessie's interpretation has been attributed to the joyous earthiness with which she sang one line of the song, "I've got the world in a jug; got the stopper in my hand."

This was just the beginning and, in the next decade, Bessie was to become an institution at Columbia. She was to sell between eight and ten million records before the collapse of the record business.

One of the facets of Bessie's great talent was her ability to select musicians who were a perfect complement to her own artistry. In this respect, she resembles Duke Ellington. Her favorites included Joe Smith, trumpet; Charles "Big" Green, trombone; Buster Bailey, clarinet; and James P. Johnson, piano. She also used Louis Armstrong, cornet; Fletcher Henderson, piano; Iriving Johns, piano; Fred Longshaw, piano and harmonium; Don Redman, sax and clarinet; Tommy Ladnier, trumpet; Eddie Lang, guitar; Porter Grainger, piano; and others. On her last date she was accompanied by an all-star group put together by John Hammond. It included Jack Teagarden, trombone; Benny Goodman, clarinet; Frankie Newton, trumpet; Chu Berry, tenor saxophone; Buck Washington, piano; Billy Taylor, bass; and Bobby Johnson, guitar.

At first, Bessie sang the songs assigned to her. Clarence Williams handled the selection of tunes and musicians for Walker. This situation did not last long, however, and Walker chose Fletcher Henderson as her recording supervisor. Bessie was happy with this arrangement because she could dominate Fletcher. After this, most of her accompanying musicians were men from Fletcher's band. Once she was furious with Fletcher for sending her a young cornetist from Chicago in place of another Henderson hornman, Joe Smith. In spite of Bessie's skepticism, the Louis Armstrong accompaniments resulted in several of her greatest records.

As she grew older and more experienced, Bessie began to assume complete control of her recording activities. She also began to write her own tunes and lyrics, and these became some of her more memorable recordings.

Sometimes, on her road tours, her stage setup resembled an old-fashioned recording studio, with an old-time horn featured. She would explain to her audience how she made her records and then sing the tunes she had recorded. Whatever she sang turned into blues. She could take the popular tunes of the day and transform them. For example, hear her *Aggravatin' Papa* and *Baby, Won't You Please Come Home?*

The blues can be broken down into categories. Among them are: happy blues songs and satirical blues; blues based on catastrophes of nature; poverty and work songs; blues for a city, street, or some other locale, like the jailhouse or cemetery; drinking blues; and sex blues built around a complete man-woman relationship.

There are Bessie Smith records illustrative of each of these types of blues.

Bessie's happy blues renditions include such numbers as *Jazzbo Brown from Memphis Town, At the Christmas Ball, Cake Walking Babies, There'll Be a Hot Time in the Old Town Tonight,* and *Alexander's Ragtime Band.*

With the exception of *Jazzbo,* all of these tunes were recorded by Bessie in an attempt to attract a wider audience. She may have been making a play for some of the popularity that Ethel Waters was enjoying. Both *Cake Walking Babies* and *At the Christmas Ball* were rejected by Columbia when they were made in 1927 as being too far from the style of the commercial Smith records, and it was not until the middle 'forties that they were finally released. Bessie's excuse for making them was that her people were tired of the "depressed" type of blues.

In 1930 there was another radical departure. With James P. Johnson on the piano and a male quartet called the Bessemer Singers, she assailed the field of the spirituals. Bessie's lusty shouting wasn't enough to make successful records of *On Revival Day* and *Moan, You Mourners.* The quartet drowned out James P.'s piano and the sides were unsuccessful both musically and commercially.

Representing the satirical type of blues, there was, among others, *Trombone Cholly,* high-lighted by the unique trombone style of "Big" Green, star trombonist with the Fletcher Henderson orchestra. This is lusty satire showcasting Green's incomparable dirty tone and his muted phrasing. Most often, the lyrics furnish the humor in the blues, and this was the case with Bessie's *Mean Old Bed Bug Blues.*

One of Bessie's finest records is *Back Water Blues,* on which she was accompanied by James P. Johnson's fine solo piano. Bessie once witnessed the Mississippi flooding the Louisiana backlands, and in this song her original words are movingly poetic. It is a simple twelve-bar blues with overtones of social protest. She sings a complaint addressed to God against the five days and nights of rain that forced the people from their homes. James P.'s accompaniment is beautiful in its spare and lyrically poignant power.

Poverty has always been a familiar subject in the literature of the blues. Again, one of Bessie's classics can be cited as an example —her May, 1929, waxing of *Nobody Knows You When You're Down and Out.* It is significant that this record was made when Bessie was already on the decline. Her road tours no longer brought her two thousand dollars a week, and her records were not selling. The depression was yet to come, but Bessie had little left of her fabulous earnings, except possibly the twenty-thousand-dollar house that Frank Walker had insisted that she buy in Philadelphia when she was in the chips. Bessie's mood was sadly prophetic when she put all the pathos, bitterness and protest she could muster into her performance of that song.

Of the many blues songs about places, some are just praise for a locale, others have to do with traveling back somewhere to see a woman, and some are songs of identification. Many people consider Bessie Smith's version of *St. Louis Blues,* with Louis Armstrong's cornet and Fred Longshaw's harmonium, the finest rendition of the classic song in existence.

Bessie recorded two sides on which she discusses her favorite beverage. They are autobiographical in content and are entitled *The Gin House Blues* and *Me and My Gin.*

A considerable part of Bessie Smith's output had to do with men and women in love, and the universal interest in the subject accounts for her great success with such recordings. She was the master storyteller of love tales for her own people. They understood all the symbolism, the frustration, and the seesaw of joy and sorrow. When Bessie sang of love, there was no expurgation. She was able, in some non-mailable cases, to convey meanings through voice inflections, without using the exact words.

Bessie preferred to sing her blues in slow tempo; she left the fast-stepping dance tunes to others. The Empress progressed from the early twelve-bar country blues she had learned from the Georgia blues singer, Gertrude "Ma" Rainey, to the more complicated sixteen-bar blues style. The latter were the artificial "rag-blues" of the vaudeville and musical-comedy stage. The two forms became combined and intermixed in Bessie's renditions.

At the peak of her career in 1926, she made several sides that can be classified as formal city blues and that are jazz landmarks. Included are *Young Woman's Blues, One and Two Blues, Baby Doll,* and *Lost Your Head Blues.* On all of these sides, there are beautifully organized accompaniments by Joe Smith's mellow cornet. Smith's unique use of the mute was pure artistry. He played intense, precisely conceived notes in answer to Bessie's phrases on *Lost Your Head,* while on *Baby Doll* he is in another mood, projecting light, floating tones with an open horn. Very rarely in jazz have there been two artists whose work blended as beautifully as did Joe's and Bessie's.

Bessie also had perfect rapport with trombonist Charlie Green, with whom she made the two-part *Empty Bed Blues*. This 1928 release was one of Bessie's records that found its way into white homes, although for all the wrong reasons. There is a report that *Empty Bed* was banned in Boston. It is hard to believe that a Boston censor could have understood the words or even the music. The word, "bed," must have done it.

These three artists—Bessie, Joe and "Big" Green—all died at about the same time. Bessie ended in an automobile accident under horrifying circumstances; Charlie Green was found frozen to death on a Harlem doorstep; and "Little" Joe succumbed to tuberculosis in a mental institution.

One visual remainder of Bessie is the film drama, "St. Louis Blues." It was made in 1929 but was immediately banned because it was considered too uninhibited. Ten years ago it was found in Mexico and is now shown from time to time at the Museum of Modern Art in New York. It is still not available for public exhibition because of the frankness and realism.

The two-reel short was made from a scenario by W. C. Handy, in collaboration with Kenneth W. Adams and was directed by Dudley Murphy. He later became famous for his direction of "Emperor Jones." An executive of Warner Brothers, for whom the picture was made, was overheard to remark during the filming that, "It's too bad that we didn't make a feature out of this."

Bessie plays the role of a cast-off woman, and the most impressive aspect of the film is the beauty of her movements and the sensitivity of her facial expressions. She apparently had considerable talent as a dramatic actress.

Musically, the film is limited because of the inadequacies of early sound techniques. A primitive crystal microphone was used, and the sound track is muddy. Even so, the great blues singer's magnificent and powerful voice is very much there. She was accompanied by a forty-two voice choir, under the direction of J. Rosamunde Johnson, and a band which included James P. Johnson, Joe Smith, drummer Kaiser Marshall, and Happy Cauldwell on clarinet.

After 1929, Bessie's star plunged straight down. Even without the impact of the depression, the record industry was temporarily doomed by radio. Where Bessie had been accustomed to receiving

a one-thousand-dollar advance against a five per cent royalty for
her recordings, she had to settle for fifty dollars a side in 1933.
Frank Walker, who had managed her well through the preceding
years, was forced to drop her. Bessie had to give rent parties in
Harlem in order to pay for her keep. She tells about these gatherings very effectively in *Gimme a Pigfoot,* made on her last record
date in 1933.

Unfortunately, it was sometimes necessary for her to resort to
pornographic songs and even a "mammy" getup in order to get
jobs. In 1930 she lasted only two nights in a Negro musical at the
Belmont Theatre in New York. She was unable to compromise her
art for Broadway audiences, and engagements at Manhattan's Kit
Kat Club and Connie's Inn were also "flops." She finally went back
on the road with a show similar to the ones with which she had
started barnstorming the South twenty-five years before. The days
of her bigger productions, like "The Harlem Frolics," "The Midnight
Steppers," and "The Whoopee Girls," were gone, as was the
T.O.B.A. circuit on which she had been a star attraction. The
T.O.B.A. was Milton Starr's top Negro vaudeville circuit in the
South.

Yet, strangely, some jazz researchers found a newspaper interview with Bessie Smith in 1936, in which she is quoted as being
very optimistic about the future and feeling that she was on the
brink of new successes. The interview gave her birth date as April
15, 1898, which would have made her only thirty-nine when she
died in 1937. Most reports gave her age at death as being between
forty-five and fifty. She may, when she died, have appeared older
than she was, or she may have wanted the story to make her as
young as possible.

She may have been utilizing press agentry when she stated
that she had won the Tennessee roller skating championship with
a pair of skates bought with her first week's salary on her first job
at the age of eight, on the stage of the Ivory Theatre in Chattanooga.
While professing her love for diamonds, fur coats, and sporting events
on the one hand, she said that her ambition was to retire in 1960 to
a farm in the country where she could settle down with her pets.
After all, she was The Empress Bessie.

These years, 1936 and 1937, were the early days of the acceptance of jazz by the white public, and this may have given Bessie
hope. In February, 1936, she sang her blues at a jazz concert held
at the Famous Door on Fifty-second Street. Eddie Condon has writ-

ten that her performance was wonderful and added that Mildred Bailey was also there but refused to sing after Bessie.

September, 1937, found Bessie traveling with Winsted's "Broadway Rastus" show through her home state. They had been to sites where Bessie could recall former triumphs—like Nashville, where, in August, 1923, the papers reported, "Bessie Smith really hits 'em in Nashville. She knocked all the tin off of the theatre roof. People cried for more and refused to leave the theatre." And then there was Beale Avenue in Memphis, where, in February, 1924, she had given a special performance for whites at eleven P.M. on the stage of the Beale Avenue Palace.

Early on Sunday morning, September 26, 1937, Bessie was riding in a car bound for Memphis. Near Coahoma, Mississippi, the car piled into a panel truck, parked on the side of the road, and overturned. Bessie sustained an arm injury. It was reported that her arm was almost severed from her body. She also suffered bruises about her face and head, and internal injuries.

There were many conflicting stories of what happened after the accident. Some of these have undoubtedly been exaggerated because of the racial issues involved. Piecing together the various reports, however, the following appears to be reasonable.

The accident took place on the outskirts of Coahoma, a town too small to have a hospital. The closest town of any size was Clarksdale, Mississippi, a few miles away. A prominent Memphis surgeon came upon the accident a few minutes after the crash. An ambulance had already been ordered, but the doctor could see that Bessie was in danger of bleeding to death. He was attempting to put her into the back of his car (she weighed about two hundred pounds at the time), when another car rammed into the back of his car, wrecking it completely. Five minutes later, the ambulance arrived and rushed Bessie to the Negro ward of the G.T. Thomas Hospital in Clarksdale, where one of the town's best surgeons amputated her arm. She died fifteen minutes past noon that same day. The doctors reported that her death was probably due more to her internal injuries than to the loss of blood.

Bessie's brother, Clarence Smith, of Philadelphia, had her body sent to Philadelphia for burial in Mount Lawn Cemetery. Reports of the funeral state that she had an expensive coffin, pall bearers and a long line of mourners.

Bessie Smith set a pattern for many blues singers among both her contemporaries and those who followed her. She was outstanding in her own time, the day of the direct, driving blues shouters. There were five other blues-singing Smiths—Clara, Trixie, Mamie, Laura and Hazel—and not one was related to the other.

The Bessie Smith influence on the jazz that followed has been deep. Louis Armstrong recorded with her early in his career and has been quoted as saying, "She used to thrill me at all times, the way she could phrase a note with a certain something in her voice no other blues singer could get. She had music in her soul and felt everything she did. Her sincerity with her music was an inspiration."

Bix Beiderbecke used to throw money at her feet at the Paradise Gardens in Chicago every time she hit a note or phrase that pleased him. Eddie Condon has said that the Chicagoans were raised on her records.

Billie Holiday used to run errands for the girls in a Baltimore bagnio just for the privilege of coming into the parlor to listen to Bessie Smith's records.

The outstanding gospel singer of our day, Mahalia Jackson, whose vocal style is very reminiscent of Bessie's, tells how, as a child, she had to sneak away from her religious household to go to a New Orleans theatre to hear Bessie whenever the great blues singer came to town.

As recently as 1954, an English blues singer named Beryl Bryden showed up in Paris singing the words and using the intonations of Bessie Smith—with a British accent!

When you hear Jack Teagarden or Joe Sullivan improvise, you are very likely to hear a phrase or an idea that originated with Bessie Smith. Her phrases and ideas, and the life-filling sound of her, will be remembered as long as there are reasons for the blues.

SELECTED DISCOGRAPHY—BESSIE SMITH

The Bessie Smith Story, Vols. 1-4, Columbia CL 855-858

Thomas
"Fats" Waller

*   *   *   *

By John S. Wilson

Both Fats Waller and his principal tutor, James P. Johnson, lived lives of aching frustration. Johnson ached openly because he could find no audience for his serious compositions, but Waller's desire to find acceptance as a serious musician was buried under a heavy coating of pervasive geniality. And while Johnson plodded steadily downhill in puzzled despair, Waller's blithely ironical attitude carried him up and up and up in the material world—eventually to a level that even his enormous energy could not cope with.

He was one of the most massively talented men who has ever turned up in the world of popular music—an inimitable entertainer whose charm has, if anything, grown in the nostalgic decade and a half since his death; the writer of some of the great evergreen songs in the popular repertoire (*Honeysuckle Rose, Ain't Misbehavin'*); a jazz pianist whose playing was a landmark in the development of that instrument and whose influence on pre-bop pianists was surpassed only by that of Earl Hines; and a section man who could swing an entire band as no one else could. All of these gifts were his and yet, like the inevitable clown who wants to play Hamlet, he had a consuming desire to bring to the public his love of classical music and of the organ. His need to offer this gift and have it accepted was almost childlike and, childlike, the hurt when it was rejected was deep and long.

Gene Sedric, the saxophonist and clarinetist in Fats' little band from 1938 to 1943, remembers times when Waller was so full of his feeling for serious music that he couldn't help playing, even in a night club, with all the musicality of which he was capable. But this wasn't the Fats that the customers had paid to hear.

"People in the audience would think he was lying down,"

141

Sedric says. "They'd yell, 'Come on, Fats!' He'd take a swig of gin or something and say resignedly, 'Aw right, here it is.' "

And he'd plod into some tawdry trifle from Tin Pan Alley.

Waller's serious ambitions were all entwined with his love of the organ. The Chicago critic, Ashton Stevens, once observed perceptively that "the organ is the instrument of his heart, the piano of his stomach."

Fats had an organ in his apartment in New York and, later, in his house at St. Albans, L.I. Wherever he went, he sought out opportunities to play the organ. In Paris, in 1932, on an otherwise rambunctious trip with song-writer Spencer Williams, he climbed up to the organ loft of the Cathedral of Notre Dame with Marcel Dupré, the Cathedral's organist. His report on what happened there was typically Wallerian: "First Mr. Dupré played the God-box and then I played the God-box."

When he was working in the film, "Stormy Weather," in 1943, shortly before his death, he found an organ on the set. He sat down to play and for three hours production was held up as the entire company listened entranced. One of his few opportunities to play the organ for a wide audience, and to play as he wanted to play, came during a year he spent on the staff of WLW in Cincinnati in the early 'thirties. He had an enormously successful late night program there, "Fats Waller's Rhythm Club," on which he sang and clowned and played the driving stride piano that was his specialty. And then, a couple of hours later, in the early hours of the morning, the station offered a program of quiet, peaceful organ music. The organist never received any billing. It was Fats Waller, playing with a full contentment that rarely came to him.

There must have been something of the same contentment for him on a day in 1927 when he sat down at a pipe organ in Victor's Camden studios and recorded two fugues by Bach (who ran third in Fats' book as the greatest man in history—Lincoln and Franklin D. Roosevelt were first and second), Moszkowski's *Spanish Dance No. 1,* Liszt's *Liebestraum,* Rimski-Korsakov's *Flight of the Bumble Bee* (which, thirty years ago, had not yet been galloped to death by accordionists and Harry James), and Friml's *Spanish Days.* None of these recordings has ever been released, but the rumors about them suggest that Waller felt the stern eye of studio expectations burning over his shoulder: he played them through straight and then dressed them up in a hot treatment.

A Chicago musical instrument store often sent a Hammond organ (compliments of the house) to Waller's hotel room when he was playing there. In the small hours, he would lull a roomful of guests with spirituals, Bach and hymns. One morning, after three hours of music, Fats sat back and suggested to his guests, "Have another glass, and I'll play you my favorite piece." His friends refreshed themselves and Waller launched into his favorite —*Abide with Me.*

This was something that came out of the very marrow of Thomas Wright Waller. It was part of the continuing evidence of the enormous sense of loss that he felt when his mother died. He had been sixteen at the time. Adeline Lockett Waller played the piano and the organ and, of the dozen children that she bore, Thomas, her youngest son, was her favorite. Her death was a shock from which Waller never really recovered. Shortly before his own death at the unseemly age of thirty-nine, he composed a melody which "really shook his soul," according to his last manager, Ed Kirkeby. He called it *Where Has My Mother Gone?*

"Several lyrics with different titles were written," Kirkeby recalls, "but none were accepted by Tom. None satisfied him nor adequately expressed the anguish of that melody."

This anguish pursued Waller for the full twenty-three years that he was completely a part of the world of music. It led him, hard on the heels of his mother's death, to an impetuous marriage to Edith Hatchett. It quickly foundered and left him with an unending stream of alimony troubles which, at one point, landed him in jail. But it was his mother's death, too, that led to his real entrance into the music world of Harlem.

He was born May 21, 1904, into a deeply religious family. His father, Edward Waller, minister of the Abyssinian Baptist Church, looked on jazz as "music from the devil's workshop." But young Tom heard sounds coming out of the cellars of Harlem that intrigued him. A brief try at formal piano instruction had little effect on him. He taught himself and quickly gained a reputation as a musical clown at P.S. 89. Later in life he listed his hobbies as "music, music, music and more music." By then he had also acquired abiding interests in food and liquor, but in his school days this listing would have been reasonably accurate.

When he was fourteen he regularly wormed his way into the Lincoln Theatre, a movie house, and battled his way down to a

front-row seat right in back of Maizie Mullins, who played piano
for the silent films. She let him slide under the brass rail and onto
the piano stool beside her and, when she wanted a rest, young Tom
was allowed to play along with the picture. When the theatre's organist fell ill, the boy filled in for him and later, when the organist
left, Tom got his job. He was a professional, making twenty-three
dollars a week.

Waller soon had a chance to pass along the kindness that
Maizie Mullins had shown him. Just as Waller had sat entranced
in the seat behind Miss Mullins, another youngster, Bill Basie, was
soon sitting behind Waller, watching him play the organ. One day
Waller asked Basie if he'd like to learn the instrument ("I'd give
my right arm," said Basie), and invited him to join him in the pit.
Basie sat on the floor, watching Waller's feet work the pedals. Then
Basie worked the pedals with his hands while Waller played. Then
he sat beside Waller and learned the keyboard. And finally Waller
found a convenient excuse for leaving him alone and Basie found
himself playing accompaniment to the film.

Waller was a big wheel to his schoolmates by now and the
next year, when he won a piano contest at the Roosevelt Theatre,
playing James P. Johnson's *Carolina Shout,* his reputation began
to spread beyond the precincts of school.

And then his mother died. His world suddenly fell apart. It no
longer had gaugeable boundaries and edges. Shortly after his
mother's death, Waller was found disconsolate on the steps of the
home of a friend, Russell Brooks, a pianist of some local fame.
The Brooks family took the boy in and, through Brooks, he moved
into the heart of the hectic Harlem night life of the early 'twenties.
Brooks introduced him to the rent-party scene, to such rent-party
stars as Willie the Lion Smith (his appraisal of Waller: "Yeah, a
yearling, he's coming along, I guess he'll do all right"), and, most
importantly, James P. Johnson.

James P. was the big man at the Harlem rent parties then and
after he heard young Waller play the pipe organ, he told his wife,
"I know I can teach that boy." So Waller practiced on the John-
sons' piano far into the morning, until three or four o'clock when
Mrs. Johnson would order him to go home. Johnson got Waller
his first night-club job when Willie the Lion decided to quit Leroy's
at One Hundred and Thirty-fifth Street and Fifth Ave. Johnson was
asked to take over but he couldn't and recommended young Fats.

Johnson also took Waller over to QRS, where he was making piano
rolls, and introduced him there. This resulted in nineteen rolls by
Fats, at one hundred dollars a roll.[1] The next year he made his
first record, a pair of piano solos, *Muscle Shoals Blues* and *Birmingham Blues,* for Okeh. And 1923 found him on the radio for the
first time, broadcasting from the stage of the Fox Terminal Theatre
in Newark.

By then, too, Waller had written the first of what was to be a
long series of brightly melodic tunes. He based his first effort on a
ribald lyric, *The Boy in the Boat.* He was in Boston at the time, taking a leave from his organ chores at the Lincoln to accompany a
vaudeville act called "Liza and Her Shufflin' Six." So he called his
tune *Boston Blues.* By the time it was published in 1925, however,
Clarence Williams had provided it with lyrics that could be used
anywhere, and the title had been changed to *Squeeze Me.*

Waller was very pleased with his first composition, and he
played it endlessly. Don Redman once visited him at the Lafayette,
where Fats presided at the organ after the Lincoln was sold. Redman sat beside Waller, chatting with him while the newsreel filled
the screen above them. As they talked, Waller pounded out *Squeeze
Me* which at that time was still *The Boy in the Boat* set to music.
Glancing up at the screen, Redman noticed with horror that a
funeral was being shown.

"Hey, Fats," he whispered, "they're showing a funeral. You
shouldn't be playing that."

"Why not?" exclaimed Fats with a satanic grin, pumping
sturdily at the keyboard. Then, beckoning an usher, Waller gave
him fifty cents to get him a pint of gin.

The pint was the modest beginning of what was to become a
standard drinking setup for Waller. At a recording session he invariably had one quart on the piano, another in reserve underneath.
In his later days, when he was touring with his little band and had
switched from gin to whiskey, his dressing room was supplied with
three fifths every day—two for Waller (and *nobody* else) and one
for visitors. At the end of the day, there were invariably two dead
Waller soldiers while the visitors' bottle, as frequently as not, hadn't
been finished.

When he got up in the morning, his regular dosage was four
fingers neat ("my liquid ham and eggs"), followed by four fingers

[1] Many are now available on LP on Riverside 12-103.

after shaving. For excursions (anywhere out of reach of a bottle), he carried a suitcase equipped with collapsible cups and, of course, proper cheer.

Waller's customary procedure on entering anyone's office was to walk over to the desk, pull open a drawer and exclaim, "Where's the bottle?"

One day, with his good friend, Redman, he strode into the office of music publisher Harry Link, examined Link's desk and made his usual request. While Link was sending out for a bottle, Waller fooled around the piano. Redman's fancy was caught by some chords Waller was playing. He took them down and, by the time the bottle arrived, the two had worked out a chorus. Just then Andy Razaf, Waller's most frequent collaborator, walked in.

"Listen to this, Andy," said Redman, and Waller played over the chorus. Razaf immediately picked up a pencil and started writing a lyric. Before the three left Link's office, they had written a complete tune, words and music, gotten an advance and killed a bottle. The tune was *If It Ain't Love*.

Waller's speed and facility as a composer were fabulous. When he was writing scores for the shows at Connie's Inn in Harlem, he would be playing piano at a rehearsal when Leonard Harper, the producer, asked him, "Have you written anything for this next number, Fats?"

"Yeah, yeah," Fats would reply. "Go on with the dance man."

And while the chorus danced, Fats composed the number that they were to dance to.

His delicate *Jitterbug Waltz* was written in ten minutes after he woke up one day with the tune floating through his mind (the inspiration, possibly subconscious, was a finger exercise his son, Maurice, had been playing). In one two-hour session, Waller and Razaf turned out *Honeysuckle Rose, My Fate Is in Your Hands* and *Zonky. Ain't Misbehavin'* was created in forty-five minutes. His six-part *London Suite* was composed in an hour to fulfill a commitment so that Fats could leave England. Waller sat at the piano playing while his manager, Ed Kirkeby, described the various sections of London which Waller portrayed in his music.

Waller, in fact, was so fluent as a composer and so eternally in need of money that he was very casual about all but giving away many of his compositions.

There were times when it seemed as though composing was just as easy as breathing for Fats. There was one occasion when it was as easy as eating hamburgs. This was one early morning when he was out with Fletcher Henderson and some of the men in Henderson's band. They stopped in a hamburg joint where Fats quickly consumed nine specialties of the house. He was broke and he offered Henderson one tune per hamburg if he'd pick up the check. Henderson agreed and Waller called for manuscript paper. He quickly wrote out nine tunes and handed them over to Henderson who upped the price per tune from one hamburg to ten dollars. Waller's hamburg numbers included *Top and Bottom* (named after a Harlem drink made of wine and gin) which was later retitled *Henderson Stomp, Thundermug Stomp* which was changed to *Hot Mustard*, and other tunes that were subsequently known as *Variety Stomp, St. Louis Shuffle* and *Whiteman Stomp*.

Another time when he was hard up, Waller tried to peddle an entire folio of manuscripts to QRS for ten dollars (offer refused); and once, in a moment of deep financial desperation shortly after his second marriage (to Anita Rutherford), he offered every song in his possession to Redman for ten dollars (again refused). However, he wasn't always so unsuccessful in his efforts to rob himself. On one occasion he managed to sell his rights to *Ain't Misbehavin', Black and Blue* and seventeen other songs for a total of five hundred dollars.

Waller's fortunes started to take a turn for the better in 1932 when he acquired a manager, Phil Ponce, who placed him on the staff of WLW in Cincinnati. His late night "Rhythm Club" program there made his name known throughout the East and Midwest. It was on this program that he was tagged "the harmful little armful," and the Waller personality began to make itself felt beyond the confines of a small group of friends. The personality got even wider exposure when he started recording for Victor in 1934 with the little band called His Rhythm. At the same time, the popular appeal of his sometimes brutal desecrations of the finest flowers of Tin Pan Alley shadowed his talents as a jazz pianist and as a song writer.

Fats, the pianist, had one of the strongest left hands in jazz. This is an important consideration for anyone attempting stride piano, the style brought to an initial peak by James P. Johnson and then polished off by Waller. In stride piano, the left hand plays alternate single notes and chords. Rudi Blesh has aptly described Waller's solid left as rolling on "like heat thunder on a summer day." For Bennie Payne, who recorded some duets with Waller, the high point of the show, "Keep Shufflin'," was the fact that the two best left hands in jazz were playing together in the pit—the hands of James P. Johnson and Fats Waller. Along with his strength, Waller had unusual delicacy, a remarkable lightness of touch which gave his stride playing a romping airiness that Johnson's never achieved.

His pianism, however, became subordinate once the path for his display of personality had been marked out. The system was the essence of simplicity. Fats just relaxed and did whatever came to mind. And the Waller mind had always been wryly direct. During a period in the middle 'twenties, when he was playing with Erskine Tate's Vendome orchestra in Chicago (Louis Armstrong was in the band then, too), it was the custom for song pluggers to hand out new tunes to the men in the band and have them play them at sight. Inevitably, this led to some treacherous tangles as the band waded through strange material. One night, when confusion was more rampant than usual in the orchestra pit, Waller leaned down from his elevated piano and asked, "Pardon me, boys, but what key are you all strugglin' in down there?"

There is a claim, made by the late Lips Page, that the term "bop" was created by Fats in one of his offhand remarks. It happened, said Lips, when Fats was playing with a small group at Minton's.

"Late one night some of the younger generation of musicians would bring along their instruments in the hope of jamming with the band," Lips related. "Waller would signal for one of them to take a chorus. The musician would start to play, then rest for eight or twelve bars in order to get in condition for one of his crazy bop runs. Fats would shout at them, 'Stop that crazy boppin' and a-stoppin' and play that jive like the rest of us guys!' "

The interjected comments that became his trade-mark both on the air and on records were often tinted with blue and his manager was repeatedly asked to muzzle him, to put him under wraps. But there was no wrap that could contain the effusive Fats. If he chose to wind up a recording of *Spring Cleaning* by remarking, "No, lady, we can't haul your ashes for twenty-five cents. That's bad business," there was nothing much that could be done about it because no one, including Waller, had the slightest idea he was going to say it until it popped out.

He went along, as he said, "livin' the life I love," pouring out himself, creating laughter everywhere he appeared. If he failed to find acceptance for the serious side of himself that he wanted to show, it was not through any lack of musical technique so much as his lack of personal discipline. He could never pass up a good time. What should have been one of the high points of his career occurred in January, 1942, when he gave a concert at Carnegie Hall. The auditorium was packed. Fats had a few anticipatory drinks but he went out and played the first half of his program in controlled, quiet form. During intermission he found that he had as many friends backstage as he had out front, and he tried to have a drink with each of them. When he returned for the second half, he played a medley of Gershwin tunes, including *Summertime,* and everything else that he played for the rest of the concert kept turning into *Summertime.* It was not a notable performance.

He had been warned a couple of times to stop drinking and once he tried—for a while. But zest alone could not keep him going and finally the 270 pound body gave out. It was on a train near Kansas City in December, 1943, when he was on his way home to spend Christmas with his second wife and their two children.

He left behind a legacy of laughter.

"Every time someone mentions Fats Waller's name," said Louis Armstrong, "why you can see the grins on all the faces as if to say, 'Yea, yea, yea, yea, Fats is a solid sender, ain't he?' "

For James P. Johnson, who looked on Waller as a son, his death was particularly hard to take. He went into into seclusion, emerging only to play a *Blues for Fats,* which he had composed, at a Waller memorial at Town Hall. He came to the concert still shrouded in his sorrow but backstage, as memories of Fats were exchanged, each recollection ended in an uproarious laugh. Soon all the mourners, including Johnson, were chortling with happy memories of an irrepressible spirit whose gift for provoking laughter has given him a form of immortality.

On another level, his memory is kept green in the work of the many pianists who responded to his brightly swinging style—in the playing of Ralph Sutton and Joe Sullivan and Johnny Guarnieri. And in the records Art Tatum has left us. Tatum was particularly proud of his musical origin.

"Fats, man—that's where I come from," he once said. And he added with a sly grin, "Quite a place to come from."

SELECTED DISCOGRAPHY—FATS WALLER

PIANO ROLLS:

Young Fats Waller, Riverside 12-103

PIANO SOLOS:

Young "Fats" Waller, "X" LVA-3035

ON THE ORGAN:

Swingin' the Organ with "Fats" Waller, Victor LPT 3040

VOCALS WITH PIANO AND ORGAN:

The Amazing Mr. Waller, Riverside 12-109

AND HIS RHYTHM:

"Fats" Waller Plays and Sings, Victor LPT 1001
Ain't Misbehavin', Victor LPM 1246
"Fats," Victor LPT 6001 (two 12-in. disks)
Fats Waller Plays and Sings, Jazztone J 1247

Art
Tatum

* * * *

By Orrin Keepnews

"Art was probably the last man left who had no trouble finding a place to play after hours."

That's the way Roy Eldridge put it, and the key words in his sentence—"after hours"—are ones that recur most regularly in the story of Art Tatum, and are inevitably stressed when one of his friends or old associates gets to reminiscing about the man who has been called the last, and perhaps the greatest, of the *big* piano players. "After hours" is a term that has a very specific, very evocative meaning in jazz. It is a bit outdated now, but not too many years ago there were places in almost any big city, not too difficult to find, where there was no curfew for the music short of exhaustion: back rooms where the emphasis was apt to be on the big man hunched over the battered, well-used upright piano. The world of after-hours jazz was, by and large, a private world. So it was altogether fitting that it was home for Tatum, whose personal world always had to be a physically restricted one.

For the other basic point to start with in any consideration of Art Tatum is, of course, his blindness. He was not totally blind— there was slight vision, probably no more than twenty-five per cent, in one eye—and he did not like being referred to as a blind man. He took pains to demonstrate how much he could do for himself unaided; he delighted in any situations that enabled him to participate as an equal or even to have an advantage over normally sighted people (Eldridge can tell of a mock fight in the snow, when Roy's brother Joe, another musician, and Tatum all joined in burying Roy in a snow drift; and he retains an equally vivid memory of Art leading him down a dark flight of cellar stairs). But the fact remains that Tatum was a man with a serious physical handicap. No other of the twenty-one performers singled out in this book as jazz greats has or had a similar burden. Yet, it is important to note, these

151

chapters surely deal with few if any lives on a more even keel than Tatum's.

It is not easy to set this down in cold print without seeming patronizing, either to Art or to others, but it might be put this way: his life was an apparently happy one, notably untortured, free from the ups and downs, the frustrations and maladjustments that so often batter the creative artist. "Calmness" is not the word for it; that doesn't come close to fitting a man for whom (as one obituary tribute aptly phrased it) life was "a vast maw of sound," a pianist whose talent placed him well ahead of his time. It must be granted that there is danger of oversimplification here: there certainly were specific areas and times of doubt and frustration. And it should also be stressed that this is no aesthetic value judgement: it is neither "better" nor "worse" for a twentieth century jazz musician to be relatively non-neurotic, or to achieve quickly a widespread and lasting acceptance by both the public and his fellow professionals. Nevertheless, it seems highly significant that, unless there were secret torments that eluded the attention even of those who knew him best, Tatum can be described as fundamentally a confident and fulfilled, though never satiated, man.

It would seem that this can be explained undeviously in terms of the fact that Art's greatest problem was one he had to face early and deal with permanently. So nearly blind (he could distinguish colors to some extent and, by holding the cards quite close to his face, play an above-average game of pinochle, but that was about all his eyes could do for him), he had a tremendous adjustment to make. He found the way to accomplish this, through his music, while still in his 'teens, and it stayed with him all his life. His world was necessarily an inward-turned one; but it could very satisfactorily be just that. For he could know that he was supremely capable as a pianist; he need not doubt that he was deservedly a focal point of his self-chosen world of music. The people who mattered to him, who were similarly enmeshed in jazz as a way of life, came to him because his talent made him the man to come to. If this had not been so, if Tatum had not been a superior musician or if he had been one of those who have to struggle long, darkly and alone for recognition, it would have been very different. But Art's dazzling technique and full, rich way of playing were appreciated almost from the first. Jazz had to be his life, and it was. There were very few occasions when it failed to work out just that well for him.

"Art was not an easy man to get to know," Roy Eldridge has

said. Roy, who feels that he "knew him as well and as long as anyone," helps build the picture of a lusty, convivial man—his rather
awesome drinking capacity was one, though not the only, point of
similarity to Fats Waller—but a man who picked his friends with
caution. "If he accepted you, that was one thing; but not just anyone could get close to him." Not just anyone could get to hear Tatum
at his best, either. It is generally accepted (and in keeping with the
pattern that has just been described) that his most formidable playing was displayed only in circumstances and before audiences largely
of his own choosing. After hours a man played strictly as he pleased
(when you're not being paid for your services, there are, after all,
certain basic privileges you can expect). He played as long and as
late as he pleased (while these sessions didn't necessarily *start* after
closing time, many musicians literally came there after their regular
night's work was done, and as often as not they'd keep going until
long after dawn). And he played primarily for friends and fellow
musicians. It was then, according to the stories, that more than a
few performers reached peaks they could never duplicate under
more normal and formal conditions. And quite specifically, it was in
the after-hours spots that Tatum really came to life. (If there were
other piano players on hand worth hearing, the owner of one such
place recalled, "we could never let Art sit down until real late, because once he started, he'd never get up.")

The after-hours joints probably reached their peak in the nineteen thirties; they lasted somewhat into the 'forties, but not beyond
that point; and their special aura and flavor will probably never be
recaptured. In Harlem, and in the Negro districts of some Midwestern cities, they would seem to have been direct offshoots of the fabulous all-night "rent parties." Like them, they were at least semi-
selective about admittance: they weren't exactly private affairs, but
it helped if you were known. Like rent parties, such sessions were
apt to have pianists as the center of attraction, and "cutting contests" of incredible length and intensity were the rule. You might
say that legalisms brought about the virtual end of the after-hours
club: tougher enforcement of legal closing times; or the musicians
union cracking down on the once-prevalent habit of unpaid "sitting
in." (Tom Tilghman, whose Hollywood Bar in Harlem was practically home for Tatum for many years, points out that "no club
could ever have afforded the going price for all the men I'd have in
my place on a good night.") But you could also say that the temper
of the times has changed, that there aren't that many musicians in-

terested in playing all night just for the love of it and maybe a few
free drinks, not that many who still feel it vitally important to prove
their mettle in all-out personal competition.

In any case, after hours was Tatum's time as long as he lived.
He could guard it jealously, too, against intrusions by outsiders who
failed to grasp the distinction between it and the standard night-
club setting. Billy Taylor, the young modern pianist who was one of
Art's closest friends during the last dozen years of his life, notes
that Tatum "would usually sit around for quite a while before he'd
feel ready to play;" sometimes he might wait until maybe seven or
eight A.M., "when the others gave out," before starting. So there
would be nights, Taylor recalls, when "someone in the audience
would come up to him and ask, 'When do you play?' He might have
been just about ready to start, too, but he'd say something like
'I play at the Three Deuces,' and hold off for maybe another
hour."

Even the earliest stories about Tatum place him in this setting
that he loved best. The basic statistics are that he lived forty-six
years, having been born in Toledo, Ohio, on October 13, 1910; his
father was a mechanic who had come north from North Carolina
just before that. He showed an early interest in music, which his family encouraged with violin lessons when he was about thirteen, and
then with piano lessons. His fully professional debut came at about
the age of eighteen, when he was hired as staff pianist at a local
radio station, WSPD, and, as Barry Ulanov puts it in his book *A
History of Jazz in America,* he began "to get a reputation (when)
his extraordinary fifteen-minute morning programs on that station
were picked up and piped across the country by the Blue Network
of the National Broadcasting Company. . . ." But that would have
to be later than 1926, the year in which the N.B.C. network was
first formed, and there would seem to have been a basis for a Tatum
reputation—built in less conventional surroundings, of course—
even before that. June Cole, bass player with McKinney's Cotton
Pickers, who played throughout the Midwest from the mid 'twenties
on, recalls first meeting Art in Toledo (he believes it must have
been as early as 1924 or '25) when young Tatum was playing at
"what we called chittlin' dinners, like house-rent parties, where the
landlady would slip him maybe five dollars." Cole was doubling,
after his night's work with McKinney, as a singer at a late-running
gambling joint called Big Noble's. He remembers quite clearly the
night when, just after he had finished *Dear Old Southland,* with Todd

Rhodes of the McKinney band accompanying him, "this young blind fellow came up to me" and, very quietly and shyly, asked, " 'Mr. Cole, could I play that number for you again later?' I said he could, and I can still remember just how good he was." According to Cole, the big, crashing chords, the sweeping runs, the richly elaborate fill-ins were part of the Tatum style even then. "He used to play behind me all the time after that, and he didn't have to ask permission again."

Art's local activities, including radio and night-club work, brought him to the attention of singer Adelaide Hall, and when he came to New York for the first time, in 1932, it was as her accompanist. His first records were made with her in that year, and in 1933 came his first, highly impressive, records as a soloist, for the Brunswick label. By then, Art had already begun to have a great impact on musicians, many of whom were making the most of their first chance to hear him at the Onyx Club on Fifty-second Street, which with the repeal of Prohibition was coming out from underground as a jazz center. It was also possible then, and only then, to spring Tatum as a devastating surprise on unsuspecting musicians. Roy Eldridge, who had met Art in Cleveland in about 1931 while working with the McKinney band, recalls the first time he, along with his brother Joe and the great tenor man, Chu Berry, took Tatum to the Rhythm Club, a Harlem musicians' hangout. The three horns jammed for a while, and then installed their unknown friend at the piano. "We turned Art loose, and goodbye. . . ."

Tatum next settled briefly in Chicago, leading a small band at the Three Deuces for a couple of years, but then switched to solo work. This was clearly the best procedure for a man who was, as Billy Taylor has put it, "a whole band, complete in himself," and whose preference was for intricate extemporaneous choruses that even rhythm accompanists often had trouble following. Until 1943, he worked alone: most often in New York, but in 1938 as far afield as London. The pattern was set; his reputation was firmly established; not only was he the idol of most jazz pianists, but it has been fairly reliably reported (although such items can sometimes be considered dubious) that his work was praised by Horowitz, Godowski, and/or Rachmaninoff. (As for the opinions of his jazz colleagues, the largest chunk of statistics are those to be gleaned from Leonard Feather's 1955 *Encyclopedia of Jazz:* of forty-six pianists who gave specific answers to a question about their "favorites" on their own instrument, thirty included Tatum's name.)

He was not exclusively a solo pianist: even while working in clubs as a single, he recorded with small bands, some of his most highly regarded work, for example, being a group of recordings made in 1941, on which he led the backing for blues singer Joe Turner on numbers like *Wee Baby Blues*. And Eldridge's earliest recollection of Tatum is his jamming with horn men at a Cleveland after-hours spot called Val's Alley ("It's just too bad there weren't tape machines in those days; somebody should have taken down *those* sessions"). But Art belonged primarily to the early solo tradition of "two-handed piano players" who supplied their own rhythm with their own left hand. It was a tradition exemplified by Fats Waller, whom Tatum looked on as his basic influence. Barry Ulanov has written of a conversation in which Art insisted, "Fats, man. That's where I come from." (Waller, for his part, had immense admiration for Tatum, once stopped playing to introduce him to a night-club audience by saying: "I play piano, but God is in the house tonight.") An important part of that tradition of the earthy "big" piano men of the 'twenties and 'thirties were the "cutting contests." The first thing to do on arriving in any town was to look up the best players in town and have at them. Thus, in New York in the 'thirties and early 'forties, Tatum would head uptown for places like Reuben Harris's or the Chicken Shack (where, briefly, young Charlie Parker was a dishwasher). There, he knew, he would find men like James P. Johnson, the dean of the Harlem "stride piano" school, and Clarence Profit, and lesser-known (to the public) but scarcely secondary figures like Donald Lambert and The Beetle. Tatum's high regard for Waller actually extended to the whole stride style, elements of which could always be heard in his own driving pace. As Billy Taylor describes what he heard in the early 'forties, Art was sometimes a bit slow in getting under way: "He hadn't played much stride for quite a while, but once he got warmed up . . . look out!" Taylor also recalls one particularly amazing encounter between Tatum and Clarence Profit, when both men decided to play straight melody, varying only the harmony, each improvising five or six choruses of a number at a time that way! Staying power was inevitably an important part of any such rivalries, and Tatum was apparently always proud of his stamina. Guitarist Everett Barksdale, who worked with Tatum in his last years, had known him back in the early Ohio days. He insists that young Art was once involved in an argument with a drummer who felt he could keep playing longer than any pianist. They decided to battle it out, each using only one hand, and according to Barksdale, it was five hours before the drummer quit. Tom Tilghman claims that Tatum once battled a pianist for a full day—"from two A.M. to two A.M."—in his back room, and he also says it was not uncommon for Art to stay up for forty-eight hours at a stretch, playing most of the time and taking only occasional cat-naps. (On the other hand, when he did sleep, it was with unusual soundness—although "you could always wake him up just by touching one of his hands.") And, of course, even if there is exaggeration in such accounts, or in Barksdale's estimate that "ten shots and ten beers" was not an unusually heavy night's drinking for him, the point remains that Tatum was a man regarded by his associates as larger than life-sized, as truly capable of such feats.

It was not all a matter of bravura competition, of course. Tilghman's bar was, from 1936, a home port for Tatum, a place where, among other things, the nearly blind man knew every foot and every angle well enough to move about without tension. It was Waller, Tilghman notes, who first "coaxed" him into the spot, at a time when just about every bar in the city was trying to persuade him to be a regular visitor. Waller, it seems, had arrived unannounced at dinner time one day, and began playing. Tilghman, not recognizing him, and deciding that his dinner customers should be protected from annoyances like this, tried asking Fats to stop. When that failed, he resorted to turning on the jukebox, and loudly. Finally Fats, on the way out, got into conversation with the owner about the trouble he'd had "with that guy who kept playing the juke box" and, Tilghman recalls, "we got to talking and I admitted I hadn't known who he was, and we got pretty friendly. He told me he liked the place, but he was going out of town, so he was going to tell his friend to come by." The friend, Tatum, kept coming, "because he got to know he wouldn't be bothered here. He'd play cards here, or fall asleep in that booth over there, and we'd kid him—you could always get his goat by calling him a *jazz* piano player. He didn't like to be called that; said he was a *piano* player, a *musician.*"

In 1943 came the formation of the Art Tatum Trio, with Slam Stewart on bass and Tiny Grimes on guitar. It was a move that seems to have been dictated by commercial considerations, adding two showmanlike performers to the act. Both men were capable musicians, particularly Stewart, who was far more of a driving rhythm man and far less a clown than he was later to become, and there were even those who felt that for Tatum, no less than for any other current pianist, the newly prevalent idea of working as a trio

in order to relieve the pianist of a part of the rhythmic burden
was a sound one. Others, however, felt that Art, the "complete in
himself" piano player, needed no such thing, and Billy Taylor (who,
like virtually all modern pianists, consistently uses the trio format)
sees Tatum's going along with this idea as the first instance of musical conflict and of compromise in Art's career. But, whoever had
had the idea seemed fully supported by results. Tatum, playing as
well as ever, became even more of a drawing card. Whether it was
because of a general wartime boom, increasingly aware audiences,
or the appeal of the lightning interplay between Tatum and his two
colleagues, is difficult to say, but in any event Art became a very
major Fifty-second Street attraction, equalled only by Billie Holiday. If there were changes in Tatum, they could be considered almost
inevitable ones. His playing style became somewhat more florid in
its intricacy; his personal attitude became somewhat more detached
and Olympian. He remained a very warm man to those he accepted:
To Taylor he was "so much like a big brother . . . I played way
over my head when he was around, and it was the same way with
lots of young musicians." But in place of the lusty, direct rivalries
of the old-style cutting contests, there were scenes like some in Los
Angeles that have been described by Taylor, who was there briefly
at the same time as Tatum during the mid 'forties. "I was with
Eddie South, and Art would come by the place where we working,
pick me up, and take me to sessions at Ivie Anderson's and places
like that." Tatum would still search out the top local man, but his
procedure after that was different. "He'd know that fellow's best
number, and he'd ask me to play it, to sort of bait the guy. I
wouldn't know what was going on, so I'd play it. . . . Of course if
I (or any of Art's boys) were getting carved, he'd just step in and
take over."

Still very much in evidence was an innate politeness towards
other musicians. Only to his very closest friends did he ever have
anything negative to say about others, Everett Barksdale has reported; and, as Tom Tilghman has put it, "he could correct someone's mistakes without ever seeming insulting." Taylor notes that
he "listened to everyone, even the worst," and he was apt to find
something for himself to develop in the work of the most unlikely
third-raters. There was one really bad pianist around in California,
as Taylor tells it, whom Art would do a devastating imitation of. But
then Art would play "straight," using touches adapted from this

fellow's playing, "but most people just don't listen closely to the bad ones, so they never did catch on to what Art was doing."

By the late 'forties, however, came a period that Ulanov has written of as "disillusionment, diminishing audiences, declining interest." Ulanov attributes this to an eventual awareness among critics and fans that Tatum was really not full perfection, that he had "several limitations as a pianist and musician," among them "excess of hyperbole" and "the quotations, endless interpolations of the familiar phrases of Gershwin's *Rhapsody in Blue,* perhaps; Sousa's *The Stars and Stripes Forever,* maybe." Actually, there had always been those who objected that Tatum's style was overly ornate, lacking in taste, more concerned with effect than content, shallow, even (an inevitable complaint against any performer with an inordinate amount of technical virtuosity) "not really jazz." There was nothing very new in what Ulanov refers to as a discovery of the late 'forties, the feeling that "Art was taking himself more seriously than he should have." And there was undoubtedly some truth in this; yet on the other hand a doggedly traditionalist critic like Fred Ramsey has referred to Tatum's "easy, lilting style wholly suffused with a refreshingly humorous approach." However, Ramsey, too, wrote, in his *Guide to Longplay Jazz Records* that "his tendency to display his accomplishments sometimes gets in the way of a performance."

Such negative comments, though, must be considered a minority report. The majority would go along with a musician like Barksdale, who worked alongside Tatum for the last few years of his life and stresses the "ease—no apparent effort at all" with which Art developed his "startling" ideas, the sort of seriousness that led Tatum, even in the nineteen fifties, to work "long hours at home, by himself," and the "far out dissonances and harmonic variations, the augmented elevenths and thirteenths that others are just now beginning to get to." Barksdale's emphasis is on the awe so many musicians have felt: "He leaves you with a sense of futility. . . . What you've studied maybe years to perfect he seems able to perform with such ease" and "He'd always say he didn't 'hear' what he was going to play in advance, he'd just feel it; and since so much of what we did was extemporaneous, not routined, sometimes he'd get off on something and just leave me out in left field. . . ." To Billy Taylor, the so-called floridity came about because Tatum "heard so much. There was always a desire to fill in all the other things he could hear besides just a normal piano part. But he was basically a melodic pianist;

not like some other pyrotechnic pianists: his playing was always melodic, not just exercises."

Nevertheless, it is fact that the period from about 1947 to '50 represents the one important dip in the otherwise even plane of Tatum's popularity. One theory—which has also been advanced in the cases of Eldridge, Coleman Hawkins and other greats of the pre-modern jazz idiom—is that their confidence was actually shaken by the fact that supposedly aware and opinion-forming writers, as well as much of the jazz public, were paying attention to nothing except bop and its variously named successor forms. Everything else was being down-graded; there was no room for what it later became fashionable to refer to favorably as "mainstream" jazz.

One story belonging to this period tells of a duel that never came off, but which might conceivably have been a basic test case. Bud Powell, Tatum and Billy Taylor were all on the same bill at Birdland, and Taylor tells of an overheard conversation between the other two. (It should be obvious by now that Taylor's views and recollections were vitally helpful in the preparation of this chapter.) Billy recalls that Powell, "who was pretty juiced," said in effect that Tatum wasn't *that* great, that he didn't do as much as it was claimed he did. Unquestionably Tatum could scent the prospect of the sort of contest he loved so well. "I won't take you on now," he said, "but tomorrow come in sober and anything you play with your right hand I'll play with my left." Powell was in early the next night, practicing with his left (admittedly the weaker) hand in anticipation of a two-handed battle, but the duel never took place. Actually there was great mutual admiration, and it is not farfetched at all to suggest that a lot of Art can be heard in Powell's solo work, such as *Over the Rainbow*.

By 1950, Art was back up near the top again. There was club work and there were concert tours; he recorded for promoter Norman Granz, who issued eleven long-play records forthrightly titled *The Genius of Art Tatum*. But the years of full living were catching up with him; the all-night sessions and the prodigious drinking were taking their toll. Everett Barksdale went with him to Washington, D.C. in 1953, for a check-up by a doctor who was a long-standing friend of Art's. Although Tatum was told nothing specific, it was made clear to Barksdale that the end was just a matter of time. The pianist must have been aware that all was far from well with him, though, for Barksdale notes that a joint three-day binge following a Birdland engagement in 1954 was the very last time he saw Tatum drink.

The clearest indications, though, were in his playing, which normally was of impeccable accuracy. "He's absolutely infallible," Barksdale once told a British interviewer. "With a man like that there's no such thing as a mistake. The only time I ever heard him goof was when the piano was at fault—a mechanical flaw." And Tatum had once suggested to Taylor that it was helpful to practice deliberately making mistakes, "to see how quickly you can recover." Tatum himself, Billy notes, could be playing arpeggios at great speed, hit a wrong note ("playing that fast, you're past it as soon as you hit it") and nevertheless make so swift a recovery that the flaw couldn't be detected and thus, in effect, couldn't really be considered a mistake. Yet in the *Genius* set, recorded in 1953, Billy noted, to his surprise, places where he could actually hear Tatum falter.

The first time Barksdale heard him falter was also the last. It was during their final engagement, although it was supposed to be the middle of a tour. One night in mid-October of 1956, Tatum was almost too tired to continue after the second set, and the guitarist knew then that the end was near. Tatum returned to his Los Angeles home, "to rest for a while," telling Barksdale he would be in touch with him shortly as to when they would resume. No such word ever came. On November fourth, Tatum was rushed to a hospital. Six days later he was dead. The cause of death was uremia, a kidney ailment.

There were many sincere tributes from musicians, but most seemed generalized, inevitably rather standard stuff. The sorrow and the respect were genuine enough, but the trouble is that once past the statements about his having been a great pianist of far-reaching influence (and in how many different ways can that possibly be said?), you've covered all that most people knew. It is surprising that a musician of his stature was scarcely ever interviewed; but it is not so surprising, at that, when the musician was Art Tatum. He would probably not have enjoyed having his personality pieced together as it has been done here. He might have enjoyed the fact that, since the Tatum story must be assembled from the not always mutually consistent, quite subjective views of associates and friends, there are unreconcilable loose ends. More than one source, for example, has said that he was a tight man with money. Yet Tom Tilghman has said that "no one could buy Art a drink without his buying another right back"; Roy Eldridge recalls Art flashing a five-hundred-dollar bill, the first time Roy had seen a bill that large; and Tilghman again tells of his pressing a thousand dollars on a once-well-off man who had befriended him when he first hit New York. There is, from one source, a story of his reluctance to be helpful to white musicians who asked how he played something (unless it were a close friend, like Nat Jaffe, he might say, "Why should I show him my stuff so he can go use it at a place I can't get to play at?"). But from another source comes vehement denial that color, rather than talent, was ever a consideration with him.

However, although there are areas of contradiction, the pattern as a whole seems to be knowable. Two final points can help pin it down. Once, rather late in his life, he was told of an operation that might improve his sight considerably but might also, if it were unsuccessful, cost him the small percentage of sight he did have. He was afraid to try it: he would not risk being literally and entirely a blind man. And, although it remained possible for him almost always to find a place to play as long after hours as he wished, he resented the passing of the era in which those high-spirited but deadly serious "cutting contests" were the rule. They were both the symbol and the reality of the world he wanted and needed: the world in which Art Tatum, a winning pinochle player and a truly awe-inspiring piano player and a man with good, chosen friends, need never be alone or entirely in the dark.

SELECTED DISCOGRAPHY—ART TATUM

The Genius of Art Tatum, Vols. 1-5, Clef 612-615; 618

The Genius of Art Tatum, Vols. 6-10, Clef 657-661

The Genius of Art Tatum, Vol. 11, Clef 712

Art Tatum Quartet (with Roy Eldridge), Clef 679

Here's Art Tatum, Brunswick 54004, (reissues of 1930's Brunswick and Decca recordings)

Coleman Hawkins

* * * *

By Leonard Feather

Coleman Hawkins recalls that he was ten years old when he began to use his father's razor: "By the time I was twelve I had a mustache and everything." The virility he showed in this early hirsute life carried over into his musicianship not long after, when he became the first jazz musician ever to earn a reputation as a tenor saxophonist. Hawkins's sound on the instrument had a puissant, Atlantean sonority that was the envy of his peers; in later years he developed a ballad style, warm and richly sensuous, that gave a new dimension to jazz by revealing its potentialities as a vehicle for the melodic portrayal of popular songs. Everything Hawkins has played in his thirty-five years as a major jazz force has followed the path symbolically suggested by that early glance into the shaving mirror.

The length of Hawkins's tenure has led to much speculation about his age. Whenever he and his good friend Roy Eldridge get together there follows a series of sardonic jokes in which they kid each other about such matters as who saw Admiral Dewey, how many Roosevelts they have voted for, and similar implications of longevity. It was reported during the early years of the draft that Hawkins made a great show out of having to register. He has often given varying and conflicting dates and ages for events in his life. "I think I'll start telling people I was born in Egypt," he remarked recently after wearily dispensing the vital statistics for what may have been the thousandth interview of its kind. On another occasion he earnestly informed an interviewer that he was born at sea, on a transatlantic liner. As for his age, he has claimed that on joining Mamie Smith's band he was so young that he had to have a guardian; however, a book published in 1935, when he would have no reason to falsify the records, gives November 21, 1904 as his birth date. The true birthplace was St. Joseph, Missouri.

Hawkins's reluctance to admit the accident of his comparatively early birth (early only in comparison with that of the average tenor saxophonist popular with today's jazz fan) is understandable in view of his undimmed vigor in performance, thought and action. He is a fine specimen of what is connoted by the cliché "young at heart." "You know, I can hardly believe it," he says of his seniority. "I feel the same; I'm the same person inside that I was years and years ago. It's hard to realize you are older than a lot of people." Hawkins need not concern himself. It is unlikely that he will ever, in effect, be any older than he feels, or feel any older than he looks. At fifty-three he is a handsome figure, a little trimmer around the waist than during the years of physical and mental self-indulgence in Europe. His features are regular; he is always well groomed; his hair has thinned, though not too conspicuously; his voice, warm and full-blooded like the voice of his horn, explodes now and then into a hearty and slightly Mephistophelean laugh.

The facts of Hawkins's professional life are few and simple and can be recounted briefly: his only two important associations as a sideman were with Mamie Smith's Jazz Hounds (1921–3) and Fletcher Henderson's orchestra (1923–34); in 1934 he left for London and toured with Mrs. Jack Hylton's band, later working on the Continent, mostly as a single, until 1939, when he returned home and promptly recorded the *Body and Soul* that made him, for the first time in his life, the creator of a top-selling hit record. He led a wonderful but short-lived big band in 1939–40; ever since it broke up he has fronted various small groups, worked as a single with local rhythm sections, appeared in concerts such as Norman Granz's JATP, and has returned twice to Europe (in 1950 and '54).

From the time his name first became familiar to musicians, in his earliest days with Henderson, right up to the late nineteen forties, Hawkins (who was known as "Bean," a nickname still sometimes used by fellow musicians) was the mental-reflex first choice whenever his instrument entered a conversation. Though he only once won a *Down Beat* readers' poll, in 1939 (in later years he was disqualified, as a band leader), he was the *Esquire* experts' choice for the Gold Award every year the poll was held (1944–7). *Down Beat,* in October, 1950, called him "the most influential reed man, even now, in the world."

Though it may not seem to the neophyte jazz fan that Hawkins can be the world's most influential reed man in a population that includes Stan Getz and Lester Young, it is safe to predict that in the year 2000, if jazz is recalled at all, it will be Hawkins who will be named as the most dynamic and crucial tenor-sax figure of the first half of this century. The earth citizens of that year will probably be able to consult such collectors' items as *Stampede,* recorded with Henderson in 1926; *One Hour,* with the Mound City Blue Blowers in 1929; *It's the Talk of the Town* with Henderson in 1932; *Lost in a Fog* under his own imprint (London, 1934); *Crazy Rhythm* (Paris, 1938), *Body and Soul* (1939), *The Man I Love* (1943), *Stuffy* (1945), and the unique *Picasso,* a five-minute performance cut in 1947 entirely without accompaniment after more than ten hours of perfectionist preparation. These are the best-known prototypes, of the thousand-odd titles he has recorded, of the various phases in Hawkins's career.

The key to Hawkins's continued eminence—for although he no longer wins magazine polls, he is respected by fellow jazzmen who keep track of him—is his refusal to blend obediently into the limbo of atavistic nostalgia to which some of his earlier fans would consign him. Their conviction that only the Hawkins of the nineteen twenties and thirties was the truly great man, that his willingness to go along with and even encourage new developments in jazz indicated the onset of degeneracy, is met only by scornful laughter from Hawkins. When Hawk's ever-open ears observed the bebop trend in its earliest stages, he was the first to encourage it; it was under his leadership that the first real bop record session took place (the February 1944, date with Dizzy). While *Esquire* conferred its second annual award on him and Rudi Blesh desperately urged *Record Changer* readers to "combat the Feather-*Esquire* clique and get *good* musicians publicly playing *real* jazz," Hawkins blithely hired a group of musicians that represented his concept of the real jazz—among them Howard McGhee and Oscar Pettiford—and took off for Hollywood. Bop musicians have been a part of his entourage more often than not since then, though he is comfortable in a more neutral setting and can even settle untroubled in the lap of a Dixieland ensemble.

Hawkins refuses to accept any of the clichés generally attached to his name. One of the most popular is that he "invented" the tenor saxophone to all jazz intents and purposes. "Why, I heard saxophones on records when I was just a little kid. There was one trio with a tenor sax that was about the earliest music I can remember. There was a whole lot of ofays playing tenor, even when I was just beginning; and before I'd really started making records and everything,

there was Happy Cauldwell in Chicago and Stomp Evans out of
Kansas City, and Prince Robinson . . . no, I certainly wasn't the
first." But then, after a negative answer to the question, "Did you
try to play like anyone else?" and a reminder that his records with
Henderson were the first to make musicians conscious of the tenor,
he shifted his ground: "Well, yes, I guess maybe you *could* say I
was responsible for the making of the tenor. . . ."

Nobody paid saxophones any mind, Hawkins conceded: "the
good ones couldn't improvise too much. And some of the fellers
used to play with these little bitty mouthpieces just like clarinet
mouthpieces; I always used a hard reed and developed an open
mouthpiece."

Hawkins's early and profound impact was at least partly born
of formal and functional training. His father was an electrician; his
mother played the organ, encouraged him in piano lessons from
the age of five and 'cello studies at seven; on his ninth birthday she
presented him with a saxophone. Though he never took music too
seriously, he would devote many dutiful hours to practice and would
follow these sessions with attempts at playing jazz for the rest of
the day. He became aware of jazz mainly through records, and of
classical music through concerts to which his mother took him.
(This was in Topeka, Kansas, where the family would buy season
tickets at the Auditorium.) He attended Washburn College in Topeka for two or three years, studying harmony and composition and
gigging with local bands. Later, at school in Chicago, already fully
grown though in his early teens, Hawkins would run around the
South Side to hear jazz. He was seventeen when he joined Mamie
Smith in Kansas City. He and the late Joe Smith, the cornetist, left
the band together in California after touring for a year or two.

Later, in New York, Hawkins was gigging and playing jam
sessions around town: "We used to call them cuttin' contests—like
you'd hear about a very good tenor player in some night spot, and
I'd have to go down there and cut him, you know! That was the
exact expression they used, 'Bean, you got to come down and cut
this kid,' they'd say. And that's how Fletcher and his men happened
to hear me play. Fletcher had been accompanying blues singers and
then he used a larger group for some record sessions and I made
some dates with him. Then he finally got a band together and went
into Roseland. Fletcher didn't have that much of a reputation at
the time; it seemed like just another job to me."

The Henderson incumbency turned out to be more than just

another job. It lasted a full decade and produced a magnificent flowering of Hawkins's style. From a crude slap-tongue technique that now sounds so corny that he winces when some elderly fan forces him to listen to one of his first recordings, he evolved into a smoother, less staccato style, with finesse and subtlety, always listening and learning. "Maybe the rest of the fellers would be out looking for chicks or something, and I'd be in these honky-tonk joints, listening to the musicians, and I'd hear things I liked, and they'd penetrate and I'd keep 'em. If I hear something I like, I don't go home and get out my horn and try to play it; I just incorporate it within the things that I play already, in my own style. I still do. I don't believe in just getting a record and practicing from it; that's why so many of these boys now sound all alike."

The band had it easy; about nine months were spent in Roseland, the Broadway ballroom, the rest of the year being given to a summer road trip. Sometimes they would spend a winter month at the Greystone in Detroit, where they learned about the much-respected Jean Goldkette band. "Then the owner of Roseland booked Goldkette in and they cut the Henderson band—that is, individually we were better, but my goodness, they played like a machine! After a while, though, we got to where we could blow Goldkette right out of the place, and Duke's band too. The Casa Loma orchestra came up a little later and that was tough competition too."

Gradually more and more of Hawkins's personality imposed itself on the band; he was its most celebrated soloist and an occasional contributor to the library of arrangements. A remarkable Hawkins composition called *Queer Notions,* recorded in 1933, made extensive use of augmented chords, almost to the point of creating a whole-tone scale effect.

Early in 1934 Hawkins began to observe, through the London *Melody Maker,* that his fame had spread overseas. "I didn't know until then that they knew me over there. I was too busy around here just striving hard to stay in front of some of the boys that were coming up—Herschel and Chu and everybody—trying to cut me all the time."

Interviewed by Paul Bacon in a tape recording of reminiscences for issue on a Riverside LP, he revealed that his first trip to Europe came about as casually as if it had been a one-night stand. Chatting with June Cole, a one-time Henderson bass man who had recently returned from Europe, he remarked, "You know, I kind of believe

I'd like to go over there." "If you want to go to London, why don't you write to Jack Hylton? He's got the biggest band in England," said Cole. Hawkins promptly got in his car, drove to the nearest Western Union office around St. Nicholas Avenue and One Hundred and Twenty-fifth Street, and sent a cable addressed simply to "Jack Hylton, London, England." The message read, "I am interested in coming to London," followed simply by Hawkins's name and address. The next afternoon he had a cable from Hylton, and in less than a week Hawkins was aboard the *Ile de France*. The combined pressure of his wanderlust and of an offer even better than the $150 weekly paycheck from Henderson (itself a very high salary in those days) made the trip mandatory.

"I told Fletcher I'd take a leave of absence—said I'd stay over about a month or two. Well, I stayed five years, and the next time Fletcher and I met was about six years later, I think it was in Chicago. Fletcher was playing, and he knew I was out in the audience. He sent the waiter over with a note saying 'Hope you have your saxophone with you. I think it's about time for your leave of absence to be over.' "

Hylton's idea originally was to co-star Hawkins with Louis Armstrong, who was then in England with his own big band: "The concerts were fixed and the tickets were sold; house was sold out and everything, but Louis cancelled the concert; he refused to do it." There was some disagreement as to whether Armstrong or Hawkins had been responsible. As a result of this incident, the thousands of young English fans to whom Hawkins had been a mere mythical name on a record for so many years had their first opportunity to see the legend brought to life when he toured with an undistinguished orchestra led by Mrs. Jack Hylton, the band leader's wife. Later he worked with Hylton's own unit, spending about a year in England before taking off for France and Holland. After a couple of years of combat with palsied rhythm sections, he was happy to run across an old friend one night at a small bar in Amsterdam—Freddy Johnson, an American pianist, who soon teamed with Hawkins and a competent Dutch drummer to open at the Negro Palace.

Hawkins was in demand for record sessions in every country he visited. The best-remembered date was one that inaugurated a new label in Paris, Swing Records, in 1937, for which he headed a saxophone quartet that included Benny Carter and two Frenchmen, with Django Reinhardt in the rhythm section.

Hawk enjoyed every aspect of his life, the life of an American jazz celebrity in Europe in the 'thirties. It was a rare and voluptuous existence, in sharp contrast with the constrictions into which he had been molded at home.

Arriving back in New York August 1, 1939, Hawkins soon took a small band into Kelly's Stable, a jazz club on Fifty-first Street near Seventh Avenue. It was there that he was approached for the record session that was to prove the most eventful of his life, the date that produced *Body and Soul*.

"I never thought of *Body and Soul* seriously as being anything big for me. I'd used it occasionally as an encore, something to get off the stage with. And at Kelly's, sometimes at night, after a couple quarts of Scotch, very late, I'd sit down and kill time and play about ten choruses on it, and then the boys would come in and play harmony notes in the background while I finished it up. That's all there was to it. But then Leonard Joy came in the club and asked me to record it. I said, 'Why? I don't even have an arrangement on it. Who wants to hear it?' " Hawkins was informed that "the big boys in Camden" [1] were raving about it. In the Victor Studios on October eleventh, Hawkins and his nine-piece band recorded three numbers for which the music had been written by Hazel Scott, Gene Rodgers and himself; as a sop to Joy, he threw in *Body and Soul* as the final number on the session. Only one take was made. Actually, it was no more, no less inspired than many ballads recorded before it in Hawkins's lushly erotic style, but Hawkins had been away five years and the American public had heard nothing quite as wonderful. Hawkins has played *Body and Soul* at least 6,500 times in the 6,500 days that have passed since the session, and has steadfastly refused to memorize the original improvised solo, though he has the sheet music on which it was printed for aspiring Hawkins mimics. Customers have complained, after he has answered their requests for the tune, that it "doesn't sound like the record," but unlike Louis Armstrong, Tatum and other jazzmen who have often repeated note for note what is supposedly an ad lib solo, Hawk prefers to create, not recreate, whenever he holds the horn.

[1] The session was for Bluebird, RCA-Victor's 35¢ subsidiary headquartered in Camden, N.J.

The slightly saturnine grin that is a typical Hawkins expression returns as he reflects on the controversy that accompanied the release of *Body and Soul*. "When the record first came out everybody, including Chu, said I was playing wrong notes. Everybody had their own set ideas about the changes on a tune like *Body and Soul*. A lot of people didn't know about flatted fifths and augmented changes and they thought that to go to a D-flat chord you had to go from an A-flat seventh—where I might go from a D ninth. Of course, that sort of thing is extremely common now, but it certainly wasn't before I did *Body and Soul*.

"Thelonius Monk once said to me, 'You know, you never did explain to me how did these people, these old folks and everybody *go* for your record of *Body and Soul*.' I said, 'Monk, I don't know.' So he says, 'I can't understand it.' He says, 'That's one thing I'll never understand. I don't see how they went for it.' He says, 'Cause I've listened to the record,' he says, 'and I could understand if you played melody,' he says, 'cause that's what they like—that kind of people, they like melody. They sure won't listen to anything else that's jazz.' So I just told him, 'Why, that's just one of those cases, you know, just one of those rare cases. I mean . . . gracious! I play like that all the time! I made thousands of pieces of that same thing, and played the same thing but they didn't mean nothing. Ever since then the studios have kept telling me to do another one like *Body and Soul* and I said, 'No, I made a hundred of them—we don't need none.' What happened with *Body and Soul,* it just so happened that at the right time it just happened to catch on with the right people, and that's all there was to it—just a lucky thing."

Self-analysis is no problem for a man of Bean's articulate and sensitive disposition. Of improvisation he asserts: "Good phrasing is dependent on good breath control; but perhaps more than that, it's the way you think. Actual playing experience on the job is the best way to learn to think. Improvising is playing with a lot of thought behind it; but none of the hard work that goes into thinking should show up in your playing. Too often improvising is really copying. To really improvise, a musician needs to know everything—not only his instrument, but harmony, composition, theory, the whole works. It's more important than ever today. Years ago, if you just didn't have it in here"—indicating the heart—"you couldn't play jazz; but today you can, because jazz moves. Years ago it was so far away from classic music, you didn't have to move. Real stomplike. It called for another type of feeling.

"Take this boy Urbie Green now. He's a good trombone player, you know? Because he's been studying that trombone since he was a kid, and he knows that trombone and can play it *back!* When you don't have that control, you can't incorporate the ideas that you hear and feel into your style. That's what's wrong with so many of the players coming up today.

"Sure, I was advanced for my time in those early days, for just that reason—I had studied hard since I was five, and studied classics all my life, and it gave me an advantage over the other fellows I was playing with. But those early records still sound ridiculous to me today, because of the advance in jazz musicianship. To go back as far in classic music as those records go in jazz, I mean to find something that would seem equally ridiculous, you'd have to go back hundreds of years, behind Bach, before anything you and I have ever heard. And I'll tell you a funny thing—what Bach and them were doing in classical music is what's happening right *now* in some jazz music. These quartets and things that call themselves 'modern' jazz quartets, all they're doing is trying to play Bach; they're playing Bach and Handel, that's all it is. They aren't playing *modern* classical, because the jazz ear couldn't stand a modern classic."

While firmly settled in the pro-evolution camp, Coleman at times feels certain ambivalences. Of Louis Armstrong he will observe: "Now he's playing just like he did when he was twenty years old; he isn't going any place, musically. So sometimes you may say to yourself, why beat your head against the wall; because as far as commercial value he's bigger than he ever was, and after all, there'll never be anything to compare with Louis."

He feels no sense of competition as he felt it when new tenor men first began to contest his monopoly; today he can survey the scene benignly, a quasi-emeritus dean. Once on a record session under my supervision at Victor, when I was ill-advised enough to suggest a chorus of fours with Allen Eager, he reluctantly tried one lack-luster take, then wisely withdrew from the microphone and let Pete Brown take over. To force a man of Hawkins's dignity and stature to play fours "against" anyone would rank with a request that an unfinished Dylan Thomas poem be completed by Nick Kenny; he has earned the right to consider himself *hors concours*.

Nevertheless, from the day Hawkins left for Europe, a free-for-all was on to fill the temporarily vacant throne. Lester Young, who took Hawkins's place in the Henderson band, failed to fill the requirements of that chair at that time; his thin tone contrasted too shockingly with the vigor of its predecessor. But Young, because he was the first to show that there was another way to play the tenor and because he showed it with the strength of a potent new personality, was a major figure by the time Coleman returned home.

"I first heard Lester way back, in Kansas City," he recalls. "He sounded then just the way he does now. Or rather, he sounded better, because I don't think he's too interested in his music any more. He can't even play on the beat any more, doesn't have any beat at all; he just slurs, never tongues anything. A lot of these boys around play better Lester than he does himself. Paul Quinichette— he's just like him; he's been trying his best to do something else but can't do nothing to save his life.

"Charlie Parker used to could play some good tenor. He played tenor every night at the Uptown House for a while. He got an open, full sound; not bad at all. Never used these tight sounds like these boys are using. Loud; he sounded loud. I used to notice about a lot of the boys that were trying to copy Charlie, a majority of them had a little tiny sound and had to use a microphone."

Had he run into much opposition when he first championed Parker and the other bop pioneers?

"Oh, good gracious, yes! One of the worst things I went through in those days was with Monk, when he was working in my group. I used to get it every night—'Why don't you get a piano player?' and 'What's that stuff he's playing?' One of these days I'm going to write a story about that."

Asked about Getz, Hawk said, "The one I prefer is Zoot. He used to play plenty on the beat, like eight to the bar all the time, but in the last year or two he's changed. I heard him down at the Bohemia the other night. . . . I'll tell you who else is really trying to get something different. Sonny Rollins. I've been digging him a long time. . . . I listen to all these boys and I know what they're trying to do; I get a great kick out of it. Now you take Sonny Stitt —he's strictly eight to the bar, that's all; no matter what he plays, baritone, tenor, soprano, anything—that's what it is."

Hawkins in the past few years, except for his trips to Europe has stayed firmly rooted in New York, only leaving town for a one-night concert date or an occasional club week. "The last thing I was out on, I was out to Cleveland for ten days this past winter, and since then I've been on gobs of gigs and that's all. Go to New-burgh, New York, play a fair, get in the car afterwards and come right back in town and the bars are still open." He laughed. "I did all the proms this past season. I guess I've been in practically all the big hotels, and schools. Those are the things that are paying, you know." In addition to these profitable dates, Hawkins has a comfortable royalty income from old records and from his compositions, which he supplements with jam-session appearances, mostly on weekends, at numerous clubs in and near the city. He has six dependents: his mother and grandmother, and the four who share his apartment (six commodious rooms) on West One Hundred and Fifty-third Street: his wife Dolores, and their three children, whose names originated in one of his preferred countries: Colette, fourteen; Mimi, twelve; and a son, René, eight. The apartment is liberally equipped with the electronic accouterments of modern living; TV, hi-fi phonograph and radio equipment abound.

Playing from two to five or six gigs a week, and record sessions, he has no need of traveling; if there were no financial restrictions, he says, he might like to take out a big, flexible orchestra "with a lot of strings, a lot of brass, a lot of reeds, a lot of woodwinds, and definitely a harp." He was particularly pleased with the results of two albums he made in 1956, *The Hawk in Paris* and *Hawk in Hi Fi.* "I'm glad I tongued a lot on *Hawk in Paris*—I'd stopped tonguing for a long time. I got tired of so much slurring. I like a lot of things I made in that album with Billy Taylor and them, too, on Jazztone. And several of the things I made in the 'forties, with Shavers and with Roy. But back in the 'thirties—I can't think of nothing I particularly like from then. Not now! As I said, your ears change!"

The theory that creation is something sublime and intangible is not for him: "There's nobody that can sit down with nothing in front of them or nothing in their mind, and create; any creator has to get it from something. Marconi got it from out of books. Others had been studying the same things he had for years, and somebody eventually had to hit on it. There was a lot of things I was obviously listening to, too. You can't create in a vacuum."

He rejects, too, the theory, so stubbornly upheld by certain French critics, of a "Crow Jim" racial concept of jazz: "Now there's something I'd like you to quote me as saying. Way back as far as the days when I went to England I had the same trouble with people believing it over there, probably from reading about it in magazines; after all, I played with Benny Goodman and all of them and I didn't know any clarinet player that played any more than Benny, you know what I mean? And the famous old Dixieland Jazz Band wasn't colored, and that was before *my* time! I used to have to tell people over there, I never did believe in that."

He is a nonconformist again if conformity requires acceptance of the proposition that all jazzmen have to remain true to the spirit of New Orleans: "They sent me up to Boston to go up on a TV program and when I go on the program they start asking me about this *Guide to Jazz,* and I realize that RCA is busy selling this book and the record, see? So I said, well, Panassie can't help it; he's all right, but the man just has a one-track mind. I didn't say what I wanted to say: that for him, if it don't sound like Louis Armstrong, it's not jazz. Louis and Johnny Dodds and a few people like that, that's where jazz stops for him. Anyhow, I was up there saying just the opposite of what they wanted me to say; I know they must have been glad to get rid of me! Now if Panassie had been talking about Kenton I might have gone along with him, to an extent; because jazz has got to swing. I'm talking about the stuff *I've* heard, because maybe Stan has a band that's swinging like mad today. I don't know."

He laughed at the recollection of the broadcast, of the attempt to make him fit into a stereotyped pattern. Hawk is no more of a Philistine today than he was when he first set the Henderson band and the jazz world aglow, when he and jazz were in the thrall of an adolescent romance. Rejecting the trite and the truism, he remains alert, his enthusiasm unquenched, a man still in love with his music, a little like the husband who sees in his sedate and stuffy wife the fancy-free, simple youngster he courted as a youth. If there are gray hairs on the mustache he grew forty years ago, the modern fluorescent lighting that seems to irradiate his personality has failed to betray them. "Whether it's singers, players, anything," says Coleman Hawkins, "all I like to do is listen. After all, you know, music is still my life."

SELECTED DISCOGRAPHY—COLEMAN HAWKINS

Accent on Tenor, Urania 1201

Documentary, Riverside 12-117 and 12-118

Hawk in Hi-Fi, Victor LPM 1281

Hawk in Paris, Vik LX 1059

Hawk Talks, Decca 8127

Hawk in Flight, Victor LJM 1017

Coleman Hawkins & His All-Stars, Concert Hall CHJ 1201

Jazz Concert, Grand Award 33-316

Benny
Goodman

*   *   *   *

By Nat Shapiro

Benny Goodman has always presented something of a problem to the serious student, historian, annotator and critic of jazz. In behavior and appearance, Goodman seems to be the prototype of the sober, conservative and somewhat staid bourgeois. He is in fact, a successful businessman, cultural dabbler, suburbanite, devoted husband and father, and most unsporting of all, a millionaire! In other words, he is everything that a self-respecting jazz musician (using romantic novels and films as a frame of reference) shouldn't and wouldn't be caught dead being.

But, of course, the foregoing characteristics are only anomalous if we subscribe to the Greenwich Village, Paris expatriate, creation-through-suffering approach to art—an approach now accepted for the most part only by Greenwich Villagers, Paris expatriates, and creators-who-suffer.

But even if we discount such misconceptions we must still conclude that Goodman is not in the least typical. As the recipient not only of the serious consideration and appreciation of jazz and concert-music devotees throughout the world, but also of the sometimes hysterical adulation of millions of "jitterbugs," Benny Goodman has become, in the most unsettling meaning of the words, a public figure.

He has been profiled in just about every mass-circulation magazine; his life story has been dramatized to the point of absurdity on celluloid; and, as a final "honor," he has had batteries of TV cameras strategically placed in his Connecticut home while he, his wife, and his children traded chit-chat with Mr. Murrow in full view of a gallery of approximately twenty million sight-seers.

From the millions of words, many of them silly, that have been written about Goodman, it has become increasingly difficult to extract not only the significant facts about his life, but the facts them-

175

selves. Goodman, who is conscious of his value as a "commercial" property, has often submitted to the exigencies of his position by willingly, if somewhat uncomfortably, lending himself to the often flamboyant procedures necessary for the creation, protection and maintenance of a legend.

The tons of propaganda that have emanated from the publicity mills of the booking agencies, record companies, radio networks, film studios, advertising agencies, theatres, ballrooms and music publishing firms—all with heavy financial stakes in the prosperity of the Goodman band—somehow convinced (and still continue to convince) the general public that it was Benny Goodman who single-handedly invented the music called "swing."

The use of this term itself was probably another inspiration of those interests concerned with the music's commercial value. According to jazz historian Marshall Stearns, its origin may have been in the early reluctance of the British Broadcasting Company to use the expression, "hot jazz" on its band broadcasts, and its subsequent decision to call it "swing music" instead. Whatever its origin, this loosely descriptive phrase caught on, was exploited, and went on to glory as the name not only of a musical style but of an entire era as well. But more of swing and its relation to Benny Goodman later.

The real difficulties inherent in any attempt to assess the artistic stature of Goodman have very little to do with his appearance, social standing and/or pretensions, financial status or with the popular impressions of him which are a product of the publicity factories. The real problems for those who are concerned with piecing together the untidy story of jazz and separating the genuine from the false have to do with the character of the music that Goodman created, the times in which it was created, and the unique set of circumstances, social and personal, surrounding its creation.

Another basic question that arises from any study of the commercially successful band leader of the Swing Era is: where does jazz stop and popular music begin?

The Benny Goodman story (not to be confused with the cinematic fantasy of the same name) examined in the light of the questions posed above might indicate some of the answers.

The lives and careers of most of the musicians dealt with in this volume, as difficult and complex as some of them may be, are characterized by an almost complete identification with jazz. While many of them may, for all of the obvious reasons, have been forced on occasion to work in commercial dance bands, in theatre, night-club, or radio orchestras, as accompanists, or even in non-musical jobs, one can never doubt their devotion to jazz. Indeed, it is impossible to visualize Louis Armstrong, Count Basie, Charlie Parker, Duke Ellington or most of the others as anything but what they are —dedicated men completely at home in the world of jazz, a world with its own traditions, language, folklore and geography.

Not so Goodman. Almost from the beginning there has clearly been an ambivalence towards jazz. At any one of a dozen different points in his professional career he might easily have changed his course and lent his talents to some other area of musical activity.

Benjamin David Goodman, born in Chicago's ghettolike West Side on May 30, 1909, was the eighth of twelve children. His father, who had fled from anti-Semitic terror and poverty in Russia, was a tailor employed in a clothing factory. Like almost all Jewish immigrant parents, the Goodmans lived for the day when their children would have the social and economic security that had been denied to them in the old country. Every opportunity, especially for educational and cultural advancement was seized upon, and among Benny's earliest memories are visits by the whole family to the free band concerts held in nearby Douglas Park.

When he was ten, along with his brothers Harry and Freddy, he began his musical studies. He obtained a clarinet from a neighborhood synagogue, which not only sponsored music lessons for the younger members of the congregation but also had a small band as well. When the synagogue ran out of money shortly thereafter and could no longer support its musical activities, Benny and his brothers were maneuvered by Papa Goodman into another boy's band at Hull House, Chicago's great social service institution.

The first clarinet player who might be said to have influenced Goodman was Ted Lewis. At the age of ten, the precocious youngster was able to carry off a reasonably faithful imitation of the then-popular musical entertainer and band leader. In fact, Benny was to earn his first professional fee as a musician doing an impersonation of Lewis in an amateur show in a large Chicago vaudeville theatre.

It was not long after this triumph that he began a two-year course of clarinet lessons with Franz Schoeppe who, in Benny's words, "did more for me musically than anybody I ever knew." Schoeppe, who had taught at the Chicago Musical College and who looked upon jazz as "the music of the streets," was a strict disci-

plinarian, intent upon giving his pupils a faultless foundation for a
legitimate clarinet technique. It is interesting to note that two other
first-rate jazz clarinetists also studied with Schoeppe—Buster Bailey
and Jimmie Noone.

Chicago, in those early post-World War I years, was fast becoming a primary center of jazz activity. The New Orleans Rhythm
Kings found a home at the Friars' Inn, and young Goodman soon
came under the spell of the NORK's clarinetist, Leon Rappolo. He
wasn't the only Chicagoan to be influenced by the New Orleans pioneers. At Austin High School, where Benny sometimes played at
school dances, he met Dave Tough and Bud Freeman and, through
them, another clarinetist named Frank Teschemacher, whose weird
and wonderful music was silenced when he was killed in an automobile accident in 1931. (Among other Windy City kids who were
to become the founders of so-called Chicago-style jazz were Eddie
Condon, George Wettling, Muggsy Spanier, Gene Krupa and Jimmy
McPartland.)

While still literally in knee pants, Goodman discovered that his
skillful musicianship was in demand and he began playing at dances
and proms in and around Chicago. His first steady job was with a
small band in a neighborhood dance hall, and for four nights work
a week he was able to bring home forty-eight dollars, a healthy contribution for a fourteen-year-old to make toward the rent and household expenses.

In 1925, came the first big break—an offer from Ben Pollack,
who had played drums for a time with the New Orleans Rhythm
Kings and who was in the process of building what was to be one of
the first large white jazz bands. The breaking-in was taking place
in the resort town of Venice, California, and Goodman (in long
pants) traveled to the Coast to join Pollack at the monumental
salary of a hundred dollars a week. Just a few days later, another
promising young musician named Glenn Miller was also to join the
new band.

The Pollack crew soon headed East but found the going rough.
They disbanded temporarily in Chicago, and Goodman went to work
for saxophonist Bennie Krueger, who was leading a band at the
Uptown Theatre. It was at about this revolving stage of his career
that he re-established contact with Bud Freeman, Dave Tough,
Teschemacher and the other Chicago jazzmen who were just beginning to be known professionally, and he occasionally jammed with
them at the Three Deuces and other musicians' hangouts.

**Jelly Roll
Morton**

Riverside Records

**Warren
"Baby" Dodds**

**Louis
Armstrong**

Columbia Records

**Jack
Teagarden**

Capitol Records

**Earl
Hines**

**Bix
Beiderbecke**

Columbia

Pee Wee Russell

Van Vechten

Bessie Smith

Thomas "Fats" Waller

Art Tatum

Coleman Hawkins

Benny Goodman

Duke Ellington

Clef Records

Charlie Parker (left) and friends

Fletcher Henderson

William "Count" Basie

**Lester
Young**

**Billie
Holiday**

Verve

...cords

Roy Eldridge

**Charlie
Christian**

Clef

John "Dizzy" Gillespie

The Pollack band reassembled and had made its first records for RCA Victor, but Benny, offered $175 a week by Isham Jones, left Pollack only to rejoin when the band received an offer to play in New York and he was asked to come along.

Even in those early years in Chicago, apart from his never really having fit into the New Orleans-influenced musical patterns taken up by Condon, McPartland, Freeman, *et al.,* Goodman seemed never to identify himself with jazz with quite the same intensity as did his contemporaries. Any one of several explanations might have accounted for this apparent aloofness. Perhaps it was his extreme youth. Or parental influence. Or an unwillingness to commit himself to an objective he didn't completely believe in. Or maybe there was a feeling that his drive for commercial success would not be satisfied on the road to jazz.

The Pollack band opened at the Little Club in New York in February, 1928, and for the next year played in and around the city, finally settling in as a sort of resident band at the Park Central Hotel. Goodman made many records that year, not only with Pollack but with many pick-up groups, some of them under his leadership and released under his name. The most notable were *Jungle Blues* and *Room 1411,* which also featured Jimmy McPartland and Glenn Miller.

In October, 1929, Goodman left Pollack to join the Red Nichols band and shortly thereafter worked with Nichols, Babe Rusin, Glenn Miller and Gene Krupa in the pit band for George Gershwin's musical comedy, "Strike Up the Band." Nichols's theatre and recording contacts made for steadier and better-paying jobs than Pollack could offer, and supplemented by radio and recording work obtained on his own, Goodman did exceptionally well in those early depression years with an estimated income of from $350 to $400 a week.

In the fall of 1931, with the itch for leadership making an early appearance, Goodman took some of Nichols's men and led the pit band in a revue called "Free for All." The show ran for fifteen performances, and back to radio and recording work went Benny.

In his autobiography, *The Kingdom of Swing,* published at the height of his career in 1939, Goodman described his feelings about his future in that musically dark period: "Radio was just beginning to spread out," he wrote, "and it seemed to me that a musician's future was going to be tied up with it. . . . I felt that I could work along and find a pretty secure living in that field. . . .

I guess I was in kind of a bad groove mentally at that time, with not much desire other than to make money, keep the place going for my mother and the kids, and have as much fun as possible."

While the market for jazz, live and recorded, had just about dried up in the United States at that time, a new and very vocal audience was being heard from abroad. Duke Ellington and Louis Armstrong had made appearances in England and on the continent with astonishing critical and financial success and American jazz records were in demand.

In 1933, a young American jazz fan and recording executive, named John Hammond, went to England and returned with a deal whereby he would produce some sixty jazz sides for release by the English Columbia and Parlaphone companies. Enthusiastic about Goodman's playing, Hammond approached the clarinetist with a proposition to record eight sides.

In an article in the English paper, *Melody Maker,* Hammond described Goodman's attitudes toward jazz in that period: ". . . [He] had the idea that real improvised jazz was uncommercial and that you had to have a compromise in order to sell any records. . . . I'm pretty sure that Benny Goodman's musical tastes were those of a jazzman who was beaten and discouraged by the commercial life then prevailing at American radio stations, and the complete lack of appreciation anywhere for the great improvising jazz artist.

"Benny was comparatively out of touch in those days with what was happening in the Harlem world; and he had very little use for the type of music that was represented, let us say, by the Casa Loma Orchestra, the various Dorsey combinations, and so on. . . . In general, Benny had the attitude of a fairly slick professional musician, one who had lost hope and interest in jazz."

From this point forward in Goodman's story, it becomes difficult to determine to whom the credit for his subsequent commercial success should go. It seems safe to say, however, that for the next ten years Goodman made few major decisions that involved the band and its personnel without the counsel of John Hammond. During its most prosperous years, just a few of the major talents brought into the Goodman band upon the recommendation of Hammond were Gene Krupa, Teddy Wilson, Fletcher Henderson, Jess Stacy, Charlie Christian, and, of course, Lionel Hampton.

A full account of the very considerable influence that Hammond has had on the history of American music from 1930 to the present day is yet to be made. The list of musicians discovered, sponsored and recorded by this remarkable man reads like a *Who's Who* of jazz. He has in his own way become a legend, and his devotion to jazz is equalled only by his hatred of injustice. There are few Americans who can match his record both of effort and achievement in the fight against racial discrimination—not only in music but in all the areas where this cancer exists.

The year 1934 was a decisive one for Goodman who, with the enthusiastic support and guidance of Hammond, formed the band that was soon to become the most popular musical organization in the world. For the first time since the pre-crash days of 1929, there was a note of optimism in the air. Prohibition was over, the Roosevelt administration's initial efforts towards economic recovery were showing signs of success, and the depression-weary American public was ready for something new in the way of entertainment.

The foundation had already been laid. Big-band jazz had been on the scene since the middle 'twenties and top-flight Negro bands led by Fletcher Henderson, Don Redman, Chick Webb, Andy Kirk, Cab Calloway, Duke Ellington, Jimmy Lunceford, Earl Hines and William McKinney had led the way. (A few of the successful white swing bands preceding Goodman's were Casa Loma, Isham Jones and the Dorsey Brothers.)

Acting as the unofficial "man behind the Goodman band," John Hammond made full use of his encyclopedic knowledge of who-was-who and what-was-what in even the most obscure corners of the jazz world. His most vital contribution to the band, aside from his infectious enthusiasm and his well-placed contacts in the talent agencies, record companies and other show business citadels, was his almost unerring ability to find for it the best musicians in the business. His getting Fletcher Henderson to write the arrangements, however, was, if not a stroke of genius, at least one of the luckiest things that ever happened to Goodman.

The new band's first job was at Billy Rose's Music Hall on Broadway. Nothing happened. Then came the big break. The National Biscuit Company decided to sponsor a three-hour dance-band show on network radio—one hour devoted to Latin American music, one hour for sweet music, and one hour—well, for something a little livelier.

Hammond has described in the pages of *Down Beat* what took place during the early weeks of the program: "When it seemed to me that the band was making less of an impression than it should," he wrote, "I took a trip to Chicago where Gene Krupa was imprisoned in Buddy Rogers' orchestra. . . . It wasn't too difficult to persuade him to turn in his notice to Buddy and join the *Let's Dance* program in New York. . . .

"Gene's arrival marked a turning point in the Goodman organization. Fletcher Henderson's arrangements began to take on excitement. . . . It was at about this time that Benny let Fletcher make arrangements of current pop tunes with a beat and irreverence he had never dared to employ with his own band. I firmly believe that it was this approach to ballads that gave the Goodman band the style that made it conquer the nation the following year."

Although the sponsor of the radio show didn't pick up the band's option after the first twenty-six weeks, Goodman was now enthusiastic about his future as a band leader.

"We are moving along," he recalled in a magazine article a few years ago. "Our success on the radio got us a record contract, and our first two sides, *Dixieland Band* and *Hunkadola,* had a pretty fair initial sale for a jazz record. We hired Bunny Berigan, . . . and for piano we got Jess Stacy, whom John Hammond had found in a run-down Chicago saloon. . . ."

After a few months of indifferent engagements on the road during the early part of 1935, a mildly dispirited Goodman crew opened at the Palomar Ballroom in Los Angeles. Audiences had been unresponsive since the band had left New York, and Goodman wasn't quite sure about what and how to play to the West Coast youngsters. After a few sets of routine dance numbers, he decided to let loose:

"I called out some of our big Fletcher arrangements for the next set," Goodman wrote, "and the boys seemed to get the idea. From the moment I kicked them off, they dug in with some of the best playing I'd heard since we left New York. . . . The first big roar from the crowd was one of the sweetest sounds I ever heard in my life. . . ."

While there are some musicians and critics who question Goodman's qualities as a *true* jazzman (whatever that may be), few will deny that he is one of the most accomplished musicians ever to appear on the jazz scene. His complete mastery of his instrument, extending beyond jazz to highly creditable performances of both classical and modern concert and chamber works for the clarinet; his imaginative, if not intense, improvisational powers; and the exceptional taste, sensitivity and intelligence that have almost always characterized his playing would be enough to qualify him as a major musical figure of our time.

Still another aspect of Goodman's talents, which distinguished him from many of his less-disciplined, if more inspired contemporaries, was his dynamic musical leadership. Sparked not only by his first-rate instrumental powers, but by his authoritative direction, the Goodman band at its peak was a near-perfect musical unit.

"I didn't just ask for good musicianship," Goodman once wrote, "I insisted on it. I've never been a particularly patient guy where music is concerned. When somebody let me and the band down, I got sore and let him know it. Nothing less than perfection would do: I lived that music, and expected everybody to live it, too."

But Goodman's most significant contribution to the development of jazz is not his superb skill as an instrumentalist or his ability as a leader. Neither is it the scores of magnificent recordings made by the band, the trio, the quartet, and other groups which he has led. Earlier we posed a question about "the character of the music that Goodman created, the times in which it was created, and the unique set of circumstances, social and personal, surrounding its creation."

Before the Swing Era, instrumental jazz was principally a part of urban Negro culture, which happened to have a few enlightened white followers. Post-swing jazz—call it "modern" for want of a better word—has taken more than a decade to find an audience capable of supporting it. It is still far from a popular music, and it continues to be difficult for the majority of today's jazz musicians to find either public acceptance or financial security.

In the years from 1936 to the outbreak of World War II, for the first and perhaps for the last time in its history, a segment of jazz became *the* popular music of the country.

Musicians like Tommy and Jimmy Dorsey, Artie Shaw, Duke Ellington, Count Basie, Jimmy Lunceford, Gene Krupa and many more became national idols, known not only to cultists and readers of musicians' journals but to nearly everybody who danced, listened to the radio, and read mass-circulation newspapers and magazines. But the "King of Swing" was Benny Goodman.

The band's popular, critical and financial successes in almost every entertainment medium from those frantic early years of swing even to the present day have been chronicled far too often to be dealt with in detail here. One accomplishment, however, can not be stressed or repeated enough. This is the integrity and courage displayed by Goodman in his consistent efforts to break down Jim Crow barriers in the popular music field. It is all too easy for a star performer to go along with the tide and to keep away from controversial issues which might "alienate sponsors" or "hurt the box office." It is to Goodman's credit that he continually resisted the enormous pressures imposed on him to play down or even completely eliminate Teddy Wilson and Lionel Hampton from engagements in theatres, clubs, concert halls, ballrooms and hotels where "there might be trouble." Needless to say, there was never any really serious problem connected with Goodman's use of Negro musicians. And, apart from the tradition-shattering precedents that he set, his featuring of such top-flight jazzmen as Wilson, Hampton, Henderson, Cootie Williams, Charlie Christian and, in his most recent bands, Buck Clayton, Budd Johnson and Hank Jones, displayed fine musical talents to vast audiences which might otherwise never have had the opportunity to hear them.

It is comforting to believe that the sometimes hysterical adulation that Goodman received from the "jitterbugs" of the 'thirties was just a little healthier than that bestowed on subsequent American musical heroes such as Frank Sinatra, Mario Lanza, Liberace and Elvis Presley. It seems evident, though, that it was his music rather than his sex appeal that thrilled his followers.

The Goodman band played good dance music. It had a beat. It *moved*. There was a strength and excitement about it, and within the band were soloists like Harry James, Ziggy Elman, Vido Musso, Gene Krupa and Lionel Hampton—all of them skilled technicians and all of them able to produce the pyrotechnics that were entertaining if not always musical. Often, however, especially with the trio and quartet, and later the sextet, honest, exciting and occasionally inspired jazz was presented to literally tens of millions of people all over the world. Because, and not in spite of, his great popularity, Goodman was able to introduce jazz to friendly and therefore receptive listeners. Certainly, this was a major accomplishment.

The Swing Era died quietly sometime during World War II, and with the subsequent decline of the commercial dance and large jazz band business, and the emergence of new musical heroes, new audiences and even a new kind of jazz, Goodman has comfortably and quietly gone into semi-retirement.

Although he periodically returns to musical life for concert tours, television appearances and occasional one-nighters or ballroom engagements, Goodman is no longer a dynamic factor in the world of jazz. The arrangements his band plays are the same arrangements that it has always played. The musicians (as ever) are first-rate, but the music lacks the excitement and sparkle that it had when it fit into the framework of the era in which it was created. It is only fair to state that the isolated attempts that Goodman has made to change the band's style have met with the disapproval of his fans. "They want to hear *Don't Be That Way, Stompin' at the Savoy, Sing, Sing, Sing* and the rest of the old things," complained one of the members of a recent Goodman crew. "Play something modern, and they complain."

Commercial success has always been a prime concern of Goodman's, and it is unreasonable to expect that he will change—especially to conform to musical ideas for which he has shown no sympathy. As a master of his instrument, he still is peerless.

Benny Goodman is one of the finest jazz musicians the idiom has known. But ironically enough, his major and inestimable contributions to jazz—giving it the largest audience in its entire history and helping to tear down racial barriers—were achieved not so much through his musical abilities as through his talents as a leader and organizer of a great popular dance band.

In his admirable book, *Jazz, A People's Music,* critic Sidney Finkelstein more or less summed up the appeal and the significance of swing and indicated still another aspect of Goodman's influence. "A great mass of hot jazz," Finkelstein wrote, "falls into a narrow, light-entertainment category . . . the line between good music and bad becomes difficult to trace. The commercial music begins to take on qualities of hot jazz . . . the hot music begins to take on something of the commercial, due to the conditions under which it has to work, the language it must use, the weak forms, and passive audiences. . . .

"If hot jazz was apparently to merge with much of what was loosely termed 'commercial,' the level of commercial music was immeasurably raised . . . the irrepressible efforts of jazz players, most of them Negro, made a creative music out of popular song idiom. The great American public was hearing a music more interesting and distinctive in instrumental texture, cleaner in melodic profile; a music of stimulation and surprises that began to teach audiences how to listen to music."

Benny Goodman—1927–34, Brunswick 54010
The Vintage Goodman, Columbia CL 821
Carnegie Hall Jazz Concert 1938, Columbia OSL 160
Jazz Concert No. 2 1937/38, Columbia OSL 180
Trio, Quartet & Quintet, Victor LPM 1226
Benny Goodman Combos, Capitol T 669

Duke Ellington

* * * *

By Leonard Feather

Though it often falls to the lot of a handsome, dignified, low-blood-pressured, lusty, euphoric composer and conductor named Edward Kennedy Ellington to be informed that he is a great man, such assurances seem entirely superfluous, for Duke Ellington knows full well that he is a great man. His denials, if and when they are made, are made in the full knowledge that it is part of the make-up of a great man to include modesty among his self-evident characteristics.

What Duke Ellington has known, and has gladly accepted for three decades, is that his peer has yet to be found among jazz composers, arrangers and conductors. Cushioned by this knowledge, lulled by it into a permanent state of glossy, gauzy emotional comfort, Ellington glides through his daily life as one on a throne with pneumatic wheels, in a world where such factors as box-office failures, moochers, swindlers, Jim Crow, narcotics addicts and the need to meet deadlines simply do not exist. When one of these problems touches him, he will shrug off the bruise, look the other way or simply convince himself that the incident happened to somebody else.

Barry Ulanov, whose book *Duke Ellington* was the first entire volume ever devoted to a jazzman of Ellington's caliber, made it clear on the first page that Duke's self-confidence was not of recent origin. "When he was late in getting up for school, his mother or his Aunt Florence would shake him and push him and rush him out of bed into his clothes. Once dressed, Duke's tempo would change. He would come downstairs slowly, with an elegance. At the foot of the stairs he would stop and call to his mother and his aunt.

" 'Stand over there,' he would direct, pointing to the wall. 'Now,' he would say, 'listen. This,' he would say slowly, with very careful articulation, 'is the great, the grand, the magnificent Duke

Ellington.' Then he would bow. Looking up at his smiling mother
and aunt, he would say, 'Now applaud, applaud.' And then he would
run off to school."

The great, the grand, the magnificent Duke Ellington has been
on display before a world-wide audience for some thirty years. Most
experts place the turning point at December 4, 1927, the night
the Ellington orchestra, augmented a few months earlier to the
then-healthy complement of ten, opened at the Cotton Club, which
was to Negro show business what the Palace was to vaudeville.
(The Palace itself was to open its stage to the band less than two
years after.) Ellington was then, and is now, an imposing figure.
An inch over six feet tall, sturdily built, he had an innate grandeur
that would have enabled him to step with unquenched dignity out
of a puddle of mud. His phrasing of an announcement, the elegance
of his diction, the supreme courtesy of his bow, whether to a Duchess
in London or a theatre audience in Akron, Ohio, have lent stature
not only to his own career but to the whole of jazz. Since the music
he represented was stifled for many years by several kinds of segregation—social, esthetic, and racial—this element certainly played
a vital part in bringing jazz fuller recognition, just as his music itself brought the art he epitomized to a new peak of maturity.

Though he and his band have slipped from first place in some
of the popularity polls, musicians and critics remain almost unanimous in their undimmed respect for the Ellington legend and in
their conviction that nothing and nobody, no matter how loud the
fanfare, how fickle the votes, can replace or surpass his position
as the greatest figure in the fifty-year dynasty of jazz. None but
Ellington can claim the reverent respect of an eclectic unofficial fan
club composed of Woody Herman, Milton Berle, Arthur Fiedler,
Peggy Lee, Percy Faith, Deems Taylor, Pee Wee Russell, Lena
Horne, Lennie Tristano, Benny Goodman, Guy Lombardo, Dave
Garroway, Cole Porter, Morton Gould, Lawrence Welk, André
Kostelanetz and Gordon Jenkins, each of whom, on the occasion of
the silver anniversary of his Cotton Club debut, not only tossed
verbal bouquets at Ellington but also added a personal selection of
five favorite Ellington records. No other band leader alive could
persuade such a galaxy even to name five of his records, far less select
the five best.

The Ellington legend has retained its power among the more

esoteric record collectors, including one Charles Mitchell of Oak Park, Illinois, who may have been the most dedicated Ellington discologist of all. After tracking down every item ever recorded by the band, he found only one disc missing, an obscure piece on the Blu-Disc label. He advertised for it, offering to give any price for a copy in any condition, and at length was able to obtain one for a hundred dollars. As might be expected, the strain of completing this collection was too much for him; he sold the entire set, moved to China, and when last heard of was bidding inordinate prices for Oriental prints.

The Ellington orchestra, which aside from a few leaves of absence (including a Hollywood jaunt for its movie debut in a slightly sleazy Amos and Andy feature, "Check and Double Check"), spent all of 1928, 1929 and 1930 at the Cotton Club, was to subside in later years into a pattern more familiar to dance orchestras, that of the floating band with occasional home bases. By 1957 Ellington and his sidemen had long been accustomed to the necessity of interminable one-night stands, with only an occasional one- or two-week stand at a major city and, very rarely, a few days of comparative leisure in New York to complete some recordings. Duke has been under pressure from well-meaning friends and relatives who point out that his income might be augmented rather than diminished if he were to keep the band on salary, and on tour, for three or four months out of each year and spend the rest of his time at ease in New York, stretching his legs and mental muscles, writing music for shows and possibly acquiring the permanent television program that has long been one of his dreams. But Ellington without his musicians would be like a celibate Tommy Manville. "I want to have them around me to play my music," he has often said; "I'm not worried about creating music for posterity, I just want it to sound good right now!"

Ellington's background upsets most of the convenient legends that tend to envelop jazz pioneers. After having the poor taste to be born not in New Orleans but in Washington D.C., he was raised not in poverty but in relative security, the son and nephew of two successful butlers who worked at the White House and at many great parties held in Washington's embassies. Despite the rigid Jim Crow system that obtained in Washington, with its attendant humiliations, Ellington grew up a well-adjusted child "with a happy awareness of the strength of families, the length of their affections and the vigorous loyalties which could and often did arise out of these groups."

Ellington earned his nickname in a manner that similarly defies legend. It was simply a name chosen arbitrarily by Ralph "Zeb" Green, a young neighbor who tended to bestow nicknames on all his friends. Zeb and Duke's mother both liked to play piano and were among Ellington's childhood influences, but apart from a few piano lessons when he was seven, there was little direct musical impact on his life until his middle teens. In the meanwhile, studying at Armstrong High, Washington's leading Negro manual-training school, he became absorbed in art, revealed a nimble talent for sketching and even won a poster contest sponsored by the NAACP. The pleasure of making posters and working with colors paled as he developed a more intense concern with tone colors; by the time the Pratt Institute of Applied Arts in Brooklyn had offered him a scholarship, just before he left high school, his interests had switched to music, and he turned the offer down.

During this period the ragtime surrounding Duke Ellington provided ample evidence that jazz had long been flourishing far away from New Orleans, often wrongly credited as its sole birthplace. Talking of the "two-fisted piano players" of that era, he recalled "men like Sticky Mack and Doc Perry and James P. Johnson and Willie 'The Lion' Smith. . . . With their left hand, they'd play big chords for the bass note, and just as big ones for the off-beat . . . they did things technically you wouldn't believe." He had little time for the garrulous Jelly Roll Morton, whose reputation was built on his own ego and its acceptance by credulous cultists rather than on musical values: "Jelly Roll played piano like one of those high-school teachers in Washington; as a matter of fact, high-school teachers played better jazz. Among other things, his rhythm was unsteady; but that's the kind of piano the West was geared up to." ("West" meant New Orleans, Duke explained: "In those days there was no other West to speak of.")

Ellington's informal music education, acquired from the pianists he heard around Washington and later in New York, combined with his slight formal training, enabled him to make a substantial living out of music almost from the outset. Engaged in sign-painting by day and combo gigs by night, he was well enough fixed financially to be married in June, 1918, to Edna Thompson, whom he had known since their grade-school days. The following year Mercer

Ellington was born. By 1919, supplying bands for parties and dances, Duke was making upward of $150 a week. He attributes much of this early success to his decision to buy the largest advertisement in the orchestra section of Washington's classified telephone directory.

Ellington's first sojourn in New York in 1922—with Sonny Greer, Toby Hardwicke, Elmer Snowden and Arthur Whetsol—was the only period in his life marked by real poverty. Jobs were so scarce that, according to legend, they were reduced at one point to splitting a hot dog five ways. Then Fats Waller, visiting Washington, induced them in 1923 to return. Through the influence of Ada Smith, who was later to become a legend herself in Europe under the cognomen of "Bricktop," they worked under Snowden's nominal leadership at Barron's in Harlem. Duke became the leader and Freddy Guy took over Snowden's banjo chair when they moved into a cellar club called the Hollywood at Forty-ninth and Broadway. This was their first downtown job, and it was during their incumbency at the Hollywood, later known as the Kentucky Club, that they made their first records.

The Kentucky Club era, four and a half years off and on, accumulated a warm storehouse of memories for the Washingtonians; memories of wild breakfast parties after the job; of the patronage of Paul Whiteman and his musicians, working a block down Broadway at the Palais Royale; of fifty- and one-hundred-dollar tips; Duke's first attempt to write the score for a show ("The Chocolate Kiddies," in 1924, never did get to Broadway, though it ran for two years in Berlin); the uninhibited antics of Bubber Miley and Toby Hardwicke and Duke in the very face of Prohibition—during all those years in which the Kentucky Club was never raided; Sonny Greer was the instinctive expert on those customers to whom drinks should or should not be served.

Ted Husing, one of the early and regular ringsiders, helped to secure the band its first broadcasts out of the Kentucky Club. *East St. Louis Toddle-O,* a minor-to-major lament with an acute accent on plunger-muted brass, became the band's first radio theme.

"I'll never forget the first time I heard Edward's music," says his sister Ruth. "Of course, we'd heard him at home, playing ragtime, but here he was playing his own music with his own band on the radio from New York, coming out of this old-fashioned horn-speaker. I think radio had just about been invented, or at least just launched commercially; I was about eight years old.

"It was quite a shock. Here we were, my mother and I, sitting in this very respectable, Victorian living room in Washington, my mother so puritanical she didn't even wear lipstick, and the announcer from New York tells us we are listening to 'Duke Ellington and his *Jungle* Music'! It sounded very strange and dissonant to us."

Black and Tan Fantasy, on which Bubber growled the famous closing interpolation from Chopin's *Funeral March,* may have horrified the Ellington family but succeeded in attracting the attention of a man named Irving Mills. A successful song publisher who was beginning to extend his practice by dabbling in the management of artists, Mills soon formed a corporation in which he and Duke each owned 45 per cent and a lawyer the other 10 per cent. It was the start of a partnership that lasted through the nineteen thirties, through the first great years of the Ellington legend. Confident that his counsel was tantamount to full collaboration, Mills published the Ellington songs and also appeared on record labels and sheet music as co-composer of famous hits of the 'thirties, among them *Mood Indigo, Sophisticated Lady, Solitude* and *I Let A Song Go Out of My Heart.* Mills wrote years later that he "withdrew" from his relationship with Duke because he sensed that Ellington had "fallen into a different attitude toward his music, and was taking off into what I thought to be a wrong direction." This claim was never disputed, nor was Ellington ever quoted on his side of the story; his characteristic avoidance of subjects that could not be discussed constructively, and without personal recriminations, precluded any public comment.

Matters that Ellington felt more suitable for comment were those he recalled in an article that appeared under his by-line in November, 1952, listing the ten most memorable events in his career since the opening at the Cotton Club.

Cautiously, he prefaced his recollections with an escape clause: "If I recall certain events and pay tribute to certain beautiful people, I may be unconsciously offending certain other beautiful people."

The band's opening at the Palace was the first big moment. ("We opened the show with *Dear Old Southland* . . . the men hadn't memorized their parts, and the show opened on a darkened stage. When I gave the downbeat, nothing happened—the men couldn't see a note!") Then came "Check and Double Check"; next, the opening night at the London Palladium in 1933 when the international impact of the band was belatedly brought home to Duke

("The applause was so terrifying—it was applause *beyond* applause.")

"Europe was responsible for the next big kick . . . it was my fortieth birthday celebration in Stockholm, April 29, 1939. I was awakened by a sixteen-piece band from a local radio station which marched into my hotel room serenading me with *Happy Birthday.* All day long huge bouquets of flowers kept arriving. . . . At the Concert House hundreds of people flocked to the dressing room. The whole audience rose to sing *Happy Birthday,* and there was a ceremony onstage, followed by a big banquet for the entire orchestra. . . . It all brought a very glowing end to our second European tour."

Two years later, in 1941, the next high-light proved to be one that flickered out prematurely: "Jump for Joy," a stage revue in which the whole band took part, was presented in Los Angeles. "A number of critics felt this was the hippest Negro musical and has remained so to this day," said Duke, perhaps a little wistfully, for after a run of only three months the show never got the New York unveiling every Ellington well-wisher had hoped for.

The evening of Saturday, January 23, 1943, brought the event that may have been the most auspicious not only for Ellington but for jazz itself. The first Ellington concert at Carnegie Hall was given in circumstances that could not be duplicated today. A concert by a jazz orchestra was a rare novelty (the last comparable event had been Benny Goodman's, exactly five years and one week earlier). The occasion had been transformed into an event at which the evening gowns and tuxedos lent a social note to which only the Ellington music could do rhythmic justice. The orchestra played a new work, *Black, Brown and Beige,* a "tone parallel to the history of the American Negro," which in its original form ran fifty minutes and was at once the most ambitious, spectacular, variegated and successful attempt to translate Ellingtonia into terms of extended forms.

"That first night at Carnegie was the only time in my life that I didn't have stage fright. I just didn't have time—I couldn't afford the luxury of being scared. But I did walk onstage without my music. Somebody signaled to me from the wings that they had it—but I didn't need it anyway; I remembered it all."

As Ellington pointed out, the quality of the appreciation, the attentiveness of the three thousand who listened that night, was "a model of audience reaction that has proved hard to duplicate." It was a far cry from the mob of caterwauling, leather-jacketed, seat-ripping jackals who were to constitute so much of the typical jazz concert audience a decade later. (Ironically, when an Ellington jubilee concert was set for November, 1952, the presentation of a self-sufficient orchestra introducing new original works, was no longer considered desirable; it was announced that the show would also include Billie Holiday, Charlie Parker, Stan Getz and others. The concept of a jazz concert as Ellington had visualized and designed it was dead.)

Concerts provided the seventh, eighth, ninth and last of Ellington's ten brightest memories. One, in January, 1945, in Los Angeles, was his participation in the then annual *Esquire* awards, with Lionel Barrymore presenting the gold Esky statuette to Duke and Lena Horne making a similar presentation to Billy Strayhorn. The next memorable concert, in 1949, offered the band at Robin Hood Dell in Philadelphia "with this beautiful ninety-six-piece symphony orchestra, conducted by Russ Case, wrapped around ours." In 1951 the band played what was, in effect, the last of its original annual series of concerts, transferring the scene this time to the Metropolitan Opera House. The beneficiary was the NAACP, an organization with which Ellington was to tangle unpleasantly a couple of months later. The Mayor appeared onstage to pay tribute before Duke introduced the premiere of *Harlem,* an extended work that reached a new apogee in the Ellington orbit.

Lastly, there was a concert held at the Municipal Stadium in Philadelphia, of which Duke's chief memory is: "When I did *Monologue,* I had the whole audience giggling—and believe me, it's quite impressive to hear 125,000 people giggling."

To bring his memory book up to date and his list to a total of eleven, Ellington would have to add the chaotic scene at the open-air concert given in Freebody Park at Newport, Rhode Island, during its three-day jazz festival in July, 1956. In the course of an extended and revitalized version of a fast blues, entitled *Diminuendo and Crescendo in Blue,* first recorded in 1938 and extended on this occasion to fourteen minutes and fifty-nine choruses, Paul Gonsalves whipped the audience into such a frenzy during his twenty-seven-chorus tenor-saxophone solo that elder jazz statesmen present could recall no comparable scene since the riots occasioned in the aisles of New York's Paramount Theatre two decades earlier during the Benny Goodman band's first wave of glory. It was a cogent reminder of Ellington's philosophy, expressed some months later:

"Skill is a wonderful thing to have if and when the four points converge—being at the right place, doing the right thing, before the right people, at the right time."

During the years of his undisputed acceptance as leader of the world's foremost jazz orchestra, and as the most distinguished of jazz composers, Ellington's career moved forward on three levels. From the economic standpoint, the most important of these three was his work as a songwriter. Some of his biggest hits were written casually in taxis, trains and recording studios (but never in planes; his aversion to flying has on several occasions cost him a European tour) and are simple single-note lines designed to be set to lyrics; others, whether written casually or more formally, were primarily instrumentals for the orchestra but were later furnished with lyrics. On this level, Ellington is in the field with Cole Porter, Richard Rodgers and Jimmy McHugh.

From the esthetic standpoint, Ellington's true significance as a contributor to the culture of the twentieth century lies in his orchestrations of original music for the instrument he plays best—his own orchestra. These range from simple blues and stomps to such elaborate efforts as the *Liberian Suite, New World A-Comin', Blue Belles of Harlem* and *Blutopia,* all of which were heard during the annual Carnegie Hall series, but few of which have been preserved on records. At this level Ellington's contemporaries are Jimmy Giuffre, John Lewis, Shorty Rogers, Ralph Burns and a large number of other men of unquestionable talent, none of whom has yet achieved anything of a stature likely to remove Ellington from his pedestal.

Thirdly there is Ellington the dance-band leader, who occasionally tries for a hit record and comes up with something like *Twelfth Street Rag Mambo* or *Isle of Capri Mambo* in an attempt to sail with a prevailing trade wind. This Ellington, more acutely conscious in recent years of the implacable exigencies of the commercial world in which he lives, is wont to open a dance date or even a stage show with an arrangement of *Stompin' at the Savoy,* which was neither composed nor arranged by anyone in the band and has about as much of the Ellington stamp as a Sammy Kaye arrangement of *Solitude.* At this plateau, Ellington's competitors include Ray Anthony, Count Basie, Les Brown, Woody Herman.

Juggling these three levels, Ellington has found time to perch himself perilously on a few other niches. As a composer of words he was responsible in 1956–57 for *A Drum Is a Woman,* a sort of jazz-tinged oratorio in which he was the slightly specious narrator; earlier he had shown himself capable of achieving a simple beauty in the pyramid-lined construction of *The Blues,* the only lyricized passage in *Black, Brown and Beige;* and a sophisticated brand of hip humor in *Monologue.* As a librettist he has had a few misadventures; generally on his visits to New York one hears of his plans to stage his own Broadway musical, or a straight drama, or a comedy with music, or some other venture that fails to materialize after months of rumors. "What the hell, you have to have some direction, you've got to go somewhere," he was heard to remark recently when his insistence on entering this field was questioned. Having scaled every mountain peak available to him and having seen that the hills are only lower on the other side, he has had to look for new promontories to tackle. "I'm so damned fickle," he once told a reporter. "I never could stick with what I was doing—always wanted to try something new."

Ellington's personality is riddled with paradoxes. "I may be a heel," he is reported to have said, "but I hate for people to think so." His warm personal attachments are few. When his mother died a lingering death in 1935, he was at her bedside for the last three days, his head on her pillow, inconsolably grief-stricken. Two years later his father, who had grown very close and had lived a life as fast and intense as Duke's own, died in a New York hospital with both his children beside him. Duke's sister Ruth, sixteen years his junior, an attractive and sophisticated girl who was to study in Paris the following year to supplement her work in biology, in which she had taken a Master's degree at Columbia, became Duke's closest friend and confidante. Dr. Arthur Logan, the family physician for the past twenty years, caters to his hypochondriacal tendencies. Fundamentally strong and healthy, Ellington gave up his heavy drinking proclivities around 1940, but never stopped conceding to his insatiable appetite until, in 1956, he suddenly decided on a diet and reduced his excessively expanded contours by some thirty-five pounds.

Ellington's vanity takes strange turns. His son, Mercer, tall and handsome like his father, has had a chaotic life in and out of various careers—band leader, trumpet player, band manager, liquor salesman, record-company executive, and general aide-de-camp to his father—and has suffered from Duke's unpredictable vacillations between parental pride and the desire to hide from the calendar. Mercer played E Flat horn in the Ellington band for a few months in

1950, but was dropped without notice and without any direct communication from Ellington Sr. There are three fine, attractive grandchildren: Mercedes, eighteen, Edward, twelve, and Gay, eleven.

With strangers or casual friends, Ellington's customary demeanor is one of sardonic badinage, of sarcasm so subtle that the victim is unaware of it. "We are indeed honored by the presence of such luminous company," he will say with a low bow to a song publisher with whose company he would be delighted to dispense. His capacity for small talk is endless. Complimented by a feminine guest on a rather striking blue and gray checked jacket he wore during a recent Birdland engagement, he promptly rejoined, "Yes, I was up all afternoon sitting at the loom, weaving it to impress you." Women of every age group, from fashion models to crones, learn to expect a string of fulsome compliments on each encounter. Ellington skids along on the surface of life in his less rarefied social relationships. It is difficult to coax him into a serious intellectual discussion; his reluctance to bruise any feelings and his desire to remain noncontroversial are jointly responsible. In a "blindfold test" interview to which, after much prodding, he submitted himself some years ago, he was slow in releasing his honest reactions and refused to follow the custom of rating the records.

Ellington is a magnificent and magniloquent mixer, as befits one who, alone among jazz musicians, enjoys the respect of Leopold Stokowski (who came in alone to the Cotton Club, sat discussing the music with Duke and invited him to his own concert the following evening at Carnegie Hall), President Truman ("whom I found very affable and musically informed," during a half-hour private audience at the White House), the Prince of Wales (now the Duke of Windsor: "He sat in with us on drums in London and surprised everybody, including Sonny Greer"), George, Duke of Kent ("I fluffed off the guy, who kept asking me for *Swampy River,* then found out he was the King's son"); the Pope ("he had a great deal to say to me, but I must have been overawed because I don't remember a single thing he said"); Jackie Gleason, who once commented that "Ellington is Wellington without Waterloo"; Orson Welles, for whose aborted movie history of jazz he wrote only twenty-eight bars of music in twelve weeks, lost the manuscript, and received $12,500 in recognition of services not rendered; and a kaleidoscopic array of old friends and poor relations, ex-sidemen, camp followers and riffraff who congregate near the bandstand nightly.

"When we were living on Edgecombe Avenue, it was a constant

mystery who these strange people were that kept coming to the door asking for money," says Ruth Ellington James, recalling her brother's generosity in his treatment of ex-employees and casual acquaintances.

Some of Ellington's fans have wondered why he, who used to set so many trends, has tended to follow others in recent years. His was the first band to use the human voice as a wordless musical instrument,[1] first to devote an entire work to a specific jazz soloist; first to use extended forms beyond the standard three-minute record length of the 78-r.p.m. record (the six-minute *Creole Rhapsody* and twelve-minute *Reminiscing in Tempo* in the nineteen thirties), first to use the bass as a melody solo instrument,[2] first to make elaborate use of Latin rhythms, of rubber-plunger mutes. Asked why he now makes such extensive use of arrangements like *In the Mood* and *One O'Clock Jump,* which have none of the Ellington sound, or of interminable drum solos, and why he writes so few new long works, he remarks brusquely that nobody can dictate to him what is meant by "the Ellington sound," that the pieces thus criticized are warmly received by the audience, and that there is no call for the long works. Understandably, it is one of his greatest frustrations that *Black, Brown and Beige* was coolly received by a number of critics and was never recorded in its entirety. The other major frustrations have been his failure to be identified with a hit Broadway show —to date the only stage shows for which he has written the scores have folded prematurely before or after coming to Broadway—and the failure of the TV networks to bring to fruition the long-cherished dream of his own television series. He resolutely refuses to recognize the irrefutable fact that racial discrimination has been responsible for this last disappointment.

His ability to turn the other way when real problems arise has immersed him in water a little too hot for comfort. A *cause célèbre* in the Negro press was his alleged statement to a Negro newspaperman that Negroes were "not ready" for full equality, which he later angrily denied. A few weeks after his concert for the NAACP, he violently denounced its Richmond, Virginia, chapter after canceling an appearance in that city because of threats that the NAACP would picket in protest against segregated seating. He complained that the NAACP represented "old people who live their lives in filth and dirt. What about the toilets and water fountains in colored

[1] On *Creole Love Call*, in 1927.
[2] Jimmy Blanton, 1939.

waiting rooms, why don't they do something about that? Why pick on entertainment investments?" He did not inveigh against the white Southerners but for whom the segregated waiting rooms would not need to exist; the sole object of his annoyance was the organization that had, in effect, thrown the smooth-running Ellington temperament, and the Ellington band itself, temporarily off the tracks, thus disturbing an equilibrium that he sometimes seems to value above any moral or political consideration. The flare-up proved temporary and not indicative of Ellington's true feelings. Today he and the NAACP are on the best of terms and the organization recently inaugurated plans to honor him at a testimonial banquet.

Ellington's oldest and closest friend within the band is Harry Carney, now in his thirty-first year as an Ellingtonian, and usually Duke's driving companion between one-night stands. Musically, his closest ties are with Billy Strayhorn, his "write-hand man" for almost two decades.

Ever since he joined the orchestra, Ellington has had an almost telepathic understanding with "Strays," whose writing for the band so closely resembles his own that veteran bandsmen are sometimes unable to discern where one left off and the other began. A symbolic statue of the diminutive Strayhorn might show him with manuscript paper just out of reach, eyes twinkling behind large shell-rimmed glasses, features fixed in a confident grin, hand raised in demonstration of some point in an intellectual dissertation, and one foot on a bar rail. Despite his tendency to procrastinate and to act as if he were trying to live the lyrics he wrote for a delightfully effete fragment called *Lush Life*, Strayhorn has retained through the years a charm that matches his extraordinary talent. Ellington, a lenient employer after his own heart, gives him complete freedom to come and go as he pleases, a freedom he exercised not long ago to the extent of wandering off briefly into a job as accompanist to his friend Lena Horne.

The Ellington employment policy has always been unique. The idea of firing anyone is so repugnant to Duke that he will tolerate unparalleled degrees of insubordination on the ground that the end justifies the means. It is no less painful to him to find a sideman quitting without due cause, which in his eyes is denoted only by such hazards as complete physical disability or retirement. Men quitting to form their own groups have hurried off the bandstand to the echo of Ellington's voice laconically commenting: "He'll be back," and in a matter of months or years this has almost always been true.

Johnny Hodges, Ray Nance, Harold Baker and Cat Anderson, all members of the 1957 orchestra, had at one time left to launch ventures of their own that petered out.

Observers of Ellington rehearsals, and even of public performances, at which two or three men may amble in an hour late, find it hard to believe that the apparently complete lack of morale can produce such exemplary music. They are no less bewildered at the reflection that the team spirit in the brass, reed and rhythm sections has at no time been audibly affected by the fact that at one time or another certain men have not been on speaking terms with Ellington or each other or both.

Duke's escapism has had the valuable effect of keeping him clear of any musical hybridization, any involvement with other musical forms. He rarely listens to classical music and has a list of preferences that many modernists may find slightly bland: Ravel's *Daphnis and Chloe,* Debussy's *La Mer* and *Afternoon of a Faun,* Delius's *In a Summer Garden* and Holst's *The Planets.*

Except for its complete independence from classical and modern concert music, Ellington's orchestration technique cannot be said to have founded any particular school within jazz itself. Direct imitation has often been found in the recordings of Charlie Barnet, Woody Herman and others; the impact of Ellington (and *ipso facto,* of Strayhorn) on Ralph Burns and other contemporary writers is unmistakable. Yet there is no true parallel between Ellington and any lesser jazz writer comparable with that which exists, say, between Milhaud and Rugolo, or Fletcher Henderson and Bill Holman, Sy Oliver and Billy May. The reason is simple: Ellington's works remain as inscrutable as the man himself. He has never allowed his orchestrations to be published, preferring to take the secrets of his voicings on an unaccompanied journey to posterity.

This is Ellington's greatest accomplishment: that he has reached a pinnacle of glorious achievement, originating without imitating, and has withheld his throne from the grasp of thirty years of pretenders, imitated but inimitable. What he has done in those thirty years was best summed up one evening at the Opera House in San Francisco by André Previn, a musician who was not born when the Cotton Club era began. "You know," he said, "Stan Kenton can stand in front of a thousand fiddles and a thousand brass and make a dramatic gesture, and every studio arranger can nod his head and say, 'Oh, yes, that's done like this.' But Duke merely lifts his finger, three horns make a sound, and I don't know what it is!"

SELECTED DISCOGRAPHY—DUKE ELLINGTON

Ellingtonia (early Ellington), Brunswick 58002, 58012, 54007
Liberian and Harlem Suites, Columbia CL 848
Duke Ellington, Allegro-Elite 3074
At Newport, Columbia CL 934
Drum Is A Woman, Columbia CL 951
Ellington's Greatest, Victor LPT 1004
Hi-Fi Ellington Uptown, Columbia CL 830
In A Mellotone, Victor LPM 1364
Plays Ellington, Capitol T 477
Presents, Bethlehem 6005

Charlie Parker

* * * *

By Orrin Keepnews

Charlie Parker died quietly, shortly before nine o'clock on the evening of March 12, 1955, having been seriously ill for only three days. The doctor attending him had seen him no more than a half hour earlier and had expressed the opinion that he was much improved; and Parker was propped up in an armchair watching television when death came. He was not yet thirty-five years old, but considering that he had led a physically punishing life and had a poor medical history, it was not notably surprising that he should die so young. Described this way, then, it was the sort of death whose circumstances must have been duplicated countless times.

But it must also be noted that this man was very probably the most significant jazz figure of his time, that he died in the New York apartment of a wealthy and titled woman, that his body lay unclaimed in the morgue for two days, that the precise cause of death is still open to argument. With such additions, the passing of the man known as "Bird" (a nickname of at least three supposed derivations and no vital significance, but consistently used), can be seen as mysterious or even sinister, as part of a contradictory, colorful, seething legend about a foredoomed folk-hero.

Actually, there are rather unsensational explanations for most of the elements of "mystery" associated with Parker's death, but the really important point may be that most people have automatically elected to accept at face value the assumption—and this is true with anecdotes about his life as well as his death—that the weirder stories were the truer ones. There is no question that Bird is going to be one of the larger-scale jazz legends; he was well on his way to that status long before he died. It cannot be denied that Parker himself, by his attitudes and by many of his quite verifiably non-standard activities, did much to help create and build the legend. But it is equally undeniable that a great many people (including many who knew him closely, in addition to those who merely knew *of* him as a public figure) seem to have shown a positive *desire* to turn him into legend as quickly as possible. In part, this tendency can be seen as no more than the very familiar urge to romanticize the "artist." Bird is just one, and certainly not the last, of a very long line of writers, painters, musicians and what-have-you to be quickly converted into myth. But it may also be that it is more comfortable to accept Parker as fiction, rather than as reality. It is not without importance that at this writing (early 1957) there are at least four people or sets of people reported at work on books about Bird and that, of the four, the only one that has been completed is a novel! (Its author is Ross Russell, who in the nineteen forties operated the independent jazz label, Dial, for which several of Parker's first important recordings were made. Russell, on the other hand, is to-day reluctant to reinvolve himself emotionally with the facts by discussing such rather strained circumstances as Bird's committal to Camarillo State Hospital in 1946, immediately following a Dial recording session in Los Angeles. For the record, the other three Parker works currently in progress are by his last wife, Chan, with a collaborator; by a musician-turned-writer friend who also helped handle Bird's business affairs in his last years; and, jointly with a professional writer, by a New York librarian who has doubled as a jazz night-club operator and promoted a number of public "jam sessions" that were among Parker's last appearances.)

The diversity of approaches to the man's life that can be assumed as forthcoming from such a list of potential authors is a fair clue to the diversity of opinion, fact and pseudo-fact that currently exist about Bird. There is, by now, little argument about his position in jazz history: he was a (very possibly *the*) major force in the creation of current modern-jazz forms; his approach, his tone, insofar as possible his musical ideas have been followed, adopted, understood, imitated, aped, unintentionally parodied and misunderstood by performers on all manner of jazz instruments in a way that far transcends any cliché about "the sincerest form of flattery." Musically, there is near unanimity. But concerning the man, it is something else again.

The major problem faced by any researcher into Parker lore is a problem of overabundance. It is almost literally true that everyone involved with modern jazz in the 'forties and thereafter feels, whether justifiably or not, that he really "knew" Bird and is en-

titled to make definitive, strongly felt statements. Asked for suggestions as to helpful subjects for interview, one musician, who
actually did know Parker well, came up with a list of twenty-two
names almost without pausing for breath, and then apologized that
with a little thought he could make the list much longer. And, no
matter how many or how few sources are actually turned to, there is
such a welter of conflicting report and reaction that it hardly seems
possible that everyone is discussing the same man. Of course, to a
great extent there is truth in that contradiction: few men are fully
consistent; the sensitive creative artist is apt to be far less so than
most and far more inclined to be reshaped over and over again by
subjective pulls; and Parker, addicted to narcotics for a substantial
portion of his life, could easily be considered to have been several
men.

Do you accept French jazz critic Charles Delaunay's impression of him as a sort of Rousseau-ian Noble Savage: "a big, dreaming child; a natural inspired force . . . good-natured, shy and quite
boyish, (with) curiously juvenile thoughts." Or do you turn to
other writers who have been impressed with the "searching clarity"
of his comments on music and have quoted him as discussing with
considerable insight why Bartok had become his favorite composer
or the possible similarities of aim between his own work and Hinde-
mith's? How much attention do you pay to friends' reports on how
intelligently he could discuss philosophy or science? What valua-
tion do you place on Chan Parker's conclusions that "he was very
mature and wise about the world and life; just immature about
himself," and that "Bird was a very gentle man, although he hid
it much of the time"? There are stories of his having been crudely
cruel and openly contemptuous towards musicians he considered not
up to his standards; but there are other stories to balance against
those. Pianist Randy Weston recalls a night in the late nineteen
forties—he was not yet even a professional and when Bird had
heard him play only once—when he was literally snatched up from
the bar at one New York club, hustled over to another on Fifty-
second Street ("where, of course, they treated Bird like a god when
he walked in") and installed on the bandstand with Parker for
almost an hour of playing with the band—"the most wonderful thing
that could have happened to me." And Bird's close friend, alto
player and arranger Gigi Gryce, insists that his awareness of music
was so strong that he could "hear right *through* to something good"
in the most unlikely places. "We might be walking along and pass

someplace with a really terrible rock and roll band, for instance, and he'd stop and say 'Listen to what that bass player's doing,' when I could hardly even hear the bass. And then he might go inside and play with that band and try to teach them things."

There are stories that can't be ignored of his borrowing money and even instruments and never returning them ("You had to pay your dues with Bird"), but Gryce, who says simply "I lent him my horn plenty of times and always got it back," can tell of Parker's visiting him in Boston wth a little money in his pocket, finding a bar in the "really poor" part of town and spending all he had on whipping up an impromptu party for the patrons there. "Of course, then he'd have to find someone to lend him the money to get back home. . . ."

Doris Parker, who married him in 1945 (when his impact both on musicians and on the jazz-listening public was at its first high point) and thus was with him both during that "up" period and the extreme "down" period that followed it rather closely, expresses deep, hurt surprise at a number of prevalent attitudes and stories. She is an admittedly prejudiced source ("To me he was Charlie, not 'Bird,' not the fantastic character . . . but the guy I loved . . . gentle, soft-spoken, withdrawn") but presumably not interested in whitewashing his memory ("Really, he did so many things that were bad, they don't need to manufacture any"). Commenting on an article in one of the current crop of shock-value men's magazines, a piece that claimed in reasonably lurid, if non-specific, anonymous-quote detail that Parker "may have had the most advanced case of satyriasis ever known," Doris has remarked: "This I find very hard to believe. For long periods of time I'd be with him twenty-four hours a day. . . . At no time did I know Charlie to be vulgar about sex . . . and I can't believe he could ever change so completely." She similarly discounts stories about his inventing "new" ways of drug-taking: "Let's not let anyone kid about that. He didn't invent addiction—everything he did has been done many times before, even the destruction."

If the stories fail to balance, there is at least little difficulty in setting forth the basic facts of Parker's life (although there is some clouding at both ends). He was born in Kansas City, Kansas, and brought up in the larger city of the same name across the river in Missouri. The usually accepted birthdate is August 29, 1920. There has been some claim that he must have been born earlier (trumpeter Harold Baker has been quoted as saying he recalls Bird

playing with a Kansas City band in about 1931), but Doris reports
that his mother verified the 1920 date. His mother bought him an
alto saxophone when he was about eleven. He subsequently told
interviewers that he had become interested in this instrument by
hearing Rudy Vallee on the radio, but it's questionable that this
should be taken seriously, particularly since it later seemed important to him to stress that he was not influenced by any of the
noted horn players of his youth, Lester Young in particular. Parker
has also spoken of taking up the baritone horn in high school because "it was loud and boisterous and dominated the band so much
the judges could scarcely ignore it" in awarding prizes, another
comment that can be taken as indicating more about Bird's later
cynicism than about early motivations.

At about age fifteen he left school and decided to take up
music professionally. As much as has ever been stated about his
reasons was set forth in a 1949 *Down Beat* interview, in which he
noted the necessity of earning a living and that music "seemed easy,
looked glamorous, and there was nothing else around." But it doesn't
call for much guesswork to add to this another reason, one that can
be equated with his mother's motives in so readily buying a saxophone for an eleven-year-old presumable Rudy Vallee fan. This
was Missouri; as in the Deep South, then and earlier, a great many
Negro parents were more than willing to encourage any musical
leanings in their children: however dubious its moral reputation,
at least the entertainment business was one of the very few open
avenues leading to other than menial jobs.

But if music "seemed easy" to young Parker, that decidedly
was a wrong impression. It is clear that he was not much of a musician at the start. Bassist Gene Ramey, who came to know Parker
very well in later years, has written that when he first met Bird, "he
was barely fourteen years old (and) wasn't doing anything, musically speaking." Ramey wrote of one early humiliation when
Parker began to play during a jam session with members of Count
Basie's band. "Jo Jones, . . . as an expression of his feeling, took
his cymbal off and threw it almost the complete distance of the
room. . . . Bird just packed up his horn and walked out." Parker
himself has told of a similar incident at the High Hat club when "I
tried doing double tempo on *Body and Soul*. Everybody fell out
laughing. I went home and cried and didn't play again for three
months."

Parker's main reaction to all this, according to Ramey and

others, was a "just you wait and see" kind of determination. Bird has noted that he had first seriously learned to read music at about this time, and Ramey has written of the "unbelievable" transformation that came about during his sixteenth summer, which was spent at a summer resort with George E. Lee's band, where a guitarist named Efferge Ware ("a great chord specialist, although he did no solo work") educated him on "the cycles—the relationship of the chords and how to weave melodies into them. . . . After which, of course, Bird expanded on his own. . . . After this sudden development in his style, Bird began to get lots of work."

There is a theory that Parker was a "natural genius." Gigi Gryce, for example, believes that he just "happened" to take up music, and would have made an important mark in any field. ("If he had become a plumber, I believe he would have been a great one.") In support of this, there is his late enthusiasm for painting. (I have seen an impressive sketch of his friend Baroness Nica Koenigswarter and have been reliably informed of highly interesting, more ambitious work.) The accounts of his rough start in music might seem to weaken this natural-genius theory, but under the circumstances perhaps the wonder is not that Parker did not play better, but that he played at all well. He lacked any sort of formative jazz background: he had heard little if anything of the music of early jazz greats; it seems clear that the swing of the mid-'thirties meant little to him musically; and his immediate reaction to the heavily vibrato-filled style of just about all jazz saxophonists of the time was simply, "I didn't like it." In addition, he had been introduced to narcotics almost as soon as to music. The accounts vary, but whether it was "an actor friend (who) told me about a new kick," or older musicians, or "a stranger in a washroom," the fact is that, by 1935, he was firmly addicted. Bird's own statement to writer Leonard Feather was that "It all came from being introduced to night life too early. When you're not mature enough to know what's happening—well—you goof." Perhaps that doesn't really say it all, but there seems no need to get overly devious about a sensitive fifteen-year-old, working as a musician in the heart of Kansas City (then in its Pendergast heyday and probably the most wide-open town of all), trying to be as hard a guy as the next and accepting heroin as part of the "glamor" of it all. Very little is known about Bird's childhood. (Doris Parker, denying that he was particularly "closemouthed" about his youth, makes the point that "he didn't have much youth to talk about. What can you say about being

'hooked' at fifteen? That rather limits the conversation.") It does
seem reasonable to take the known teen-age circumstances and add
to them whatever you care to accept of the sexual-appetite stories
and also his lately, strongly demonstrative affection for children—
his own or those of friends—and conclude that he was looking for
a warmth and acceptance he had been unable to find in childhood.
Chan Parker has been quoted as saying, "He had been hurt early
and he had been hurt bad. He was cynical sometimes as a result,
but he was also sentimental. When he came home, whether he had
much money or barely any, he'd bring presents for the kids."

As for the practical problems of addiction, Parker later commented forcefully that "any musician who says he is playing better
either on tea, the needle, or when he is juiced, is a plain straight
liar." For a Bird who was just learning his trade, this must have
been true many times over.

Nevertheless, he was developing as a musician, accepted by
that time at the plentiful jam sessions, and working briefly with Jay
McShann's band, a top local group. Then came a now-cloudy unpleasantness involving his refusal to pay a cab fare. Apparently his
mother refused to help him out and he spent twenty-two days in
jail, after which he abruptly left town—leaving his horn behind. One
story places him briefly in Chicago in 1938, where (as singer Billy
Eckstine has told it) he walked into the Club 65 during a "breakfast
dance" and sat in, using a borrowed horn and looking "like he just
got off a freight car, . . . but playing like you never heard." A
short time later he was in New York, still without an instrument.
For three months he was a nine-dollars-a-week-and-meals dishwasher at a Harlem after-hours spot; then he just "bummed around
awhile." He had been in town eight months when some by-now-
anonymous musicians bought him a horn (presumably after hearing what he could do on a borrowed alto at some session); shortly
thereafter he was hired at Clark Monroe's Uptown House, soon to
become known as one of the key breeding grounds for the new jazz.

This was in 1939, which seems to have been the year in which
things really began to jell. On one subsequent occasion (during a
Down Beat interview ten years later) he was inclined—or induced—
to pin it down to a specific month (December, 1939) and place (the
back room of a Harlem chili house, where he was jamming with a
guitarist named Biddy Fleet). Bored with "the stereotyped changes
being used then," Parker is quoted as thinking "there's bound to
be something else. . . . I could hear it sometimes, but I couldn't

lay it." Then, while playing *Cherokee*, "Charlie suddenly found that
y using higher intervals of a chord as a melody line and backing
hem with appropriately related changes, he could play this thing
e had been 'hearing' . . . and bop was born."

This somewhat technical version is a good deal more apocalyptic
and less plausible than the way Bird told it on other occasions, when
t was merely that he used to "hang around with Fleet at . . . spots
uptown" and "we'd play around with flatted fifths" and the like.
But both ways of putting it have their merits. The assumption that
Parker's new approach came about gradually jibes with accounts
that trace at least some elements of his eventual style back to his
Kansas City days. Both Jo Jones and Ben Webster have mentioned
an alto player named Buster Smith, who played with Bennie Moten
and then with Count Basie's earliest band, as being (in Webster's
words) "the only man I ever heard to whom you could attribute
anything Bird ever did." Jones has flatly called Smith "Charlie
Parker's musical father." Doris Parker recalls Bird telling her of
"a tenor (?) player who influenced him greatly" at the start, and
some of Bird's friends have cited mention of "a guy who played
alto in an old band." Unquestionably, Parker's "modernism" did
not suddenly spring into full-blown life one fine day; but on the
other hand, the *Down Beat* sudden-flash account does have the
virtue of dramatically indicating that, by the end of 1939, Parker
had found himself. For by early 1940 he had returned to Kansas
City and rejoined Jay McShann; and his sound on his first records
with McShann, as well as stories of how he was a leading force in
the band, make it clear that he had come a long way since he ran
home and cried in 1935.

It does seem strange that Bird found himself during a period
of rootless wandering and odd jobs, not even owning a horn most
of the time, but it is simply a fact that must be accepted. It must
also be kept in mind that he was certainly on narcotics at this time,
that this was part of a period in which, as he once put it, he was
"always on a panic." Pain, poverty and loneliness were among
the ingredients—whether because of them, in spite of them, or
both, Charlie Parker was about to become a focal point of the new
jazz forms that were just beginning to take shape.

For many reasons, among them various personal jealousies and
musicians' habit of supplying interviewers with the answers they think
are the ones wanted, regardless of accuracy, the precise beginning
of the music first known as "be-bop" will most probably always be

shrouded in confusion, contradiction and double-talk. It was no
necessarily recognized by the participants as a glamorous period
of creativity: pianist Thelonius Monk says, "Nobody was sittin
there trying to make up something new on purpose. The job at Min
ton's was a job we were playing, that's all." But at Minton's Play
house, the number-one proving ground for bop, the job was at leas
one where men could play as they pleased, with a sympathetic clu
manager (ex-band leader Teddy Hill) and a growing crowd of in
terested musicians eager to listen or to sit in. There, and at Mon
roe's and at other side-street Harlem spots, Monk could play a
he had always wanted to; drummer Kenny Clarke, another membe
of the Minton's band, could work on the ideas that had bee
frowned on when he was with Hill's band; Dizzy Gillespie an
guitarist Charlie Christian and so many others could come by
(Monk does not recall Parker having been there at the very start
nor that there was any single memorable moment when he firs
appeared; but he does say that Bird's ability and authority wer
immediately accepted as exciting and important additions.) Thei
various new concepts were similar enough to merge—or perhap
it was something like the classic stories of inventors separately, bu
almost simultaneously, achieving identical results. Clarke has bee
quoted on this subject of mutuality, noting that he, Monk and Gil
lespie would often end up at Monroe's after Minton's closed for th
night: Bird had left the limited confines of McShann's rather routin
Kansas City riff-and-blues outfit and returned to New York, an
"we went to listen to Bird," although at first it was "for no othe
reason than that he sounded like Pres." ("Pres"—Lester Young—
was perhaps the only no-vibrato sax man before Parker, and Bir
had spoken of admiring his "clean and beautiful" sound, althougl
disclaiming any influence from Young's jazz ideas, which "ran o
differently" than his own.) But they found, Clarke added, that Bir
also had something new to offer: "Things we'd never heard befor
—rhythmically and harmonically," and it aroused the interest o
Dizzy and Monk because they *were working along the same lines.*
(my italics—O.K.).

Earl Hines's band was becoming a home for several member
of the bop clique; men like Eckstine and Gillespie helped persuad
Hines to hire Parker. The only opening was on tenor, so Bir
played that instrument exclusively during the ten months of 194
he spent with Hines. But, although there is a story that Ben Web
ster was moved to open admiration the first time he heard him, Bir

was never at home with the tenor; and when he joined Billy Eckstine's big band in 1944, as one of several ex-Hines men involved
in that musically ambitious but short-lived orchestra, he was back
on alto for good.

After 1944 bop broke out into the open, beginning its rather
brief, hectic and heavily publicized period of more-or-less acceptance by the public. Parker was making his first important records
with small groups for the small jazz labels and no one since Louis
Armstrong's early heyday had ever had so overwhelming an impact on
his fellow musicians. Parker was working on Fifty-second Street, first
with Dizzy and then heading a group that included eighteen-year-old
Miles Davis. He was, everyone around him agreed, playing wonderfully well. He was also living hard; but so were most of his co-
workers, and so have most jazzmen of most eras, particularly when
times are good for them and the clubs are crowded. When you spend
each night working hard at playing what you want, when your work
is being enthusiastically received, and when your setting is a place
that does nothing but serve drinks all night long—well, the atmosphere is hardly conducive to sedate living, or to rationing either
your emotions or your appetites. There are stories of eccentric behavior (with the Hines band he had once missed a theatre show
because he arrived early and was asleep under the bandstand
throughout the performance), and it can be said with hindsight
that Bird was close to a breakdown late in 1945 when he went to
Los Angeles with a group that included Gillespie and vibist Milt
Jackson. But the unanswerable question is whether he would have
gone over the line at that time if Los Angeles had not turned out
to be a terrible place to play. "Worst of all," Parker told Leonard
Feather in an interview a few years later, "was that nobody understood our kind of music out on the Coast," in sharp and bitter contrast to the Eastern scene, where he and Dizzy were the newest of
idols. And through it all there was the narcotics habit, which among
other things is expensive, so that even when he was working regularly, he was painfully unable to "buy good clothes or a place to
live."

It all came to a head on the night of July 29, 1946. At a record
session for Ross Russell's Dial label, Bird, despite having drunk
"a quart of whiskey to make the date," was beset by uncontrollable
muscle tics. He cut only two numbers, one of them an almost in-
coherent *Lover Man*. (Parker's later comment was: *"Lover Man*
should be stomped into the ground," but it was released, and an

embarrassing number of listeners didn't seem to know enough to dis
like it.) Later that night he broke down completely, was arrested and
then committed to Camarillo State Hospital. He was released seven
months later, seemingly quite recovered: he was playing well on
records made in February, 1946. There are contradictory detail
concerning his release; although he worked for Dial again, there
was some feeling that Russell had taken advantage of him by in
sisting that he sign a recording contract before agreeing to help
gain his release, although, according to Doris's account, they later
determined that he could have been released, and even sent back
to New York by the state of California, without outside aid.

In any event, the next few years were successful and seem
ingly happy and stable, although by taking a long hindsight view
again it is possible to say that the road was leading down toward
its end. Bird was in demand at New York clubs, and was a big
enough name to make it a commercially appealing idea for a club
that opened in 1950 to be called "Birdland." He was in Paris and
the Scandinavian countries in 1949 and '50, was featured on sev
eral of promoter Norman Granz' "Jazz at the Philharmonic" tours
and eventually recorded (for Granz' Clef label) an album with a
rich string background. This, Doris Parker says, "had been one of
Charlie's pet dreams . . . for so long."

But the with-strings recordings can be taken as marking an
other turning point. Although some have found these selections
especially a version of *Just Friends,* among his most moving work
others considered them a sign that he was going "commercial"—
always the most insulting word in jazz.

Bird had for some time been talking about the potentialities
of the "variety of coloration" and "new sound combinations" offered
by strings and other primarily symphonic instruments, and several
friends were aware that he was deeply disturbed by the negative
reactions. He went ahead with plans for a tour with a string group
but it was unsuccessful. Entering the 'fifties, he was moving into
a period of personal confusion and erratic behavior. Bookers and
club owners were growing impatient with his unreliability; there
was a falling out with the management of Birdland (in his last year
he played in "his" club only twice; both times with disastrous re
sults). He apparently was fighting to keep "straight" as far as nar
cotics were concerned, but there are conflicting reports as to how
successful he was. One prevalent self-cure among musician addict
has been to drink heavily as a sort of substitute (what medica

authorities might say about the effectiveness of this is another matter), and it is a fact that Parker drank more heavily at this time than ever before, to the point where he was hospitalized by a serious ulcer attack. For the first time (except for the actual breakdown in 1946) his physical condition was affecting his playing, and although he was still vastly appreciated and widely copied by musicians, many of them placed him in a sort of *emeritus* status that didn't sit at all well with him.

Bird had left Doris, and Chan had borne him two children. Early in 1954, the girl, Pree, died of pneumonia. Many people consider this tragedy to have been the real finisher. Leonard Feather has called the next few months a "pattern of apparently intentional self-destruction." The immediate culmination came in September of that year, when he was booked into Birdland with a string group. The strings began playing one tune; Bird began on an entirely different one, screamed wildly at the musicians, and "fired" them on the spot. Later that night he drank iodine in an apparent suicide attempt.

There was one last attempt at regeneration, sparked by Chan. She rented a house in Bucks County, Pennsylvania; Bird attempted to stop drinking and for a while actually commuted to New York, over an hour away, almost daily for sessions with a psychiatrist. But this rather demanding routine didn't last too long. He went back to work, usually as a "single," backed by a "house" rhythm section. It was an oddly unreal existence; Baroness Nica Koenigswarter (in whose apartment he was to die), who came to know him well during his final months, insists that he was not moody—except when Pree was mentioned—but was for the most part quite cheerful, warm and witty. But she also notes that he told her, "I've been dead for four years." And there were times when he would ride the subways all night long, alone.

There was no question but that he had deteriorated badly. Frank Sandiford, a Chicago writer who was a close friend for several years, tells of a night at The Beehive in Chicago, "just before he left . . . to go back East and die."

"It began with the owner begging me to go to the room behind the bar to get Charlie to go on the stand. It was a small room used to store cases of beer and other things. . . . Bird met me at the door by throwing his arms around me as though I were the only person left in the world to whom to plead for rest. He couldn't go on, he said. Didn't want to, was in no condition. He looked it. The house was packed. I reminded him that there were many people out there who had come just to hear him play. I opened the door and . . . he glared at them. 'They just came out here to see the world's most famous junky,' he grumbled. I will always feel guilty about this, but I did get him to get up and face the crowd. He couldn't play. All he did was to make a few awful bleating sounds . . . spilling out his disgust, his fears, his frustrations. He made a pitiful figure. . . . He was a beaten man and he knew it. That made it most painful."

Birdland tried him again, on March 4, 1955, but someone misguidedly and unthinkingly arranged to have his group include pianist Bud Powell, who was far from fully recovered from his own mental illness. It was, according to eyewitnesses, a thoroughly painful experience, with a full-scale verbal battle between Bird and Bud on the bandstand the first night.

The following Wednesday, just before he was to leave for a Boston engagement, Parker stopped at the Baroness Koenigswarter's apartment. While there he had a bad coughing spell that brought up blood and left him breathing with difficulty. The baroness called a doctor, who asked a few briskly routine questions (including "Do you drink?", to which Parker answered: "Sometimes I have a sherry before dinner") and recommended hospitalization. Bird refused insistently, and the baroness agreed to keep him there; she and her daughter could nurse him. He was very weak for two days, tried to eat only a few canned peaches during that time, couldn't retain even that, but drank great quantities of water from a jug at his bedside. He remained very alert, however. The doctor knew, if somewhat unclearly, who he was, and there was much discussion as to which of Bird's records would be most suitable to play first for the doctor. (Parker finally decided on *April in Paris,* from the with-strings album.) He also talked, near the end, about the future: about forming a large new band "that would knock them all dead." "On that third day," Nica Koenigswarter says, "he seemed much better; then he died." (He died while watching the Dorsey brothers' television program; he had always admired the Dorseys as technicians.) As the baroness recounts it, the doctor was called three minutes later; he immediately sent for the medical examiner; and thereafter it was out of her hands. She says she was most anxious that Chan not learn of Bird's death from the radio or newspapers, but it was more than a day later before she could locate Chan. (Bird had refused to tell her

Chan's whereabouts, saying that he didn't want her or anyone else to know where he was until he was better.)

As for the cause of death: the baroness knew of no heart attack or pneumonia, which were mentioned by most newspaper accounts, and says that the doctor specified ulcers and cirrhosis of the liver. Doris Parker, on the other hand, says, "The district attorney told me they did a very thorough autopsy on Charlie and he died from lobar pneumonia and nothing else was mentioned." This mystery may never be fully clarified, but there is no doubt that it can be said, without excessive sentimentality, that Charlie Parker, like more than a few others before him, died of being a naked, stubbornly and inevitably unadjustable genius.

"Genius" has become a rather cheapened word in our times, but it tends to have its old, formal dignity when musicians talk about Bird. What might be called the omnipresence of music in his life is something on which several have commented. Gene Ramey has been quoted as saying, "Everything had a musical significance for him. He'd hear dogs barking, for instance, and he would say it was a conversation and . . . he would have something to play that would portray that thought to us." Similarly, Gigi Gryce has noted his ability to "augment anything. You might be humming a couple of bars of something, without thinking about it, and in a couple of minutes he'd be giving it back to you so changed and developed you wouldn't even recognize it."

Yet, like many artists to whom creativity is, at least in part, a sort of natural function, he tended to minimize his own abilities. This might have been simply a not-uncommon urge towards perfection. "Basically, he was never satisfied with what he did," Doris has said. "There wasn't a record he didn't think could have been better." And Bird himself once answered a question as to what he'd recommend to anyone wanting to buy his three best records by saying, "Tell him to keep his money." Gryce, however, feels that he was bothered by his lack of formal training, that he thought, incorrectly, that the fact that he could write and arrange so readily without schooling did not just mean that it came easily to him, but rather that he wasn't doing it as well as he might. Yet, Gryce notes, he had a phenomenal ability to read, and even to transpose, music at sight.

The extent to which he was disturbed by imitators, or made unhappy by varying degrees of non-acceptance by the public, is hard

to define and obviously was itself quite variable. Gryce believes that
part of the unhappiness of his last years stemmed from a feeling
of "What's the use? People didn't really dig him," and there is agreement that he felt his "disciples" were overdoing it to the point of
stultifying their own creative potentials.

But any opinions about Parker must be looked at with an
understanding that, to an amazing extent, people saw in him what
they wanted to see. Take even so apparently simple a matter as
whether he was more, or less, reliable during his best periods.
Doris says, "When Charlie was on his feet, he made time" (*i.e.*,
showed up on time for engagements). But Gigi feels that he was
simply unable to adjust to business routine—"he wanted to create
like a painter, when he wanted to; not like a commercial artist
working on schedule"—and that, when he was feeling best, he was
most apt to get wound up in a session someplace and just neglect
to show up for work.

Of one thing there can be little doubt: he had given up the
fight towards the end. He spoke often about his death as close
and inevitable ("I'm just a husk," he told Nica Koenigswarter); and
in 1954 he sent Doris a poem, which he may have written but more
probably had copied down (judging from the rather ornate style),
and which he seems to have considered fitting. In part it sets forth
a credo that might easily have been his own ("Hear the words! Not
the doctrine. Hear the speech! Not the meaning. . . . Don't look
at the sun! Feel it!") and in part is concerned with dying ("death is
an imminent thing"), though also with hope ("My fire is unquench-
able"). There can also be little doubt that he was a tortured man,
and there are several who emphasize the loneliness. One friend of
the last years, Chips Bayen, never thought it unusual that he had
long talks with Bird, and discovered only after his death that most
people considered it something unique. Gigi Gryce puts the blame
on Bird's position of eminence: "The pressure of being on a pedestal, which he didn't like at all." Gigi feels that he wanted and needed
companionship, but that many musicians were wary of approaching
him on a personal level: "People wouldn't talk to him because they
didn't know what to say—but, really, all they had to do was say
'Hello.' "

Although so many writers of fiction have turned the concept
of the artist as a soul in torment into something approaching a
stereotype, it still seems the clearest way to sum up this man. The
basic paradox must be that the same qualities that made him play

as he did made him unable to find "normal" happiness and acceptance. Frank Sandiford calls him "a man of violently opposing urges: one towards greatness . . . the other towards defeat." In a letter, Sandiford tells of seeing him at his worst: ". . . when he would beg dimes and quarters, anything, from those that came to hear him play . . . sweaty and looking sick and tired (and trying) to keep his words together so as to make some sense. There were times when I would see him sneer, trying hard to believe in the cynical statements he made, when I knew he made them only to keep pain at a safer distance." This is a friend speaking, of course, and perhaps being considerably more tolerant than, say, someone at whom the cynicism was directed or from whom the money was begged. But at the very least a man is entitled to have a friend speak the final words. And there is another portion of Sandiford's letter that seems a suitable epitaph for Bird (and probably for more than one other musician whose living presence was sometimes less than pleasant for those who knew and worked with him):

"He was an artist who paid a great price to be able to get out of himself some of the things that most disturbed him. He might have cheated a little, he might have stolen from some, he might have hurt many. But he cheated, stole and hurt himself more than anybody. And he did give us something far more wonderful than he took from us. Our bill was far smaller than the one he couldn't pay."

SELECTED DISCOGRAPHY—CHARLIE PARKER

Charlie Parker: All-Star Sextet, Roost 2210
(reissues of Dial recordings)
Charlie Parker with Strings, Clef 675
Charlie Parker Memorial, Vol. 1, Savoy 12000
The Charlie Parker Story, Savoy 12079

Fletcher Henderson

* * * *

By John S. Wilson

The figure of Fletcher Henderson looms over big-band jazz in a commanding yet strangely diffuse fashion. He was leading the musicians' swing band a full decade before Benny Goodman reached a mass audience with a slicked-up version of the same thing. Henderson had the first band which can logically—and with equal emphasis on both adjectives—be called a big jazz band. And his arrangements were the crucial element in the musical brew that brought Goodman his fantastic popularity.

But despite these seemingly solid factual achievements, Henderson personally remains a somewhat misty, equivocal contributor to jazz. Granted that his band was the first big jazz band, did Henderson really have much to do with making it a *jazz* band? The arrangements for that early band were written mostly by Don Redman, not Henderson. The jazz stars of that band were the likes of Louis Armstrong, Coleman Hawkins, Joe Smith, Jimmy Harrison—not Henderson, who was a relatively indifferent pianist. And later, in his writing for Benny Goodman, Henderson has been pictured by some jazz commentators as contributing not to the glorification and expansion of jazz but to its dilution and diminution.

At the root of these apparent contradictions can be discerned the consequences of that difference of opinion brought on by the first great schism in jazz. It was a schism which Henderson, more than anyone else, helped to create and for which he has had to take the bulk of the brickbats from those who opposed his course. Before the appearance of Henderson's band, there had been only one way to play jazz—the New Orleans way, the extemporaneous, polyphonic, small-group way. By moving away from this format, Henderson committed a heresy for which he has never been forgiven by the uncompromising traditionalist segment of jazz opinion. But Henderson was no consecrated-ground breaker who envisioned new vistas for jazz. He did not deliberately set out to do what he did. Like most of the developments in Henderson's life, it just happened. He was an easygoing, generous person who probably kicked away, through casual business methods and a lethargy that sometimes approached laziness, as many opportunities as he managed to use to advantage.

In a day when almost all jazz musicians were still receiving their education in back-room dives, Henderson was an oddity—a college graduate. Born in Cuthbert, Georgia, on December 18, 1898, he got a degree in chemistry from Atlanta University in 1920 and went north to continue his studies. But there he was led astray by his talents as a pianist.

He had started studying piano when he was six, taught by his mother, Ozie Henderson, a pianist and music instructor. His father, Fletcher Hamilton Henderson, Sr., was principal of Randolph Training School. During his first summer in New York, he went to work as a song demonstrator for the Pace and Handy Publishing Co., and when Harry Pace and W. C. Handy organized the Black Swan Recording Co., Henderson was installed as house pianist. That ended his interest in chemistry, much to the relief of his mother and father who felt it was too dangerous a career.

For Black Swan, Henderson was a piano soloist, leader of a house band, the Black Swan Troubadours, and accompanist for several blues singers. One of these was Ethel Waters who was singing at Edmond's, a Harlem cellar spot. After she had made her first Black Swan records, Pace and Handy suggested that it would help sell them if she went on tour with Henderson's band which, for this purpose, was called the Black Swan Jazz Masters.

Henderson was dubious about the propriety of a man in his position—a recording-company executive, a man with a college degree—being the piano player for a girl who sang blues in a cellar. "Before he would go out," Miss Waters recalls in her autobiography, "Fletcher had his whole family come up from Georgia to look me over and see if it would be all right. They not only put their stamp of approval on me but they all fell in love with me at first sight."

The Jazz Masters that Henderson took out on this tour were Joe Smith and Gus Aiken, trumpets; Buddy Aiken and Lorenzo Brashear, trombones; Garvin Bushell, clarinet; Raymond Green, drums; and Henderson, piano. The inclusion of Joe Smith was significant for he was the first of a long list of topnotch jazzmen who were to be drawn into Henderson's orbit.

Smith, a master with a plunger mute, was one of the earliest jazz musicians to be noted for the sweetness of his tone. Henderson has called him "the most soulful trumpeter I ever knew, and when he used a felt hat for a mute, it was difficult for me to tell if *he* was playing or if it was one of the saxophonists." A restless type, Smith was in and out of Henderson's band throughout the middle 'twenties.

The Waters tour wound up stranded in the Middle West and Henderson returned to New York where, through contacts made while he was at Black Swan, he set up numerous record dates for a variety of labels both as a band leader and as an accompanist. In April, 1923, he made his first records with Bessie Smith, an association that was to continue for four years during which Henderson or members of his band backed up the great blues singer on almost every recording she made.

Between 1923 and 1925, Henderson was the accompanist for an incredible number of blues singers. He worked with all of the famous Smiths—Bessie and Clara on Columbia, Trixie on Paramount. He backed the illustrious Ma Rainey on Paramount, as well as Ida Cox, Alberta Hunter, Coot Grant, Faye Barnes, Gladys Bryant, Maude De Forrest, Edna Hicks, Ozie McPherson, Mary Straine, Hannah Sylvester, Inez Wallace and Isabelle Washington. His accompaniments were used on Victor (Rosa Henderson, Emma Lewis), Brunswick (Rosa Henderson again and Viola McCoy), Emerson (Hazel Meyers), Gennett (Josie Miles), Vocalion (Rosa Henderson, Edna Hicks, Hazel Meyers and Lena Wilson) and Columbia (Bessie and Clara Smith, Ethel Waters, Maggie Jones, Carroll Clark, Rosa Henderson, George Williams and Bessie Brown).

Buster Bailey, the clarinetist who worked many of these dates with Henderson, has recalled what "accompanying" meant in those days.

"We didn't have any rehearsals for Bessie's records," he said. "She'd just go with us to the studio around Columbus Circle. . . . Fletcher would get the key. This applied not only to Bessie but to almost all blues singers. The singers might have something written out to remind them what the verse was, but there was no music written on it. On a lot of the records by Bessie you'll see lyrics by Bessie Smith and music by George Brooks. That was Fletcher."

That Henderson was as adept an accompanist as he was may have been due to the combination of his early legitimate training and the practical experience of working with Ethel Waters. On their tour, Miss Waters found his playing leaning too far to the classical side to suit her taste. She kept demanding what she called "the damn-it-to-hell bass, that chump-chump stuff that real jazz needs."

"When we reached Chicago," she has recounted, "I got some piano rolls that Jimmy Johnson had made and pounded out each passage to Henderson. To prove to me he could do it, Fletch began to practice. He got so perfect, listening to James P. Johnson play on the player piano, that he could press down the keys as the roll played, never missing a note."

Throughout his career, Henderson's piano work had an academic air, but the most predominant jazz element was the slightly ragtimey quality of Johnson's stride style. Henderson himself thought so little of his talents as a pianist that he rarely featured himself with his band in more than the briefest of solo spots, and when he recorded a number that had an opening for a good piano solo, he was as apt as not to bring in his friend, Fats Waller, to take over the piano for the record session.

It was after a record date at Columbia's Columbus Circle studio in 1923 that the small pool of musicians on which Henderson drew for records and gigs (they played frequently at Broadway Jones', a club at One Hundred and Twenty-ninth Street and Lenox Avenue) jelled into what was to become the first big jazz band. It happened with typical Henderson casualness.

The session had been one for the band. Afterwards Henderson and his six sidemen—among them Don Redman, Coleman Hawkins and Joe Smith—drifted down to Roseland at Fifty-first Street and Broadway, which was the midtown center for musicians in those days. There they learned that auditions for a Negro band were being held by the Club Alabam, a cellar spot under the Nora Bayes Theatre on West Forty-fourth Street, where *The New York Times* is now located. Henderson's group was urged to go to the audition, but Henderson was reluctant because he had neither a drummer nor a bass with him, since they weren't allowed in recording studios then. Despite this, the drummerless, bassless seven-man band went to the Club Alabam and got the job.

Joe Smith took off almost immediately on one of his wanderings, this time to play in a show called "Chocolate Dandies," and the band which became known as the Club Alabam Orchestra, an expanded version of the audition group, was made up of Howard Scott and Elmer Chambers, trumpets; Charlie "Big" Green, trombone; Don

Redman, alto saxophone; Coleman Hawkins, tenor saxophone; Henderson, piano; Charlie Dixon, banjo; Bobby Escudero, tuba; Kaiser Marshall, drums; and Allie Ross, a violinist, who fulfilled the requirement of that day that every band had to have somebody in front of it waving a stick.

This band was primarily a dance band and a show band despite its display of names which are now known for their jazz abilities. At that time, however, their talents as jazzmen were more potential than real. One of the strongest influences on the group was the alto saxophonist, Don Redman, a conservatory-trained musician, who had been playing in and arranging for a Paul Specht unit, the Broadway Syncopators, before he joined Henderson's select circle. Redman wrote the arrangements for the Club Alabam band and continued to write almost all the arranged material played by Henderson's band until he left in 1927 to whip McKinney's Cotton Pickers into one of the more striking bands of the late 'twenties. His early writing for Henderson was, in jazz terms, rudimentary and stiff but, as a result of the shocking impact occasioned by the arrival of Louis Armstrong in Henderson's trumpet section in 1924, Redman received a jazz education which he was able to bring to bear on his arrangements.

It was during and immediately after Armstrong's year as a Henderson sideman that the band really began to swing, both in its arranged work and in its more free-blowing sketches. Redman developed the use of an entire section—the reeds or the brass—in a way comparable to the use of the single instruments in the smaller, extemporizing jazz bands. And he left open spaces for hot soloists, backing them up with prodding riffs, sometimes in the form of call-and-response between sections. In essence, this was the basic outline of big-band arranging as it was to remain for twenty years.

It was the Armstrong and post-Armstrong band that can rightfully be called the first big jazz band. The Club Alabam Orchestra, on the other hand, was little more than a seedbed, although one that had been brilliantly planted. It quickly became popular, helped by radio broadcasts over station WHN, and an offer came to move to Roseland. The band was inclined to turn the offer down until one evening when Edith Wilson, one of the stars of the Club Alabam show, asked to have Hawkins come on the floor and play the blues behind her. Hawkins was willing, but he felt he should get extra money for doing it. The management said "no" and when Hawkins refused to go on, Henderson was told to fire him. This riled the band

so that they told Henderson to give two weeks' notice. At the end
of the two weeks, they moved over to Roseland which was to be
Henderson's base of operations for the next decade.

Henderson's was the second Negro band to play this huge
Broadway dance palace. The first had been a group brought north
by the pioneer New Orleans clarinetist, A. J. Piron. It had included
Bobby Escudero, Henderson's first tuba player. Henderson found
himself sharing the twin bandstands much of the time with Sam
Lanin's band, which included the nucleus of white New York jazz
of the early 'twenties—Red Nichols, Miff Mole, Irv Brodsky, Vic
Berton, Joe Tarto. The rivalry between the two bands was intense
even though Lanin's was essentially a sweet dance band. Working
in close proximity with Henderson's increasingly jazz-conscious
group, however, Lanin's men became more and more interested in
jazz. Their desire to outdo each other was carried to such extremes
that when either band brought in a new arrangement, the title
of the piece was torn off and a fake title substituted. One night
Lanin came in with a new arrangement which drew a wildly enthusiastic response from the crowd. Henderson got a peek at the
title, found it was called *Tin Can*. The next day Henderson and his
men were out scouring the town for a copy of *Tin Can*. They
couldn't find a trace of it. A month later the number was published, with its real title—*Milenberg Joys*.

The Henderson band's reputation began building in its first
year at Roseland, and it moved onto the high road when Louis
Armstrong left King Oliver in Chicago in September, 1924, to come
East and join the Henderson trumpet section. Henderson had waited
three years to get Armstrong. He had first heard him in New Orleans in 1921 when he was touring with Ethel Waters. He was so
impressed then that he offered Armstrong a job on the spot. Armstrong thought it over for a while and finally agreed to join Henderson if Zutty Singleton, Armstrong's drummer, could come along,
too. Henderson had to turn down this suggestion because, as he
pointed out to Armstrong, he had a drummer with him, and he
couldn't strand him so far from home.

But by 1924 Armstrong had been playing under King Oliver
for two years in Chicago, and he was ready to move on. When
another offer came from Henderson, Armstrong accepted it.

His arrival had an electrifying effect on the Henderson band.
It was made up almost entirely of Eastern musicians, men who had
had little direct contact with the mainstream New Orleans tradi-

tion. Suddenly they found the finest flower of that tradition blowing lustily in their midst. The presence of Armstrong proved a challenge and an education to the other men in the band.

Armstrong brought with him a number by Joe Oliver which the Oliver band had played as *Dippermouth Blues.* Rechristened *Sugar Foot Stomp,* set in a framework by Redman and featuring some inspired playing by Armstrong, it became the prototype of the Henderson big-band style with its mixture of driving beat, swinging ensembles and brilliant solo work. A quarter of a century later, looking back over all his recordings, Henderson chose his original disc of *Sugar Foot Stomp* with Armstrong as his favorite.

The exchange between Armstrong and the Henderson band was not entirely a one-sided affair, however. It was a helpful association for Armstrong, too, for he became an adept reader during his year with Henderson. The Henderson band was also a proving ground for Armstrong's singing. About three weeks after he joined the band, he asked Henderson to let him sing a number—the first time, to Henderson's knowledge, that he had sung—and he continued to clown with the band throughout his stay.

By this time, Roseland had become a magnet that drew every jazz musician in town. There were, one veteran recalls, more musicians in the place than dancers. Henderson's band was rated with Jean Goldkette's (with Bix Beiderbecke) as the best in the country and on rare occasions both bands battled it out at Roseland. The Henderson band was gradually becoming an all-star group. When Louis Armstrong left to return to Chicago, he lined up Rex Stewart as his replacement, but Stewart was so awed by the prospect of taking Armstrong's chair that he couldn't pull himself together sufficiently to report for the job for several months. Later Stewart was replaced by Tommy Ladnier. Early in 1927 the trombones were expanded to a section with the addition of Jimmy Harrison to the incumbent Big Green.

To most followers of Henderson's band, 1926–28 is usually viewed as its great period. It was a time when soloists—great soloists—dominated the band. Hawkins began to develop the tenor style that revolutionized the jazz use of the saxophone in 1927 and was adding his strong voice to those of such other great individualists as Harrison, Green and Benny Morton on trombones; Stewart, Ladnier and Joe Smith on trumpet; Buster Bailey on clarinet and, towards the end of this period, Benny Carter's alto saxophone. There were times at Roseland when Henderson, plowing happily away at the piano, became so hypnotized by what his band was playing that he forgot to play.

In those days the band was riding high and Henderson's casual attitude towards the normal requirements of a leader was of no particular consequence. This was the band that the best jazz musicians of the day wanted to play in because they knew they would have the freedom that they might find in no other big band. (Abe Lincoln, a white trombonist who is now an outstanding Hollywood-studio musician but who was then with Ace Brigode's band, once begged Henderson to let him join his band: Henderson, amazed, had to point out that it was unheard of for a white musician to play in a Negro band.) Moreover, as a Henderson sideman, a musician could become a name in his own right, a circumstance that was then relatively unusual.

But new and shrewdly managed competition in the form of such bands as Duke Ellington's and Cab Calloway's was on the way up to challenge Henderson. As opportunities narrowed with the coming of the depression years, his nonchalance in business matters became an increasing handicap. His wife, Leora, attributes his strangely lackadaisical attitude to an automobile accident which occurred late in the 'twenties when he was driving through Kentucky to a date. Swerving to avoid another car, Henderson's Packard plunged over an embankment and rolled over. Joe Smith, Big Green, Hawkins and Bobby Stark were in the car with him at the time, but Henderson was the only one who was hurt. His left arm was broken and his head was gashed so deeply that he was left with a scar all the way across his forehead which glowed white when he was tired. There were stitches over both eyebrows and from then on he played the piano with his left shoulder hunched up higher than the other.

"He had been a good business man before that accident," Mrs. Henderson has said. "But afterwards everything seemed amusing to him. He didn't care. All he wanted was a little money in his pocket. It was a gradual change—a little bit each year. But he was different."

His lack of direction in business matters is reflected in the recording work of his band—once the type of contact work at which he excelled. There was a period of almost two years—from December 12, 1928 to October 3, 1930—when the Henderson band recorded a total of two selections!

During the next few scuffling years, the band stayed together despite sporadic bookings (often at scale) through a combination of loyalty to Henderson and the circumstance that there were few other jobs around. During 1931 and 1932 the band had long stands at Connie's Inn in Harlem, and it got back into the recording studios more frequently. But this was a low point in Henderson's recording career, for he turned out a succession of dreary pop performances, enlivened only by an occasional solo by Hawkins, J. C. Higginbotham, Rex Stewart or Benny Morton.

The morale of the band was understandably low. In the course of a week's engagement at a theatre on New York's lower East Side, the band managed to accumulate almost one hundred tardy marks. At a recording session in December, 1932, the band was so slow in arriving that only forty-five minutes of the three-hour session was left by the time the last man showed up.

The band was dying slowly, but the crucial blow came in a roundabout fashion. John Hammond, less than a year out of Yale and brimming with enthusiasm for jazz, was in England in 1933 when he was asked by both English Columbia and Parlophone if he could arrange some American jazz dates for them since they had exhausted their supply of American jazz and nothing more was being sent to them. Hammond immediately drew up plans for fifty sides, most of them devoted to some version of the Henderson band (Hammond has called the 1932–33 Henderson band "the greatest band I have ever heard, outside of possibly Basie"). He envisioned twelve Fletcher Henderson sides for English Columbia; twelve Horace Henderson sides (the same band with Fletcher's brother, Horace, playing piano) for Parlophone; eight Benny Carter sides, built around Henderson sidemen, for English Columbia; four sides by the same group disguised as the Chocolate Dandies for Parlophone and so forth.

Part of this project was carried out. The release of the records in England led to an offer of a year's work to Hawkins by the British Broadcasting Corporation. Hawkins took the offer and left the band in the spring of 1934. He was the last of Henderson's early stars to leave and to Henderson his departure, added to the uncertain conditions under which the band had been working for several years, seemed to be the last straw.

Early in 1934 he talked of firing his whole band and replacing it with a band he had heard out in Kansas, led by a pianist named Bill Basie. Hammond, who knew Basie only as the second pianist in Bennie Moten's band, dissuaded Henderson from this, but when Henderson insisted that at least he wanted Basie's saxophone player to replace Hawkins, Hammond helped him send for Lester Young.

Young's stay with Henderson was brief and unhappy on all sides. He arrived when Henderson was hopefully rehearsing to audition for the Cotton Club. The band, accustomed to Hawkins' strong, heavy tone, took an instant dislike to Young's light, airy way of playing. He was accused of making the tenor sound like an alto, and he was soon on his way back to Basie, replaced by Ben Webster who played a tenor with hair on its chest.

The Cotton Club job didn't materialize, but Henderson did land a recording contract with the fledgling Decca label which was to prove an important showcase for him. The year before, after having always depended on a string of able sidemen, from Redman to Benny Carter, to supply his arrangements, Henderson started writing himself. (Leora Henderson remembers his first arrangement for the band as "the prettiest thing—it wasn't real rough, you know; it was nice.") In September, 1934, he recorded for Decca several of his earliest arrangements—*Wrappin' It Up, Down South Camp Meetin'* and *Rug Cutter's Swing*. Relatively unnoticed at the time, within a couple of years they were to be the heart and pulse of Benny Goodman's fabulously successful band.

Henderson's association with Goodman began with a bit of typical Henderson generosity. Goodman, fronting a band for the first time, had gone into Billy Rose's Music Hall playing stocks and a few arrangements by Deane Kincaide. To strengthen his book, Henderson lent Goodman a few of his scores, including *Down South Camp Meetin'*. A couple of years later, Henderson did much the same thing on a larger scale when Count Basie's newly expanded band, fresh out of Kansas City, followed Henderson into the Grand Terrace in Chicago. Basie lacked the varied material needed for a spot like the Grand Terrace, so Henderson lent him most of his library. ("He was the only leader in the business who ever went out of his way to help me," Basie has said. "Without those arrangements, there's no telling what would have happened to my band.")

The picture for Henderson had changed radically by the time he reached the Grand Terrace, but in 1934 he was in a tight spot. His band rarely worked, and there were no recording dates in sight. Then, in October, Goodman's band landed a spot on the three-hour National Biscuit Company, and Goodman was given the money to buy eight new arrangements a week. Three of these were regularly assigned to Henderson at $37.50 apiece. For thirteen weeks he got a steady check from these arrangements.

While the program was on the air, Goodman was recording with indifferent success for Columbia. In March, 1935, he switched to Victor and things began to pick up. He got his first resounding hit in July, the pairing of *Sometimes I'm Happy* and *King Porter Stomp*, the former one of Henderson's $37.50 National Biscuit arrangements. These two selections, particularly the latter, which had been recorded by Henderson in 1932 in the arrangement he gave Goodman, set the tone for the Goodman band and outlined the idiom that was to be known as "swing."

The writing leaned to simplicity and clarity. Henderson scored for the sections as though they were a single improvising instrument, punctuating the rhythmic pulse with brief bursts from the brass or reeds. At first Goodman's band played them stiffly, but as his men relaxed into the arrangements, they began to achieve the ease and flow that gave them their excitement.

With his success as an arranger bringing him new fame, Henderson found himself accused—as he had been before, when arranged jazz was new—of turning jazz into a mechanical operation by planning everything in advance. Henderson denied this vigorously.

"To say that a swing arrangement is mechanical whereas a jazz solo is inspired is absurd," he said. "A swing arrangement can sound mechanical if it's wrongly interpreted by musicians who don't have the right feeling, but it's written straight from the heart and has the same feeling in the writing as a soloist has in a hot chorus. That's the way, for instance, my arrangement of *Sometimes I'm Happy* for Benny was written—I just sat down not knowing what I was going to write and wrote spontaneously what I was inspired to write. Maybe some arrangements sound mechanical because the writer studied too much and wrote out of a book, as it were—too much knowledge can hamper your style."

Henderson's new fame as an arranger turned him to band leading again. This time, instead of centering on the New York area, he went out to the Middle West, to the Grand Terrace in Chicago, where Earl Hines had been holding forth for eight years. There he organized his last great band, a band which included only two veterans of his earlier groups—Buster Bailey and bassist John Kirby—along with a new generation of Hendersonites: Roy Eldridge, Fernando Arbello, Chu Berry, Sid Catlett and later, Omer Simeon and Israel Crosby. Like his band of the early 'thirties, this one is quite inadequately represented on records. After making four fine sides for Vocalion—*Christopher Columbus, Blue Lou, Grand Terrace Swing* and *Stealin' Apples*—it ground out pop material for Victor and later for Vocalion once more.

The band made little impression on the public even though swing was then the thing. Henderson was still writing occasionally for Goodman, who was playing his arrangements, old and new, with the kind of precision and polish that appealed to the vast audience conjured up by Goodman's advent as the King of Swing. Henderson found himself in the awkward position of being popularly viewed as an able arranger who needed someone like Goodman to interpret his arrangements. Yet the qualities that had made the Henderson band great in its heyday were quite the opposite of those shown in Goodman's smooth-surfaced interpretations of Henderson's arrangements. Summing up Henderson's situation in 1939, Wilder Hobson astutely commented:

"Many currently popular bands . . . have a polish which Henderson seldom, if ever, had and for which I imagine he never tried. But his best combinations had a quality beside which a high polish seems a rather routine, if difficult, achievement. It might be called ensemble ease and spontaneity—listen to the records of *Fidgety Feet* or *New King Porter Stomp*. There was a sense of relaxation, lack of strain, reserve strength. This was perhaps largely a matter of individual talent. With a brass team such as Russell and Joe Smith, Ladnier, Green and Harrison, it would have been too bad to insist on precision. They might have delivered it, but the music would have lost the spirit of these men attacking with their natural enthusiasm."

In 1939, Henderson gave up his band and returned to Goodman as a full-time arranger. When Jess Stacy left the band in July, Henderson took over the piano chair and held it until the following January when Johnny Guarnieri joined the band. The best recorded examples of Henderson's pleasant but limited piano style come from this period: *Stealin' Apples* and *Henderson Stomp* with the full Goodman band (both arrangements originated in Henderson's bands), and *Rose Room* and *Soft Winds* with the small groups.

For months before he left Goodman, he had been having trouble with his sight and in July, 1940, he had an operation on his left eye.

The remaining twelve years of Henderson's life spun grimly downhill. During the war he had a band at the De Lisa in Chicago for fifteen months. In 1945 he went to the West Coast and wrote once more for Benny Goodman, whose band by this time had pretty well run its course. Some of these latter-day Henderson arrangements were recorded by Goodman for Capitol: *Sweet and Lovely, Slow Boat to China* and *Back in Your Own Backyard.* In 1948, Henderson reached even further back into his past: He went on the road as accompanist to Ethel Waters. That job wound up when Miss Waters went into the Broadway production of "The Member of the Wedding."

By then Henderson's blood pressure was up to 240. He was thin, sick, depressed. He took nine months off, away from music, in seclusion, saying, "I'd rather relax and live a little longer."

When he came out of his brief period of retirement, he wrote the score, with J. C. Johnson, for "The Jazz Train," a production which played at Bop City, New York, for six weeks to good reviews and no business. Then he took a sextet into Café Society in Greenwich Village, a sextet which included three one-time Henderson men —Dick Vance, trumpet; Eddie Barefield, clarinet, Lucky Thompson, tenor saxophone—along with the old Lunceford drummer, Jimmy Crawford, and John Brown, bass. He was leading this group on December 20, 1950, when he suffered a stroke from which he never fully recovered. For the two years of life that were left to him, he was an invalid. He died December 29, 1952, eleven days after his fifty-fourth birthday.

In those fifty-four years, Henderson helped to bring big-band jazz into being, saw his arrangements rouse an interest in jazz among the broadest audience the music had ever had and lived to see arranged big-band jazz go down under the onus of its own pretentious weight. Although he was not a performer of any special distinction, although his casual, easygoing attitude prevented him from being an effective leader, and although his arrangements clung tenaciously to a format which had already been worked out by other members of his band, Henderson holds a remarkable place in jazz as a catalyst, as the attracting force that brought together the fantastic pool of talent which made up the Henderson band in the middle and late 'twenties, and as the creator of that bridge between popular dance music and jazz which made possible the Swing Era in the middle and late 'thirties. Despite the fuzziness that mists a definition of his particular talents, he must be counted as a major figure in jazz because, without him, at least a decade and a half of jazz history could not have happened.

SELECTED DISCOGRAPHY—FLETCHER HENDERSON

FLETCHER HENDERSON'S BAND:

The Birth of Big Band Jazz, Riverside RLP 1055

Fletcher Henderson and His Connie's Inn Orchestra, "X" LVA 3013

Harlem Jazz, 1930 (two selections), Brunswick BL 58024

Boyd Raeburn-Fletcher Henderson (four selections), Allegro 4028

Gems of Jazz, Vol. 4 (four selections), Decca DL 5384

Fletcher Henderson Memorial Album, Decca DL 6025

FLETCHER HENDERSON ACCOMPANIMENTS:

The Bessie Smith Story, Vol. 3, Columbia ML 4809

Louis Armstrong Plays the Blues, Riverside RLP 1001

FLETCHER HENDERSON ARRANGEMENTS:

Benny Goodman Presents Fletcher Henderson Arrangements, Columbia
CL 524.

William
"Count" Basie

* * * *

By Nat Shapiro

A quite funny phonograph record was released a few years ago on which a plausibly obtuse disc jockey carried on a somewhat harried interview with a purported jazz musician. Justice triumphed when in the course of their talk, the interviewer asked the jazzman what his music had to do with Art. "Art?" replied the puzzled musician. "Well, man, like he blows the most, you know?"

Except when directed to a vocal handful of "serious" modernists, a question with the word "Art" in it put to a jazz musician is likely to elicit any one of the following responses: (1) a glassy stare, (2) patronizing double talk, (3) an incredulous "Huh?", or (4) an embarrassed "Man, I don't know anything about that stuff!"

Contrary to almost all of the well-intentioned nonsense disseminated about musicians in romantic novels of the *Young Man With a Horn* genre, on television, and in the movies, the percentage of tortured souls with messages in the world of jazz is small indeed. To most of the musicians of the "old school," jazz was and is a way of life as well as a skill or craft that one masters and takes pride in mastering. But most important of all, it is a means of earning a livelihood; the conscious desire to communicate ideas and emotions, if it exists at all, is of little consequence.

Since jazz musicians are notoriously inarticulate verbally, a good deal of analytical and creative writing about jazz during the past three decades has been speculative, fanciful, romantic and wrong. It has been especially wrong when it has concerned itself with problems of intent and motivation on the part of the practitioners of the idiom.

Throughout the years, for the Negro especially, music has been one of the few professions in which some degree of freedom, prestige, dignity and—most vital—decent compensation has been possible. Before the revolution at Minton's, the music, with all its limitations,

232

was blessed with an absence of self-consciousness, pretension and verbosity.

None of the foregoing blights apply in the least to either Bill Basie the man, or the Count Basie band.

To those who know him, the idea of Basie theorizing about his music is absurd. Comfortably ensconced in his recently acquired and tastefully appointed saloon at One Hundred and Thirty-second Street and Seventh Avenue in New York's Harlem, he will talk. He will talk about baseball, prize fighting, food, Western movies on television, "the good old days," and his elaborate plans for an electric railroad installed in the basement of his Long Island home. He will talk about the many things that men enjoy talking about in saloons, living rooms and on street corners everywhere. But about the "meaning" of music? Never!

William Basie, who has lived his life and made his music with sincerity, dignity and a seemingly effortless grace, was born, an only child, in Red Bank, New Jersey, on August 21, 1904. His "formal" musical training was taken care of first by his mother and then by "a wonderful German lady named Holloway," who charged twenty-five cents for her piano lessons. Actually young Willie Basie had his heart set on being a drummer, but became disenchanted very early in his career after some friendly competition with a boyhood friend, named Sonny Greer.

Along with Greer and hundreds of other young musicians from all parts of the country, Basie gravitated to Harlem in the early 'twenties. While the most fertile period of New York jazz was still to come, Harlem, in the years of Basie's professional apprenticeship, was developing a feeling and tradition of its own. Pianists ruled the roost, and such masters of ragtime as James P. Johnson, Lucky Roberts and Willie "The Lion" Smith were setting an example for dozens of young men, among them Fletcher Henderson, Duke Ellington, Fats Waller and Basie.

The training grounds for young pianists were the scores of small cabarets, theatres, saloons, and dance halls that were springing up in a community teeming with thousands of post-World War I refugees from the South. Racial barriers in the entertainment business were beginning to break down, and a few musicians were beginning to boast of real prosperity. Of vital import were the facts that there seemed to be work for anybody with real talent, and there was always someplace to go to talk and drink and play.

According to Basie, the most important direct influence on his

piano style was Thomas "Fats" Waller, whom he first heard playing
the pipe organ in the pit of the Lincoln Theatre on One Hundred
and Thirty-fifth Street. Fascinated by the instrument as well as the
man playing it, Basie became a daily visitor, invariably sitting as close
to Waller as possible, watching the organist's magic fingers and foot-
work. Waller noticed Basie one day, invited him into the pit, and
soon afterwards permitted his new disciple to sit alongside him at
the console.

One of the principle sources of revenue in those days was vaudeville, and for the Negro entertainer and musician there was the famed
T.O.B.A., the Negro equivalent of the Keith circuit. Traveling the
T.O.B.A. "wheel" meant playing everything from big houses in Chicago, St. Louis, Memphis and New Orleans to store-front and tent
theatres in the most rural areas of the Deep South.

One of Basie's earliest jobs was with an act called *Kattie Crippin and Her Kids*. Another was with a show called *Hippity Hop*. He
also played in June Clark's band in a Fourteenth Street dance hall
and accompanied such blues singers as Clara Smith and Maggie
Jones.

The next, or "Horace Greeley" phase of Basie's career was his
participation in a road show presided over by one Gonzel White—
an act that spent a good deal of its time touring the South and Southwest and eventually, in true vaudeville tradition, found itself stranded
in Kansas City.

Jimmy Rushing, who before achieving wide recognition as a
Basie vocalist had been an itinerant blues singer, monologist and
pianist, remembers his first meeting with Basie in Tulsa, Oklahoma.
"I was with Walter Pages's Blue Devils," he recalls, "and Basie was
still in the Gonzel White show, playing piano in the four-piece band
and even acting the part of a villain in one of the comedy skits.

"It was on a Saturday afternoon and both bands were 'bally-
hooin' ' from horse-drawn wagons. The Blue Devils were trying to
entice customers to the Southern Barbeque, an open-air beer garden,
(they served great ribs) and Basie's band was advertising the White
show. We were playing a piece called *Blue Devil Blues* and up comes
Basie and sits himself down at the piano. Man, but he played!"

Projecting forward to Basie's eventual membership in the Blue
Devils, a group that Basie has called "the happiest band I've ever
been in," Rushing remembers many instances when he and Basie
would visit the jazz haunts in Southwestern cities, challenging all
comers to piano contests. "If Basie decided to go somewhere and

break up the place, he'd just sit down and play. Then, watch out! Nobody could do anything after that."

The Blue Devils broke up in the early nineteen thirties and several of its members—Page, Rushing and Basie included—joined Bennie Moten, a well-established Midwestern band leader. Basie insists that he played "third piano" with Moten. "Bennie was the big man at the keys," he says, "and his brother, Buster, played piano-accordion."

In 1935, after Bennie Moten's death, his brother Buster took over as leader for about six months, and shortly thereafter, the band broke up, Basie returning to Kansas City, a place he fondly and realistically remembers as "a cracker town, but a happy town."

A few months later Basie, along with several other former members of the Moten band, settled into the Reno Club which was described by John Hammond in *Down Beat* as follows: "The Reno Club was a place that had nickel hot dogs and hamburgers, nickel beer, and whiskey for 15 cents. It also had a floor show, complete with chorus line and three acts. The 'scale' for the musicians was $15 a week, and the hours were from eight 'til four, except on Saturday, when it was 12 solid hours from eight to eight. It was a seven-day week, naturally, and nobody got rich, least of all the club owner."

Hammond, the first recording executive who not only took jazz seriously, but did something about it, was and is one of the most perceptive talent scouts the idiom has ever known. In December, 1935, Hammond heard the Basie band for the first time on his car radio. It was, curiously enough, broadcasting from the far-from-chic Reno over W9XBY, an experimental radio station in Kansas City. Hammond began writing about this exciting nine-piece combo in the pages of *Down Beat* and the *Melody Maker*, and six months later persuaded one of the large booking agencies to take on the band. Four more men were added and, in October, 1936, the Count Basie band as we know it was on its way.

On the night before leaving Kansas City, with all of twelve written arrangements in his book, Basie played "against" Duke Ellington at a dance. Looking back at that "first time out," Jimmy Rushing insists that rough as the band was, the men were convinced that they outswung Duke that night. "We were anxious to play against all the big-name bands—even without arrangements we knew we could rely on the blues and swing as well as any of 'em."

Although the band wasn't an immediate success on its first two dates, it did begin recording almost immediately—with a contract that called for Basie to receive all of $750 for twenty-four sides with no royalties and tied him up exclusively for three years.

"It was," according to Hammond, "probably the most expensive blunder in Basie's history . . . typical of some of the underscale deals which record companies imposed on unsophisticated Negro and 'country' artists." When Basie finally reached New York, Hammond was able to achieve some modifications in the contract, bringing payments up to minimum union scale. But Basie has never received one cent of royalties for such tremendous popular hits as *One O'Clock Jump, Swingin' the Blues* and *Jumpin' at the Woodside*.

The news about the Kansas City band spread and then, as now, musicians were the first to carry the word. The dry, airy sound of Lester Young's tenor saxophone was a revelation and, as set against the relentless repetition of riffs laid down by the brass section, became one of the most inspirational new experiences in jazz. But more than Young or Buck Clayton or even Basie himself, it was the band—this happy, highly integrated organization with a unified feeling and uncompromising dedication to the beat that marked it as something quite new and extraordinary on the musical scene.

A review in the February, 1938, issue of *Metronome* was indicative of the degree of Basie's acceptance.

"Count Basie did it! For years, nobody was able to lick Chick Webb and his Chicks within the walls of his own Savoy Ballroom, but on January 16, notables such as Duke, Norvo, Bailey, Duchin, Krupa and Goodman . . . heard the Count gain a decision over the famed Chick. . . . (It was a matter of) solid swing to the heart triumphing over sensational blows to the head."

That was more than two decades ago, and, apart from a short period in 1950 when the band business was at a particularly low ebb and Basie relinquished the big band for a small combo, this has been, as Barry Ulanov so definitively put it, "a band that sums up, that shows you how it was done and how it is played, what was good and what is still good in the jazz of 20 years ago and of today."

Bill Basie's keyboard style is one of the happiest and most readily identifiable sounds in jazz. To the casual listener, it is no more than a formless and spontaneous series of interjections, commas, hyphens, underlines, quotation marks and interrogation and exclamation points.

Actually, Basie's piano is the energizing source of his band's power, vitality and astonishing drive. "He contributes the missing things," says Freddie Green. "Count is just about the best pianist I know for pushing a band and for 'comping' soloists. I mean the way he makes different preparations for each soloist and the way, at the end of one of his solos, he prepares an entrance for the next man. He leaves the way open."

With characteristic modesty, Basie disclaims any special pianistic prowess. "I'm a pace-setter," he admits, "but, really, I'm only part of the rhythm section. I figure that my job is to sort of feed the soloists and the band."

Basie does his "job" extraordinarily well. As a supplier of musical nourishment for his fifteen healthy dependents, he is a peerless provider. He seems instinctively to be able to strike the precise chord, indeed the one note, necessary to thrust the soloist, or even the whole band forward. His dry, rugged and intensely rhythmic punctuation can be as effective as a blinding stab of brass or a sensuous slur by the reed section. It can increase the tension or offer release. It can spur the sections or soloists on to climax after climax, and it can simply and unerringly bridge a progression from one chorus to the next.

But even more, the Basie piano has a quality that is as revealing as it is engaging and functional. More than anything else, Basie's keyboard presence and sound is a reflection of the whole man. The modesty and wit are there. So is the rugged virility, the nonchalance, the assurance and—so important—the sense of joyous participation. A charming illustration of the last quality can be found in Basie's response to an interviewer's inevitable query about the de-emphasis of his left hand. "You know," he said, "it's because I want the bass to be heard. I've always enjoyed the bass. We talk back and forth."

Watch Basie at a dance or a concert or a night club. It would be difficult to imagine this man "performing" in the accepted tradition of the successful band leader. A Basie performance has none of the fakery and flummery that is so often proffered in the name of showmanship. With benign dignity, Basie sits at the keyboard and, as Joe Newman puts it, "feels the crowd, calls the tune, and then sets the mood and pattern for the band. He *knows* and puts us all into just the right groove."

Despite his casualness, Basie knows what is happening "out front" all the time and paces his performances accordingly. A nod, a lifted eyebrow, and a signal chord on the piano convey his directions to the band. Riffs are dictated, soloists encouraged, and coloration delineated with subtle sureness.

Basie's modesty is one of his most remarkable personal characteristics, and for the past few years, it has become increasingly difficult to persuade him to play very much solo piano. "The kids don't want my kind of piano any more," he says. "A few old-timers maybe, but the kids who can listen to Phineas Newborn, Oscar Peterson, and Erroll Garner don't want to hear the old-fashioned kind of stuff I play."

Basie's piano, as distinctive as it is, cannot be separated from the living pulse that is the rhythm section of his band. On its own, his playing creates the mood and then sustains and heightens it. But with the guitar, bass and drums, it becomes an integral part of a near-perfect power unit that drives and motivates the entire band. In a sense, one can say that the Basie band was built around the rhythm section, a section with a beat that probably did more than any other factor to influence, rhythmically, both big- and small-band jazz in the past three decades.

Jo Jones describes the origin of that special beat thus:

"Bennie Moten's band played a two-beat rhythm such as one-and-three. Walter Page's band played a two-and-four. It wasn't that they would stop to accent that beat, it was sort of like a bouncing ball, and when those rhythms met in the Basie band there was an even flow—one, two, three, four—like a bouncing ball."

The Basie rhythm section of the late nineteen thirties and the early nineteen forties, made up of Basie, Page, Green and Jones, was the most brilliant unit of its kind in the history of jazz. These four superb musicians together were able to produce a rhythmic flow that was at once solid and supple, disciplined and yet unconfined.

Much of the rocklike stability of the Basie rhythm section can be attributed to Freddie Green, who has been with the band since 1936, when John Hammond found him working for eleven dollars a week in a Greenwich Village cabaret. Basie calls Green his "tieup" man. "Not only because he's very steady," says the Count, "but because he actually holds the band together." Green himself, who almost never takes a solo, once described his function as follows: "A performance has what I call a rhythm wave, and the rhythm guitar can help to keep that wave smooth and accurate. I have to concentrate on the beat, listening for how smooth it is. If the band is moving smoothly, then I can play whatever comes to mind, but that doesn't happen too often."

Arranger Quincy Jones sums him up this way: "That man is sort of a spirit. He doesn't talk loud and he doesn't play loud. But man! You sure know he's there. The brass and reeds can be up there shouting away, but there's Freddie, coming right through it all, steady as a rock and clear as a bell. He's something special. What he represents is the only one of its kind in existence."

There is evidence to support the often-made claim that Walter Page was the foundation of the Basie rhythm section. As leader of the Blue Devils, Page, known as "Big One," was one of the first of the rhythm tuba players to switch to the string bass. Jo Jones has called him his musical father: ". . . without him I wouldn't have known how to play drums." Testimony to Jones's debt to Page also comes from Mary Lou Williams, a pianist nurtured in musically fertile Kansas City. "Page," she said, "showed Joe what to do and when to do it, and it was really something to dig those two great musicians. I have caught Basie's orchestra at times when there was no one on the stage except Page and the horns, and, believe me, 'Big One' swung that band on his bass without much effort."

As for Jo Jones, described by a fellow drummer as "the man who plays like the wind," there are a great many musicians and critics who seriously consider him the greatest rhythm percussionist that jazz has known. John Hammond summed him up as follows: "He combines an incredible technique with lightness, humor and imagination. . . . Great drummers like Chick Webb, Gene Krupa, and even Sid Catlett had provided the rhythm section and the entire band with a driving power and beat. Jo relaxed the drive of the right foot, using it for just the necessary accents, reminding the listener of the beat rather than insisting on it. . . . He added a variety of timbres, establishing the jazz battery of drums as a musical instrument of great beauty. . . . Jones and Basie, with the inspired collaboration of Freddie Green on guitar and Walter Page on bass, brought richness of sound and subtlety to jazz rhythm, providing at the same time an unequalled lift and support for the soloists."

If a band is only as good as the musicians in it, then a listing of some of the men who have worked with Count Basie ought to be strong proof of how wonderful the Basie organization has been throughout the quarter of a century that it has been making music.

Basie once admitted that he has always "been queer for tenor men. The band's always been built from the rhythm section to the tenors, and then on to the rest." A brief tour through the Basie discography reveals the astonishing fact that Basie's predilection for tenor men has resulted in his having employed, at one time or another, just about every good saxophonist in jazz. The following list, by no means complete, reads like a *Who's Who* on tenors: Lester Young, Herschel Evans, Chu Berry, Buddy Tate, Don Byas, Illinois Jacquet, Paul Gonsalves, Paul Quinichette, Lucky Thompson, Wardell Gray, Ben Webster, George Auld, and his present first-rate men, Frank Foster and Frank Wess. Incidentally, even the "daddy of 'em all," Coleman Hawkins, recorded with Basie in the early nineteen forties.

While favoring tenors, Basie didn't neglect the other reeds, and Jack Washington, Earl Warren, Tab Smith, Ernie Wilkins and Marshall Royal have worked with him on alto. Although Lester Young occasionally doubled on clarinet in the early days, and Buddy De Franco worked with Basie's small group in the early 'fifties, Basie has never really found a place for the clarinet in the band. And, while Frank Wess has worked out some fanciful settings for his flute in the current Basie book, it has not really become part of, or had any basic effect on, the band's over-all sound.

Basie brass has almost always been a source of fabulous musical strength. Both as a section and as a collection of superb soloists, it has always managed to produce some of the richest and most exciting moments in big-band jazz. Discussing what he expects from his brass section, Basie explains, "I want those four trumpets and three trombones to bite with real guts. But I want that bite to be as tasty and subtle as if it were the three brass I used in Kansas City. . . . say that the minute the brass gets out of hand and blares and screeches instead of making every note *mean something,* there'll be some changes made."

Further discussing the role of both his brass and reeds, Basie told a critic a few years ago, "I want those solid ensembles and want that brick wall behind the solos. There's nothing like those shout licks. But they gotta be able to play those shout licks softly too."

Through the years, the list of men charged with making notes mean something as well as shout in the Basie brass section also reads like a roster of jazz immortals. Among Basie's trumpet players have been Oran "Hot Lips" Page, Buck Clayton, Harry Edison, Shad Collins, Emmett Berry, Al Killian, Joe Wilder, Clark Terry

Joe Newman and Thad Jones. Some of the trombonists were Dickie
Wells, Ed Durham, Benny Morton, Vic Dickinson, Don Minor, J. J.
Johnson, Ed Cuffie and, most recently, Henry Coker and Benny
Powell.

For the past few years there have been remarkably few changes
of personnel in the Basie band—testimony to its excellent morale.
Almost without exception, Basie's musicians are loyal and devoted
to the Count, and none of the prevailing ills of the band business
—among them, drug addiction, alcoholism, gambling, lateness and
jealousy—have affected the organization.

"I usually look for a type of guy," says Basie, "for a certain
kind of character in a man. I think it's important to have a likeable
guy, a happy sort of guy as well as one who is also a nice musician.
Those things put together make a happy band. . . . And I like to
keep adding things to the book all the time. It inspires the men, I
think, to have new arrangements to work out."

The Basie library which still contains such durables as *One
O'Clock Jump, Jumpin' at the Woodside* and *Every Tub* is constantly being replenished by arrangers of such stature as Neal Hefti,
Quincy Jones, Ernie Wilkins, Nat Pierce, Sy Oliver, Johnny Mandel and Frank Wess.

The fact that many of the instrumentalists and arrangers associated with the current Basie band live, think, write and play in the
modern idiom doesn't in any way detract from a basic (or Basie)
concept of what a jazz orchestra should sound like. Basie's insistence
on the strong steady beat doesn't seem to deter or compromise either
the soloist or the arranger. On the contrary, even the most avant-
garde members of the organization are consistantly inspired and
stimulated by the propulsive drive of the rhythm section. Indeed, at
this moment, Basie's is the only band of stature that manages to
achieve the rhythmic impact of main-stream jazz along with contemporary conceptions of both playing and arranging.

A recently published evaluation of the Basie band pointed out,
with a note of patronizing regret, that although here "is an almost
definitive example of the exuberance available in big-band jazz,"
it is a limited exuberance "dwelling too longingly and caressingly
on the 'balling' side of life."

But what on earth, we incredulously demand, are you talking
about? Is this just another tiresome example of a critic taking an
artist to task for not reflecting the *critic's* aesthetic outlook? This is

the band of Bill Basie of Red Bank, New Jersey; Harlem and Kansas City. This is Basie, the disciple of "Fats" Waller; Basie the healthy warm and happy purveyor of a music that has been consistently exciting and *profoundly* joyous.

Basie is no pretentious seeker of sounds, no hostile introvert or dabbler in form or formlessness. He doesn't submerge a personal or social bitterness in private musical messages. But neither is Basie the court jester, the Uncle Tom, or the user of funny hats. He is a mature and exceptionally talented man, who knows what he is, what his limitations are and what he wants to say. He is a reasonably happy man, who has had the talent, craftsmanship and doggedness necessary to communicate his message effectively to millions of people throughout the world for more than twenty years. If his principal preoccupation has been a "longing and caressing" musical exploration of "the 'balling' side of life" and its communication, so much the better for all of us.

It is hard to imagine a more valid *raison d'etre*.

SELECTED DISCOGRAPHY—COUNT BASIE

Count Basie, Brunswick 54012

Count Basie & his Orchestra, Decca 8049

Basie's Back in Town, Epic LN 3169

Blues by Basie, Columbia CL 901

Count Basie Classics, Columbia CL 754

Lester Leaps In, Epic LG 3107

The Swinging Count, Clef 706

Lester Young

* * * *

By Nat Hentoff

Billie Holiday awarded Lester Young his nickname. "When it came to a name for Lester," she said in one of the few mellow pauses in her autobiography, "I always felt he was the greatest, so his name had to be the greatest. In this country kings or counts or dukes don't amount to nothing. The greatest man around then was Franklin D. Roosevelt and he was the President. So I started calling him the President. It got shortened to Prez."

And Prez (or Pres) it has remained. In one sense, Pres's term —among musicians—is not likely ever to run out. It is not that he has or ever had unanimous recognition from his peers as the nonpareil jazz tenor. There are those who prefer Coleman Hawkins; there are younger men who look to Sonny Rollins; and several other tenors have had their determined bands of constituents.

Yet Lester Willis Young has continued to be Pres to nearly all in so far as he has personified consummate relaxation in the act of creative improvisation. The relaxation may sometimes have been more apparent than real; some feel that in recent years it has occasionally approached resignation.

But the memory and occasional present power of Pres invariably evokes a particular musical effect—pulsating ease. He has several corollary achievements of major importance in the evolution of jazz; and these, of course, contribute to his stature. A large part of the essence of Pres, however, is the flowing quality of his phrasing, his rhythmic development, and even his tone. In the process of sustaining this uniquely muscular ease of playing, Lester, as French composer-critic André Hodeir has noted, was also greatly if perhaps unwittingly responsible for "a new conception of jazz."

Off the stand, without a horn to speak through, the ease of Pres has frequently turned into a fiercely shy, unpredictable independence. An independence of movement, of speech, of dress. An

243

independence that for many years was stubbornly self-destructive.

A booking-agency executive has said bitterly of Pres: "He's an aloof goof. He's in a world all by himself. He's oblivious to people. I don't think he regards people as anything. I'd talk to him and all he'd say was 'Bells!' or 'Ding! Dong!' I finally decided I'd go to Bellevue if I wanted to talk to crazy people. So he's a talent! He's a nut!"

John Lewis, who was Lester's pianist for several months, disagrees: "Lester is an extremely gentle, kind, considerate person. He's always concerned about the underdog. He always wants to help somebody. It is true that he doesn't like unpleasantness and that he'll avoid it if he can, but isn't that true of most of us?

"The basic mark of Lester," Lewis added, "is that he's always young; he stays young in his playing and in his person. Some people are always crying for love and kindness; but Lester doesn't cry. The way he seems to see *being* is: 'Here we are. Let's have a nice time.' "

Lester, it is true, does not *cry* for love and kindness. But he has searched for them for a long time while trying to look as if he weren't looking. And he spent many of his years in a forest of petrified emotions, petrified into surface numbness by gin and pot, behind a mask that was only removed before those he trusted. And he trusted very few.

Where and how the first crack in his sense of security began to widen is difficult to trace. But in going back to his beginnings and to his growth as a jazzman, there is illumination to be found concerning the growth of a significant part of jazz itself. And while Lester, more than most of us, will probably always be seen quite differently by quite different people, a unified perspective of his life in music may help outline him somewhat more clearly as a man, as an intently casual individualist for whom the self-expression of jazz has been a life-sustainer.

Lester Willis Young was born in Woodville, Mississippi, August 27, 1909. The family moved to New Orleans and remained there until Lester was ten.

Lester's father, William H. (Billy) Young, was once described succinctly by Pres in an interview with Leonard Feather for the British *Melody Maker:*

"I really appreciated what my father did for me. He'd been a blacksmith, but he studied at Tuskeegee and he knew so much. He tried to teach me *everything*. He played violin, and was a teacher with choirs. He could play all the instruments and liked trumpet best. He was a carnival musician and kept up traveling with carnival minstrel shows and teaching music until he died, in the 'forties."

While the family was in New Orleans, Billy Young entered the music life of the city, and Henry "Red" Allen, the New Orleans trumpet player, remembers that his father was once hired by the senior Young for a date.

Lester still has memories of the city. "I liked to hear the music in New Orleans. I remember there were trucks advertising dances and I'd follow them all around."

At ten, Lester joined his brother Lee and his sister Irma as all three went to live with their father who had left New Orleans. "He took us to Minneapolis where we went to school. During the carnival season, we all traveled with the minstrel show, through Kansas, Nebraska, South Dakota, all through there."

He began at ten as a combination drummer and handbill-carrier. "I played drums until I was about thirteen, but quit them because it was too much trouble to carry the traps and I got tired, too, of packing them up. I'd take a look at the girls after the show, and before I'd get the drums packed, they'd all be gone.

"So I switched to alto. Frankie Trumbauer and Jimmy Dorsey were battling for honors in those days, and I finally found out that I liked Frankie Trumbauer. Trumbauer was my idol. When I had just started to play, I used to buy all his records. I imagine I can still play all those solos off the record. He played the C-melody saxophone. I tried to get the sound of a C melody on a tenor. That's why I don't sound like other people. Trumbauer always told a little story. And I liked the way he slurred the notes. He'd play the melody first and then after that, he'd play around the melody. I did like Bud Freeman very much. Nobody played like him. That's what knocked me out."

Lester has been entirely self-taught except for basic lessons from his father. "He wrote out the scales for me when he got me an alto, but I'd get to listening to a lot of music, and I'd goof off and play everything but the scales. My sister was a better reader than I was. She played saxophone, too, and so did my brother Lee. I always played by ear. Whatever she would play, I would play a second or third part to. One day my father spied me. He had my sister play her part alone and then he had me play my part alone. I couldn't play a note. He put me out of the band and wouldn't let me back in until I could read. That hurt me real bad, so I practiced every day and was back in the band in about six months. I was about thirteen. [Editor's note: he has also said another time he was sixteen when he was temporarily expelled from the family band.] Pretty soon I could cut everybody and I was teaching other people to read."

As for his other schooling, "I got to the third or fourth grade at school," he told Feather, "but I've been earning my own living since I was five—shining shoes, selling papers. And I was a good kid. I would *never* steal. Mother was a seamstress and a school-teacher."

Another view of Lester's father comes from Ben Webster, who also became an important jazz tenor. Webster was playing piano in Amarillo in the late 'twenties "when Lester Young's father came to town along with Lee Young to pick up a piano player. I took the opportunity to ask Lester's father if he needed a sax player. He said he did, and I told him I didn't have an instrument. He laughed and said he'd find an instrument for me. Then I told him I couldn't read. He really fell out laughing then, but told me he'd teach me. So I went to Albuquerque with the Youngs, and for three months, Lester's father taught me how to read. He was a very good musician. I remember Pres used to sit and practice with me every day, and he'd try to help as much as he could."

For Lester, the carnival seasons continued. "I was raised up in a carnival, a week in each town. I liked it, but in the wintertimes my father wanted to go down South. I didn't like the idea and I'd run away." When he was eighteen, Lester broke with his father. "We were in Salina Kansas," he later told Pat Harris of *Down Beat,* "and he had a string of dates down through Texas and the South. I told him how it would be down there, and that we could have some fine jobs back through Nebraska, Kansas and Iowa, but he didn't have eyes for that. He was set to go.

"I ran away and went to a cop who asked me whether I could take care of myself. I had nothing but the clothes on my back. But this fellow Art Bronson from Salina, Kansas, who had a band called the Bostonians, accommodated me. The only horn he could get me was a baritone, so I joined the Bostonians; and later on, when the tenor man goofed off, they switched me."

The story became amplified years later when Lester explained: "The way I switched to tenor with the Bostonians was the tenor player kept grandstanding all the time. So I told the leader, if you buy a tenor for me, I'll play it. You see, the regular tenor was a boy from a well-to-do family. He didn't have to play. I remember we'd go by his voice sometimes and beg him to play. I got sick of it."

A time with King Oliver followed. The New Orleans giant was in decline in popularity from the greatness he had achieved at home and in Chicago in the early 'twenties. "He had a very nice band, and I worked regularly with him for one or two years around Kansas and Missouri mostly. He had three brass, three reeds and four rhythm. He was playing well. He was old then and didn't play all night, but his tone was full when he played. He was the star of the show and played one or two songs each set. The blues? He could play some nice blues. He was a very nice fellow, a gay old fellow. He was crazy about all the boys, and it wasn't a drag playing for him at all."

At this point, the exact pattern of Lester's subsequent band alliances is as hazy as are the memories of the principals of the story, some seven of whom were interviewed in this connection. Lester remembers spending some time around Oklahoma City where, incidentally, he met Charlie Christian. "We used to go out in the alley and jam." He then apparently went back to Minneapolis and worked around there for a while. It was in Minneapolis that Lester joined Walter Page's Blue Devils. Page concurs that he picked Lester up in Minneapolis, but feels it was before Lester played with Oliver.

Around 1930–31, Page remembers, he went to a "joint" in Minneapolis where he heard a group that wasn't very good except for the tenor. He talked to Lester, and Lester left with him that night, staying about ten or eleven months. (The reference books support Lester's chronology, but John Hammond recalls hearing Lester with Oliver around 1933, presumably after his stay with the Blue Devils.)

"Those were tough times," Lester once told Leonard Feather. "The Blue Devils band was getting bruised. I mean really bruised, playing to audiences of three people. One time all our instruments were impounded in West Virginia, I think it was, and they took us right to the railroad track and told us to get out of town.

"There we were sitting around with these hobos, and they showed us how to grab the train. We made it—with bruises. We got to Cincinnati, no loot, no horns, all raggedy and dirty, and we were trying to make it to St. Louis or Kansas City.

"I found a man who had an alto and he loaned it out for gigs, so I managed to play a couple of dates. Finally we all had a meeting—

Walter and the boys—and we decided it was 'every tub,' every man
for himself.

"Well, I got to Kansas City, got hold of a tenor, borrowed
some clothes from Herschel Evans—he was playing with Bennie
Moten. Moten was stranded, too, and all the men put him down;
Count Basie had been playing with him but they'd been squab-
bling, so Count cut out and took over most of the band while Benny
Moten and George Lee formed another group and I went with
them."

Here the story becomes even more tangled in the multiple
telling. Jo Jones relates a story which neither Lester Young nor
Walter Page remembers of one night when Lester was with the
Moten band and tenor Herschel Evans was with Basie. Lester was
growing bored, Jones recalls, with having to play sedately in Moten's band at the Harlem club with too little chance to solo, while
Evans preferred the added money that being with Moten would
bring. So, the story goes, they switched jobs. Later, said Jo, Lester
went back to Minneapolis when times became tough.

Lester and Basie remember differently. Both agree that Lester
first joined Basie as a result of a telegram Pres sent from Minneapolis. "I had heard of him before," Basie recalls, "but he didn't
play with me until that wire. It was a strange and convincing wire."

Count Basie had a band at the Reno Club in Kansas City
that broadcast regularly. "I was working at the Cotton Club in
Minneapolis," says Lester, "and I used to hear the Basie broadcasts when I was off from work. Everything was fine with the band
but the tenor player. I couldn't stand him. I sent Basie a telegram
and asked him if he could use a tenor player. He'd heard me before.
We used to go back and forth between Minneapolis and Kansas
City. So I joined Basie. It was very nice. Just like I thought it
would be."

Some time before he joined Basie, an incident occurred in
Kansas City that had a sequel. While working with Bennie Moten
and George Lee, Lester had had his first chance to hear the Fletcher
Henderson band which was traveling through town.

"That was the time I first heard Coleman Hawkins. I'd always
heard so much about Hawk—he was from St. Joseph, Missouri—
and while I was working at the Paseo Club, Fletcher Henderson was
in town. I ran over to dig him between sets; I hadn't any loot so I
stayed outside listening. Herschel was out there, too.

"Then one night Fletcher said his tenor man hadn't showed up, and wanted to know if there was someone around that could blow. I went in, read the book—clarinet part and all—blew Hawk's horns, then ran back to my own job at the Paseo."

In 1934, after Lester had joined Basie, the Basie band was in Little Rock when Lester received an offer of more money from Fletcher Henderson if he would join the Henderson band. Coleman Hawkins, the dominant tenor stylist of the time, had left Henderson to go to Europe. Lester went to New York, and auditioned for Henderson at the Cotton Club.

John Hammond was there. "I thought he was the greatest tenor I'd heard in my life. He was so different. There was a terrific scene. The guys in the band all wanted Chu Berry to replace Hawkins because Chu had a sound like Hawkins. They complained that Lester's tenor sound was 'like an alto.' Buster Bailey, Russell Procope and John Kirby outshouted me that day," says Hammond.

It is Hammond's recollection that Lester soon went back to Kansas City, but Lester and Mrs. Leora Henderson, Fletcher's widow, state that Lester was with the Henderson band for from six to eight months. It was a painful period for him.

"The whole band was buzzing on me," Lester remembers grimly, "because I had taken Hawk's place. I didn't have the same kind of sound he had. I was rooming at the Hendersons' house, and Leora Henderson would wake me early in the morning and play Hawkins's records for me so I could play like he did. I wanted to play my own way, but I just listened. I didn't want to hurt her feelings.

"Finally I asked Fletcher to give me a letter of release saying that he hadn't fired me, and that was it. I went back to Kansas City. I had in mind what I wanted to play, and I was going to play that way. That's the only time that ever happened, someone telling me to play differently from the way I wanted to."

Back in Kansas City, Lester worked with Andy Kirk for about six months ("He was wonderful to work for.") and then returned to Basie. One night, Lester remembers, Basie asked him if he'd mind if Herschel Evans were to rejoin the band. Lester said he didn't, and from then on there were two tenors with Basie, which may have been the start of the two-tenor "battle" that was later to become a prevalent phenomenon in big jazz bands.

Lester first began to attain a significant reputation with Basie when the band moved on to Chicago and farther east and Lester began to make records. Several critics and musicians feel, in fact, that Lester did a key percentage of his most creative and influential (in retrospect) work while with Basie. But there came a time when "Basie was like school. I used to fall asleep in school because I had my lesson, and there was nothing else to do. The teacher would be teaching those who hadn't studied at home, but I had, so I'd go to sleep. Then the teacher would go home and tell my mother. So I put that down.

"In Basie's band," Lester continued, "there always would be someone who didn't know his part. Seems to me that if a musician can't read, he should say so, and then you help him. Or you give him his part before. But Basie wouldn't. I used to talk to him about it, but he had no eyes for it. You had to sit there and play it over and over and over again. Just sit in that chair. . . ."

He remained with Basie until 1940, quit because a record session had been called for Friday the thirteenth, headed his own combo the next year, had a sextet with his drummer brother, Lee, in 1942, and rejoined Basie in 1943 until he was inducted into the army.

Lester wanted to play freely, and never quite wholly enjoyed his big-band experiences. He will never return to a big band. "You don't get a chance to play. You walk to the mike for your eight bars or sixteen bars and then you sit down. You're just sitting there and reading music. There are no kicks for me that way."

While in Kansas City, Lester had experienced his formative years and they may also have contained many of his most enjoyable hours musically. There was little money to be made then in music in Kansas City. In 1934, Lester was earning about $1.50 a night at the Reno Club working from ten P.M. to five A.M. And in the summer of 1936, he was only making a dollar an hour more. But there were strong compensations.

Kansas City in those years was a non-stop jam-session after-hours town, and a man could play at these sessions as long as he had something to say. There were tenor battles of the titans, often with Lester Young, Herschel Evans and the late Dick Wilson of the Andy Kirk band confronting each other.

Mary Lou Williams has written of a characteristic 1934 Kansas City jam session: "The word went around that Hawkins was in the Cherry Blossom, and within about half an hour there were Lester Young, Ben Webster, Herschel Evans, Herman Walder and one or two unknown tenors piling into the club to blow. Bean (Coleman Hawkins) didn't know the Kaycee tenor men were so terrific, and he couldn't get himself together though he played all morning. I happened to be nodding that night, and around 4 A.M., I awoke to hear someone pecking on my screen.

"I opened the window on Ben Webster. He was saying, 'Get up, pussy cat, we're jammin' and all the pianists are tired out now. Hawkins has got his shirt off and is still blowing. You got to come down.' Sure enough, when we got there, Hawkins was in his singlet, taking turns with the Kaycee men. It seems he had run into something he didn't expect. Lester's style was light, and . . . it took him maybe five choruses to warm up. But then he would really blow; then you couldn't handle him on a cutting session.

"That was how Hawkins got hung up. The Henderson band was playing in St. Louis that evening, and Bean knew he ought to be on the way. But he kept trying to blow something to beat Ben and Herschel and Lester. When at last he gave up, he got straight in his car and drove to St. Louis. I heard he'd just bought a new Cadillac and that he burnt it out trying to make the job on time."

Lester kept up his after-hours vocation in New York when the Basie band moved East. In her memories of New York during the 'thirties, in *Lady Sings the Blues,* Billie Holiday writes that it was at a jam session that she first met Lester Young.

"From then on," she continues, "Lester knew how I used to love to have him come around and blow pretty solos behind me. So whenever he could, he'd come by the joints where I was singing, to hear me or sit in. I'll never forget the night Lester took on Chu Berry, who was considered the greatest in those days. Cab Calloway's was the biggest band and Chu Berry's was one of its big sounds.

"Well, this night Benny Carter was jamming for a session with Bobby Henderson, my accompanist. And then there was Lester with his little old saxophone held together with adhesive tape and rubber bands. Chu was sitting there and everybody started arguing as to who could blow out whom, trying to promote a competition between Lester and Chu.

"Benny Carter knew Lester could shine in this sort of duel, but for everybody else the end of the story was considered a pushover: Chu was supposed to blow Lester right out of the place. Chu had this pretty gold horn, but he didn't have it with him. Benny Carter wouldn't let that stop him. He was like me; he had faith in Lester. So he volunteered to go and pick up Chu's horn. He did and came back.

"And then Chu Berry . . . suggested they do *I Got Rhythm*
. . . Lester blew at least fifteen pretty choruses, none of them the
same, and each one prettier than the last. When the fifteenth one was
down, Chu Berry was finished. . . . Chu's gang were die-hards and
they were sick. All they could say to console themselves was that Chu
had a bigger tone. What the hell that meant, I'll never know. What
difference how big a tone is or how small, as long as Lester's line
was moving in that wonderful way, with those changes and those
notes that would positively flip you with surprise? . . . There ain't
no rule saying everybody's got to deliver the same damn volume or
tone.

"But anyway, this talk about a big tone messed with Lester for
months. And me, too. So I said, 'What the hell, Lester, don't let them
make a fool of us. We'll get you a big horn with big fat reeds and
things and no damn rubber bands around it holding you back.
We'll get us a tone.'

"So every time Lester could get a dime together he'd get him
some more reeds and start cutting them up all kinds of different
ways. He got him a new horn, too, and thought that would end
him up with a big fat growl. But his tone never got any bigger. He
wasn't meant to sound like Chu and he soon gave up trying."

And Jo Jones remembers how Lester always loved to jam.
"There were thirty days in Chicago in 1936. Lester and I were with
Basie at the Grand Terrace, and Roy Eldridge would pick us up in
front of the Terrace after work every night, and we'd jam from four
until ten or eleven in the morning. We'd often wind up with just
the three of us playing."

Although the necessary confines of the Basie band didn't allow
a constant jam-session spirit, there was one presence in the Basie
band that particularly spurred Lester to keep challenging himself.

Herschel Evans, a tenor from Texas, was co-featured on that
horn with Lester in the band until Evans died in 1936. Evans was
a remarkably sensitive, powerful soloist with roots in Coleman
Hawkins.

"Herschel Evans," Jo Jones recalled for *Hear Me Talkin'
to Ya,* "was a natural. He had a sound on the tenor that perhaps
you will never hear on a horn again. As for the so-called friction
between him and Lester, there was no real friction. What there was
was almost like an incident you would say could exist between two
brothers. No matter what, there was always a mutual feeling there

Even in Lester's playing today, somewhere he'll always play two to four measures of Herschel because they were so close in what they felt about music.

"I was always a sort of go-between with them. I roomed with Herschel and I had a liking for Pres, and I was always trying to get them together in a café or in a restaurant booth. It was some childish thing that had started it—I never knew exactly what. It may have started in part that night Coleman Hawkins came to Kansas City with Fletcher Henderson, and Herschel, Lester and Ben Webster played for him.

"That night Herschel played all over the horn—played it the way it was supposed to be played because Hawk was his idol. You couldn't say anything bad about Hawkins to Herschel. Some of that friction between Herschel and Pres may have had something to do with that night and with Hawkins. Lester, you know, has always been an unlimited soloist, and he was still playing at the session when everybody else was finished.

"And then, too, there was something about tone. Hawkins had a full tone and Herschel's was full, too. But Lester's tone was different. It was lighter. Some people would tell Lester that he didn't have a good tone, that he should change his tone. And that would cause friction. These people never think in terms of the physical features of an individual and how each one has different physical characteristics and that these make him play the way he does play."

Billie Holiday illuminates the Evans-Young ambivalence further: "Pres and Herschel Evans were for ever thinking up ways of cutting the other one. You'd find them in the band-room hacking away at reeds, trying out all kinds of new ones, anything to get ahead of the other. Once Herschel asked Lester, 'Why don't you play alto, man? You got an alto *tone*.' Lester tapped his head, 'There's things going on up there, man,' he told Herschel. 'Some of you guys are all belly.'"

Lester himself summarizes the relationship: "Herschel Evans was a Hawk man. That was the difference between the way we played. He played well, but his man was Hawk like my man at the beginning was Trumbauer."

Recently, Jo Jones returned to the subject: "In a way they were almost like twins. When Herschel died, it was like part of Lester had died. The difficult thing was to keep him in the band after Herschel died. Their rivalry wasn't a vicious thing. Herschel wanted Pres to get what he felt was the *tenor* sound, but he wouldn't change. As for the band, the more musical rivalry we could get, the more distinctively things kept going."

And Jimmy Rushing adds, "Basie used to like to make them angry. He'd make one follow the other. They'd turn their backs on each other and play like mad."

Rushing's sidekick, altoist Rudy Powell, discloses, "You know how Lester first started holding his horn at that 45-degree angle he used for so many years? When he first joined the band, he said, 'Herschel is playing so much, nobody is paying any attention to me.' So he held his horn a different way."

Perhaps the most traumatic event in Lester's life was his army experience. A friend of Lester in Chicago says, "He once told me how he got in. He kept getting notices as to when and where to report; and later, urgent telegrams. Finally, he said, someone from the draft board came down to the club where he was playing at the time and 'grabbed me off the stand and took me away!' In that last sentence, he may have been speaking figuratively although I'm sure he wasn't too happy to go into service."

The fifteen months in the army turned into a nightmare.

A musician, a close friend of Lester who was also stationed at Fort McLellan, Alabama, tells the story. "First of all, Lester didn't get into the band. The warrant officer was from Atlanta, Georgia. He said he wouldn't select Lester for the band because 'he'd be hard to manage.' Now that was absurd. Here was a man who had broken no rules doing something he disliked, soldiering. He certainly wouldn't be apt to break any if he had been put to something he wanted to do so much. He'd already been throwing hand grenades in the mud, and he wasn't hard to manage *then*.

"Anyway, we had a sympathetic captain, a 24-year-old drummer, and a sergeant major who also understood Lester, his sensitivity, and how difficult it was for him in the army. There was a move under way to have Lester discharged because of 'maladjustment to the confines of the army.' Lester, meanwhile, went into the hospital for minor but painful rectal surgery. He was returned to the company, and to relieve the post-operative discomfort, he was given pain-deadening pills."

When he had entered the hospital, according to one version, Lester had filled out the usual forms, and with characteristic ingenuousness, had answered "Yes" to a question as to whether he smoked marijuana. After his discharge from the hospital, a search was conducted of his belongings.

In charge of the search was a major from Louisiana who was Jim Crow. In going through Lester's locker, the major found the pills. He also found a picture of Lester's wife. Lester's wife (they have since been divorced) was white. The major also knew of the plans to obtain a discharge for Lester.

The major brought charges against Lester. The exact nature of those charges has been difficult to find, but they were connected with the pills and with Lester's admission on the questionnaire concerning his use of pot. The feeling of the captain and the sergeant and Lester's friends was that the major was primarily driven by prejudice. Pot was probably found.

The trial resulted in a five-year sentence, later reduced to one year. Lester was remanded to the detention barracks at Camp Gordon, Georgia. (He later recorded *D. B. Blues*). An intimate of Lester says, "Lester has yet to talk in any detail of that year. He'll say a few words once in a while, but then he'll stop. It was a horrible time.

"He did a wonderful job of rewinding himself when he was discharged, but he was very bitter. He didn't say anything, but he acted out certain things."

When he was finally separated from the army, Lester refused to appeal his case. He just wanted out. He came back to Los Angeles, began playing, headed his own unit, and began touring with Jazz at the Philharmonic.

Among other scars, the army experience had made him more suspicious.

One promoter, an honest man, gave Lester a large sum of money one night after a particularly successful concert a few months after he had left the army. Three weeks later, Lester called the man in California and charged him with having stolen his money. The promoter flew back to Chicago, found Lester very high, impossible to reason with. "How much did I steal?" "You know, about one thousand dollars or something." "All right, here it is," and the promoter left in disgust. He's still not sure why he gave him the money except that he wanted to be done with the whole affair.

The story sounds apocryphal, but the action is entirely characteristic of this particular promoter.

In the years since, Lester has traveled the night-club circuit with small combos, usually a quintet, toured with Jazz at the Philharmonic and the Birdland All-Stars throughout the States and Europe. He has also recorded prolifically for Norman Granz.

As of this writing, Lester is probably in better condition—physically, emotionally and musically—than he has been in several years. He lives in a small, comfortable home in St. Albans, Long Island, with his lovely, considerate wife, Mary, a nine-year-old son, Lester Young Jr., and a new daughter, Yvette. He enjoys his family, and the ties remain strong during his long travels. While strolling in Paris recently, Lester had his picture taken before a huge statue at the Museum of Modern Art and immediately had it sent to his son.

Since a hospital stay in the winter of 1955, Lester has played consistently well and with a strength and confidence that had often been missing in the previous decade. There are several musicians who feel he has long passed his creative apex of the Basie years and the early 'forties. Others are moved no less by his horn now—at its best—than they were then. They are, to be sure, moved in a different way, but they're convinced he can still be an unusually distinctive, eloquent improviser.

Lester had gone to Bellevue in the winter of 1955, knowing with what must have been an awful awareness that the effects of having been almost constantly high on gin and marijuana for a long time were finally impossible for his body, his nervous system, to ignore. The period of self-appraisal his illness made mandatory has apparently resulted in a Lester Young whose personality is more integrated, whose fears and insecurities are more under control, if not conquered.

Pres still wears a mask, although it is more often a cheerful one than the familiar phlegmatic, almost somnolent face and posture with which he faced strangers, particularly white strangers, for many years. His voice remains soft; he speaks slowly and with deliberation when he's serious. In his frequent teasing, good-humored moods, his tone can be lightly mocking, though almost never malicious.

With strangers he is courteous but still guarded. Lester is a fairly large man but the primary physical quality he projects is a looseness, an ease of movement.

A Swedish writer whose house Lester visited several times a few years ago, wrote: "As soon as I tried to get him to make statements on musical problems, Lester changed the subject. What night clubs were there in Stockholm? Could one make a round trip to Paris in one night and could one get 'schnapps' there? . . . in his wide-brimmed hat and down-to-his-feet overcoat he reminded me quite a bit of 'the wolf dressed as a sheep' . . . but he is really a lost child."

A young girl in Chicago grew to know him somewhat better. She is not a musician, but spends much of her time with musicians, and many of them trust her. "About Lester," she says, "once I had made known to him my own personal attitudes on various things, he would take it into consideration, not by strictly conforming, but by not pressing *his* divergent attitude on those things. This fell into his over-all philosophy that he expressed as 'to each his own.' I don't recall that he ever forcefully tried to talk me—or anyone that I observed—into anything or out of anything."

Another perspective on Lester is that of George Wein, a Boston jazz-club owner. George also plays piano, and occasionally will work with an attraction at his club. When Lester Young was booked for a week last year, Lester had not been told that the boss would be playing piano.

"It was the first set of the first night," recalls Wein. "No customers were in the place yet. I got up on the stand with the rhythm section. Lester wouldn't. He sat on a chair by the bandstand, waiting until I played. It was like an audition. I played one chorus, two choruses, three. Finally he said, 'You and I are going to be all right, Pres.' He calls whomever he's working for, a club owner or a promoter, 'Pres.' Fellow musicians he addresses as 'Lady.'

"I have a feeling," Wein concludes, "that if Lester hadn't liked my playing, he would have walked out. The week's work wasn't as important as working for a week with a man whom he could get on musically."

With regard, however, to being on time, Lester is very conscientious. "He's of the old school," says his manager Charlie Carpenter who has been with him for ten years. "He feels obligated professionally to be on time. In fact, Al Cooper, who used to promote concerts around New York, once said: 'The one thing you have to worry about Lester is he gets to town *too* early.' "

There is a famous (or notorious, depending on who tells it) story about Lester that has been much changed in the re-relating of it through the years. Most people tell it to prove how "eccentric" Lester is. But his manager tells it to show how self-compelled Lester is to make time.

"It was in 1949," says Carpenter. "Lester had missed a train in Washington because he'd fallen asleep in the station. He was due in New Bedford, Massachusetts, for a one-nighter. Instead of waiting for the next train, he became panicky. He hired a taxi to Newark, chartered a plane to Providence, and then took another taxi to New Bedford. I think it cost him at least $250. He was an hour late and worked three hours overtime for nothing.

"About Lester being aloof," Carpenter goes on. "He's very sensitive and he's been hurt so much through the years with people telling him about his tone and his style and with many personal problems complicated by a lack of being understood, that he feels if he says nothing, then he won't get hurt."

Jo Jones, who has been close to Lester for some twenty-six years, adds, "Lester never did a malicious thing. He's very sensitive. Anything that hurts a human being hurts him. He's very sincere. When he meets phonies, he makes himself scarce. He's also religious. I remember in the Kansas City days when we were all traveling with Basie, we'd go to a different church every Sunday. Basie would play organ; Jimmy Rushing would sing. We weren't doing that to bribe the people in the community. That's the way we were.

"Lester doesn't like unpleasant situations, but he'll break up a fight if he can. They ought to send him to the UN; he's that kind of person. To avoid his own conflicts, he'd always grab his horn, and go out and play. We had facilities for jamming then. Anything he wanted to say, he'd say on his horn. He spent most of his time playing in those years."

One of Lester's problems through the years has been a fear of doctors, and Jo has been one of the very few people who have been able to break through Lester's obstinacy on the subject. "There was a time when his teeth were practically falling out of his mouth until I got him to a dentist. Another time I had to take him to see about his tonsils."

Some of those who have been associated with Lester claim he has no interests aside from music, and one goes further to claim he hasn't much intellectual capacity for any other subject.

Jo Jones disagrees. "He has depth. He used to read a lot of comic books, but that doesn't indicate lack of intelligence. He's very interested in baseball too. He's definitely a Giant fan, and he keeps abreast of other sports. He can discuss practically anything."

Young pianist Bobby Scott, with whom Lester became friendly

during a 1956 Jazz at the Philharmonic tour, adds, "He's bright, very bright. A lot of his trouble in communicating is the vernacular he uses. A lot of people just can't understand him." (Norman Granz tells of the times Lester used to try to pretend to speak a foreign language. "It was gibberish, but he did it with a straight face and with conviction.")

"Lester," Bobby Scott continued, "is an avid sports fan, and we also talked a lot about music. A few other musicians of his era don't keep their ears open. But Lester has always had his open. He's very broad. He may vote for Harry Edison in a poll, but that doesn't stop him from listening to Miles Davis. He hears everything. He wants to. I had records on the tour with me, and he was always on me to play them. Modern records—Bird, Milt Jackson, Bud Powell, Jimmy Giuffre.

"As a person," Bobby added, "I'd say he's pretty pure. I mean good-hearted. To me he can almost be like a father-image. He was encouraging. He took an interest. He used to bother me about my right hand, and said I wasn't playing enough with my left hand. He'd ask me about my 'left people,' as he would put it."

While in England in 1953, Lester met a young English modern tenor, Ronnie Scott. He spent time and a considerable amount of patience teaching Scott his fingering secrets, how to achieve two different sounds from the same note.

A man for whom Lester has toured and recorded frequently has yet another view of Pres: "I knew him in 1941 in Los Angeles. I'd see him a lot. I'd go to rehearsals of the first band he and his brother Lee had. I've never known two brothers who were more completely antithetical. They profess to love each other, but I don't think they really get on. They never ran together.

"Lee, for example," the prompter continued, "runs a boys' club, is a wonderful golfer, basketball player, an all-round athlete. I don't think he ever got high in his life. He's been with Nat Cole for a long time now, and is a thoroughly consistent musician. Lester is undoubtedly the genius of the two.

"He's been a strange guy as long as I've known him. I remember watching Lester walk to a rehearsal. He was a block down the street. They were waiting for him. Lee yelled, 'Hurry up, Lester.' But Lester dragged his horn on the sidewalk and took his time. You never could rush him. We've been with him with planes to make, curtains going up. I've never seen him make a hurried move. Coleman Hawkins once told me: 'I think *I* can get relaxed but I don't know anyone who can get as relaxed as *he* can.' The way I heard his troubles in the army was that he just wouldn't do anything."

A French writer, Frank Tenot, who spent some time with Lester in Paris, observes, "Lester expresses himself with a minimum of gestures, words, notes."

"He's a loner," the promoter says. "On our tours we'd all check in at the same hotel. But he'd wind up in one of his own. 'I'll go for myself,' he'd say. And it was always a colored hotel.

"Except for the time he was in the hospital, there was no period when I knew him when he wasn't high. You could wake him up in the middle of the day and he'd be high. As for his drinking, he'd go for strange combinations. Gin with a sherry chaser. Courvoisier and beer. He could drink incredible quantities of liquor, more than anyone I've known. And he wouldn't eat. I remember one tour when he'd gone four days and we had to force-feed him. I think he has a strong death wish."

"He didn't always drink," explains a musician who knew Lester well in the Basie band. "A lot of people go in for drinking as a substitute companion. And he happened to acquire a taste for one specific drink, gin, and stayed on that. Now he's happy with a half-pint of Henessey's that he can sip at during the night."

"He has a lot of phobias," says the promoter. "When I knew him well, he couldn't sleep unless the radio was on full blast and the lights were on. I've never seen him in a dark room. He's frightened of life. But fear turned him into a lotus eater. He lived in a lassitude. Not his playing though, not in those years. He had a vigor then that the "cool" modernists today haven't approached.

"There was sometimes a resentment in him. The people who have been with our show a long time take pride in our grosses. But Lester would come to me with glee and point out what a competing show had done. 'They smothered you in Minneapolis!'

"He'd get into business problems. He either can't or won't read a contract. Once, he got into a tax jam, and I had to save his home for him. And later, when he had himself put into Bellevue, I sent his wife money. Yet when we talked about his going on my tour after he got out, he first agreed to his usual $750 a week. Then he talked with his manager, called back and asked for $850. That was O.K. Ten minutes later he called and asked for $950. O.K. Finally he said he'd have to have $1,000. That was very strange conduct for him. Anyway, we had a blow up, and he made another tour instead.

"The thing with him is that if anything's making him unhappy, he'll walk away from it. If he's bugged on a session, he'll pack up his horn and go. He won't face up to things. On a European tour, he came to me in Paris in the middle of the night and said, 'Please give me my money, I'm not happy. I want to go home.' I didn't and he was all right the next day.

"I said he was a loner. Like on the bus, his was always the last seat. He never dressed in a room with the rest of the guys unless that dressing room was the only one there was. At Carnegie Hall, they would have to open up the symphony room so he could have it by himself. He almost never mixed socially with the group. The other guys would always pair up and run for girls. But not Lester. His relationships with women seemed strange to me. Those I saw looked alike. Same size. Fragile.

"The only guys he would pair up with on the tour would be the misfits. The few weirdos. One of them, a drummer, was a guy whose playing he didn't like. But he hung around with him.

"Another thing is he won't write. At least, he was the only guy on any of my tours for whom I had to make out his own immigration slip with his name and passport number.

"He does have a great pride in being a musician. He has a great tolerance for a wide variety of music, too. He could probably tell you Perry Como's latest record.

"Lester likes to be different; he apparently needs to be. Like the ridiculous things he'd eat. Buttermilk and crackerjacks. There was a period too in which he was affecting effeminacy although he's never been a homosexual. At one point he had let his hair grow so long in back, it fell in natural curls, and he was going to put ribbons in it. We had to stop him.

"Anything that's weird attracted him. Anything that's weird and different he buys. He used to wear his hat backward. Then he started wearing the porkpie hat that's become identified with him. He would always wear dark clothes, black or dark blue. I once took him to Brooks Brothers, selected and paid for some suits, but he never picked them up.

"There's also something masochistic about him, I feel. At one time, a business associate was cheating him. He knew it, but he kept him. Another time a guy who was part of his entourage was playing Uncle Tom to some white girls. 'Look at him Tomming,' Lester said in disgust. But he never said anything to the guy."

"He was always different," Jimmy Rushing and Rudy Powell

remember. "If he'd follow a guy's solo, you'd think he'd go one way, but he'd always go the other. He always did the opposite. He could play an odd note, and you'd think, 'Gee, he'd better leave it alone because now it's going to be all wrong if he goes on with it.' But it wasn't. He'd always have another note next to that one to slip into. He played on a note like you would play a word."

"Lester sings with his horn," Billie Holiday wrote. "You listen to him and can almost hear the words. People think he's cocky and secure, but you can hurt his feelings in two seconds. I know, because I found out once that I had."

"Everyone playing an instrument in jazz," Jo Jones commented on the same theme, "expresses what's on his mind. Lester would play a lot of musical phrases that were actually words. He would *literally* talk on his horn. That's his conversation. I can tell what he's *talking* about in 85% of what he'll play in a night. I could write his thoughts down on paper from what I hear from his horn. Benny Goodman even made a tune out of a phrase Lester would play on his horn—'I want some money.'

"But Lester also has continuity," Jo emphasizes. "He tells a story. A lot of the little kiddies today aren't saying anything. They'll start talking about Romeo and Juliet and in two measures, they're talking about William S. Hart."

Nearly all musicians who have worked and traveled with Lester agree that, as John Lewis puts it, "Lester has a subtle and playful sense of humor."

"He's always a lot of fun," says Jo Jones. "There's always something going on, never a dull moment when he's around."

The seeming conflict between Pres as an introvert and as a humorist may be resolved in the realization that by making people laugh, by using his unique gift for language-sketching to amuse, Lester can feel he is accepted. By his wit he can shore up his ego, and gain pleasure from the exercise of an unusual skill.

"He's always performing," says Bobby Scott. "He does it for other people. Without him on that one tour I made with Jazz at the Philharmonic, I might have shot myself."

Lester is most renowned avocationally for his ability to select nicknames that stick. Billie Holiday was christened Lady Day by Pres. "Lester was the first to call Mom 'Duchess'—and it turned out to be the title she carried to her grave. Lester and I will probably be buried, too, still wearing the names we hung on each other after he came to live with us. Back at the Log Cabin, (where Billie worked in Harlem in her early time in New York) the other girls used to try and mock me by calling me 'Lady,' because they thought I thought I was just too damn grand to take the damn customers' money off the tables. But the name Lady stuck long after everybody had forgotten where it had come from. Lester took it and coupled it with the Day out of Holiday and called me 'Lady Day.'"

Pianist Charles Thompson is now irreversibly Sir Charles because of Lester. Bobby Scott became Bobby Sox on the tour they worked together, and bassist Whitey Mitchell, since it was World Series time, was dubbed Whitey Ford. And Harry Edison has been Sweets since 1936 because of Lester.

It's likely that Lester originated much of the onomatopoetic "rooney" material on which Slim Gaillard later expanded. And he is credited with having originated the widely used phrase (among Negro musicians mostly), "I feel a draft," which can mean the detection of Jim Crow in a person or a general feeling of not being wanted for other reasons.

Lester's way of inviting a sideman to take another chorus may be, "Have another helping." If he'd like you to take three choruses, he's apt to advise, "Have a trio."

Pres has also been known to slip into song during a set at Birdland, slyly enjoying the effect. And he has been known to engage in water-pistol battles with members of the Basie band at Birdland.

As for his verbal wit, the pleasure of others in this aspect of Lester's humor may be deepened for some by their feeling that he respects their intelligence enough to expect they'll understand his highly idiomatic subtleties. The softly deft humor that is Lester's basically is an expression of personality that, whenever possible, seeks fun and warmth and the security of communication among soul brothers, to use a current term among jazzmen.

In November 2, 1951, Lester took a *Down Beat Blindfold Test* given by Leonard Feather. The test consists of Feather playing a series of records for a musician without telling him personnel or name of the selections. The test serves as some index of how familiar a musician is with his contemporaries' styles, and it often doubles as a forum for a particular musician's likes, and more often, dislikes.

Pres, while discriminating, was gentle with all the entries. And throughout his comments there was evident an insatiable love of music. In the afterthoughts section of the test, he said, "Just all music, all day and all night, music. Just any kind of music you play for me, I melt with all of it."

Some kinds of music, however, do not "melt" Lester at all. There are the honking hornmen by whom he has sometimes been flanked on the Jazz at the Philharmonic tours.

"Those tenors who stay on one note, I don't go for that. I like to see a person stand flat-footed and play the instrument. When I'm on the stage with honking going on I never pay it no mind. I don't buy that no kind of way when a person gets on one note for an hour. But they sell it like hot cakes. Yet it's dying out, if you notice. I wouldn't go to see nothing like that."

Occasionally, depressed by colleagues who honk and by the easy rise they get from audiences, his own performances have suffered. Once he played France with Jazz at the Philharmonic, and French editor Charles Delaunay recalls, "The first time he came over with JATP, his short, mediocre stage appearance disappointed nearly every one of his fans. But pianist Henri Renaud and a few other musicians managed after the concert to take him to the Tabou where he sat in with the local band and really *blew*. There we discovered that Lester could still blow when he wanted to, when he was in a proper environment or mood." And another night, in the warming empathy of a French jazz club, following a formal concert, Lester was seen dancing for hours.

Lester's love of playing in a context he likes has not diminished. "After all these years, there's still kicks for me in music. I don't practice because I think I've been playing long enough. But I love to play."

In Paris, during a JATP tour, Lester spent his free time for five days sitting in with French jazzmen, and finally played all night from two A.M. on.

Wrote Frank Tenot: "Lester and Barney Kessel were the two musicians of the JATP troupe that year who played as much as they could. . . . One night Lester said, 'There are too many people at the concerts and I don't think my music interests them; they've come for something else. I bore them. I prefer to play before those who like my music."

Tenot concluded: "Lester Young has never gone commercial. What Louis Armstrong, Dizzy Gillespie, Charlie Parker have not been able to avoid, Lester Young has not tried yet."

Lester Young's insistence on being Lester Young has resisted more than commercial pressures. Ralph Gleason has written: "Lester Young was himself when all pressures were on him to be something else. The way he chose to go was the way everyone else chose, eventually."

Lester's advice to young musicians is: "Every musician should be a stylist. I played like Trumbauer when I was starting out. But then there's a time when you have to go out for yourself and tell *your* story. Your influence has already told his."

He is aware that he has influenced so many of the young modern tenors. Bill Simon wrote: "Oddly enough, while there were some Lester followers during his Basie period, his influence didn't really catch a firm hold until the late 'forties. Then it did so emphatically, virtually obliterating [editor's note: for a time] other tenor styles. The Woody Herman band, with its 'Four Brothers' sax section, actually at first consisted of four tenor saxophonists, all playing with Lester's sound. To fashion that sound, Woody at times employed such men as Stan Getz, Zoot Sims, Herbie Steward, Al Cohn and Jimmy Giuffre. Others in the idiom included Paul Quinichette (called the 'Vice Pres' and often indistinguishable from Lester whom he followed into the Basie band), Allen Eager, Brew Moore, Dexter Gordon, Wardell Gray and such latter-day stylists as Arno Marsh, Dave Pell, Bill Perkins, Bob Cooper, Warne Marsh, and alto saxophonists Lee Konitz and Paul Desmond."

Konitz's tribute to Young, as reported by Barry Ulanov, was eloquent: ". . . the sound of Lester Young on the old Basie records —real beautiful tenor saxophone sound, pure sound. That's it. For alto, too. Pure sound. How many people Lester influenced, how many lives! Because he is definitely the basis of everything that's happened since. And his rhythmic approach—complex in its simplicity. How can you analyze it? Shall we tag some words on it? Call it polyrhythmic?"

Charlie Parker, *the* influence in modern jazz, claimed not to have been influenced by Lester, but said that in his formative years, "I was crazy about Lester. He played so clean and beautiful. . . ." It's interesting to note that when Charlie Parker first began to attract attention among New York musicians by his playing at Monroe's Uptown House, "They began to talk about Bird," according to Kenny Clarke, "because he played like Pres on alto. . . . We thought that was something phenomenal because Lester Young was the style setter, the pace setter at that time. We went to listen to

Bird at Monroe's for no other reason except that he sounded like
Pres. That is, until we found out that he had something of his own
to offer."

"Have any of the younger tenors," Lester was once asked,
"said anything to you about your having influenced them?" "No,"
said Lester, "none have. I hear a lot of things from what I play in
some of them, but I never say anything. I mean I hear a lot little
riffs and things that I've done. But I don't want it to sound like I
think I influenced everybody."

The problem, George Wein once pointed out, is that "his
imitators have played so much of him, he sometimes doesn't know
what to play."

Charlie Carpenter tells the story of the night Lester and Paul
Quinichette were leading units on alternate sets at Birdland: "Lester
came off the bandstand and said, 'I don't know whether to play like
me or like Lady Q, because he's playing so much like me.' He wasn't
putting Paul down. Why, Paul is the only man I've ever known him
to lend a tenor to. But that night, Paul sounded so much like Lester
that Lester was at loose ends as to what to do."

Lester's concern with being original, with being his own man,
extends to not wanting to copy himself. "I feel funny listening to
my own records. I think I enjoy them too well. I might repeat them
when I play so I don't like to listen to them over and over. If I
listened to them too much, I'd be thinking about them when I'm playing or recording new ones instead of creating.

"Among those of mine I like the best are *Lester Leaps In; Clap
Hands, Here Comes Charlie; Every Tub; Swingin' the Blues; One
O'Clock Jump* and *Shoe Shine Boy,* the first record I made."

Lester has always encouraged younger modern jazzmen prag-
matically. Trumpeter Jessie Drakes worked with him for a long
time, and more recently, Art Farmer and Idrees Sulieman have
played trumpet with him. John Lewis has been his pianist, and Gildo
Mahones was a later Young pianist.

"He never put the kiddies down," Jo Jones says.

" 'I've got to give the kiddies a gig,' he'd tell me before a record
session," Norman Granz adds. "So we'd have to use his people.
Afterwards, he'd sometimes admit the records weren't as good as
they could have been if we had used better-known guys."

Lester is not as *laissez-faire* as he sometimes appears on stand.
On the matter of solos for his sidemen, he is more generous than

ome leaders. But he has firm ideas of what he wants—and requires
—in a rhythm section: "The piano should play little fill-ins. Just
ice little full chords behind the horn. I don't get in his way, and
let him play, and he shouldn't get in mine. Otherwise, your mind
ets twisted. That's why I always let my little kiddies play solos.
'hat way they don't bother me when I solo. In fact, sometimes I
et bawled out by people who want to hear me play more, but I
elieve if you're paying a man to play, and if that man is on the
andstand and can play, he should get a chance to tell his story.

"A bass should play nice, four-beat rhythm that can be heard,
ut no slapping. I can't stand bass players when they slap the
trings. I love bowed work. It's very nice on ballads. But not all
ass players can play good with a bow, and yet it's nice to have
ne who can in a small group.

"On drumming, I don't go for the bomb. I want the drummer
o be straight with the section. He's messing with the rhythm when
e drops those bombs. In small groups, I like the drummer to
lay a little tinkety-boom on that one cymbal, four beats on the
edal. Just little simple things, but no bombs.

"The Basie rhythm section was good because they played to-
ether and everybody in it was playing rhythm. They played for you
o play when you were taking a solo. They weren't playing solos
ehind you.

"On a date, I play a variety of tempos. I set my own tempos
nd I take my time. I wish jazz were played more for dancing. I
ave a lot of fun playing for dances because I like to dance, too.
'he rhythm of the dancers comes back to you when you're playing.
Vhen you're playing for dancing, it all adds up to playing the right
empo. After three or four tempos, you find the tempos they like.
Vhat they like changes from dance date to dance date."

"That's what I especially noted, playing with Lester," says
jeorge Wein. "He very seldom played the same song at the same
empo. It would change from night to night."

"Another thing about Lester," contributes Jo Jones, "is his
hoice of tunes. He's often a year or a year and a half ahead of
verybody else. He catches something on the radio he likes, and he
tarts playing it—like *How High the Moon*. He and Marlowe Mor-
is were playing it at Minton's before it became so widely popular
1 jazz. He was the one who first started playing *Polka Dots and
Aoonbeams* and *Foggy Day* again. He finds things that have mean-

ing to them, and soon, other people are playing or singing them again."

Lester spends much of his time at home listening to the radio or watching TV. He keeps up with popular records. "I usually hear records over the radio and the TV, but I also collect some. I like to get records with singing. Really my man is Frank Sinatra. And I like Lady Day, Ella, Sarah and others like that. Al Hibbler too. Most of the time I spend in listening to records is listening to singers and getting the lyrics to different songs.

"A musician should know the lyrics of the songs he plays. That completes it. Then you can go for yourself and you know what you're doing. A lot of musicians that play nowadays don't know the lyrics of the songs. That way they're just playing the changes. That's why I like records by singers when I'm listening at home. I pick up the words right from there."

Even when abroad, according to Frank Tenot, "as soon as Lester arrives in a hotel, he has a radio installed. He can't do without music."

One of the best analyses of Lester's style and of the permanent effect he has had on the direction of jazz was written by Ross Russell in the April, 1949, *Record Changer:*

"Lester was the first to junk the machine-gun style of Hawkins, with its reliance on eighth note-dotted sixteenth patterns. This is the phrasing method of Sedric, Berry, Webster, Wilson and Young's Basie section mate, Herschel Evans. Lester used more notes and less notes than his predecessors, but abundances were balanced against bareness within the structure of his solos.

"In his solo on *Lady Be Good* (small-band version), Young employs a bare ten notes for the first four-bar section. A classic stylist would have doubled the amount. These ten notes are set with lapidarian skill in the rhythmic and melodic framework. The opening phrase, so succinctly stated, leads to longer and complex improvisations upon the melody, the whole of which is a masterpiece of economy, subtlety and logic.

"Lester's musical thought flowed, not within the accepted confines of two or four-bar sections, but more freely. He thought in terms of a new melodic line that submitted only to the harmony of the original as it reworked the melody into something fresh and personal.

"Harmonic sense that enables a jazzman to improvise readily is a talent. Melodic vision of Young's quality is a mark of genius

Iis example and that of the Basie band restored to the jazz language tool which had been dulled by improper usage.

"Lester Young's chord and bar changes are arranged with uch adroitness that the listener is frequently not aware of them ntil after they have fallen. Lester's method is to phrase ahead—to repare for and gracefully lead into the next change several beats efore its arrival. To be able to move so freely, in and out of the armonies with an ear so keen and a step so sure, to always come ut on the right note and the right beat—this is a mark of genius. azz had known nothing like it since the first daring improvisations f Louis Armstrong.

"As an innovator of harmonic change, Lester employed the ght polychrome orchestral palette of the Debussyians. Lester's pirit was pleased by the sound of the sixth and ninth intervals which e adjacent to the dominant and tonic notes. It was typical of his ubtle and inquiring nature to play just off what the ear expected nd thereby extend musical structure on a horizontal plane.

"Lester added variety to the melodic line, but he knew well how ɔ balance the parts. He is complex, but he is never complicated. Vild crescendoes are contrasted with hammering repetitions, irides- ent multi-note passages with sections where notes are massed like locks. Short statements lead to long flowing sentences. Lester's solos re replete with dips and soaring flights, surprises, twists, hoarse houts and bubbling laughter. The holes—and like Basie, Lester eaves many—are deliberate and meaningful. The dry bite of the ttacking notes, the fatness of the slurs and periods—all are parts of ne deliberate style of a master virtuoso of the tenor saxophone.

"Like all of the giants, Lester possesses a tremendous beat. He ɛ one of those rare musicians who can swing an entire band. The nassive swing of the Basie orchestra became even more exciting vhen Lester soloed. Very often, when he had the first solo, as on 'axi War Dance, Young would divest the opening statements of ll but their rhythmic elements. Here Lester underlines the first and nird beats, giving greater emphasis to Jo Jones's high-hat accents, vhich fall on two and four. In rhythmic language, this solo develops $\frac{4}{4}$, a $\frac{2}{4}$ and a $\frac{1}{3}$ pattern simultaneously and results in rhythmic omplexity that goes beyond that of any contemporary. No one be- ɔre him, neither Armstrong, nor Morton, nor Hawkins, had created nelodic lines as rich in rhythmic interest as did Lester Young.

"New Orleans bands achieved this rhythmic complexity col- ectively. The quality deteriorated during the following period when jazz emphasized romantic and individualistic tendencies. Leste Young, the arch-romantic, recreates this quality in an individu style.

"Lester's insistence on the rhythmic priorities of jazz came a a tonic to a music which was drifting away from the drive of earl New Orleans music. Lester did more than reaffirm these prioritie He replenished the stream polluted by the arrangers and thus mad possible the even more complex rhythmic developments of the be bop style. . . .

"Lester's detachment was unshakable. He always seemed t be in a world of his own. . . . The Lester Young style is esser tially romantic. It is uninhibited and relaxed, sensitive, imaginativ deeply subjective. . . . Less disciplined than Hawkins, he is non the less a musician whose product is orderly and structural. B these qualities—balance and unity of parts, clarity of concept— lie beneath the surface, under the luminous texture of notes.

"When Lester first appeared on the jazz scene he had con mand of a completely integrated style. . . . It was as if he had bee planning a frontal attack on orthodoxy for years.

"The roots of Lester's style extend in many directions. On on side they are indisputably in the reed tradition of the early clarinetis who emphasized the melodic and lyrical qualities of jazz, an thought in terms of the blues scale. . . . But Lester draws equal from sources of a much different nature—Debussyian harmony . . and the spiritual qualities which are attached to the . . . jazz trad tion of Bix Beiderbecke and Bud Freeman, both of whom Youn listened to in his early period. . . . It is this synthesis of opposin attitudes and ideologies—the profound tradition of the blues con bined with the infusions of European harmony and . . . romant cism—that gives Lester Young's music its special appeal. The var ous materials are combined in a style which has no eclectic qualitie but is fused, integrated, and intensely personal. . . .

"(The young tenors who came to be influenced by Lester were in revolt against the orthodoxy of the Armstrong-Hawki school of jazz, with its powerful vibrato, emphatic periods . . rigid harmonies and severe solo architecture. What they admired i Lester Young was his lighter and purer tone, his broader harmoni concepts, his greater extension of the solo line—with the resulta freedom from its bar division—his . . . more lyrical style . . his melodic gifts, inventiveness, and above all, his tremendou swing."

Sidney Finkelstein in discussing Lester's freedom from bar
mitations, points out in *Jazz: A People's Music*, ". . . this free-
om from strict bar limitations is not unknown to other music, but
s a reassertion of a basic truth of music, a 'humanization' of music
. . the great recitative, chanson and madrigal art of early musical
enturies shows a similar flexibility, and interplay of beats" (as do,
e goes on, the songs of Mussorgsky and Charles Ives).

Along with the flexibility, humor, warmth and relaxation of
ester's playing, the blues have always been present in his work.
Blue" tonality and the coursing virility that its rich tradition con-
otes. On occasion, there has been a completely individual evoca-
ion of sadness in Lester's playing. "There is a poignancy," Norman
Granz feels, "in the bending of the notes that is peculiarly, espe-
ially his."

In an image that "makes it" musically as well as visually, Barry
Ulanov has described one key aspect of Pres's style: "His phrases
vere longer than the traditional riff; when at a loss for fresh ideas,
e would extend his statements by hanging on to one or two notes in
 kind of auto-horn honk that gave his solos a quality of cohesion;
is lines hung together, even if suspended precariously from a single
ote. And how they swung!"

Further insights into Lester's style can be found in André Ho-
eir's *Jazz: Its Evolution and Essence:* "(Sometimes Lester) . . .
acrifices everything else to swing, concentrating all his rhythmic
owers on one or two notes repeated at greater or less length. . . .
Young's veiled sonority and his almost imperceptible vibrato, which
ends to disappear completely in quick tempos, brought into being
n unprecedented musical climate, the first fruit of the revolution
egun by men like Carter, Goodman and Wilson . . . . the inde-
inable charm that is all Lester Young's own comes chiefly from his
stonishing muscular relaxation. Good jazzmen have always had to
e supple, but Lester has gone beyond being merely supple to achieve
 kind of relaxation that has become something of a cult among
is disciples . . .

"(He can sometimes effect) a thorough, essential renewal of
he melodic raw material and its emotional content. . . . Lester
Young took over the element of relaxation at the high degree of per-
ection to which Armstrong and Hodges had brought it and carried
t even further by developing muscular relaxation and suitable rhyth-
nic conceptions."

As for the quality of Lester's rhythmic mastery, John Lewis, in discussing ways of varying and developing the jazz potential for improvisers, said, "If you have a melodic design that is strong enough, you can build on that design and on the accompanying rhythm patterns without relying on any particular harmonic progression. This is especially true if there is enough rhythmic character. Lester Young has been doing this for years. He doesn't always have to lean on the harmonic pattern. He can sustain a chorus by his melodic ideas and rhythm. The chords are there, and Lester can always fill out any chord that needs it, but he is not strictly dependent on the usual progression.

"That's why he needs first-rate musicians to play with him. This is something you can't tell a musician. He has to know and feel it."

French critic, Frank Tenot, has written of the fact that the relaxation of Lester's playing does not preclude his ability to project tension, that half of the tension-release equation that propels nearly all artistic achievement for the creator and for those with whom a communication is established.

A less realized part of Lester's musical equipment has been his clarinet playing. Except for a few sides with Basie and several solos on a series of Kansas City Six sessions for Commodore, Lester's clarinet does not appear on records. Yet the few solos extant indicate to several listeners, this one among them, that Lester could have been as important and influential a creator on clarinet as on tenor.

"I never could find the one I wanted," he explained in 1956. "I used a metal clarinet on those Kansas City Six records for Commodore, but I never could find one like that afterwards. I got a tone on that metal one like I wanted."

At the beginning of 1957, an admirer sent Lester a metal clarinet, and it's to be hoped he resumes playing the instrument.

Lester Young, in transitory summary, is a musician who has found emotional sustenance in jazz, and has helped provide that essential nutrition to many others. A man who has often found it difficult to articulate his feelings verbally, Lester has been able to make his emotions, thoughts, inside humor and sadness—his life experiences—meaningful to others and perhaps clearer to him through his horn.

The result has been a continuing enrichment of a significant part of the whole of the jazz language, for Lester's story has proved more universal than he himself might have imagined.

In telling so personal, so introverted a life tale, Lester has

communicated enduringly to listeners throughout the world; and he
has marked hundreds of younger musicians, men who have taken
parts of his speech, adapted it to their own needs, and in the process
have made Lester's voice a permanent part of the sound of jazz.

Allan Morrison of *Ebony,* who has known Lester well for seventeen years, recently tried to summarize his feelings about Pres:
"There are really two Lesters—prewar and postwar. You can tell
by just listening to his playing. In jazz more than any other way of
music, a man's music will reflect the man, his thoughts, his emotions.

"Those who knew Pres before the war felt deep changes in
him when he returned from the army. His experiences in the Southern army camps embittered, soured, changed him profoundly. He
had been a boy in the South, so he had known the cruel humiliations
of Jim Crow as only a Negro in the South can. He came out of the
South early in life with distrust of whites and a loathing for second-
class citizenship.

"The years barnstorming with his father's band and later in
Kansas City were free-wheeling and gay. Lester laughed and loved
and lived it up. Life was one long romp with little time out for
serious reflection or depression. He was a happy man, bursting with
vitality and constantly visiting beyond the pale. He ran unfettered
and confident in his strength and stamina. The prewar years stimulated him and gave him seemingly endless opportunities for self-
indulgence and release.

"He was one of the great dissenters of his own jazz age, the
man who took the 'wrong' turning, and ended up the most pervasive
personality of his time. He turned his back on Hawkins, and told
the jazz world that he was going to be himself and they could take
it or not. He found his own voice and, in a wonderful way, he expressed it eloquently and with increasing power between 1933 and
1942.

"His army service was marked by tragedy, tension, appalling
indignities, spiritual and physical torture. When he came out of it,
his spirit was twisted and sore and he hated with an intensity he had
never before known. He deeply distrusted practically all whites and
realized as never before the injustice and inhumanity under which
Negroes in the South lived. And not only in the South. A feeling of
revenge lingered in him for years.

"Whether or not he knew it, his spirit had been defaced. His
postwar music showed it and conveyed moods that had been alien
to him before. He became withdrawn, less forceful, hesitant, often

pitifully unsure at times. For a while, in 1946, when he grossed close to $50,000 working for Norman Granz and captured many new admirers, he seemed about to reclaim his former glory. But it didn't last. The reasons were more than commercial. Two marriages failed and he gathered and sustained deep hostilities to people he felt had wronged him. He remembered hurts, slights, defeats.

"He accepted the fact that the postwar world was much different from the one he had known in the happier 'thirties. He made his adjustment and peace, but it was more of a surrender. He knew he could never return to the world he had known.

"In the past decade Lester has often aligned himself in his choice of sidemen with those who were working for musical change evolution in jazz. I once heard him turn down an offer to play with a group of ex-Basie musicians and reconstruct the style of that era for an album. 'I can't do it,' he said. 'I don't play like that any more. I play different; I live different. This is later. That was then. We change, move on.'

"His children have softened and gladdened him, and given him a new grip on life. But he often remains a man drifting sadly through a world he fears and dislikes."

SELECTED DISCOGRAPHY—LESTER YOUNG

Lester Leaps in, Count Basie Orchestra, Epic 12" LP LG 3107 (1936–40)

Count Basie and His Orchestra, Decca 12" LP DL 8049 (1936–39)

Count Basie and his Orchestra, Brunswick 12" LP BL 54012 (1936–39)

Let's Go to Prez, Count Basie Orchestra, Epic 12" LP LN 3168 (1939–40)

Blues by Basie, Count Basie Orchestra, Columbia 12" LP CL 901 (Lester Young is on three 1939–40 numbers).

Lady Day, Billie Holiday, Columbia 12" LP CL 637 (Lester Young on five 1937 numbers). Lester can also be heard on some numbers of *Billie Holiday Sings,* Columbia 10" LP CL 6129 and *Billie Holiday Favorites,* Columbia 10" LP CL 6163.

Kansas City Style, Kansas City Six, Commodore 10" LP FL 20, 021 (1938 and 1944). Lester plays clarinet on some of the 1938 numbers. Seven of the eight titles on this 10" Commodore were also made available on *Prez and Chu,* Jazztone 12" LP J-1218.

Lester Young Trio, Aladdin 10" LP 705 (1942).

Lester Young and his Tenor Sax, Vols. 1 and 2, Aladdin 12" LP 801 (1945–47). Also available on Intro 12" LPs 602, 603.

Jue Lester, Savoy 12″ LP MG 12068 and *The Master's Touch,* Savoy 12″ LP MG 12071 (1944 and 1949).

Jazz Royalty: Earl Hines-Count Basie, EmArcy 10″ LP MG 26-23 contains edited versions of four 1944 numbers by Kansas City Seven. Also available on *Giants of Jazz,* Vol. 1, EmArcy 12″ LP MG 36048.

Pres Meets Vice-Pres, EmArcy 10″ LP MG 26021 contains four numbers by Lester Young quartet (1943). Also available on *Giants of Jazz* series, EmArcy 12″ LPs MG 36050, 36051 (two numbers in each).

Lester Young Trio, Vols. 1 and 2, Clef 10″ LPs MG C-104, 135 probably 1942 or 1943.

The following LPs represent Lester Young from mid-40s to the present:

Lester Young Collates, Mercury 10″ LP MG C-108

Lester's Here, Norgran 12″ LP MG N-1071

Lester Young, Norgran 12″ LP MG N-1022

The President, Lester Young, Norgran 12″ LP MG N-1005

The President Plays with the Oscar Peterson Trio, Norgran 12″ LP MG N-1045

Pres and Sweets, Norgran 12″ LP MG N-1043

Pres and Teddy, American Recording Society 12″ LP MG 417

The Jazz Giants '56, Norgran 12″ LP MG N-1056

Billie
Holiday

* * * *

By Charles Edward Smith

"There was nothing about living on the sidewall
that I didn't know," Billie Holiday told a writer for *Tan*.[1] "I kne
how the gin joints looked on the inside; I had been singing in afte
hour joints, damp, smoky cellars, in the backs of barrooms.

"It was slow, this attempt to climb clear of the barrel. But a
I grew older, I found those trying to keep me in it were not alwa
the corner hoodlum, the streetwalker, the laborer, the numbers ru
ner, the rooming-house ladies and landlords, the people who existe
off the twenty-five and thirty-dollars a week salaries they were pa
ing in those days.

"They, I found, were the ones who wanted to see me 'go,'
get somewhere. It was their applause and help that kept me inspire
These 'little people,' condemned as I have been ever since I ca
remember, gave me my chance long before the mink-coated lorgnet
crowd of Fifth Avenue and Greenwich Village ever heard of me."

Which could be said of most outstanding hot musicians. N
one begins at the top; few even reach it. And if Lady was condemne
now and again—and she has been, plenty—it was by essential
smaller minds and smaller people than the "little people" she kne
in Harlem during the Prohibition era. But her talent has never bee
without recognition. Indeed, it was in the small spots of Harle
that people like John Hammond, Paul Muni, Mildred Bailey ar
others heard her, encouraged her and got others to listen to her u
usual voice. This has not always meant popular acclaim or financi
success, though in plain sober fact Miss Holiday has made mo
luscious loot in a few good years than most of us can expect
make in a lifetime.

[1] A Johnson publication, February, 1953.

276

She is an altogether remarkable singer and, like her great predecessor, Bessie Smith, deserves the best. In backgrounds, the two have little in common. Bessie, when she was a kid, sang in a choir in Memphis and left home to become a protege of Gertrude "Ma" Rainey in Negro minstrels, in the South, the only place where the blues were "big" until Bessie, Louis and others rescued them from an unfair charge of country contamination. Billie ran errands for a Madam in East Baltimore, so that she could listen to records on the parlor phonograph by Bessie and Louis. But when she began singing in second-string Harlem hot spots, the material most in demand consisted of pop songs and show tunes, especially Negro show tunes, for few Negroes in those days could afford the charges in the swanky night clubs (such as the dicty Cotton Club, where oftentimes there were more whites than colored at the pink-lit tables).

In joints such as those Billie worked in there were any number of kids doing miserable imitations of Ethel Waters. She was different. Not that her style was perfect, but it was shaping up and already the direction was clear. For whatever she sang, she had a voice born of blues. And if she sang in the cellars, as she says, she probably sang more blues there—her rather sophisticated vocal style still shows the influence of lowdown and "dirty" blues intonation—than she ever did in the lesser night clubs of the Harlem circuit. There was a speakeasy around the corner from Jerry's Log Cabin, for example, where, at the very time Billie sang at the Log Cabin, at this basement bistro (which hardly deserved the name; there was a dirt floor and old boxes for chairs), one could hear harshly sung, moaning blues and "primitive" polyphonal and antiphonal spirituals that, years later, were to give root-nourishment to Rock and Roll. And this, too, was part of the Harlem scene but one the visiting public seldom got to know—"down home" blues and spirituals close to the field holler and the chant, gone underground in the urban North. But Billie knew it and, mixed up in her singing, as she went to work on the latest romantic ballad, was the beat and burning fire of the blues.

Essentially, hers has been a jazz, an *instrumental* style of singing for as long as critics have known it. She may have got it mostly from Louis, from his records and from hearing him at theatres, but style comes in bits and pieces, so infinitesimal that not even a singer can be aware of every last influence. What is significant is that she has been, and is, an artist in reshaping songs and ballads, and in this, of course, Louis was the first great master.

Billie Holiday (Eleanora Fagan Gough), was born in Baltimore, April 7, 1915, of teen-age parents who married three years later. When she says she was a woman at six she may have been thinking of other things than physical development. Her father, Clarence Holiday, was a musician (McKinney's Cotton Pickers, guitar; he'd formerly played trumpet) almost always on the road. He and Billie's mother had separated when Billie was little more than a baby so that she was, in effect, a fatherless child (as were so many during slavery days); the little mother called "Mom" was the rock she clung to. And even her mother left her with relatives, to go up North in search of work. It wasn't merely that Billie had traumatic experiences—life slaps all of us around—but it slapped her viciously, when she was very young and didn't know what it was all about.

Albeit she lacked Job's eloquence, her recital of grievances reminds one of him, as he inculpated the powers of darkness with a kind of sulky solemnity. Job in his way, was salty, and so was Billie, and in each case there seems an obvious merit. For instance, Billie was accused by her arch-tormentor, a cousin named Ida, of having indirectly caused the death of her great-grandmother, one of the few people who gave her love and to whom she gave love in return. Her great-grandmother had been a plantation slave (and Billie is descended from the owner), who used to entertain her with stories of the old days. She couldn't read or write but knew the Bible intimately. When her great-grandmother—who was not supposed to lie down (but rest in a chair) because of illness—asked Billie to let her lie down, she only thought to ease the old woman's pain. She spread a blanket on the floor and, being tired, lay down herself. She woke up hours later, with her great-grandmother's arm around her neck, and the arm was growing stiff and cold with death. She was scared and panicky and couldn't free herself and began to scream. After that she was in a hospital for a month, recovering from shock.

At the age of ten she was attacked by a man who lived in the neighborhood. The man was sent to prison and Billie was sent to a Catholic home where, as a punishment for infringement of rules, a refractory girl had to wear a raggedy red dress; once, Billie claims, she was locked in a room where a girl (who'd met with an accident) was lying out dead. In between such harrowing experiences she lived the "normal" life of a slum kid, snitching stuff from the dime store and sneaking into movies. When her father nicknamed her "Bill" because of her tomboy ways, she changed it to Billie, after Billie Dove, her idol of the silent films.

As she describes her early years in her autobiography she sounds like a tough little kid, running scared, and makes one realize how meaningless terms like "juvenile delinquent" can be when applied to specific persons. She didn't run in gangs. She was a lone wolf and a lonely little girl who, when barely old enough to be out on the streets, learned to spit and scratch and howl. Years later at the Grand Terrace in Chicago she threw a lethal threat and an inkwell at the manager, exploding in blind hostility just as she had as a small child when a boy teased her with a dead rat. On that occasion she whacked him over the head with a stick. On another, in a Fifty-second Street club, she dunked a maid (who'd called her a dirty name) in a toilet bowl, and a jurist, measuring the provocation, refused to press charges. On still another, she slapped a queer-dear down some stairs. Now that she is famous, such incidents are categorized as temperament. Yet all of these acts, and more, were less than adult and other than childish, for the child's act was defensive and, in its context, more than reasonable.

Billie came to New York when she was thirteen, in 1928, the year Louis recorded one of her favorite numbers, *West End Blues*. She decided to get off at Pennsylvania Station and visit Harlem before going on to meet her mother at Long Branch. Instead of which she got lost. A social worker for the Society for the Prevention of Cruelty to Children took her in hand and set her up in a beautiful hotel where she had a room and a bed to herself. This was living it up. Years later she looked up the place, out of curiosity, and to her amazement it turned out to be the YWCA.

In her autobiography, Billie tells of her experiences, in and out of jail, as a teen-age prostitute, and describes, at first hand, the seamy sides of seamy streets, during the late nineteen twenties, when corruption and gangsterism were rampant in many parts of the city, but nowhere more so than in Harlem, where white gangsters were in control of the more plush night clubs and street-corner loafers could steer you to after-hours joints, prostitutes or marijuana pads— whatever your wayward heart desired. Billie took to smoking reefers (marijuana) when still in her teens. This was not unusual in New York in those days and probably not unusual elsewhere—a "Kinsey report" on the subject would shock and surprise only the very sheltered.[2]

[2] I have known countless people who, at one time or another, smoked marijuana, only a few of them musicians (though I have more friends in music than any other field). So far as I know, none of them kept up the habit—

Billie didn't expect to be a call girl, even temporarily, but apparently looked upon the world of pimps and prostitutes as a way to make a fast buck. Since she was allowed to visit a house of prostitution and run errands for a Madam before she was thirteen, it i logical to suppose that she thought of the girls in the house as making a living (which, in fact, they did), without moral theorizing. To a slum kid the more affluent prostitutes may have seemed like fashion plates. Billie was sent into transports of happiness when "Mom" got a floppy big red velvet hat, such as Billie had seen on good-time glamour girls, decorated with Birds of Paradise feathers. But *she* only ran errands and, anyway, wasn't paid in money. She was paid in being allowed to listen to records by Bessie and Louis on the parlor phonograph, like the *West End Blues* that seemed to fit her changing moods. Sometimes it would make her happy and, "Some

---

except one poor guy who was baited by his own past, and not by a stick of tea—and none got "hooked" on the big H or anything else. Each to his own poison. The overweight lady with her box of chocolates and a bound volume of romantic slush and the dope addict with the handy hypo are sisters under the skin, each covering up an escape from reality with a more enveloping escape from reality. No escape solves problems; it only makes them more acute —*the monkey on your back, when you're on dope, always rides another monkey, and that goes for all such anodynes.*

Countless people have tried this or that habit-forming drug, for kicks, without forming any habits at all; others get hooked. And this last is no different —except in unfortunate choice of poison—than the plight of the alcoholic who gets hooked on good Kentucky bourbon and is finished off by sneaky Pete! The danger of marijuana is that it's an unnatural stimulant—I am not using the term medically, of course—it lets down bars (social inhibitions and endows one temporarily with extraordinary listening clarity. It appears to affect the time sense, and if the charge is effective, the most frenetic up tempo jamming by a Dixieland band or a gone Gillespie group can be as clear, individually and collectively, as though only one or two instruments in slow tempo were all the ear had to sort out. Such listening clarity may happen often, or rarely. The effect of a drug depends upon one's mood and one's tolerance to it; the more you take, the less the effect and the more damage to yourself physically. (After all, even drugs used legitimately, in medicine, are not intended to nourish the body; they are thieves set to catch thieves.) And perhaps the great danger in a seemingly harmless drug like marijuana, which many doctors have said is not habit-forming, is that when a "tea party" is drag, the escapist looks for a stronger charge and goes on to something else such as hashish. The marijuana smoker, like the drug addict, is often affected by conscious hallucination (one part of his mind the casual bystander as in some types of mental illness and delirium tremens. Until the hangover comes along, the alcoholic has a better, much less expensive, deal—he gets real lost, real fast.

times the record would make me so sad I'd cry up a storm." (*Hear Me Talkin' to Ya*).

So the two roads beckoned in a good-time parlor on the corner and she knew she would take the one that meant singing, even as she walked the streets in Harlem in a silk dress and spike heels. "I know this for damn sure," she says in her book, "if I'd heard Pops and Bessie wailing through the window of some minister's front parlor, I'd have been running errands for him. There weren't any priests in Baltimore then like Father O'Connor of Boston, who loves jazz and now has a big radio congregation listening to his disc-jockey shows."

In low-class joints where she worked for a while when young, she refused to pick up bills from tables without using her hands. She wanted to be a singer without tricks, sexual or otherwise. This was consistent. In the sort of hustling she had experienced there was nothing at all glamorous—one wonders if there ever is, except in books—and the whole pattern of life, from stealing white socks in the dime store to accepting a blue mink coat from her man, *paid for out of her own earnings as a singer,* found her trying to live up to the Lady, perhaps with an eye on the one for whom a day of the year, Lady Day, is listed on the Calendar of Saints. She had only to have known her own destiny, her own greatness, that she could not help but share with millions, to have found some measure of peace but, as with many artists, inner relaxation came only in rare moments. She was a Cinderella in reverse—it would seem at times that she could only believe, only be harassed by the phony part of herself—ragged, raw, pointless emotions, the wave peaks of choppy surface tensions, having little reference to the deeper tides. She was, like most of us at one time and another, a flagellant to appearances.

In an interview with Dave Dexter, Jr.,[3] she tells of the depression period when her mother couldn't find work as a housemaid and when she herself tried scrubbing floors and just couldn't make it. "We lived on 145th Street near Seventh Avenue," she explained. "One day we were so hungry we could barely breathe. I started out the door. It was cold as all-hell and I walked from 145th to 133rd down Seventh Avenue, going in every joint trying to find work. Finally, I got so desperate I stopped in at the Log Cabin, run by Jerry Preston. I told him I wanted a drink. I didn't have a dime.

[3] *Down Beat,* November 1, 1939.

But I ordered gin (it was my first drink—I didn't know gin from wine) and gulped it down.

"I asked Preston for a job . . . told him I was a dancer. He said to dance. I tried it. He said I stunk. I told him I could sing. He said: *sing*. Over in the corner was an old guy playing piano. He struck *Travelin' All Alone* and I sang. . . .[4] The customers stopped drinking. They turned around and watched. The pianist, Dick Wilson, swung into *Body and Soul*. Jeez, you should have seen those people—all of them started crying. Preston came over, shook his head and said, 'Kid, you win.' That's how I got my start."

The influx from downtown wasn't long in starting. Tipped off by Hammond, Benny Goodman and other musicians dropped in, and Benny used Billie on a record date for Columbia. This was before he'd organized his regular band. Teagarden, Krupa and Joe Sullivan were among those on the date that made *Your Mother's Son-in-Law,* in November, 1933, and, the following month, made *Riffin' the Scotch.* Wrote Dave Dexter of the first Holiday record (released with a Teagarden vocal on the flip side), "The disc is an item today, not only because of the fine instrumental work, but because it was Holiday's first side. She was pretty lousy. You tell her so and she grins. 'But I was only fifteen then,' she says, 'and scared.' " (I'll buy the "scared" but not the age bracket; she had to be eighteen or born in wedlock; she can't have it both ways.)

She continued to sing in Harlem night spots and at theatres but, outside the professional world of music and entertainment, she was surprisingly little known. What probably helped her more than anything else were some recording dates that John Hammond arranged for her with Teddy Wilson, Roy Eldridge, Benny Goodman, Ben Webster, John Trueheart, John Kirby and Cozy Cole, *e.g., What a Little Moonlight Will Do, I Wished on the Moon, Miss Brown to You.*[5]

Like most other hot musicians who have since become famous, Billie got very little for her work. Bernie Hanighen fought for her, to get her more money and wider recognition. "A lot of guys were big tippers uptown," she says in the autobiography, "but when it came to fighting for you downtown, they were nowhere. Not Bernie. He was the cause of me making my first records under my own name —not as anybody's damn vocalist, but as Billie Holiday period—

---

[4] A recording of this song which, in a sense, marked Billie's professional debut, was issued on Columbia CL 6129, *Billie Holiday Sings.*

[5] Reissued, *Lady Day* Columbia CL 6040.

and then the list of musicians backing me. Bernie Hanighen is a great guy."

When she opened at the Apollo, she sang one of his tunes. She had a bad case of stage fright, but by the second tune the house was with her and she was all right. There was an interesting crowd at the Apollo, as there had been at the Lafayette. They not only knew current song hits but knew the composers of them, and if they liked the composer, that was it, he was in, he was applauded just as loudly as though he'd been there in person. "There's nothing like an audience at the Apollo," says Billie. "They didn't ask me what my style was, who I was, where I'd come from, who influenced me, or anything. They just broke the house up." [6]

Billie said [7] that she'd aways wanted Bessie's big sound and Pop's feeling. What she got, as her style developed, was altogether her own sound, big, brash, subtle, soft-sensitive, a sour-sweet sound, the shape of which she manipulates so that it comes out flat, round, harsh, *pianissimo*—one of the most beautiful vocal sounds in jazz, once you get to know it—and out of a raw, emotional maelstrom, feelings disciplined in song.

She met Lester Young at a jam session. "I used to love to have him come around and blow pretty solos behind me." She once said that she was first called *Lady* because she wouldn't take customers' money off tables, an old-established (frankly obscene) gin-mill custom. Then Billie, who can use a rough, tough, nasty vocabulary when she wants to, blew a gasket at the loose and dirty talk of some Basie-ites. Whereupon Lester took the "Day" out of Holiday and that made it—Lady Day. She called him "Prez" for "President"; "Mom" was "Duchess"; to complete the list, her boxer was "Mister."

"If you find a tune and it's got something to do with you," she says,[8] "you don't have to evolve anything. You just feel it, and when you sing it other people can feel something, too. With me, it's got nothing to do with working or arranging or rehearsing. Give me a song I can feel, and it's never work. There are a few songs I feel so much I can't stand to sing them, but that's something else again."

From this statement, it is clear that the lyric is part of the material she has to work with, yet in treatment of it, melodically and rhythmically, she confutes semantics. "I don't think I'm singing," she says (*Hear Me Talkin' to Ya*), "I feel like I am playing a horn.

[6] *Autobiography.*
[7] *Hear Me Talkin' to Ya.*
[8] *Autobiography.*

I try to improvise like Les Young, like Louis Armstrong, or anyone
else I admire. What comes out is what I feel. I hate straight singing. I have to change a tune to my own way of doing it. That's all
I know."

Some of the incidents in Billie's life story, as one rereads them,
only get "curiouser and curiouser." Sometimes this is due, probably,
to confused memories, like her statement that she recorded *Night and
Day*, with Teddy Wilson, though she hadn't seen it before. (She
recorded it with Joe Sullivan and she should remember the band.
Freddie Green, a friend of hers, was in it. So were Buck Clayton,
whose horn she admired, Walter Page and Jo Jones. Hadn't seen
it before? This famous Cole Porter tune came out in 1932 or 1933,
featured in "The Gay Divorcee"; it was immediately in the hit category and has been ever since.

Such minor confusions are as negligible, really, as typographical
errors. What really floors one are yarns like the Philadelphia story,
the weirdest goof, when Joe Glaser arranged for her to appear on the
same bill with Ethel Waters. Her mother blew a week's salary on a
new evening dress for Billie, with shoes to match. Billie went into a
dime store and bought a tiny satin handbag to match, paying cash.
Her mother had once worked for Ethel Waters and both thought
that this was Opportunity, with a sparrow on her shoulder.

At this time Ethel Waters was big in show business. (Musicians
like her for her craftsmanship and showmanship, but she never rated
really big as a jazz singer.) Now, as we've indicated, audiences at
Negro theatres are among the most knowing in the country. They
know the singer, his or her theme song, and one chord is enough
to trigger the applause. Billie thought of herself as a pretty hip chick
in those days, and maybe she was. Yet she later claimed an ig-
norance of Ethel Waters' repertoire! She trotted up to the stage, gave
the piano player the nod and began blowing with both lungs on
Underneath the Harlem Moon, singing, she insists Ethel Waters said
later, like her shoes fit too tight (a remark attributed to others also).
She was still chewing up the first chorus when Ethel popped up in
the darkened theatre. "Nobody's going to sing on this goddamn stage,"
she boomed (according to Miss Holiday, *Autobiography*) "but
Ethel Waters and the Brown Sisters!" At this point in her story the
hip chick in Lady goes all naïve on us and she concludes, "I don't
know why Ethel Waters didn't like me. I never did a thing to her
that I know of except sing her big number that day."

"I'll never sing with a dance band again," Billie told Dave Dexter, Jr.[9] "It never works out for me. They wonder why I left Count Basie, and why I left Artie Shaw. Well, I'll tell you why— and I've never told this before—Basie had too many managers— too many guys behind the scenes who told everybody what to do. The Count and I got along fine. And the boys in the band were wonderful. But it was this and that, all the time, and I got fed up with it. Artie Shaw was a lot worse. I had known him a long time, when he was strictly from hunger around New York, long before he got a band. At first we worked together okay, then his managers started belly-aching."

Billie's chapters on road tours with Basie (1937) and Shaw (1938), playing dates that took them overnight from riff-raff joints to class hotels, are as frank and revealing as those on the seamy side of Harlem, when she was trying to make a fast buck the fast way. There also emerge from these pages her respect and love for musicians (some of them; for others she had no damn love at all, so to speak) and her growing maturity as a musician among musicians (though she didn't read music). For example, she says, "With Basie we had something no expensive arrangements could touch. The cats would come in, somebody would hum a tune. Then someone would play it over on the piano once or twice. Then someone would set up a riff, a ba-deep, a ba-dop. Then Daddy Basie would two-finger it a little."

Already, with groups led by Teddy Wilson and others, Billie had proved herself on blues, ballads and pop songs that in her interpretation, could be as poignant or portentous as *crimes passionels*. In handling tone and rhythm she was infinitely subtle, as is essential in a capable blues singer; usually she dragged the beat but she fooled around it (as Louie does) and sometimes gave it a nudge. The timbre of her voice changed to suit the mood of the song and her beautiful, strong vibrato could also be as delicate as an angel dancing on the head of a pin. Many of her metamorphoses of pops and ballads—some of the best vocals in jazz—are out of print, including the first version of *Summertime,* that she did in 1936 with Bunny Berigan and a small band.

By 1939, according to her (Dexter interview), she had loved three men. (There were others, subsequently, but only much later did she seem to radiate any real sense of contentment.) "One was

[9] *Op. cit.*

Marion Scott, when I was a kid. He works for the post office now. The other was Freddie Green, Basie's guitar man. But Freddie's first wife is dead and he has two children and somehow it didn't work out. The third was Sonny White, the pianist, but like me, he lives with his mother and our plans for marriage didn't jell. That's all." Even her book lacks what one could call any moving romantic interest, though it is not at all lacking in revelations of tenderness and feeling. (Frank and revealing as it is, it sometimes leaves one with an odd sense of incompletion, as though it did not always "dig" the real Billie, who is perhaps best felt in the sinuous line of a song. I was reminded, perhaps irrelevantly, of Freud's concept of dreams: that there is a manifest content, that *appears to be* the reality of the dream, and a *latent* content that is real, and that *is* the dream.)

"I'll say this about her," said Carmen McRae,[10] "—she sings the way she is. That's really Lady when you listen to her on a record. Whether it's a jump tune or a ballad, whatever you get out of a record of hers is really Lady. Singing is the only place she can express herself the way she'd like to be all the time."

When she gave a concert in 1949, Barry Ulanov wrote: [11] "The coarse yet warmly emotional quality of this sound, and the exquisite delicacy of her phrasing and dynamic nuances, were often given added lustre by the support she gained from her long association with Lester Young and other members of the Basie band on her earlier records."

The human reality of segregation—not the "race problem" of learned essays and Congressional cacaphony—dogged the Lady east, west, north, south. Unless your skin is the appropriate color, you may not be aware of the everyday humiliation that one out of ten of our citizens experience every day of the week, as regular as clockwork, but with more wheels within wheels. At a Detroit theatre she was asked to apply dark grease paint, so that she wouldn't be mistaken for off-white. Conversely, when she played a Detroit theatre with the Artie Shaw orchestra there was some apprehension about her appearing on stage (with a white band) because of her dark complexion. Billie, in her memoirs, called it "dynamic-assed Detroit."

Once, at a joint where some members of the Artie Shaw orchestra were having a snack, everybody got waited on but Lady. Chuck Peterson (trumpet) called the waitress over and Tony Pastor

---

[10] *Hear Me Talkin' to Ya.*
[11] *Metronome,* March, 1949.

(saxophone) bawled her out. "This is Lady Day," he said; "now you feed her." At some stops on the road such as roadside diners, there weren't even outdoor toilets for colored. Said Billie, "At first I used to be so ashamed. Then finally I just said to hell with it." [12]

When the band went into the Blue Room of the Lincoln (N.Y.C.) the treatment accorded Billie griped the whole band. Yet there seemed no way to cope with it. As Billie explained later, Artie and the men had taken months of hell-on-the-road for this New York engagement and a radio wire. This was the big one. So Lady came in the back door and didn't sit on the bandstand—as girl vocalists almost invariably did in the great days of swoon and swing —but went upstairs to a little room until she was called to sing her number. She was, she said, given fewer and fewer spots on the air time. It got to her, it got to her more than it ever had in the South, where it was all a part of somebody else's gracious way of living, and she blew up a storm and quit.

When Billie opened at Café Society Downtown (N.Y.C.) in the late nineteen thirties—her favorite flowers, white gardenias, in her hair—it was seven years and thousands of gut-torn, satin-sheathed songs from the Log Cabin. Café Society was filled to capacity with the sort of cosmopolitan audience for which it became famous—celebrities, artists, society people, and just people. And top-drawer jazz. Said Billie: [13] "Meade Lux Lewis knocked them out; Ammons and Johnson flipped them; Joe Turner killed them; (Frankie) Newton's band sent them; and then I came on. This was an audience."

When she sings from the guts—and that was the only way to sing her big tune there, *Strange Fruit* (Lewis Allen wrote it with her in mind, and she's the only one to sing it)—she reminds one of Bessie on a deeply felt blues. There is no hip-twisting or flirting with the microphone, but there appears to be an almost imperceptible tremor. Like Bessie, she sings with her whole body.

Once at a Miami night club a customer asked for *Strange Fruit* and *Gloomy Sunday!* She couldn't figure out why he asked for either but she finally sang *Strange Fruit* as an encore. "When I came to the final phase of the lyrics," she said, [14] "I was in the angriest and strongest voice I had been in for months. My piano player was

[12] *Autobiography.*
[13] *Op. cit.*
[14] *Op. cit.*

in the same kind of form. When I said '. . . for the sun to rot,' and then the piano punctuation, '. . . for the wind to suck,' I pounced on those words like they had never been hit before." The Commodore record of this song is one of the great vocals of jazz, described with penetrating accuracy by Glenn Coulter in *i.e.* [15] as "that uncanny expression of horror which transcends its willful lyric when Billie sings it, and becomes a frozen lament, a paralysis of feeling truer to psychology than any conventional emotionalism could be."

The nineteen forties, for Billie, began near the top and ended as near the bottom as one could get with any hope of climbing up again. She made trips to the Coast where moving-picture stars became her friends and where she met Norman Granz ("Jazz at the Philharmonic" concerts and recordings) who, in the 1950's, helped her to get back on her two feet and stand up straight professionally. She sang and acted in the film *New Orleans,* with Louis Armstrong. (She was given the usual, ignominious role of a maid, but at least she got to sing.) By the time the film had its premiere in New York she was in trouble with the law because of using heroin. Archer Winsten [16] wrote that her singing retained "the personal style that has inspired countless imitators. It is good to be able to say that some portion of her vocal and emotional sincerity makes itself felt on the screen at the very time when she herself is in sad circumstances." Previously, in 1946, her first solo concert, reported *Down Beat,* "was an event to go down in jazz history. Unsurpassed in her own field as a great and individual song stylist, and long a favorite in jazz circles, the turnout at Town Hall was far beyond expectations."

Before the timbers shoring up the roof (that was to fall on her) began to creak, Billie recorded songs that are among her most moving performances. Among these was *God Bless the Child* [17] worked out with Arthur Herzog after she had had a quarrel with her mother. She said [18] "This will gas the Duchess, I thought. And it did." In fact, it gassed a lot of people, sardonic lyrics twisting and squirming under the scalpel of Billie's membraneous reed.

"In a reversal of the usual story," wrote Glenn Coulter (*i.e.*) "Billie's popularity increased during the same time that her style became more complex. This was also the period when her life seemed

[15] *The Cambridge Review,* December, 1956.
[16] New York *Post.*
[17] Columbia.
[18] *Autobiography.*

tangled and difficult . . . if drama intensifies it may do so by means of irony. To this weapon Billie now turned and as she sang a love song, it became a cry of hatred and contempt. . . ." Of her uneven output at this time he remarks, "Most of these bad performances take place in an over-arranged, be-violined setting, and the gait never seems to be an honest jazz tempo, or indeed any tempo that allows music to breathe naturally." Mr. Coulter noted what appeared to be an attempt to convert Billie "into a super-personality cranking out million-copy best sellers. . . . It is a shock to recall that Billie saw no incongruity in this attempt; we even learn with dismay that the throbbing violins are there at her express wish; it is only the demon that kept her against her will from abandoning her art for the big money."

This is almost too neat a way of putting it. From the simplest beginnings of folk art, it would seem, artists in whatever field have taken pride in craftsmanship and found a simple joy in the esthetic end result of art, with its serene and commonplace identity with all things that breathe and have life. This directness and direction of art is modified by ego-demands for money and prestige—no artist is altogether free from both—and might also be influenced (as indeed, is often the case) by the everyday hungers, for love and food and a roof overhead. Stress and conflict in lesser and greater security needs cast impinging shadows and these, in grotesque distortion, become the demon.

Lady's demon had many faces. One was the big H, heroin. On Tuesday, May 27, 1947, she appeared in United States District Court, Ninth and Market, Philadelphia, and was arraigned for violation of Section 174, Title 21, U.S.C.A. (violation of Narcotics Act). In the course of his remarks the district attorney said: [19] "She has given these agents a full and complete statement and came in here last week with the booking agent (Glaser) and expressed a desire to be cured of this addiction. Very unfortunately she has had following her the worst type of parasites and leeches you can think of. We have learned that in the past three years she has earned almost a quarter of a million dollars, but last year it was $56,000 or $57,000 and she doesn't have any of that money."

Billie volunteered to take a government-supervised cure—she had previously tried to "kick" it off with a private hospital cure but it hadn't worked—and was committed to the segregated Federal rehabilitation establishment for women at Alderson, West Virginia,

[19] *Autobiography.*

for a year and a day. After a brief but rough "cold turkey" treatment, she was fitted into the routine, starting out as a "Cinderella," washing dishes and peeling potatoes, then for a spell was assigned to work with the pigs on the farm. Nevertheless, and despite Jim Crow, she found it a better environment than the city prison had been and remarked at one point, "There were any number of heart-warming experiences." [20]

Billie gave a concert at Carnegie Hall ten days after leaving Alderson. She played to a packed house and hundreds were turned away. Coming north from West Virginia she got off at Newark and went direct to Morristown to stay with Bobby Tucker's family. Bobby was her accompanist and the first song they rehearsed was *Night and Day,* which she described as "the toughest song in the world for me to sing." [21] "I'll never forget that first note, or the second. Or especially the third one, when I tried to hit 'day' and hold it. I hit it and held it and it sounded better than ever. Bobby almost fell off the stand, he was so happy. . . . We did all our rehearsing right there. We never went near New York, or Carnegie Hall. Bobby and his mother made me feel I was home and everything was cool."

"All dope can do for you is kill you—and kill you the long slow hard way," said Billie.[22] "And it can kill the people you love right along with you."

The user of narcotics is the eternal fall guy. Pushers, themselves *pushed* by the tycoons of the multi-million-dollar dope racket, harass them with all the slimy persistence of bloodsuckers and blackmailers. Narcotics agents keep tabs on users, and it would seem, of those who have "kicked" the habit, in the hope of getting a line on the higher-ups. In New York, Billie was refused a performer's license for work in cabarets—but this was standard procedure; she was in no sense singled out. "Billie is not self-pitying," Nat Hentoff commented in reviewing her book for *Down Beat,*[23] "but she does make several valid complaints, including a plea that America adopt the British system of treating addicts as 'sick people' under medical care."

In the interests of rehabilitation, at various times, Billie had a talk with a priest, spent loads of money on new clothes, bought a

---

[20] *Ebony,* July, 1949.
[21] *Autobiography.*
[22] *Ibid.*
[23] August 8, 1956.

sleek Cadillac the color of chlorophyll-happy green peas, and a plot of land in New Jersey. Later (she doesn't give an exact date) she went to a psychiatrist, and was proud to have fought down an urge to die and gotten back the love of life and the will to live that goes with it.

As often happens with people who've been on dope, some previous friends and acquaintances were wary of associating with her. In the vernacular, she was *hot*. Others, such as Bobby Tucker and John Simmons, acted as though she had merely been away for a while, which was the truth. John took her down to the Strand to hear Lena Horne. Lena had been told that Billie was out front and came down from the stage and up the darkened aisle to take Lady in her arms. As Billie said, people like Lena took the sting out of the others.

But grief piled up. She told a writer for *Ebony* [24] that a manager had taken her to the cleaners to the tune of six thousand dollars, "most of my earnings following my confinement. Other large sums that belonged to me were squandered by unscrupulous handlers, money that had accumulated during my imprisonment. These charges are not directed against the Associated Booking Corporation whose president, Mr. Joe Glaser, has been my friend and confidante."

The storm that blew her house of cards apart in 1947 had a vicious back-lash that caught her while on the West Coast two years later. A news item in *Down Beat,* datelined San Francisco, July, 1949, reads:

"Broke and alone after her manager, John Levy, left her to face the trial here at which she was acquitted, Billie Holiday decided to go back to work. . . . But despite the fact that the jury said they believed Billie had been framed by Levy, she said, 'If he was to walk into the room this minute, I'd melt. He's my man and I love him.'

"The trial appeared to confirm that a package of opium had been planted on Billie just before the raid. Billie came to trial with a black eye she said Levy gave her before he left. 'You should see my back,' she added. 'And he even took my silverblue mink— 18 grand worth of coat. He said he was going to give it to his sister to take care of for me. *I got nothing now and I'm scared.*

" 'I turned all my life over to John. He took all my money. I never had any money. We were supposed to get married. On January 22, John came back from Los Angeles. We had been arguing about

[24] July, 1949.

money. . . . While Levy was unpacking the telephone rang.' Immediately afterwards, she said, he handed her a package and told her to get rid of it. I went into my room. John closed the door behind me. . . . Then someone grabbed me. . . . John told me to throw some trash away. I did it. . . . My man makes me wait on him, not him on me. I never did anything without John telling me.' " And in her autobiography, she has this comment: "Somebody once said we never know what is enough until we know what's more than enough. They could have had me and Mr. Levy in mind."

The story of the San Francisco trial and her acquittal is told by Billie in her book and by Jake Ehrlich, the famous West Coast lawyer who defended her, in a paperback dealing with famous cases he's handled, *Never Plead Guilty*.[25]

In the late 'forties, Billie had her own show on Broadway, backed by Bob Sylvester and other true believers; it flopped after three weeks. She has had very successful tours of Europe, the last one in the nineteen fifties when, in a group shepherded by Leonard Feather, she wowed them in Copenhagen. Some time after the San Francisco trial she married Louis McKay. She was also once married to trumpet player Joe Guy, but this time it showed signs of taking.

During the present decade she has steadily recaptured her sureness of style and, along with it, a mellowing and maturity. Happily, however, her intonation has not lost its caustic undertones and her voice can still be as tight as Montgomery Clift's Levi's. In the spring of 1957 contracts were signed for a film-biography of her life, with indications that William Dufty, her collaborator on the book, would do the script, Billie the sound track and possibly Dorothy Dandridge would play the lead.

Sardonic and sophisticated as her singing style is, it has retained and made stronger and deeper an affinity to such honky-tonk styles as that of Alice Moore whose "I'm black an' evil an' I did not make myself . . ." sears the eardrums. No one since Ma Rainey has sung the "My man"-type blues with such sullen, sultry pathos. No one has given such point and passion to popular song lyrics. On *I'll Be Seeing You*,[26] her manipulation and control of rhythm, tone and beat, are almost flawless in a perfection you won't find in any

[25] Ballantine Books.
[26] Com. 20005.

rule book. For instance, on such words as "familiar" and "wishing well"; the rhythmic accent on the latter words, especially, is a beautiful example of a great jazz singer's awareness of and emphasis of the beat. This is style, not trickiness (though she could be tricky, at times). When young singers are so reckless as to try to imitate her, they thunder gracelessly down the stretch like Percheron colts running for the roses.

In an article on the jazz vocal, this writer remarked, "She can twist a syllable into a stabbing and lethal stiletto; she can cry without tears. . . . A surging, explosive, emotional force pushes at the orderly, almost bland lineaments that contain her song. More than any other modern singer she belongs to the blues and has extended them into jazz with a superb and dedicated craftsmanship."

Nat Hentoff called hers "the most hurt and hurting style in jazz." Reviewing a 1956 album, *Music for Torching*,[27] he said, "This is Holiday as she is now—no softening, no looking for ghosts of the past. I feel there is no one in jazz who can come close in terms of penetration to the Holiday on these tracks." In a review of a concert at which Billie sang and Gilbert Millstein did a narrative commentary based on the book, John S. Wilson [28] remarked that, "She still manages to convey that feeling of wonder that, along with her rough, throaty croon and her expressive dips, lifts and dolorously twisted notes, are the essential ingredients of a highly personal style." She has, of course, had some low lows in her singing career and it may be, as she has implied, that some critics have tried to read her out of the club. She says of American critics, "Some damn body is always trying to embalm me. I'm always making a comeback, but nobody ever tells me where I've been." [29]

In one of the most penetrating analyses of her style it has been the pleasure of this writer to come upon, Glenn Coulter says, (*i.e.*) "Billie's deadpan actually conceals a good deal of intricate treatment. She is not afraid to sound awkward if that is the best way for her to nail a song home: *Nice Work If You Can Get It* is a good example of this rigidity." And of her voice: "Many a singer has tried without success to copy its colour, clear and cold, so bitingly cold that like dry ice it can suggest great heat."

And the following paragraphs on style are very lucid indeed:

[27] Clef C-713.
[28] *New York Times,* November 11, 1956.
[29] Well, Lady, that's why you wrote a book, remember?

"Her distortions of pitch are wedded, welded rather, to her manipulations of the beat. . . . When Billie sings, we notice that nobody relies more emphatically on those modal changes.[30] But the voice is more limited in respect of melodic variation than any instrument. Billie therefore depends on other weapons, particularly on a tight control of what weapons she has, and so we have a whole spectrum of blue notes: a note may begin slightly under pitch, absolutely without vibrato, and gradually be forced up to dead center from where the vibrato shakes free, or it may trail off mournfully; or, at final cadences, the note is a whole step above the written one and must be pressed slowly down to where it belongs.

"The melodic alterations which vocal convenience made necessary now have a miraculous simplicity. Best of all, Billie has at last recaptured delight in her singing, and her sense of suffering is no longer cruel but compassionate. In place of the angry outcries so noticeable before, we now hear a sad acceptance, not only of pain but of the truth that pain is not an individual thing. An excellent foretaste of this further range may be found in the second record of *Travelin' Light*,[31] the record of a public performance, and one of the few things in jazz that can stand the word 'sublime.' It is noteworthy as one of the rare occasions when Billie has risen triumphantly above an inept accompaniment. . . . *It Had To Be You* [32] is a good example of this late warmth in tone."

Billie Holiday, born Eleanora Fagan and dubbed Lady Day, was a product of the East Baltimore slums where a star cracked on her cradle, leaving her star-born and star-crossed. Some years ago the Lady of the White Gardenias, in a Cadillac whose whiteness matched the white steps of Baltimore she'd scrubbed as a kid, drove slowly through the old neighborhood. Even in this she appeared to pay homage with the clumsiness and belligerence of the fear-ridden, the guilt-gotten. But, if so, this was a deeper guilt than the unreasonable but conventional reaction that her past might have instilled in her—of the deep and dark places of the mind, having only a tangental relationship to all manner of hustling, a hurt and a haunt that could be exorcised only by a song.

But we're all of us love hunters, some stalking the prey, some wooing it, some finding it by giving it, others folding before it like

[30] Blues style C.E.S.
[31] Clef 169.
[32] Clef 669.

night flowers in sunlight, resistless in the coils of an indiscriminate and emotional hunger. Insight is not enough. Not unless it becomes part of one, as in some precious moments when there is no longer the chasm between what one knows, deep within one's self, and what one believes and is, outwardly. Lady comes closest to this fusion of knowing and feeling when she says: [33] "I've been told that nobody sings the word 'hunger' like I do. Or the word 'love.'

"Maybe I remember what those words are all about. Maybe I'm proud enough to *want* to remember Baltimore and Welfare Island, the Catholic Institution and the Jefferson Market Court, the sheriff in front of our place in Harlem and the towns from coast to coast where I got my lumps and scars, Philly and Alderson, Hollywood and San Francisco—every damn bit of it. . . . You've got to have something to eat and a little love in your life before you can hold still for any damn body's sermon. . . ."

SELECTED DISCOGRAPHY—BILLIE HOLIDAY

Lady Day, Columbia CL 637
The Lady Sings, Decca 8215
Lady Sings the Blues, Clef 721
Music For Torching, Clef 669
Solitude, Clef 690
Velvet Mood, Clef 713

[33] *Autobiography.*

Roy Eldridge

* * * *

By Nat Hentoff

Otto "Toby" Hardwicke, for many years in the Duke Ellington reed section, is almost as famed among musicians for his accurate wit in affixing durable nicknames as is Lester Young. It was Hardwicke who first called Roy Eldridge "Little Jazz," a description that has been Roy's other name ever since.

"We were working together in Smalls' Paradise with Elmer Snowden around 1931," Roy remembers. "I was blowing all the time—on the set, between sets, on the way home, in the morning. So he called me 'Little Jazz.' "

The irresistible urge to play jazz, to keep playing it, is a motivating characteristic of Roy Eldridge. His close friend and equally inexhaustible contemporary, Coleman Hawkins, recently was lamenting the extreme present-day rarity of jam sessions as contrasted with their plenty years ago.

"But Roy finds them," Hawkins shook his head. "Even if he's the only horn there, playing with the house rhythm section."

In Stockholm one night, during a Jazz at the Philharmonic concert, Ella Fitzgerald was listening from the wings as the instrumentalists settled into a ballad medley. Roy played the first couple of notes of his selection.

"God gives it to some and not to others," Ella said. "He's got more soul in one note than a lot of people could get into the whole song."

Also to the jazz point is the fact that Roy is so personal a trumpeter that his voice can be instantly recognized on hearing the first couple of notes.

The fire that is Roy Eldridge began in Pittsburgh, January 30, 1911. In a 1950 Paris interview with Charles Delaunay of *Jazz-Hot*, Roy recalled:

"I started playing music from the age of six. I played drums then in a band made up of a violin, a horn, a trumpet, and a piano. When I was twelve and playing in a brass band, somebody lent me a trumpet. Each year, the band took part in the Decoration Day ceremonies. The trumpets were placed at the four corners of the cemetery and blew *Taps*. I remember that I was so moved by the presence of a lot of neighbors who had come to see my debut, that when my turn came to play, all that came out of my horn were quivering, strangled sounds."

Roy's elder brother by three years, Joe, a reedman, tried to encourage the youngster to continue in music. He gave him a trumpet and Roy began to take lessons. "But I was very lazy," Roy said years later. "I barely learned my solfeggio, and couldn't read music. When my teacher and I had to play duets—particularly in church—I had to pretend to read my part, and there were often some curious results."

Roy began to work evenings; and one day, having been sent home from school, he left home to join the band for a traveling show. "My only baggage was a suit, a pair of shoes and my trumpet."

The band, Eldridge told Delaunay, was called the Nighthawk Syncopators. The year was 1927. "The people who had hired us didn't know that none of us could read music. For the overture to the show, a blues singer gave us her arrangement, saying, 'Just hit it!'

"The curtain opened, and we couldn't get a sound out. She turned around and asked us what was going on. We confessed we couldn't read music. So we played a blues and it worked out. We had at the most five or six numbers in our book. The specialty was *Stampede* on which I played note for note the saxophone solo of Coleman Hawkins that I'd learned from a Fletcher Henderson record."

The promoter of the show abandoned the troupe in Sharon, Pennsylvania, and the band's trunks were locked in their rooms for non-payment of rent. Hungry, they went to Farrell, Pennsylvania, and rented a small store front wherein they presented a nightly show. Nobody came.

A samaritan took the boys to Youngstown, Ohio. At a party, the leader of a carnival band heard Roy and his colleagues play Roy's Hawkins-version of *Stampede*. "He had never heard a trumpet play like that before. So he asked me to join the show and I did.

"That carnival," Roy recalled recently, "had a thirty-two-piece brass band, but before the trip was over, I wound up playing drums. I couldn't read a note as big as this building. Also I'd never played outdoors before. I had the kind of sound that would be right in style in cool jazz. Well, they had made up an arrangement of *Stampede* for me with me playing the Hawkins solo, but I had my troubles. The first trumpeter would sometimes purposely stay out, so that I'd have to play the first trumpet part. I got away with it for a while because if he hummed it, I could play it. But one day, he didn't hum it, and it caught up with me.

"The pianist in the band kept telling me, 'You'll never be a musician; you'd be better off if you forgot about it. Don't you see that you're taking the place of a real musician?'"

"What kept me in the show was that I switched to drums. The drummer had left, and we were playing in Aurora, Illinois. Guys from Chicago were coming out every day to audition. I knew the drum part by heart, so I told them to rent some drums, and that's how I stayed with that show."

According to the interview with Delaunay, Roy's next gig was in the territory band of Oliver Moldroon out of Little Rock. He came back to Pittsburgh, headed a band under the name of "Roy Elliott and his Palais Royal Orchestra from New York," and developed a specialty on *East St. Louis Toodle-Oo* during which he used a gold-painted tin can as a "wa-wa" mute, dancing the camel walk while playing.

During this first growing period, Roy's initial major influences were Rex Stewart and Red Nichols on trumpet. "And also," he has pointed out, "saxophones. Coleman Hawkins and Benny Carter. They played so much music, Hawkins and Carter, how could you help not like them if you like music? They had and have distinctive sounds, voices of their own.

"My first major influence on my own horn was Rex Stewart. I liked his speed, range and power. He was a bad boy in those days, and he was the guy I was trying to pattern myself after. He used to play in my brother Joe's band. They came to New York, worked at the Renaissance for some time, and then they came to Pittsburgh, and stayed at our house. This goes back to when I was around ten or eleven. The band, the Elite Serenaders, would practice in our house all the time. Rex was the first trumpeter to show me breaks."

Red Nichols was another influence. "I liked the nice, clean sound he was getting for a trumpet in those days. I was doing all right playing in that style until I got to St. Louis where I went after the experience as Roy 'Elliott.' In St. Louis, every Sunday, five trumpet players came down and tore me apart. I was about sixteen, and I was playing smooth. They played with a guttural kind of sound. They were more or less on a Louis Armstrong kick, the way Louis used to play, but more guttural. I was playing what could be called cool then, and I wasn't familiar with that other style. I couldn't understand how they got around to playing like that— the lip vibrato, trills and the like. Some of the names of those trumpet players in St. Louis were Dewey Jackson, Baby James, 'Cookie' and 'Big Ham.'

"Next I worked a traveling show until my first gig in an important orchestra, the Fletcher Henderson Stompers under the direction of Horace Henderson. There weren't very big names in the band, but they were all excellent musicians. My next bands were the Nighthawks (another one in Detroit); Zach Whyte (where I met Sy Oliver and Herman Chittison); and Speed Webb (which included Teddy Wilson and his brother Gus, Vic Dickenson and Reunald Jones, now with Basie).

"That was a remarkable orchestra with no less than eight arrangers among the men. One day we decided to dispense with Speed and I was chosen leader. It was at that time that I won my first musical battle. One night we were opposite the band of Sam Hines, a pianist who had met me before. When he recognized me, he said, 'I'm sorry for you that you had to come up against a band like mine tonight.'

"Our band had never played as well as it did that night. Before we left, Whyte came up and told me, 'I always knew you'd make it.'"

When the band dissolved, Roy went on to Milwaukee to play in the Johnny Mills band. It was in Milwaukee that young, cocky Roy received a lesson he remembered as long and deeply as his informal Sunday school in St. Louis.

"That town was where Jabbo Smith caught me one night and turned me every way but loose. I was young in those days, and I guess I was modern then. One night Jabbo asked for my horn. He played *Confessin'*. It was like Louis, I guess. At that time I hadn't heard Louis in person. So I thought Jabbo wasn't playing anything much, and asked for my horn back. He said to meet him at the Rails an hour later.

"The joint was loaded with performers and musicians, and they tried to make a contest out of it. 'It wouldn't be a contest,' said Jabbo. 'Don't nobody know this boy.' That got me mad, but he wore me out before that night was through. He knew a lot of music, and he knew changes.

"Back in that time, in the 'twenties, the men who were wailing, as I began to find out, were Louis, King Oliver, Jabbo Smith and Cuban Bennett. And guys like Bobby Stark and Rex Stewart were playing a lot. Cuban Bennett, whom very few people have apparently heard of, was playing around New York in the 'twenties. He was one of the first cats I ever heard play the right changes. I knew about him because, although we didn't have any magazines in those days, you'd hear about things. You could be in California, but you'd know whether a guy in New York could play.

"Cuban Bennett was Benny Carter's first cousin. He was really making his changes in those days. You could call him one of the first of the moderns. He mostly gigged around. He wouldn't hold a steady job; he drank a lot. And he never made any records. He was a great trumpet player. He played more like a saxophone did. You see, the saxophone then, or some of them, would run changes, would run through all the passing chords and things, and then do a little turn around. Like they might play six bars, and in the seventh would start going into the release and then the eighth would be all set up for the second eight."

Roy, as Barry Ulanov pointed out in his *A History of Jazz in America*, "reached for saxophone lines when he picked up his trumpet." Roy told Barry how Hawkins and Carter had inspired him. "I'd listen to them and be stunned. I didn't know the right names for anything at first, but I knew what knocked me out. . . . Changes, man, I dug."

From Milwaukee, Roy faced the major challenge. He came to New York.

He worked with Cecil Scott's band, doubling at the Douglas Theatre alongside musicians like Chu Berry. "Chu did a lot for me when I came to New York to stay around 1930. I had been there before on vacations, but now I had to prove myself. When I came, for two weeks Chu, my brother and a piano player named Panama kept me in a house and taught me all the tunes before they took me to the Rhythm Club to play with and against people.

"When I first came to New York, I thought more of speed than of the melody. I remembered when I was kid hearing Rex Stewart play with great speed and with a lot of notes. At that time in the East, trumpets either played like Red Nichols or Bix, or they went for a lot of effects with mutes, especially 'growl' effects. I felt there were other possibilities in the trumpet, and I tried to play very fast. I had to play everything fast and double fast. I couldn't stand still.

Like a lot of youngsters today, all my ballads had to be double time. I was fresh. I was full of ideas. Augmented chords. Ninths.

"The cats used to listen to me," Eldridge once told Ulanov, "and they'd say, 'Well, he's nice, but he don't say nothing!' Consequently I didn't work. No one played as fast I did, but the other trumpet players broke it up. I didn't. Also, I was playing fine saxophone on the trumpet. Trying to hold notes longer than they should be held, trying to get a sound which I couldn't and shouldn't get. When I discovered that a trumpet has a sound all its own, and a way of playing all its own, then I began to play."

It was at this time that the most important influence yet on Roy's playing began to be felt. Roy first really discovered Louis Armstrong.

"I didn't get to hear Louis in person until 1932. The first time I heard any records by him was in 1927, I think. It was through Matty Matlock in Omaha, Nebraska. I was in a traveling show, and I met him in a music store in town. Matty was with a band from Chicago, working at a hotel there. He brought some of the records to our house, and I can remember *Wild Man Blues, Gully Low,* etc. I can still play *Wild Man Blues*. In fact, years later, I recorded it in France with the pianist Claude Bolling along with *Skip the Gutter* and *Fireworks*. They were issued here on Dial.

"But Louis wasn't an influence on me until I saw him in person. Jabbo Smith didn't have Louis' sound, but he was faster. But Louis gave me something I couldn't get off Jabbo—continuity, which makes all the sense. Louis introduces the piece and sticks around the melody, but when he has it out, you know it's out, and you know he's going to finish a whole.

"In 1932, I first caught Louis at the Lafayette Theatre in New York, and he finally upset me. I was a young cat, and I was very fast, but I wasn't telling no kind of story. Well, I sat through the first show, and I didn't think Louis was so extraordinary. But in the second show, he played *Chinatown*. He started out like a new book, building and building, chorus after chorus, and finally reaching a full climax, ending on his high F. It was a real climax, right, clean, clear. The rhythm was rocking, and he had that sound going along with it. Everybody was standing up, including me. He was building the thing all the time instead of just playing in a straight line.

"I've been digging him ever since. I started to feel that if I could combine speed with melodic development while continuing to build, to tell a story, I could create something musical of my own that the public would like. As for Louis, I began buying his records, and I let him alone. I got to know him pretty well. We never have played together at after-hour sessions. We did play on the same set at a Metropolitan Opera House concert, but the producer didn't let me do the thing I wanted to that night. Anyway, from the time I heard him at the Lafayette in 1932, new horizons were opened for me."

Returning to Roy's career, that first New York engagement with Cecil Scott and doubling at the Douglas Theatre had given Roy his initial taste of money in quantity. "It was the first time in my life that I was making one hundred dollars a week. I had my first one hundred dollars changed into one-dollar bills, and I'd enjoy looking at it and counting it."

Roy went to work with Elmer Snowden's band at Smalls' Paradise, and among his colleagues were Dickie Wells, Wayman Carver, Don Kirkpatrick, Sid Catlett and Otto Hardwicke. It was on that gig that Hardwicke gave Roy his name. Other bands with which Roy gained experience in New York were those of Charlie Johnson and Teddy Hill.

In 1933, he returned to Pittsburgh and formed, together with his brother Joe, the Eldridge brothers' band. Young Kenny Clarke, later to become the dean of modern jazz drummers, was included. Roy played with McKinney's Cotton Pickers in 1934–35, and then returned to Teddy Hill and another association with Chu Berry. He soon formed another small combo with his brother to play the Hickory House in New York; joined Fletcher Henderson for a time; and headed his own band again at the Three Deuces in Chicago for three years.

Back east, he joined Mal Hallet around 1938; worked in a radio-studio band for a few months; then played nine months at the Arcadia Ballroom in charge of his own band. Billie Holiday worked with that band for some time and the then relatively unknown King Cole trio and Art Tatum were also often on the bill.

Before joining Gene Krupa's big band as featured soloist in 1941, Roy had returned to Chicago and another period of trying to make it as a leader. In the 'forties, he intermittently headed his own big band again, and for some four months played another studio job with the Paul Baron orchestra on CBS. His most pleasant studio memories were the broadcasts he did during this time with Mildred Bailey. "I never had any trouble reading in studio work. The only reading trouble I ever had was with Fletcher's band. He used all the sharps."

But as for studio work in general, Roy has often stated his position: "It's a nice feeling at first to know that you can make it, that you can read well and fast enough. But after the thrill of reading, I mean of blowing along with everyone else and not having to have an orchestra of thirty men stopped because of you, then what do you have? Playing the same thing again and again becomes monotonous. I guess I don't have the temperament for it. That's why I've stayed in jazz."

For the rest of the 'forties, there was a period with Artie Shaw's big band in 1944–45, with Jazz at the Philharmonic, back with Krupa in 1949, with varying gigs in between.

In 1950, Roy had a chance to travel to Europe with Benny Goodman. Once in Paris, he decided to stay for a while. He needed time to reassess his career, and especially to rewind a dwindling confidence in his continuing ability to function successfully in a new world of "bop."

Charles Delaunay, editor of *Jazz-Hot* in Paris, came to know Roy well during this plateau period. "Roy ended the Goodman tour in Paris. He felt so happy in Europe and particularly in Paris that he decided to stay over awhile. He made lots of friends and really had a ball. The first thing anyone would notice was that he really felt happy, was welcomed everywhere, invited to people's homes, and was accepted. I imagine his pleasure in just being there was mainly due to his discovery that there was no racial prejudice."

The absence of Jim Crow—so far as he was concerned—was undoubtedly a major factor in Roy's delight in being in France, because Roy has always been rawly sensitive to the indignities he has had to undergo in America, and not only in travels through Southern one-nighters.

In a painful interview in *Down Beat* some years ago, Roy communicated some of his anger and grief on the subject of Jim Crow:

"One thing you can be sure of, as long as I'm in America, I'll never in my life work with a white band again! It goes all the way back to when I joined Gene Krupa's band. Until that time no colored attraction had worked with a white band except as a separate attraction, like Teddy and Lionel with Benny Goodman.

"That was how I worked with Gene at first; I wasn't treated as a full member of the band. But very soon I started sharing Shorty Sherock's book and when he left the band, I took over. It killed me to be accepted as a regular member of the band. But I knew I'd have to be awful cool; I knew all eyes were on me to see if I'd make time or do anything wrong.

"All the guys in the band were nice, and Gene was especially wonderful. That was at the Pennsylvania Hotel. Then we headed West for some one-nighters, winding up in California. That was when the trouble began.

"We arrived in one town and the rest of the band checks in. I can't get into their hotel, so I keep my bags and start riding around looking for another place, where someone's supposed to have made a reservation for me. I get there and move all my bags in. Naturally, since we're going to be out on the Coast several months, I have a heavy load, at least a dozen pieces of baggage.

"Then the clerk, when he sees that I'm the Mr. Eldridge the reservation was made for, suddenly discovers that one of their regular tenants just arrived and took the last available room. I lug that baggage back into the street and start looking around again.

"By the time that kind of thing has happened night after night, it begins to work on my mind; I can't think right, can't play right. When we finally got to the Palladium in Hollywood, I had to watch who I could sit at the tables with. If they were movie stars who wanted me to come over, that was all right; if they were just the jitterbugs, no dice. And all the time the bouncer with his eye on me, just watching for a chance.

"On top of that, I had to live way out in Los Angeles, while the rest of the guys stayed in Hollywood. It was a lonely life; I'd never been that far away from home before, and I didn't know anybody. I got to brooding.

"Then it happened. One night the tension got so bad I flipped. I could feel it right up to my neck while I was playing *Rockin' Chair;* I started trembling, ran off the stand, and threw up. They carried me to the doctor's. I had a hundred and five fever; my nerves were shot.

"When I went back a few nights later I heard that people were asking for their money back because they couldn't hear *Let Me Off Uptown.* This time they let me sit at the bar.

"Later on, when I was with Artie Shaw, I went to a place where we were supposed to play a dance, and they wouldn't even let me in the place. 'This is a white dance,' they said, and there was my name right outside, Roy 'Little Jazz' Eldridge, and I told them who I was.

"When I finally did get in, I played that first set, trying to keep from crying. By the time I got through the set, the tears were rolling down my cheeks. I don't know how I made it. I went up to a dressing room and stood in a corner crying and saying to myself, 'Why the hell did I come out here again when I knew what would happen?' Artie came in and he was real great. He made the guy apologize that wouldn't let me in, and got him fired.

"Man, when you're on the stage, you're great, but as soon as you come off, you're nothing. It's not worth the glory, not worth the money, not worth anything. Never again!"

A man who knows Roy well feels that as a result of years of tripping over Jim Crow, Roy trusts few white men. "It may be," said the friend, "that he only really trusts Norman Granz and Gene Krupa among the whites."

So, feeling free in Paris, Roy began to find it was possible to be relaxed on the Crow score all the time, or nearly all the time. But his major problem was not Crow. He had reached a difficult, acutely self-questioning stage in his career.

"I had to go away and think. Things were getting so turned around in music. I couldn't figure out which way to go. I listened to all the records, but I'd always go back to Hawkins, Carter, Tatum, Teddy Wilson, etc., because they seemed to be playing more originally, and they seemed to be playing more music all the time than the others. They didn't get so set, so involved with stock things."

Yet, though his confidence in Hawkins and Carter remained firm, Roy had gradually lost a great amount of faith in himself. He felt he was aging, and he worried whether the young "boppers" were not so pervasive a wave of the future that there would soon be no dry land for him. And if that were the case, could he change his style? Would he want to?

"Back around 1945," Norman Granz recalls, "I went out on a tour with Roy and Hawk. When we got to Los Angeles, I augmented with local cats, Howard McGhee among them. For some reason, McGhee started taunting Roy and didn't let up. Roy couldn't get himself together. He didn't know whether he should be experimenting the way they did. It got pretty bad with him emotionally, and it kept building."

And it had started before the darts of Howard McGhee. Kenny Clarke once told Ross Russell about a night at Minton's in 1941 or 1942 that really shook Roy up.

"Monday night was always a free for all at Minton's," Clarke recalled. "All the young musicians in town would be in the place with their horns, waiting for a chance to get up on the stand and blow. Big name stars used to drop in, especially if they were playing with the band at the Apollo Theatre a few blocks away—Charlie Christian, Lester Young and especially Roy Eldridge. Roy was the king.

"Dizzy Gillespie had started out playing like Roy, but had gotten on the new kick, working out his ideas with Charlie Parker, Thelonious Monk, Nick Fenton and myself. We had the regular band at Minton's starting in 1941. Dizzy could play and his ideas were new, but try as he would, Dizzy could never cut Roy. Roy was just too much. Roy had drive and execution, and he could keep going chorus after chorus. Every time Dizzy tried, Roy gave him a lesson, made him pack. But Dizzy never quit.

"Then one night Dizzy came in and started blowing. He got it altogether that night. He cut Roy to everyone's satisfaction and that night Roy packed his horn and never came back. Dizzy was the new king and the cats were already beginning to call it bop."

It's quite possible that story, at least in part, is apocryphal, particularly in the apocalyptic nature of its close. But it does symbolize the feeling of dread inside Roy as the 'forties came to a close that jazz time may have passed him by.

But in Paris he found his voice again, and was glad in it.

"Musically," Charles Delaunay remembers, "I found out in the conversations we had that year that he was pretty confused about 'bop' before he came over. He had lost all confidence in himself, and didn't know whether he should try to play 'modern' or not to keep his place among the jazz greats. I imagine he resented the fact that musicians like him were becoming more and more neglected. Jazz at the Philharmonic was one of the few opportunities left for him to play. Life and the future looked pretty dark.

"Being in France, feeling happy again, confidence growing back, his friends told him to play his own way, not other musicians' ways. He began to look for sessions, really blew again. In a way, he recovered his very personality and started a new career."

Roy agrees: "It seems to me that in the last four and five years I've been more interested and trying to make something happen."

He has been a regular and vital member of the Jazz at the

Philharmonic tours in America and Europe, and he has recorded a number of the most impressive sides of his career for Norman Granz. (It is Granz, incidentally, who has persisted in providing a forum for musicians like Roy, Ben Webster and Lester Young, despite sales apathy among the newer generation of record buyers, most of whom seem to feel either that jazz grew from Stan Kenton's forehead or that anything after Duke Ellington is jazz-in-its-corrupted-decline.)

In the past few years, Roy has also worked a few clubs as co-leader of a small combo with Coleman Hawkins, a burning, joyous listening experience for those lucky enough to hear them. He has also tried occasionally to keep a quartet of his own going, and is often found at the weekend Dixieland all-star shivarees at the Central Plaza in New York although he can hardly be termed a Dixielander by style or inclination.

"I think a musician who is a musician," Roy frequently declares, "ought to be able to play anywhere and shouldn't be limited to one style. Something's wrong if he is. I play Dixieland at the Central Plaza, but if some of the modernists had to play Dixieland, they couldn't do it. When it's good Dixieland, I like it."

He's often been asked how he likes working regularly with Jazz at the Philharmonic which used to be known for its hyperthyroid audiences and the effect these audiences often had on some of the musicians.

"Night after night on a stage like that is really difficult because, more or less, you have to play to the people. That isn't what Norman Granz tells us to do. He doesn't tell us how to play at all, and that's why I like working for him. But if you want to get those hands, you play to the people.

"Let me give you an example. Say I'm closing a tune. There are certain little things all musicians make that will get to the people. They're not great musically, but they get to the public. Well, I get in between doing one of those things and doing what I really have in mind, and sometimes I wind up doing nothing.

"Sometimes you get more of a musical crowd, and then you can stretch. Same thing happens in a club. If there's a musical crowd, you can play what you want to and break through. I can really tell when I play a ballad whether a crowd is musical because nonmusical crowds don't dig ballads. Another sign is when I do the strollers—just bass and drums with me playing soft and often with a mute. If it's a musical crowd, they'll go along with it.

"One thing about Jazz at the Philharmonic is that our choruses never get set, because some night you can feel better than another night. That's what I like about it."

"Roy has competitiveness," says Norman Granz approvingly. "He's purely my kind of musician. I always want the guy who thinks he's a bitch. Coleman Hawkins does, but in a 'quiet contempt' sort of way. He doesn't always extend himself. Roy has that extra ounce of competitiveness and because he's an emotional guy, he rises to heights. Like, if he's playing a Dixieland set, he'll attack *Ja-Da* with the same zest as he will a song more associated with him.

"Roy," continues Granz, "is completely honest, not only musically as but as a person. His zest for life is reflected even in his eating habits. He's the only one on the tour who carries bottles of tabasco sauce, hot pepper and mustard to season food on planes. He keeps them in his trumpet case. He likes hot things.

"And as for his competitiveness, he'd *love* to play opposite Miles Davis or Chet Baker."

It is true that Roy's confidence is fully back. When he was booked for a couple of weeks in 1956 at Café Bohemia in Greenwich Village, a room best known for modern groups, Roy was keenly disappointed that Miles's band wasn't opposite him. Roy's desire to test himself against the modernists is not malicious. He and Dizzy Gillespie, for example, have a solid relationship and both deny there ever having been hostility between them.

But Roy does enjoy challenges, especially when his weapon is his horn. If it were possible, he'd try for a contest with Buddy Bolden.

"Another thing about Roy," Norman Granz underlines, "is that on the tour he changes his ballads from night to night more than anybody. Dizzy almost never would. With Roy it's always an emotional experience. He plays the blues, too, in as varied ways as Lester Young does. Above all, Roy has a sense of climax.

"Roy has a lot of professional pride," Granz added. "He's proud of being a musician. Bird didn't have that. He would come on with bad reeds or a bad horn. But Roy feels a man should take pride in his horn, in the fact that he is a musician."

"Roy," says Jo Jones, "has enjoyed a full life. But he's no devil-may-care guy, because he's too sincere in his art. He's a very responsible man. He'll work just as hard for $25.00 as for $250. He's going to play, period, whatever environment they put him in, whatever the circumstances. And he has continuity in what he plays. Some guys don't have that."

"The man," concluded Norman Granz, "has robustness. I've

never seen him not try. I've never seen him not go out and break his back to get something going. When we were at Las Vegas, he did some singing as he has sometimes on records or in a club, and he sang with the same gusto with which he plays."

"Some of the younger guys with reputations are children," one club owner observed. "Roy is a man."

Another Eldridge behavior pattern about which there is complete agreement among his colleagues is that Roy loves to jam. As Bill Simon once noted, "He'll play piano, bass, drums or trumpet, as the situation requires, or as the spirit moves him."

Once in a session outside of Boston, Roy grew impatient waiting for a drummer to arrive, and rather than not play at all, he laid down his trumpet, and played drums for the kids who were sitting in with him.

One of the first cogent analyses of Roy's style and contributions to jazz was made by French critic André Hodeir in the October, 1948, *Jazz-Hot*. Hodeir began, however, by making an error that other critics have also perpetrated, ascribing Henry "Red" Allen as one of Roy's influences. Roy denies this.

"I like Red, but, oh God, no! When I first came to New York I used to wonder why people were saying he was playing such wonderful chords. But I wasn't the type of cat that would say a cat wasn't playing until I heard what he was doing and felt I understood. He used to come in and sit in with Teddy Hill, and I felt something was wrong. I didn't know exactly what it was until I went with Fletcher, and from the experience I got there, I knew he had often been playing the wrong notes."

Hodeir continued more valuably: "Roy explored the various registers of his instrument, particularly the high register. He didn't do that solely to display his virtuosity but because his imagination pushed him to this diversity."

In this connection, Bill Simon has noted, "Roy played faster and higher than Louis Armstrong because he was affected greatly by saxophonists Coleman Hawkins and Benny Carter. Much of what he plays is the result of attempts to play saxophone-type solos on trumpet."

"Eldridge's style," Hodeir points out, "alternates between a considerable sobriety of line (*Wabash Stomp, Florida Stomp*) and such a boiling point that one wonders whether he isn't going to lose control of his music. Between these extremes, his style is often agitated with a curious putting-into-relief of essential notes (*That*

Thing)—a procedure that Charlie Parker in an entirely different sense, was to do later—but is also often very tranquil (the first chorus of *Fish Market*); in both cases, he swings marvelously. Between the two can be placed a record like *Tippin' Out,* where he mingles a fullness worthy of Armstrong with a more mobile, more tied-together phrasing with bursts into the very high register followed by agitated descents into the low register.

"In *Hi Ho Trailus Boot Whip,* a series of repeated notes of a very simple effect is followed by a development in a very high register in a Cat Anderson manner that is of a seizing contrast but in good taste. . . ."

Hodeir continues to talk of Roy's "virility" and his "vehemence of expression" before examining his melodic invention. "A solo like his in *Blues in C Sharp Minor* is a treat for whoever can appreciate a handsome development garnished . . . with bold and troubling notes."

In a comparison between Roy and Louis Armstrong in the late 'thirties, Hodeir talks of the way they both can soar over an orchestra. "The melodic invention of Eldridge is less vast, less logical than Armstrong's, and Louis, who was mature, had a more stately accent and soared more. But Roy's sonority is more sensual, more ardent; it is as moving as Louis's although in a different way. . . . Very few musicians possess this *presence,* project this *joy* which pierces you when you hear Eldridge on a good day. In *Wabash Stomp* and *Florida Stomp,* there is a contained vehemence, an inner fury that are those of a very great musician."

A debatable but stimulating further comparison between Louis and Roy results in: "Louis is the triumph of equilibrium and Roy of romantic expression as contrasted with the classicism of Louis. The admirable V-discs on which they play side by side indicate clearly . . . the serenity of the one and the sensuality of the other . . . often pushed to exasperation. This exasperation of the senses is expressed in Roy's vibrato, crushed in the high register, larger in the low register, singularly personal and moving. It does not exist without a certain disequilibrium which on a musician's bad days makes one fear for . . . the form of his work. . . .

"Eldridge's influence," concludes Hodeir, "has been considerable. It extends from around 1936 to bop. It's enough to hear a record like the *Blue Rhythm Fantasy* he made in 1938 with Teddy Hill to measure all that Dizzy Gillespie owes to 'Little Jazz.' . . . Roy Eldridge appears to me a revolutionary . . . it is difficult today to call him a 'modern'—who, nourished on the classical tradition, has known how, when it was necessary, to break with it in order to express his message. . . ."

In a study of the past quarter-century of jazz trumpet in the June, 1956, *Metronome,* trumpeter Don Ferrara added this tribute: "So complete was his range of volume that he could whisper with a wonderfully warm intimacy and then shout with magnificence. And he defined and gave life to each step between that whisper and shout. So wide-open was his sound that it compelled his audiences to listen. All talk would cease when Roy played. Even when he played soft, his sound still was big. The softness never sounded pinched or crowded into a small corner, but clear and unrestrained . . . Roy's feeling pushed his valves down, not his fingers. . . . His music was so earthy and uninhibited it seemed as though he had a direct line right to his feelings. Not a schooled musician, Roy's feelings were so overpowering that he had to master his horn technique to give birth to his feelings. And this mastery he had. His music was charged with fire and vitality."

Because his emotions so dominated his playing, Roy was and is uneven. But at his best, when he played "a great freedom would fill the room," to use Ferrara's evocative phrase.

In a chapter on "Brass Instrumentation in Be-Bop" in the January, 1949, *Record Changer,* Ross Russell illuminated the place of Roy in the development of jazz trumpet even more: "The 'link' musician between Louis Armstrong and the present is Roy Eldridge. . . . Between 1936 and 1942 . . . Roy Eldridge was the most listened to, admired, and imitated trumpet player in jazz. Eldridge's records have only occasionally captured the compelling force of his playing (*Heckler's Hop*). Heard in person, especially during the 1937–39 period when he headed his own six-piece band, Roy was the most exciting of musicians.

"In effect, Roy took as his point of departure the fantastic style of the middle Armstrong period. Roy's trumpet went beyond Louis in range and brilliance. It had greater agility. His style was more nervous. His drive was perhaps the most intense jazz has ever known."

Roy, as quoted by Barry Ulanov, expressed in a few sentences the key identifiable quality of his playing: " 'I tell you what I love about the trumpet. I love to hear a note cracking. A real snap. It's like a whip when it happens. It hits hard and it's really clean, round and cracked.' "

In his recent book, *Jazz: Its Evolution and Essence*, André Hodeir returned to Roy with these added insights: "Ten years after Armstrong created an authentic language for the trumpet, Eldridge developed this language and added to it. But he could do this only by increasing its complexity. He paid for this enrichment by the loss of a collective equilibrium; when improvising in a group, Roy continued to play as a soloist."

Hodeir also talks of Roy's "disciplined but violently colored sonority."

Roy sums up the discussion of himself as soloist: "I never can say all I want to say. For one thing, it takes me a long time to get warmed up. But there are good nights sometimes. . . . I remember around 1948–49, I went into a joint in Chicago for one night. It was a strictly modern place, and I went into training for the job, practicing six to seven hours a day for a whole week just to play one night. This was when the modern scene was at its height, and I was a foreigner in that club. I had good drums and bass, and I blew that night! Wow! I didn't play anything I'd practiced. I just played.

"It only happens about four or five times a year—four tops. I mean when you break through and everything you want to make, you make. It's hard to get the right feeling, but sometimes it hits you. And then it feels while you're playing like there's something back of you. You don't actually hear it, but you feel it, and it's all knitted together, and it all jells. It's like standing and playing under a mountain by yourself.

"In the early 'forties I used to have the band at Kelly's Stables with Kenny Clarke, Ted Sturgess, Kenny Kersey, and John Collins. Charlie Christian and Jimmy Blanton used to stop by and sit in, and one night they swung so much I felt so good I had to stop playing.

"That happened to me on a record date, too, with Oscar Peterson, Ray Brown, and Jo Jones. It happens so seldom it gets me and I have to stop. Like on *Dale's Wail* with Oscar on organ, if I hadn't got so filled up that I had to stop, my first chorus would have been the best one, but I just couldn't go no farther."

When that feeling, that four-times-a-year feeling, is present, he once told Ulanov, "nothing matters. Range, speed, sound—they just come. It's nothing I use; I can be cold sober. From somewhere it comes. Afterward I sit up in my room and try to figure it out. I know I haven't cleaned my horn, but the sound was 'gone.' I know my lip isn't in that good shape, but I made an altissimo C as big and fat as the C two octaves lower. It just doesn't figure."

Roy's vigor, his love of playing haven't diminished at all as the years have increased. He has settled down in a familial sense in that he has a house in Long Island; a wife, Vi; and a young daughter just approaching her teens, Carol.

Roy is short, compact, and moves with a wiry fire that also carries through to the somewhat hoarse urgency of his voice. Even when he is relaxed, there is a drive in his gestures, in the way he tells a story, in his ready alertness to everything around him. He is a full man.

Outside of music, his interests extend to photography, to painting (for a time in France), and to writing. He wrote a large section of his autobiography while in Paris but complains that those potential collaborators and publishers who have been interested in the book, have wanted to soften it, to leave out the harsher passages, and Roy will abide no censorship. He has lived too long a free man to allow his own book to be constrained.

"Roy," says a close friend, "also gets writing out in letter writing. He's a prolific writer—to girls. He's always been a remarkably quantitative worker with women. He has first place. No one else I know has his capacity."

Roy believes in enjoying life—consistently. He is disappointed that France now, from his viewpoint, has become increasingly like America. When he was there in 1950, as Charles Delaunay notes: "He discovered . . . that, in contrast with U.S. life where people seem to fight for another dollar, people in Paris were mainly concerned with taking advantage of life—good food, fun. . . . From then on he seemed to not care at all about money problems, playing a gig or a concert occasionally when they were offered him."

But combined with his pleasure in being himself and living as completely as he can is his sense of responsibility as a musician.

"A couple was here tonight," he has said during a club date, "wanting me to play *When the Saints Go Marching in.* I don't want to play that m—— f—— of a tune but they're buying the whiskey that keeps the club going. So I'll play it." Years earlier he had said: "Basically, nothing changes. From the beginning of music, people like only what moves them and what they can understand."

And he was very hurt when he auditioned in 1956 for a studio job with a late night television show. "Because I was a jazz musician and because I was a Negro, the music director came on with warnings that I'd better not be drunk and with questions about how well I could really read. I've been a professional for thirty years, and I have to prove myself now?

" 'You're a jazzman,' he said to me.

" 'I'm a musician,' I answered."

"Ella Fitzgerald," says a friend, "always regards Roy as a little boy. The eternal boy. And there's a lot of that in him. He's very youthful for his age. Even his clothes are."

Roy has mellowed, however, in temperament as he has aged. He was recently angered by a loud customer. "Ten years ago, I would have rapped him in the head with my horn. But now—what the hell?"

Perhaps the major disappointment Roy now experiences is a feeling that there are fewer and fewer places in jazz where he and contemporaries like Coleman Hawkins can really stretch out, can really feel the presence of a large and appreciative audience.

One way he expresses the narrowing of the walls is: "One thing today is that there are not enough sessions. . . . Now if you go out to jam and don't play a certain way, the cats don't like you, and there are no kicks. So for people like me and Coleman, there are no places for jamming these days. We used to go out and play, and we'd have a ball. There was no feeling of 'I'm going to outplay you.' And we went out every night.

"Now guys who feel like I feel don't have any steady gigs where you can come and jam. The other guys have the gigs today. And they don't want you to play with them if you don't play their things. They let me, but they don't mean it, and I can feel the draft."

SELECTED DISCOGRAPHY—ROY ELDRIDGE

Trumpeter's Holiday, Epic 12″ LP 3252. Roy Eldridge is on three numbers (1937).

Lady Day, Columbia 12″ LP CL 637. Roy Eldridge is on three numbers behind Billie Holiday (1935).

Gene Krupa: Mutiny in the Parlor, Camden 12″ LP CAL-340, Roy is on four numbers (1936).

Chu Berry Memorial Album, Commodore 10″ LP FL 20,024. Roy is on four numbers (1938).

Gene Krupa, Columbia 12″ LP CL 753. Roy Eldridge is on several tracks, including *After You've Gone, Let Me Off Uptown*, and *Knock Me a Kiss* (1941, 42).

Gene Krupa's Sidekicks, Columbia 12″ LP CL 641. Contains *Rockin' Chair* (1941).

Man With a Horn, Decca 12″ LP DL 8250. Like the preceding, Roy is featured on one number, *Stardust* (1943).

Battle of Jazz, Vol. 7, Brunswick 10″ LP BL 58045. Roy is on four numbers (1943).

Giants of Jazz, Vol. V, EmArcy 12″ LP MG 36053, Roy is on four numbers (1944).

Giants of Jazz, Vol. III, Part 1, EmArcy 12″ LP MG 36050. Roy is on two numbers (1944).

Artie Shaw: Both Feet in the Groove, Victor 12″ LP LPM 1201. Roy is on two numbers, *Lady Day* and *Little Jazz* (1944, 45).

This Is Artie Shaw and His Gramercy Five, Victor 10″ LP. Roy is heard on three numbers (1945).

Roy's Got Rhythm, EmArcy 12″ LP MG 36084, Stockholm (1951).

Roy Eldridge, Dial 10″ LP 304 (label now defunct), Paris (1950).

Roy and Zoot, Discovery 10″ LP DL 2009 (label now defunct), Paris (1950).

The Strolling Mr. Eldridge, Clef 10″ LP MG C-162 (around 1952).

The Roy Eldridge Quintet, Clef 10″ LP MG C-150 (1952 or 1953).

Rockin' Chair, Clef 12″ LP MG C-704, contains four numbers from preceding (about 1953).

Little Jazz, Clef 12″ LP MG C-683 (probably 1955).

Roy and Diz, Volumes 1 and 2, Clef 12″ LPs Mg C-641, C-671 (probably 1955).

Jam Session, American Recording Society 12″ LP G-404 (probably 1955).

Gene Krupa: Drummer Man, Verve 12″ LP 2008 (1956).

The Jazz Giants '56, Norgran 12″ LP MG N-1056 (1956).

Swing Goes Dixie, American Recording Society 12″ LP G-420 (1956).

The Urbane Jazz of Roy Eldridge and Benny Carter, American Recording Society 12″ LP G-413 (probably 1956).

Charlie
Christian

*   ✳   *   ✳

By Bill Simon

The guitar had some history in jazz before Charlie Christian, but there's little evidence, if any, that Charlie was particularly aware of it.

He had his own ideas about the function of the instrument—as a solo voice, in a small combo, and in a big band. But he never talked about these ideas, he just played them—and they became the accepted, the ideal for an entire generation of guitarists.

There hasn't been more than a handful of musicians of whom it may be said that they completely revolutionized, then standardized anew the role of their instruments in jazz—Louis, Bird, Dizzy, Blanton, Chick Webb, Lester Young, perhaps a few more, but especially Charlie Christian.

Let's first take a look at the guitar-in-jazz prior to Charlie's sudden emergence, full grown, on the big time scene in 1939. . . . Going way back to the New Orleans beginnings, only one "name" guitarist survives in memory—Bud Scott (1890–1949) began early enough to join Robichaux's orchestra in 1904 and to participate in street corner "battles" with the first jazz "King," Buddy Bolden, around 1904.

Scott was a good musician, who later studied with legit teachers and was able to alternate on fiddle and even to play symphony and theatre jobs. He claimed in his later years to have been the first guitarist to play all four beats with a downstroke. Scott's influence may have reached Charlie indirectly at least, since he was the unidentified guitarist on hundreds of recordings made with blues singers and early combos, including those of Richard M. Jones, King Oliver, Jimmie Noone and many others.

From New Orleans days on until the late 'twenties, the guitar fought for its place on the scene with the jangly banjo, whose metallic ring may have been less inspiring to jazz feeling, but which carried better in the days before clubs and dance halls used amplifying systems. And, of course, before guitars themselves were amplified. The guitar, except in more intimate blues and ballad interpretations, was designed more to be felt by musicians, than to be heard by the audience. Electric recording helped change that, and consequently, in the late 'twenties, we began to hear from such guitarists as Lonnie Johnson and Eddie Lang. As these men appeared on discs, their influence spread rapidly.

Johnson came first. He began to record around 1925, mainly backing blues singers, and musicians began to notice that, more than just voice with accompaniment, he was beginning to make each side a partnership. Single-string obbligato figures, interesting chord changes and voicings, and occasional solo passages by Johnson took the guitar a giant step from the primitive rolling rhythm backings of the cotton-field pluckers, and introduced the first virtuoso elements.

Johnson was far too sophisticated to be labeled strictly a blues man: he eventually recorded with Louis Armstrong, and was guest star with Duke Ellington's band on such significant early sides as *The Mooche* and *Misty Morning*.

A Philadelphia-born white musician, an ex-fiddler who went under the professional name of Eddie Lang (he was born Salvatore Massaro), was the next important voice on the fretted instrument. He was a Johnson follower, and was to bring the idea of the guitar-as-a-voice into the public consciousness through his key position with such bands as those of Jean Goldkette, Paul Whiteman, Roger Wolfe Kahn, Red Nichols, and later as accompanist for his sidekick, Bing Crosby.

Lang patterned his full tone after Johnson's, but he also introduced new expressive elements, new chord inversions, new subtlety and sensitivity. It was his kick to sneak off to jam with Johnson and some of the colored combos in days when this generally wasn't done. In fact, he even recorded several duets with Lonnie, and other sides in a combo with Johnson and King Oliver, using the *nom-de-disque* of "Blind Willie Dunn."

It has been said that Lang was the first man to make his fellow guitarists conscious of using the proper bass notes and the best possible chord voicings.

His chordal ideas were picked up, varied and expanded by the next group of guitarists to hit the Big Time—men like George Van Eps, Carl Kress, the late Dick McDonough. Van Eps developed a style on guitar which might be likened to the "locked-hands" chordal style of some of the more modern pianists.

Then, when the single-string, one-note-at-a-time style of jazz guitar came into its own, it was an import—all the way from France. Its proponent was the Belgian-born gypsy, Django Reinhardt (1910–1953). While he had little if any influence on Christian, he did more than any other guitarist to create an acceptance for a solo virtuosic guitar, and to destroy the concept of the instrument as a device purely for rhythm. As a rhythm guitarist, in fact, Django was sadly deficient by jazz standards. With only three working fingers on his left hand, he was, of necessity, more of a single-string man than a chord man. And he was the fastest.

But Django's folk origins were gypsy, not slave or sharecropper. He brought new, exotic and showy elements into jazz; still he himself never came close to the core of jazz. One has only to compare his frothy, though fertile, inventions with the driving, earthy improvisations of young Christian to understand the difference.

Django's role in a jazz combo was also limited by his instrument, which was still the unamplified Spanish guitar. Some years later, after Christian had established the electrified box in jazz, Django converted and by this time he had lost much of his old authority via attempts to adapt himself to the new jazz sounds of the mid-'forties.

Once Django had attuned the public's ear to the notion of an audible guitar, (but still had left much to be desired as far as jazz people were concerned), the stage was set for the new six-string Messiah, and he emerged in the shape of that awkward, friendly, impossible rube of a kid named Charlie Christian.

If Charlie *had* been influenced by anyone directly, he never let on. Little is known of his formative years. It hardly makes sense, still. To anyone who knew him from 1937 on, it appeared that Charlie was the mature, original genius and had never been anything but. It was thus with Louis and Bird and maybe Tatum. Teddy Hill, who was Charlie's best friend after he hit New York, still scratches his head when he tries to explain the phenomenon. . . .

"Where did he come from?" he'll ask, of no one in particular. "When we were kids growing up here in New York, we watched Benny Carter grow from a squeaky beginner to a master musician. Or take Dizzy. When he joined my band after Roy (Eldridge) left, he played just about like Roy. Then he was influenced a lot by Bill Dillard, who played lead trumpet for me and who, incidentally, was one of the best I ever had. Then Dizzy began to work out those new things with Monk and Klook (Kenny Clarke). . . . The point is, we could see him grow. But what about Charlie. . . . Where did he come from?"

We do know that Charlie was born in Dallas, Texas, sometime in 1919, and that he was brought up in Oklahoma City. This was guitar country and, to a fair extent, blues country. Blues singers or country and Western singers—they all played guitar in those parts.

Oklahoma City also was fertile ground for the stomp bands —particularly the Kansas City units which invented a happy, danceable approach to the blues—free-flowing, four-even-beats-to-the-bar blues. And the combos that developed riffing to a fine, forceful art —all in the process of doing as many different things as they could conceive to dress up that self-same twelve-bar blues progression. In the late 'twenties in Oklahoma City there had been Walter Page, the great bass man, with his Blue Devils, who included the late Dallas-born trumpeter Oran "Lips" Page, blues singer Jimmy Rushing and pianist Bill "Count" Basie. This band had a rival in that of Bennie Moten out of Kansas City, and it was an historic day for jazz when they merged, and another historic day in 1935, when Basie picked up the baton where the lately deceased Moten had laid it down.

And the dominant sounds in jazz in that region, besides the good-rockin' blues shouters and the blues-'n'-boogie pianists, were those of the saxophonists. This was the breeding ground for many of the distinctive sax styles. Coleman Hawkins came out of St. Joseph, Missouri, though his development into a major stylist took place after he hit New York. But Ben Webster, Lester Young, Herschel Evans, Buster Smith, Harlan Leonard, Jack Washington, the late Dick Wilson, and the more recent Charlie Parker, all came out of K.C. and vicinity, and all blew their way through the Southwest.

The fluidity and freedom and individual expressiveness these men brought to their music had its effect on the way other men approached other instruments. Longer lines, shifting accents, more notes per bar, harmonic explorations, even within a single solo line. Trumpet men, trombonists and even drummers began to play more like saxophonists. And when Charlie Christian played solos on his guitar, that's how he played them—like a modern jazz saxophonist, but always as a guitarist.

Charlie, then, I believe, was a product of his region and his

time. John Hammond, who brought him into full public view, is
certain that he was influenced by Lester Young's tenor, and it's
established that he was fond of Lester's playing, but apparently no
more so than of many others'. Hammond also advances the theory
that he was indebted to Floyd Smith, the one-time Andy Kirk
guitarist, also out of that general region; and there could be something to this. But Smith's influence may have been more mechanical
than musical. He was the first capable jazz man to exploit an electrified instrument. His choice happened to be the Hawaiian guitar
—a slippery monster with which, however, he was able to cope
without sacrificing jazz feeling. It may have been from Smith that
Charlie got the idea of amplifying his Spanish-style box.

Whatever influences, Charlie, as we said, never mentioned
them, and when they were suggested to him in conversation, he,
apparently, just liked everybody and just about everything musical,
and that was about all that could be gotten out of him—in conversation.

Charlie didn't have much education. By 1934, when he was
fifteen, he was a professional musician. He was playing guitar, but
he had big, strong fingers, and for a time he also played bass, with
Alphonso Trent's band. Then he toured the Southwest with Anna
Mae Winburn's aggregation. By '37, he was playing electric guitar,
and he organized his own little combo in Oklahoma City.

Soon he was back on the road, hitting such towns as Minneapolis and Bismarck, North Dakota, but none of the big jazz centers.
He may have been with Al Trent again at that time, and Oscar Pettiford, who jammed with him in '38, recalls vaguely that he was with
Lloyd Hunter or Nat Towles.

In the program notes for a Columbia album, Al Avakian and
Bob Prince tell of the time in Bismarck when a young guitarist, Mary
Osborne, went to hear Charlie play. "She recalls that on entering the
club she heard a sound much like a tenor sax strangely distorted by
an amplification system. On seeing Charlie, she realized that what she
was hearing was an electric guitar playing single line solos, and
voiced like a horn in ensemble with the tenor sax and trumpet. She
says, 'I remember some of the figures Charlie played in his solos.
They were exactly the same things that Benny (Goodman) recorded
later as *Flying Home, Gone With "What" Wind, Seven Come Eleven*
and all the others!'"

At the same period, the annotators recall, "Christian's prom-
inence was established locally to the extent that a Bismarck music

store displayed 'the latest electric guitar model as featured by Charlie Christian.' "

Oscar Pettiford was playing with his father's band in Minneapolis in '38, when he met Charlie at a place called the "Musicians' Rest." Here the local and visiting bandsmen would come to juice and jam. "We had a wonderful time blowing with Charlie," Oscar reminisced. "I never heard anybody like that, who could play with so much *love*—that's what it was, pure *love of jazz,* and great happiness just to be a part of this thing called music.

"We exchanged instruments: he'd play my bass, and I'd try his electric guitar. I hadn't heard about him yet, but Charlie told me, "You'd better watch out for a guy named Jimmy Blanton (*Charlie may have played with Blanton for a while in the Jeter-Pillars band out of St. Louis*). I never forgot that."

Two people in Charlie's life made it their personal business to see that he found the recognition and fulfillment he deserved. Both John Hammond and Teddy Hill remain warmly proud of their roles and their friendship with this warm, generous—and grateful boy. Both remain bitter to this day towards the newer "friends" who actually killed him with their own peculiar brand of "kindness."

Hammond's total contribution to jazz has been positively staggering. He had been mentor for Benny Goodman, Count Basie, Billie Holiday and benefactor for countless others. . . . While he himself has not always been in sympathy with the new jazz trends of the 'forties and 'fifties, one of his "discoveries," Charlie Christian, was a prime influence in shaping these trends.

John first heard about Charlie from Mary Lou Williams in 1939. The fine pianist-arranger had heard Christian herself in Oklahoma City, when she had played the town some weeks earlier with the Andy Kirk band. Hammond's now brother-in-law, Goodman, was playing in San Francisco, and he had just signed with the newly reorganized Columbia Records. John was flying to Los Angeles to attend the first Columbia sessions.

He located Charlie in Oklahoma City, and wired that he'd be stopping off en route and would appreciate an audition. The plane landed at one P.M. after a much-delayed, steaming hot summer flight, and Hammond got off, as he put it, "beat and bedraggled." To the "horror" of his fellow passengers, an old wreck of a car drove up to the airport, jam-packed with six young Negroes. One of them asked for Mr. Hammond, introduced himself as Christian and reeled off the names of the others, all the members of his band.

Charlie thoughtfully had made a reservation for John at one of the "nicer" hotels, where his mother was working as a chambermaid.

But by three, the audition was on at the Ritz Café. This is the place where Charlie and his buddies were working about three nights a week at the nightly rate of $2.50 per man. Somehow, on a weekly paycheck of $7.50, the boys all looked presentable, if not prosperous.

Charlie possibly had the impression that Hammond was interested in the combo, or more likely, as with most friendly kid musicians, he just hoped this important man would like his pals, too. As Hammond recalls now, the band was "simply horrible. Charlie was the only one who could play. But he was almost unbelievable."

The next day Hammond left for Los Angeles, and found Benny in no mood to expand his organization. In addition to the band, he still had the Quartet, with Lionel Hampton, and occasionally he would add the bass, Artie Bernstein, from the band to form a Quintet. John insisted that Christian was "essential" and pointed out that Benny might take him on without jumping the budget. . . . The band was still playing the Camel Caravan shows, and these provided a "guest fee," which could be used to take care of Charlie.

BG agreed to such an arrangement, and Hammond wired Charlie the money to fly in, ostensibly in time for one of that first series of recording dates for Columbia in August, 1939.

This particular date had been going for two hours, and the band was cutting Fletcher Henderson's arrangement of Mendelssohn's *Spring Song,* with "Smack" himself on piano, Bernstein on bass, Nick Fatool on drums, and others like Ziggy Elman, Chris Griffin, Vernon Brown, Toots Mondello and Jerry Jerome in the band.

Suddenly, in walks this vision, resplendent in a ten-gallon hat, pointed yellow shoes, a bright green suit over a purple shirt and, for the final elegant touch—a string bowtie. One man in the band, who happened to be color-blind, noticed that this character also toted a guitar and amplifier.

"There he is," Hammond prodded Benny. The King of Swing took one look and shivered visibly. "Wait till you hear him play," Hammond pleaded, but BG would have no part of it.

After the date, Goodman stayed around just long enough to hear Charlie play one chorus of *Tea for Two* without the amplifier. Then he rushed out to keep a dinner engagement.

Artie Bernstein, who had observed the whole bit, felt real compassion for Charlie, who really didn't know how to interpret the course of events. He enlisted Lional Hampton and they conspired to sneak Charlie into the Victor Hugo, where the band was playing, that night. Normally, the band would take a break and vacate the stand, while Benny and the Quartet would stage a short concert.

Later, while Benny was off the stand, Artie and Hamp got Charlie in through the kitchen and set up his amplifier. Goodman strolled back into the room, spotted that awkward pile of bones on his stand and did a quick double-take. There wasn't much he could do without creating a scene, so he signalled resignedly for *Rose Room*.

They played *Rose Room* for forty-eight minutes!

Hammond had been in on most of Goodman's triumphs since he had persuaded him to stay with jazz in the early 'thirties, but he "never saw anyone knocked out as Benny was that night." Apparently, Charlie just kept feeding Benny riffs and rhythms and changes for chorus after chorus. That was Benny's first flight on an electronically amplified cloud.

In future months that "impossible rube" was to inspire and frame the most fluid, fiery, interesting and human sounds that Goodman has ever produced.

A few days later, October 2, 1939, Benny set up the first Sextet recording session. This was the one where they recorded *Flying Home,* a riff opus whose writer credits go to Eddie De Lange, Goodman and Hampton. No one ever has denied that most of the riffs that have become standard on this otherwise slight concoction were Charlie's, and the same was to apply to most of the other Sextet "specials."

Charlie was in. Benny had to agree with Hammond that Charlie was "essential." From $7.50 a week, he was now making $150, as a regular member of the Goodman organization.

But Benny still didn't like an amplified guitar with the big band, and his colored stars still were restricted to the "chamber music" group. He did use Charlie on many of the band recordings, but most of the time, the band chair was held down by Arnold Covarrubias or Mike Bryan.

Anyway, Charlie was "living." He had gone from the backshack to the Big Time in one giant step. He was bright enough, and certainly not illiterate, but he apparently had just two great interests —music and chicks. Now he could indulge his tastes until satiated, and life became one big ball. When the warning signals sounded, Charlie refused to stop the party.

When he didn't seem to be feeling right, Benny sent him to his own doctor in Chicago who spotted the t.b. scars. Charlie knew he had been afflicted, but had never let on to his new boss.

The doc warned him to get his rest, and to take care of himself generally, but Charlie was having too much fun up in the stratosphere.

It was in October, 1940, that Minton's was opened, in the Hotel Cecil, up on One Hundred and Eighteenth Street in Harlem. Teddy Hill, one-time saxophonist and popular band leader, was installed as manager. Teddy had been around for years, grown up with jazz in New York, but he was and is an insatiable fan. When Mr. Minton gave him a free hand, he opened the doors wide to the "guys" and announced that this would be the one place in town where they could come and play just what they wanted to play.

Teddy knew what was good and could tell when some of his boys began to lead jazz in new directions. He extended his hospitality to all musicians, but he took special care of the good ones. This friendly, generous, understanding man is credited with a major assist in the invention of modern jazz.

Dizzy Gillespie and Roy Eldridge before him had played with Hill's band; so had the adventurous drummer Kenny Clarke. In the 'twenties, Hill, still in his teens, had toured the Midwest and South with Bessie Smith. He took his own band to France in the 'thirties and played for some weeks at the Moulin Rouge. Nearby in Montmartre, the Harlem emigré, Bricktop—one-time benefactor of Duke Ellington—had a place, and her featured attraction was Django Reinhardt. Teddy was in the place every night to listen, and to him, Django was the greatest, until he heard Charlie Christian.

When one of the big colored bands would come to town to play the One Hundred and Twenty-fifth Street Apollo, the sidemen would make it a point to fall into Minton's for some unfettered after-hours blowing. Teddy would cook up a big batch of food and supply free drinks, and usually the place would be packed with musicians, leaving little or no room for customers.

Monday nights were a special ball for any jazz fans who were able to spoon their way into the place. Most of the musicians with steady jobs were off that night, and they would flock in from Fifty-second Street, from Harlem clubs, and from some of the name bands downtown. On Mondays, Hill would invite some special guests, and make certain that these weren't crowded off the stand.

Minton's became Charlie Christian's home. As far as the manager was concerned, Charlie owned the place.

Goodman was getting ready to open up at the Pennsylvania (now the Statler), and was holding rehearsals every afternoon. The boys had some free time, and the pianist, Mel Powell, brought Charlie up to Minton's. If you sincerely liked music, you were Charlie's friend, and Teddy Hill became his best friend. Charlie came up every night. After the band opened at the hotel, Charlie would finish his last set, hop in a cab and speed up to Minton's where his seat on the stand was being held for him. He wouldn't take the time even to change his uniform, and oftentimes he was still wet with downtown-type perspiration when he arrived. Minton's stayed open until four, which gave him about two and a half hours to wail all of the high-band jimmies out of his soul.

As long as there was somebody on the stand to play music with, Charlie never got up out of that chair. There were always chicks around waiting for Charlie, but they couldn't get more than a nod from him until the last note had been blown at four. But they always waited.

And on Monday nights, when the Goodman band was off, Charlie was in his usual chair at Minton's from note one. Musicians, good and bad, battled on every instrument, crowding each other on and off the stand. But Charlie never budged. Guitarists came to listen to him, not to cut him. That would have been impossible and everyone knew it.

Jerry Newman, a young jazz fan and then amateur engineer became a regular at the place and night after night would record the happenings with his own semi-pro equipment. He recalls that Charlie most of the time would electrify the crowd with his riffing and his long-lined solos and his powerful drive, but that sometimes the stand would become jammed with battling no-talents, and Charlie would simply sit there and strum chords.

Hill himself went out and bought Charlie an amplifier—the best one he could find—so that he wouldn't have to lug his own heavy box up there every night. It cost $155, which was a lot of money for an amplifier in those days. Charlie would put his lighted cigarettes down on the thing and forget about them while he was playing, and they'd burn all the way down. The box is at Teddy's home now, burns and all, and it will probably stay there until some official jazz museum or Hall of Fame has been established. Its owner has turned down dozens of offers for it.

Celebrities got word of Charlie's jamming habits, and began to flock in. Ella and Billie came and sang with him. Newman would take down his recordings, and after closing time, Charlie, Teddy and Jerry would listen to the playbacks over and over and over.

One night, Lena Horne and Fats Waller joined the select company. Fats, who traveled in different jazz circles ordinarily, would sit and listen to Charlie with his arms folded, for once completely ignoring the bottle in front of him. . . . This one night, Newman was playing the records back and the second time around Fats sat down at the piano. Between each number, he'd improvise an interlude, and everybody was gassed.

When Dizzy would fall by, that's when the musical sparks would fly. Diz and Charlie would "battle" for forty to fifty minutes at a time. It was the same on rarer occasions when Charlie Parker would drop around. And Christian loved it.

"It's like that back room was made for him." Hill undoubtedly heard more Charlie Christian than did any other person.

Everybody loved Charlie. The chicks mothered him, and the musicians kidded him good-naturedly. He was the Willie Mays of jazz. Teddy would tease him with, "We're going to bring that Django over here, and he'll blow you right off that stand." Charlie would break into a big grin and answer with a couple of slippery, typical Django phrases on his box.

He would discuss another musician, but only while the man was right there playing, and never in a derogatory way. He obviously loved Monk's piano, and Klook's drumming, and Diz. He even tolerated Joe Guy's trumpeting.

Guy was an Eldridge imitator whose biggest claim to fame was to be his later association with Billie Holiday and the mess he got into with her. On more than one occasion he was heard to grouse about the attention Charlie was getting. "If I was playing at the Pennsylvania with Benny Goodman, everybody would think I was great, too." But he never got in Charlie's way and he never had it as good as when Charlie was riffing in back of his mediocre inventions. Charlie could make a midget feel like a giant.

Both of Charlie's mentors, Hill and Hammond, have told us that Charlie was increasingly interested in and moving towards more "classical" ideas, though he never considered himself other than a

driving four-beat musician. In the Minton's days he was just twenty
or twenty-one, and he was getting better all the time, was evidently
far short of his potential peak.

And so life continued to be one big ball for Charlie until Spring
of '41, when he got really sick. He was sent to Seaview, a New York
City-operated sanitarium on Staten Island. He was getting routine
care there until Count Basie's physician, Dr. Sam McKinney, took
an interest in his case and began making weekly trips out to see him.

Teddy Hill was his other faithful visitor, making the long journey every Sunday. He tells about "Mom" Frazier, who had a restaurant uptown at One Hundred and Twenty-first Street and Seventh
Avenue where all the musicians hung around, and how this lady
would mother them all, but her special favorite was Charlie. Every
week that Charlie was away, she'd bake a chicken—especially prepared without spices—and a chocolate layer cake for him. When
Hill would try to pay her, she'd shrug him off with, "Now you take
this to my boy and tell him to hurry up out of that hospital."

Hammond was out in California most of those months, but he
did arrange to have a guitar sent to Charlie in the hospital.

Charlie, in his new-found "high-life" had acquired another set
of friends, and that's how he happened to die at the tender age of
twenty-two; t.b. was only part of it.

There are stories of some of the boys from the Goodman and
other bands dropping over to the Island for visits and spiriting
Charlie out of the hospital for "parties" with combustible tea and
chicks. These parties had their comic moments—if one can forget
their tragic consequences.

There was the time, for example, when the Germans had just
begun to overrun Western Europe. This one bass player, who was
more concerned than most of his colleagues with current events and
politics, buttonholed Charlie for an intense one-way discussion.
Charlie was "stoned," and he loved everybody and would agree with
anybody about anything.

"And Charlie, those German planes roared over and dropped
all those bombs and leveled just about every building in Rotterdam.
And thousands of people, women and children—got wiped out. How
about that, Charlie?"

Charlie cut through his haze and answered emphatically—
"Solid!"

He had a couple of other "friends"—a guitar player and a tap
dancer; the latter a well-known character around the bands. They

brought over the "pot" and they also brought chicks. Charlie was getting better—in fact, it looked as though he would be getting out soon, and he was feeling his oats. But it was winter and Charlie sneaked out late one special night and got excited and overheated.

Dr. McKinney learned of these extra-curricular activities and made sure they were stopped, but it was too late. Charlie had pneumonia.

It was early in February, 1942, when Hammond returned from California and received a call from a nurse at Seaview that Charlie was in bad shape. He rushed out to see him, and could tell that it was hopeless. He called Benny.

The next day, Hill made his regular call, and that night Somebody turned off Charlie's "juice" for the last time.

And so, most of the jazzmen Charlie was to influence—just about every jazz guitarist in the fifteen years since his death—have had to learn their lessons from his all-too-few phonograph records. I don't think anybody had ever asked Charlie to be leader on a disc date, and if they had, it's doubtful that he would have accepted—it might have taken time and attention from his playing. He was content to play what Benny wanted him to play, apparently, but when he got up to Minton's, his release was almost feverish. As some of those Jerry Newman recordings show, he would play dozens of choruses on end. If he ran out of ideas temporarily, he'd simply riff rhythmically for a few bars until he caught his muse again.

Although the man came from the segregated South, there was no evidence that he carried any prejudices or any resentment against any person or group. He had no regional restrictions in his make-up. He had one home—music. He was meek and humble, but never an Uncle Tom.

Even today, young guitarists hearing his recordings for the first time are convinced immediately that this is the master. Jimmy Raney, one of the top guitarists of our modern day, didn't arrive in New York until 1944, or two years after Charlie had died. He had been about fifteen when he first heard *Solo Flight,* the number Charlie cut with Benny's full band. "Jesus, I flipped!" was the typical reaction. "The only other time I felt something like that was the first time I heard Bird." Raney, like the others, believes that Charlie still stands on top of the heap, even when judged by the more modern standards. It was his sense of time, and of harmony—his way of outlining his chords without actually running them. The same observation has been made of Parker's playing on the alto sax.

Naturally, one is curious about the personal relationship between Charlie and his boss, Benny Goodman. One must look hard for any evidence that he interested Benny as a person. Charlie never discussed Benny. Benny came up to Minton's several times, but when he did, the boys played Benny's jazz, not Charlie's or Monk's or Klook's. That stuff didn't interest BG then or now. Charlie's $150 per from Benny was more money than he had ever seen before, and he could sit there at the Pennsylvania with the juice turned off most of the evening and play rhythm for Benny, because he had Minton's.

If Charlie were alive today, he'd probably be spending most of his working time in recording studios, but in the two years of his Big Time activity, jazz dates were few and far between. He did cut twenty-five sides with the Benny Goodman Sextet or Septet, which, in its best moments included Count Basie on piano, Jo Jones on drums, Cootie Williams on trumpet, Artie Bernstein on bass, and Georgie Auld on tenor sax. He also was on a flock of full band sides, but was rarely featured. *Solo Flight*—which was strictly Charlie's show piece, and *Honeysuckle Rose* are the only band numbers still available which offer any satisfying amount of Christian guitar.

Charlie also got in on two of the Lionel Hampton all-star combo sessions at Victor, cutting seven sides in a company that also included Dizzy Gillespie, Benny Carter, Coleman Hawkins, Ben Webster, Chu Berry, Milt Hinton, Cozy Cole and the late Clyde Hart —on one date! And Red Allen, J. C. Higginbotham, Earl Bostic, Hart, Bernstein and the late Sid Catlett on the other. There wasn't much "blowing" room for Charlie, obviously.

Teddy Wilson used him in October, 1940, on a Columbia date in the backing for a set of four standards sung by the pop singer, Eddy Howard, along with such other positive stylists as Bill Coleman, trumpet; Benny Morton, trombone; Ed Hall, clarinet (the Café Society clique) and Bud Freeman, tenor sax.

There were two dates—they were J. C. Higginbotham's—backing the blues singer Ida Cox for Columbia's subsidiary label, Vocalion. James P. Johnson was pianist on one, and Henderson on the other. Lips Page, Ed Hall, Hampton (on drums), and Bernstein were in on these also.

There were the Metronome All-Star sessions of 1940 and '41. Charlie had little trouble winning the polls once his first recordings with Benny had hit the market.

Charlie had one rather strange, but quite successful session for

Blue Note, the first of the independent jazz labels, in February, 1941. This resourceful outfit had Edmond Hall assemble a quartet which consisted of clarinet (Hall), celeste (Meade Lux Lewis), bass (Israel Crosby) and guitar (Christian). They cut four sides for twelve-inch 78-r.p.m. discs, thus permitting the men more than the usual blowing time for those days. But Blue Note producer Alfred Lion wouldn't tolerate an amplified guitar, and that's how Charlie happened to record, in quite traditional company, his only unamplified solos on discs.

Easily the most important, revealing work of Christian on records is the material gleaned from Jerry Newman's well-worn acetates. It was this writer's privilege to arrange for the release of several of these Minton's cuttings in a Vox album in 1947. One was an original based on *Topsy* and the other was *Stompin' at the Savoy*. The group was Charlie on guitar, Kenny Clarke on drums, Thelonius Monk on piano, Joe Guy on trumpet, and Nick Fenton on bass— the Minton's house band.

Apart from the poor balance, extraneous crowd noises and some irritating Guy trumpet, this is the biggest and best sample of jazz guitar on discs. Charlie "wails" on chorus after chorus with those long, full-blown lines, those simple riffs and those complex strung-out changes. Here was the beginning of "bop," with Clarke dropping "bombs" in unorthodox places behind Charlie's own shifting accents, and Monk beginning to play his own strange harmonies and "comping" for the soloists.

Newman himself took over these masters again when he started his Esoteric label, and brought them out on a ten-inch LP. Later he followed up with some additional gleanings, which he coupled with some early Gillespie sides, also cut at Minton's. Neither of these sets currently is in print, although there are plans to bring them out on one new twelve-inch LP coupling.

Aside from these, the most valuable Christian is to be found in the Goodman Sextet and Septet sides, many of which remain unavailable today. During 1956, Al Avakian, brother of Columbia's George Avakian, undertook the assignment of putting together a sort of Christian memorial mainly from unreleased studio material. Fortunately, some of the test acetates cut before and during several of the Goodman sessions had been retained. By transferring everything to tape, Avakian was able to do a brilliant editing and reassembling job. From bits, scraps and rejected takes, he was able to put together what, next to the Newman material, is the best, least adulterated Christian obtainable.

Through these cuttings, one may study the evolution of the Goodman combo classics and Charlie's key role in their creation.

Charlie Christian probably is the only jazz figure who would have been able to serve as the model stylist on his chosen instrument as long as fifteen years after his disappearance from the scene. There isn't an important guitarist playing today who does not recognize him as the all-time best, and who does not credit him as a prime influence. In most of the better modernists, the strain has crossed with that of a saxophonist, Charlie Parker, but basically, it's Charlie Christian. The best thing anybody can say about a guitarist today is that he could be "the closest thing to Christian."

The album annotators and the critics have said it about Barney Kessel, Tail Farlow, Sal Salvador and some of the others.

They've all been grateful.

SELECTED DISCOGRAPHY—CHARLIE CHRISTIAN

Available discs in order of importance:

Charlie Christian and Dizzy Gillespie at Minton's, Esoteric (scheduled for release)

Charlie Christian with the Benny Goodman Sextet and Orchestra, Columbia CL 652. Includes alternate takes and special compilations of: *Seven Come Eleven, Till Tom Special, Gone with "What" Wind, Six Appeal, Wholly Cats, Gone with What Draft, Blues in B, Airmail Special, Waiting for Benny, Breakfast Feud, A Smo-o-o-oth One, Solo Flight* (the original full-band version)

Benny Goodman Combos, Columbia CL 500. Includes these numbers on which Christian has solos: *Breakfast Feud* (the master originally issued), *Stardust* (excellent example of *chordal* solo style), *Benny's Bugle, On the Alamo, Shivers, A Smo-o-o-oth One* (the master originally issued), *As Long as I Live, Gilly*

Honeysuckle Rose (with full band). Available in two collections:

Benny Goodman Presents Fletcher Henderson Arrangements, Columbia CL 524

$64,000 Jazz, Columbia CL 777

John
"Dizzy" Gillespie

* * * *

By Leonard Feather

Something very strange happened to John Gillespie. It was an event that touches few men. Usually, when it happens, they react by swelling mentally, physically and psychologically, by acquiring delusions of grandeur and, in some cases, swimming pools, a set of six matching Cadillacs, and a brand-new wife to replace the mate who struggled through the poverty period. John Gillespie reacted in none of these ways, because what befell him never changed for one moment his sense of balance, of direction, of humor.

What happened to John Gillespie was that he woke up one year and found himself a hero.

The way of the pioneer can be as rough after recognition as before it, for it is no harder to achieve the recognition and establishment of a new style than to maintain its integrity in the face of economic and sociological compulsions. John Gillespie is a man who had greatness thrust upon him. Despite this, he has preserved an equilibrium that may well be unique in its area. The other musicians who took part in the incubating process that evolved into bop today are dead, or struggling intermittently with the dope habit. Gillespie apparently has never suffered any major frustration or neurosis; has kept the narcotics problem at a safe distance by screening its victims before hiring men for his band; and has never taken himself, or the music he created, as seriously as the countless students and musicians who have spent so much of the past decade dissecting, discussing and duplicating it.

The year of Gillespie's heroic accolade is generally placed at 1945, though it is a fact that even in 1943 he was the subject of much excited conversation among fellow musicians and was well on the way to becoming a cult.

The year 1945, though, was the most significant in that it

brought to records the first evidence of bop's most fruitful partnership, that of Gillespie with the alto saxophonist Charlie Parker, who was to Dizzy what Wilbur Wright was to Orville. Together they took off into the wild *Blue 'n' Boogie* yonder, to name but the first famous collaboration of that vintage year; and together they thumbed their horns at the derisive cries of critics (and even a few musicians) who told them that they would never get it off the ground.

What they were trying to separate from sea level was a new approach to the creation of improvised (and, ergo, of written) jazz. Because they were given to the use of heavy accents on the first and second eighth notes of the measure as an opening or closing statement, and because these accents could best be verbalized in the sound "be-bop!", the musicians who heard them informally referred to their music by this name. For a while they also used "rebop," which had the same onomatopoeic significance. It was several years before the impact on the music world at large reached the stage at which the abbreviation usually born of familiarity led to the now generally accepted cognomen "bop."

Musicians are divided on the question of who was the foremost force in the forging of bop. Many credit Parker; others feel that Gillespie, who was more continuously around New York and more consistent in his experimentation, was the principal figure, while many acknowledge Charlie Christian, Thelonius Monk, Kenny Clarke and others as powers behind the usurpers' thrones.

This much is certain: Gillespie, working as a sideman in name bands from 1936 to 1943, slowly developed a style that was ultimately to shape the future of jazz. By the time he started his first job as a leader, in 1944, fronting a quintet at one of the boites along Fifty-second Street, he had acquired a knot of hero-worshiping followers who not only tried to play the trumpet like him, but even imitated his clothes, his walk, the tuft of hair beneath his lower lip, and other physical characteristics. He had started, almost unwittingly, on a march to global fame that was ultimately to make him the first jazz-band leader ever to tour overseas with an official blessing (and promise of financial support) from the U.S. State Department, an honor that most 1944 jazz musicians and fans might have dismissed as ranking in probability with the addition of Mezz Mezzrow to the Gillespie band.

That this could have happened to a man called "Dizzy," and one whose adolescent record amply justified the nickname, is a tribute to the durability of his musical innovations. Gillespie is no musical avant-gardiste: confronted with a Teo Macero record during a "blindfold test" interview he commented: "Is that what you call atonal music? . . . I don't understand what it means." Yet he has changed the direction of jazz more than any other living jazzman. He is no intellectual: yet he has flirted with left politics and has been much sought after by ax-grinders of all kinds. He rose to fame as a symbol of advancement; yet he gets some of his biggest kicks out of listening to blues records or sitting in with a Dixieland or New Orleans-style band. He has impressed some strangers as a clown, who sings and shakes his can on the bandstand, giggles and has a ball when at ease; yet he can, when the occasion demands it and the mood hits him, sit down to a serious discussion of music and talk of "the place of improvisation in relation to composition" and "emotional impact applied to technique."

He is no easily pigeonholed character. If he had been, he might today be washing dishes, or driving a truck, or undertaking any of the other unrewarding chores to which life and local conditions might have been inclined to dispose him in his early years.

Gillespie was born October 21, 1917, in a modest house in South Carolina. The citizens of his natal town recently brought him home and for a day Cheraw, South Carolina resembled Kitty Hawk, North Carolina, as the mayor accorded him a hero's welcome. The ninth and last child of Mrs. Lottie Gillespie, now one of six surviving children, he was introduced to music by the convenient presence in the house of a number of instruments stored by his father, a bricklayer, on behalf of a band which Gillespie Sr. led as a sideline.

"My father treated my mother real good," Gillespie told Richard Boyer. "He got her real expensive stuff. I was scared of him though. When he talked, he roared. He was a real man. He didn't have a voice like this." Dizzy ended the sentence in a falsetto. "I got a beating every Sunday morning." He exploded into mirth. "At school, I was smart, but I didn't study much. I'd fight every day Ev-er-y day I'd fight. I was *all*-ways bad, you know."

After the death of Gillespie *père* in 1927, John's musical interests led the way to a scholarship at the Negro Industrial School in North Carolina, the Laurinburg Institute. Starting on trombone at fourteen, he borrowed a trumpet from a neighbor nine months later. Soon after, he was given a trumpet of his own at Laurinburg, where he was studying theory and harmony. He never studied trumpet at school; nor did he become an expert reader until many years

ater. When Mrs. Gillespie left Cheraw in 1935 to live in Philadelphia, John had to quit school several months before his class
graduated. Not until he visited Laurinburg in 1937 for a special
ceremony did he receive his diploma and football letter.

Arriving in Philadelphia, his trumpet wrapped in a paper bag,
Gillespie was a rough and rowdy country boy, with a smart-aleck
manner that had already earned him his nickname. Before long, he
was working in a local band led by Frank Fairfax, in which his
trumpet teammates were Charlie Shavers and Carl "Bama" Warwick. He soon found a musical idol in Roy Eldridge, trumpet star
with Teddy Hill's band, which was on the air over NBC from Harlem's Savoy Ballroom. Before long he found himself in the same
chair Eldridge had once occupied, despite an audition for Hill at
which Dizzy mounted the bandstand clad in overcoat and gloves and
remained that way throughout the rehearsal.

During his years with the Hill band, Dizzy studiously avoided
any attempt to belie his nickname. Embarking on a new arrangement, he was as likely as not to start by reading an interlude, or the
last chorus, instead of taking it from the top. While another soloist
was featured, Dizzy would stand up and imitate him, hold his horn
and pretend to blow. Often he would play an extra bar or two at
the end of a number, a habit that persists today. If Hill reprimanded
him for putting his foot up on a chair, he would remove it promptly
—and rest the foot on a music stand. By the time the band left for
Europe in the summer of 1937, several men threatened to leave
Hill if Dizzy were not fired. Their tempers calmed by the smooth-
talking leader, they retracted their demands and took off in a Cotton
Club revue that toured successfully in England and France, where
Gillespie was just the third trumpet man in a band whose other
trumpeters earned all the kudos as visiting firemen.

Dizzy had entered the Hill band more or less as an apprentice,
but before long, he was teaching more than he was learning, and
began to play some of the first trumpet parts as well as many of the
solos.

During a week at the Howard Theatre in Washington, Dizzy's
eye was caught by the charm and grace of a pretty dancer in the
show, Lorraine Willis.

"Every time I'd dance around to his corner of the bandstand,
he'd blow the horn right in my ear," recalls Lorraine. "He had short,
fat fingers, and I liked to watch him fingering his horn, but it was
a long time before I knew what instrument that was he was playing.

He kept sending me notes, but I ignored them. One day he saw me having lunch and asked if he could sit with me. I called another girl over before I would let him. . . . I really didn't pay him any mind; but later on we played the Apollo, with another band, and he came by to see me."

By this time Dizzy had sweated out the six-month waiting period transferring into New York's Local 802, during which he had had to fill in with odd jobs ("I worked with one cat in the Bronx who doubled on bass and musical saw.") During these largely idle months, Dizzy, who was a good cook, would prepare elaborate meals and take them to the Apollo Theatre for Lorraine. After getting his 802 card, he rejoined Teddy Hill at forty-five dollars a week at the Savoy Ballroom, and later at a replica of the ballroom installed at the New York World's Fair. He also spent a couple of months with Edgar Hayes, the pianist, in whose band one Rudy Powell was functioning as clarinetist and arranger. "I played one of Rudy's best arrangements over and over," he recalled years later, "and realized how much more there could be in music than what everybody was playing." This, incidentally, combined with his determination to stop copying Eldridge and to outblow him by developing a style of his own, were pivotal factors in his career. After rejoining Hill briefly, he became a member of the big band fronted by Cab Calloway late in 1939; in the short but numerous examples of his solo work recorded with Calloway during the next two years—such items as *Pickin' the Cabbage* (his own composition and arrangement), *Hard Times,* and *Bye, Bye, Blues,* attest to the developments in his style: a subtle use of grace notes, an occasional diversion in the implied harmonic contour of his solos and a thin but very personal tone.

The romance with Lorraine blossomed. One week while they were in Boston, he informed her that the Calloway band was bound for Canada, but added, "You can't go with me unless we're married." "I always wanted to go to Canada," says Lorraine, "so I got married." On May 9, 1940, in Boston, Lorraine became Mrs. Gillespie. The marriage, after surviving many storms, has settled into a firm and successful one; in recent years, Mrs. Gillespie has played an increasingly active part in Dizzy's career, touring with the band and taking a managerial hand.

The job with Calloway came to an abrupt end in September, 1941, with an incident that made headlines at the time. Cab had accused Dizzy of throwing spitballs at him in the middle of a stage how in Hartford, Connecticut. There was a scuffle backstage. "Cab made a pass at Diz," recalls Milt Hinton, who was the band's bassist, "and was nicked in the scuffle before they were separated. Cab hadn't realized he had been cut until he was back in the dressing room and saw the blood."

"Cab Calloway still has a sore rear end," said *Down Beat* delicately in a long news story on the fracas. "Cabell took ten stitches from a doctor."

For a few weeks Diz worked with the Ella Fitzgerald band, along with his old pal, Kenny Clarke from the Teddy Hill orchestra. But this time he was making strides as an arranger, placing several originals with Woody Herman, Jimmy Dorsey and Ina Ray Hutton.

One riff tune which he had put together during the Teddy Hill days, entitled *The Dizzy Crawl,* was used for background music by the dancing line at the Apollo. Diz never bothered to copyright it; later it acquired some momentum in the Count Basie band under the title *Rock-a-Bye-Basie,* the composer credits going to Basie, Lester Young and Shad Collins, the trumpet player who had been Gillespie's neighbor in the Teddy Hill brass section.

The next two years were dotted with innumerable short-lived jobs with Benny Carter, Charlie Barnet, Les Hite, Lucky Millinder and for a while back home in Philadelphia, where he formed a quartet at the Down Beat that included a local white boy, Stan Levey, on drums. In 1942–43, unfortunately a period that coincided with the first recording ban, he became a member of the Earl Hines orchestra that was a virtual nursery of bop, its personnel including Charlie Parker on tenor and Benny Green on trombone, with Billy Eckstine and Sarah Vaughan as vocalists.

This was an era of discovery, of musical experimentation that was at least beginning to crystallize. Dizzy never tired of playing; one night in Chicago he persuaded Oscar Pettiford to trudge through ten long city blocks in a snowstorm, carrying his bass, to join him in a hotel room for an all-night jam session. Often in New York, up at the Dewey Square, or at Dizzy's apartment nearby, there would be Bud Powell and Benny Harris and Freddy Webster, to whom playing and talking and thinking meant more than eating and drinking. One night Diz came home from rehearsal and remarked to Lorraine, "Do you know what the people call my music? They call it 'be-bop.'" He was clearly unimpressed by the name. Some of the musicians even addressed him with the name "Be-bop."

There was not merely experimentation in those days; there was serious devotion to music and even an occasional period of study. When Dizzy wasn't at home practicing or writing arrangements, he might be downtown taking lessons with a private teacher. Though the manner in which his cheeks distend when he plays is unorthodox and is frowned on by most teachers, he was informed that it would not affect him to continue this technique; he is perfectly capable, incidentally, of playing in the more conventional manner.

Coming off the road with Hines, Dizzy spent three weeks at the Capitol Theatre in New York with Duke Ellington. The alliance was not a happy one: Dizzy and the band didn't seem to dig each other, though Duke soon became one of Gillespie's most distinguished admirers. The frenzied wartime Fifty-second Street scene was now burgeoning rapidly, and it was time for some of the experiments conducted by Diz, Charlie Parker and others at Minton's and other places uptown to be reflected in a downtown showcase. Diz and Oscar Pettiford started a small group on "The Street" with Don Byas, tenor; George Wallington and Max Roach.

This was the beginning of the jazz revolution. By now, no longer an obscure sideman, Dizzy was acquiring an ever-larger knot of followers. One night on her way home, Lorraine passed a dance hall on One Hundred and Twenty-fifth Street and heard Dizzy practicing. On arriving home, to her amazement, she found him sitting there; the trumpet player in the dance hall had been one of the innumerable Gillespie imitators, already numbered in the dozens by 1943 and in the hundreds by 1944.

Marshall Stearns, annotating a concert given in 1947 by Gillespie's band at Cornell recalled that the premiere of Stravinsky' Sacré du Printemps in Paris in 1913 had precipitated a general riot at which sweet old music-loving gentlemen used their umbrellas a clubs; and that Gillespie was the center of a comparable controversy. In retrospect, the heat of the fury in which the pro- and anti bop factions were embroiled during the mid 'forties is almost incredible.

By dislodging jazz from the rut into which it had settled, Gillespie, along with Parker and the other innovators, had stirred up a hornet's nest of which he was completely unaware. Though musicians in general were quick to open up their ears, most of the jazz critics used him as a whipping boy in some of the most savage attacks ever leveled against a jazz musician. It might be said that the bell was sounded for the first round of the great battle of jazz in the fall of 1944, when a group of experts selected by this writer engaged in a poll for *Esquire* to name the top jazz musicians and the greatest new stars. The results, announced in December, named Dizzy Gillespie as the greatest new star on trumpet, along with several other musicians of unmistakably modern persuasion. Chaos ensued: the fight against recognition of the inevitable developments that were taking place in jazz brought attacks, not only on Gillespie and bop, but on everything that had represented evolution from the very New Orleans beginnings. Swing, big bands, polished musicianship of every kind were the butt of scathing diatribes, mostly from writers in the recherché small magazines dedicated to the oldest and simplest kinds of jazz. Thus, in a review of a broadcast featuring some of the *Esquire* winners, Rudi Blesh condemned Benny Goodman's flashy virtuosity and used such adjectives as "trite" and "turgid" in assessing Duke Ellington. Frank Stacy counterattacked in *Down Beat:* "Blesh should be confined to a small, dark room on Perdido Street where he will be allowed to go on polishing his 1905 recording cylinders."

"The so-called experts of *Esquire,*" moaned *The Record Changer,* a violently anti-modernist monthly edited by Bill Grauer and Orrin Keepnews, "by keeping good jazz hidden from the public while forcing upon them the Eldridges, Tatums and Pettifords, have created a totally false impression of real American jazz music."

Counterpoised against Gillespie as the symbol of the new in jazz was the figure of Bunk Johnson, a symbol of the past into which this group of critics wished to retreat. Bunk, a sexagenarian trumpet player who had been brought out of cold storage, equipped with new teeth and set up as a puppet hero of the old guard, appeared at such traditionalist jazz havens as the Stuyvesant Casino, where one night he informed a lady patron: "I am the greatest trumpet player in the whole world!" George Avakian was among those who solemnly agreed with Bunk's self-estimate; in addition to voting for him in the *Esquire* poll, he engaged in a long series of violent attacks on what he described as "cultism at the shrine of the up-to-the-second swing musician." When Maxie Kaminsky, the Dixieland trumpet player, was imprudent enough to express a favorable review of Dizzy in an interview with this writer in *Metronome,* Avakian devoted 3,000 words in *The Record Changer* to an attempt to prove Kaminsky had been misquoted. Kaminsky, however, held his ground.

"I don't know of a single admirer of New Orleans music who was converted to swing," declared Avakian. In 1957, Avakian had

Jay Johnson, Miles Davis and innumerable other bop and/or swing musicians under contract at Columbia Records, and was writing enthusiastic liner notes about them.

Nesuhi Ertegun, discussing the poll that brought Gillespie, Parker and Milt Jackson their first real recognition, wrote: "The American public is misled when an incompetent jury makes a confused and haphazard selection of musicians . . . I find it boring and useless to discuss in detail the various musicians who won the awards . . . The outlook for jazz is gloomy. Only by returning to New Orleans jazz can it become a living art form." In 1957 Ertegun, who now had Milt Jackson and many other bop musicians under contract at Atlantic Records, had evidently lost his gloomy feelings about the outlook for jazz.

Among the others lined up against the new jazz were Ernest Borneman ("The boppers were sophisticated, urbanized Negroes . . . the result was disastrous . . . they had sold their birthright for a poisoned mess of pottage"); John Hammond ("Bop is a collection of nauseating clichés, repeated ad infinitum"); George Frazier ("This is incredible stuff for a grown man to produce!"); Norman Granz ("Jazz in New York stinks! Even the drummers sound like Dizzy Gillespie. There isn't one trumpet player in any of the clubs except Hot Lips Page. Charlie Parker's combo is rigid and repetitive").

In 1957, Borneman was specializing, for the London *Melody Maker,* in reviews of Afro-Cuban records, many of them with an unmistakable bop flavor; John Hammond was recording Rolf Kuhn and had helped Friedrich Gulda to assemble an all-star bop band for Birdland; Frazier had publicly retracted his views on Gillespie, which he had expressed with greater frequency and virulence than almost any other writer a decade earlier; Granz had used Gillespie and Parker on innumerable record dates and concert tours, released a big Parker memorial album, and was similarly engaged in activities involving Buddy De Franco and other modern musicians, including a couple of drummers who sounded like Dizzy Gillespie. Grauer and Keepnews, whose *Record Changer* had been the most passionately persistent voice against progress, were engaged in the production of more and more bop records for Riverside.

A curious aspect of the critical uproar of the 'forties was that the musicians' voices were almost drowned out. When at last they were heard, when Mary Lou Williams wrote in *The Jazz Record*

that "Be-bop is certainly the most influential and important development jazz has known for many years; all musicians should open their
minds to it," the tide began to recede. In 1948, more than four years
after *Metronome* had paved the way by according constant encouragement to Gillespie and Parker, the *Record Changer* made a
180° turn: "In the past, most of [our] articles . . . have been based
on the theory that jazz died the night they closed Storyville. We
doubt the truth of that. We've got guys around here who love Louis,
Bix, Teagarden, Jelly Roll, Ellington, Maxie, Benny, Hodges and
Holiday with equal fervor. There's even someone who claims he
once liked a chorus that Dizzy took, but this is generally disbe-
lieved." The following month, the *Record Changer* began to review
bop releases—analytically and most often favorably.

While the critics were thus engaged in this endless esoteric
combat, Gillespie had a different and more musical fight on his
hands; first as musical director of the chaotic though significant
Billy Eckstine band, the original big-bop orchestra (again with
Parker in the line-up), which kept him on tour through the second
half of 1944; then as leader of a band that went out under his own
leadership in "Hep-Sations of 1945," and, after this folded, as the
unhappy captain of a Gillespie-Parker combo that played opposite
Slim Gaillard at Billy Berg's in Hollywood. It is questionable in
retrospect which Gillespie disliked more, Hollywood in general or
Gaillard and his disturbingly popular comedy music in particular.
Nobody in California knew or cared much about bop save a small
clique of musicians; it was a happy day for Gillespie and his cohorts
(Al Haig, Stan Levey, Milt Jackson and Ray Brown) when they
straggled back to New York. Charlie Parker, so sick that he had
been absent from the job more often than not, stayed behind, well
on his way to the nervous breakdown that took him to Camarillo
State Hospital.

The next years were marked by a gradual upsurge of public
interest in bop, enabling Gillespie to keep a large orchestra together
from 1946 to 1950. It was discovered that verbalized into nonsense
syllables, bop could be a vocal novelty; soon everyone from Babs
Gonzales to Mel Tormé was on the bop-wagon. It was also found
that Afro-Cuban rhythms blended with bop made a heady potion;
Luciano Gonzales, better known as Chano Pozo, had a short but
startling career as Cuban drum specialist with Dizzy before meeting

a violent end in a New York bar brawl. It was further revealed that
Europe was ready and waiting; in January of 1948 the Gillespie
band sailed for Sweden.

Scandinavia had already shown its bop-consciousness enough
to enable Chubby Jackson to make a successful tour with a sextet
that same winter. The Gillespie band arrived in Sweden just before
Chubby left for home.

Reactions to Dizzy's music ranged from outraged indignation
to unqualified enthusiasm. An embezzling promoter had the band
almost stranded until Charles Delaunay, first of the continental critics to appreciate Gillespie's role in jazz, rescued him by bringing the
band to France for a tour.

As 1948 came to a close, bop had achieved recognition and
success beyond the most ardent hopes of its sponsors. Gillespie's
band had played its first Broadway theatre, drawing big crowds at
two successful weeks at the Strand, and played his third Carnegie
Hall Christmas concert under this writer's sponsorship. National
magazines, hearing that Dizzy's followers were aping his goatee,
beret and glasses, as well as his trumpet playing, ran feature stories
devoted mainly to the eccentricities of the boppers: *Time,* belatedly
acknowledging Dizzy's existence, patronizingly gave the title "How
Deaf Can You Get?" to a piece on bop; a six-page spread in *Life,*
culminating in a picture of Dizzy, supposedly a Mohammedan bowing to Mecca, spread misinformation to millions. On a television
program, Eddie Condon was introduced as "the king of bebop."

Lionel Hampton compounded the confusion by telling New
York newspapers that "be-bop is the chord structure; re-bop is the
rhythm. We combine both and call it the New Movement. Music is
nothing but arithmetic—nothing but mathematics." To prove it,
Hampton recorded an album entitled *New Movements in Be-bop,*
presumably using statisticians as arrangers. Benny Goodman, not
too long after giving out heavily sarcastic anti-bop quotes, formed
a new band featuring bop soloists and arrangements, and gave a
bop party at the Stork Club, at which he was photographed wearing
a beret.

Bop had moved from a nadir of steep and apparently invincible
opposition to a zenith of national acceptance. Because it was accepted largely for the extraneous non-musical aspects, a reaction
was inevitable. A couple of years later columnists were announcing
gleefully that bop was dead. In 1950, Gillespie broke up the big
band and from then until 1956, when the State Department was in-

strumental in helping him rebuild an orchestra, he was on tour, either with his own small combos or with the Norman Granz concert unit.

Bop was an unconscionable time a-dying; in fact, in 1957 more musicians were playing it than ever. Significantly, it was no longer known as bop, but simply as modern jazz; the belated acceptance of Gillespie and Parker innovations had brought it into the mainstream of musical evolution. A book by this writer issued in 1949 as *Inside Bebop* was reissued in 1955 under the title *Inside Jazz*.

When he saw that the bop novelty balloon had burst, Gillespie was undismayed. "I think I'll change it around a little," he told Lorraine one evening. Soon the pill was sweetened for Birdland customers by the incorporation of more and more vocal novelties, mild and effortless showmanship, and a generally extrovert approach that helped to make the Gillespie combo acceptable for those to whom the musical and technical qualities of bop were still a mystery. These modifications were retained in the big band he led during most of 1956 and 1957.

On a recent evening at Birdland, the orchestra prepared to start its first set at ten P.M., while the leader, in a narrow corridor leading to the kitchen directly behind the bandstand, leaned against a wall fixing his horn as the waiters brushed by.

"Do you know what I did today?" he said to a friend. "I went and bought a record. Must be the first time in forty years that I went out and bought a record! It's a new thing by Ray Charles. Boy, that cat can *sing!* He gets a real sanctified church sound, you know? Damn! This guy's fast becoming my favorite singer!"

Strolling casually through the narrow swinging door, he crossed over to a microphone at floor level in front of the bandstand.

"Ladies and gentlemen," he said, "I'm sorry we're a little late getting started this evening, but we just came from a very, *very* important benefit. The Ku Klux Klan was giving a party . . . for the Jewish Welfare Society . . . it was held at the Harlem YMCA . . . so you can see we're very lucky to be here at *all* this evening." This introductory routine, used regularly for years, has never failed him in bringing guffaws.

The first tune was *Anitra's Dance,* arranged by the band's attractive girl trombonist, Melba Liston. After it Gillespie said, "That was an excerpt from one of the old symphonic tunes. *Anitra's Dahnce.* And now here's a tune that we are certain you will recognize the title, if not the melody." A bristling interpretation of *Begin the Beguine* followed, exotically transformed into ⅝ time. As it ended there was a smattering of applause in the sparsely filled room (it was not yet ten fifteen), at which Gillespie smiled inscrutably and said, "I'd like to thank you very much, ladies and gentlemen, for that tremendous ovation. I'd like to thank *both* of you." He proceeded to cavort his way through *The Umbrella Man,* an old popular song, the first chorus of which he sang in waltz time, later passages being delivered in a sort of bop vocalese in ¼. A blues called *Doodlin',* involving an elaborate comedy byplay between Gillespie and his baritone saxophonist, ended the set.

During the intermission Gillespie sat with a group of friends, evoking memories from an old photograph he had pulled out of his pocket. The photo showed his father and mother, standing before the front door of a house; the father was bowing a bass fiddle. "He looks like he's really wailing on that fiddle. Look at the way he's holding that bow!" said Gillespie with a touch of pride. "My father died when I was nine. Boy, I wish he were alive today—he'd sure have a ball to see one of his sons making a living as a musician."

Asked about the activities of his two non-musician brothers, he said: "One of them's still driving a taxi around New York. The other is a chef. Right now he's at a restaurant in Greenwich Village. Specializes in all that Russian crap. Ooh, you gotta try that! He's great!"

Shifting subjects abruptly, he said, "You know who's the most underrated trumpet player? Dud Bascombe. He was playing stuff in Erskine Hawkins's band back in 1939 that was way ahead of its time. He's real *bad!* I told him today, what the hell, everybody's getting all these write-ups and shit in the magazines, and nobody talks about you—I'm going to write a piece for them about you!"

Gillespie then spoke warmly of Lee Morgan, a recently hired trumpet player in his own band whom he had started to feature generously, even on such tunes as *Night in Tunisia,* a Gillespie work that used to feature its composer exclusively. Morgan had barely passed his eighteenth birthday when he joined the band in 1956, but his style and command of the horn were astonishing. "It sure scares you," said Gillespie, "seeing kids like that coming up so fast. But it's good to see it happen.

"People copy other musicians, too, nowadays; they don't all copy me. I don't mind that. I remember back to the time when I was listening to Roy Eldridge, when he was the cat everyone listened to.

You expect those things to happen; you can't be the only influence forever."

Gillespie and his friends were joined later in the evening by Lorraine, whose visits to her husband's places of business are circumscribed by her almost total lack of enthusiasm for the branch of music in which he is engaged. (In the summer of 1956, accompanying him on a business-and-pleasure trip to the summer jazz colony at Music Inn in Lenox, Massachusetts, she remained in her room the whole time, playing records by André Kostelanetz and Frank Sinatra.)

As the night drew to a close, the Gillespies began to discuss financial problems. Dizzy has, on many occasions, demonstrated an interest in the business end of the music world. In 1951, he engaged in a partnership with a Detroit friend, David Usher. Their joint venture, a company called DeeGee Records, folded after a couple of years of distribution problems. At a birthday party for Lorraine in January, 1954, at Snookie's, a bar on Forty-fourth Street, Gillespie left his horn on a music stand. A dancer fell over it and bent the horn so that the bell pointed upwards. After his anger had subsided, Dizzy tried to play the horn and found that the sound seemed to reach his ears better with the bell tilted up this way. The next day he went to a trumpet manufacturer to ask whether he could put this idea into mass production. "He even got a pad for taking orders," recalled Lorraine. Gillespie's dream of financial glory crashed abruptly when he found it impossible to get a patent: a similarly designed trumpet had been patented 150 years earlier.

One Gillespie project that has succeeded is his apartment building in Long Island, where he retains the main floor and basement and rents out, at a modest profit, the two apartments that occupy the other floors.

Gillespie is a man of impulses. On the first trip abroad in 1948, he started collecting pipes, but gradually he had to give them all away to admiring friends; at this writing he has a new collection of some thirty pipes, many of which were picked up during his tour of the Middle East.

Possibly because he has won the fight for esthetic recognition that took up so many years of his youth, he has settled into an attitude somewhat more patient than that of his radical early years. Wherever they went on the two State Department tours—first in Pakistan, Iran, Lebanon, Syria, Turkey, Yugoslavia and Greece;

later on the South American tour in Ecuador, Argentina, Uruguay
and Brazil—Dizzy and Lorraine were asked questions about the
Autherine Lucy case and other racial problems. His replies were a
model of firm conservatism; he would indicate that little by little
conditions were improving, and instead of making a speech would
point to his band, composed of eleven colored and four white musicians. "They couldn't understand it at first," says Lorraine. "A lot
of them thought that colored and white could never work together.
And they were so surprised that we live in Long Island, not in Harlem."

Marshall Stearns, who went along on the Middle East tour,
observed that Dizzy showed real statesmanship. "In Karachi," reported Stearns, "Gillespie persuaded a doubtful snake-charmer to
play a duet in his room. To the flustered management he countered,
'The man's a musician, isn't he?' You could hear the native bellboys
hissing the news. In Ankara, Dizzy declined to play at a lawn party
unless the urchins crowding outside the walls were admitted. 'I
came here to play for *all* the people,' he murmured."

Part of Gillespie's show on the tour was a miniature history
of jazz, for which the band gave its impressions of every phase from
spirituals and work songs and blues through Dixieland to swing,
including impressions of various name bands, and modern bop in
both big-band and combo formats. It was a symbol of the end of
a vituperative era: the critics having observed the validity of the
advice "If you can't fight 'em, join 'em," Gillespie was meeting them
halfway.

By now, almost the only active opposition to bop rested in the
hands and mouth of Louis Armstrong, who continued to direct his
barbs at bop in frequent interviews. Armstrong, whose bop-mocking
lyrics of the *Whiffenpoof Song* (written for him by Gordon Jenkins)
were recorded after he had heard the Gillespie parody of Louis on
a record of *Confessin'*, is an occasional visitor to the Gillespie home
where, according to Lorraine, "Louis and Diz run off at the mouth
and then go off in the back room and look at pictures and Louis tells
Diz jokes. I don't think he means all that stuff about bop; maybe he
just keeps it going because he thinks it's good publicity."

The life Dizzy Gillespie leads today is a settled and secure one
in contrast with the years when he and Charlie Parker were made to
feel that they had taken on the whole world as an adversary. His
name, once a mild joke to some and a laughingstock to others, now

is spoken of in reverence on five continents; his orchestra has been called one of the greatest in jazz; his contribution to modern music is now virtually undisputed. His only regret is that Charlie Parker, who for so long was Pythias to his Damon in a partnership that fell apart too soon, never enjoyed the fruits of the jazz revolution.

Just a week before his death Parker ran into Gillespie at Basin Street. He was desperate, pitiful, pleading. "Let's get together again," he urged Diz. "I want to play with you again before it's too late."

"Dizzy can't get over Bird saying that to him," recalls Lorraine. "His eyes get full of water even now when he thinks about it.

"He was downstairs a week later when I heard all this crying and I found out someone had called and told him Charlie was dead. I didn't say anything; what could you say? I just let him sit there and cry it out."

SELECTED DISCOGRAPHY—DIZZY GILLESPIE

Afro-Dizzy, Norgran 1003

Diz & Getz, Norgran 1050

Dizzier & Dizzier, Victor 1009

With Charlie Christian, Esoteric 4

With Strings, Norgran 1023

World Statesman, Norgran 1084

Dizzy Gillespie, Allegro-Elite 3083

Dizzy And Big Band, Gene Norman GNP 23

Index

Abide with Me, 143
Ace in the Hole, 25
Adams, Kenneth W., **137**
Adelman, Skippy, 124
Adirondack Sketches, 101
Afternoon of a Faun, 101, 200
After You've Gone, 73
Aggravatin' Papa, 134
Aiken, Buddy, 219
Aiken, Gus, 219
Ain't Cha Glad, 72
Ain't Misbehavin', 141, 146, 147
Alexander's Ragtime Band, 135
Allen, Henry "Red," 245, 309, 329
Allen, Lewis, 287
Allen Brothers, 111
All-Stars, Louis Armstrong's, 62, 76
Alvis, Hayes, 86
American Federation of Musicians, 76
American Jazz Music, 123
American Music, 40
American Record Corporation, **132**
American Stars, The, 22
Ammons, 287
Anderson, Cat, 200, 310
Anitra's Dance, 343
Anthony, Ray, 195
Apex Club (Chicago), 84, 114
Apollo, the (Harlem), 76, 87, 283, 306, 324, 336
April in Paris, 214
Arbello, Fernando, 228
Arcadia Ballroom (St. Louis), 98, 103, 113, 114, 118
Arcadians, 116
Arlington, Josie, 6
Armstrong, Louis, 8, 27, 28, 29, 30, 32, 38, 44, 49–58, 62, 63, 65, 68, 70, 76, 78, 81, 83, 84, 88, 95, 98, 110, 114, 118, 124, 125, 134, 136, 140, 148, 149, 168, 169, 171, 174, 177, 180, 211, 218, 222, 223, 224, 264, 269, 270, 271, 277, 280, 284, 285,

Armstrong, Louis (*continued*)
288, 299, 300, 301, 302, 309, 310, 311, 312, 316, 317, 318, 341, 346
Armstrong, Lil, 15, 81
"Armstrong Plays Handy" album, **53**
Armstrong's Hot Seven, 38, 83, 84
Armstrong's Hot Six, 84
Art Tatum Trio, 157
ASCAP, 14
Associated Booking Corporation, 291
Astor's (San Fernando Valley), **78**
Atlantic, 84, 340
At the Christmas Ball, 135
Auld, George, 240
Austin High Gang, 98
Avakian, Al, 320, 330
Avakian, George, 99, 128, 330, **339**
Avedon, Richard, 103

Baby Dodds No. 3, 40
Baby Doll, 136
Baby, It's Cold Outside, 53
Baby, Won't You Please Come Home?, 134
Bach, 142, 143, 171
Back in Your Own Backyard, **230**
Back Water Blues, 135
Bacon, Paul, 167
Bad Sam, 11
Baker, Harold, 200, 205
Bailey, Buster, 134, 178, 220, **224**, 228, 236, 249
Bailey, Mildred, 139, 276, 302
Baker, Chet, 308
Barbarin, Paul, 33
Barefield, Eddie, 230
Barksdale, Everett, 156, **157**, **158**, 159, 160, 161
Barnes, Faye, 220
Barnet, Charlie, 200, 337
Baron, Paul, 302
Barron's (Harlem), 191

349

Barrymore, Lionel, 194
Bartok, 204
Basie, William "Count," 87, 144,
    177, 183, 195, 206, 209, 226,
    227, 232–242, 248, 249, 250,
    251, 252, 254, 256, 258, 260,
    263, 265, 267, 272, 274, 285,
    286, 319, 321, 327, 329, 337
Basin Street, 121
Basin Street Blues, 71
Bauduc, Ray, 32, 39, 71
Bauer, Billy, 45
Bayen, Chips, 216
Beale Avenue Palace (Memphis),
    139
Beale Street Blues, 73
Bean. SEE Hawkins, Coleman
Bechet, Sidney, 36, 57, 124, 133
Beehive, The (*Chicago*), 213
Beetle, The, 156
Begin the Beguine, 344
Beiderbecke, Agatha, 92
Beiderbecke, Leon Bismarck (Bix),
    63, 65, 73, 75, 90–102, 110, 111,
    113, 114, 115, 116, 118, 119,
    125, 140, 224, 270, 300, 341
Beiderbecke, Charles Burnette, 92,
    94
Beiderbecke, Herman Bismarck, 92
Beiderbecke, Mary Louise, 92
Belair, Felix, 54, 55
"Believe It or Not," 15
Belmont Theatre (New York), 138
Bennett, Cuban, 300
Benson Orchestra, 110
Benton, Thomas Hart, 109
Berg, Billy, 341
Berger, Herbert, 110, 111, 112, 113
Berigan, Bunny, 119, 120, 182, 285
Berle, Milton, 188
Bernstein, Artie, 72, 322, 323, 329
Berry, Chu, 73, 134, 155, 167, 170,
    228, 240, 249, 251, 252, 268,
    300, 302, 329
Berry, Emmett, 240
Berton, Vic, 223
Bessemer Singers, 135
*Bessie Smith Story, Vol. 2: Blue to
    Barrelhouse,* 73
Big Eye Lil, 33

Big Gate. SEE Teagarden, Jack
"Big Ham," 299
Big Kid's Palace (Juarez, Mexico),
    111
Big Noble's (Toledo), 154
"Big One." SEE Page, Walter
"Big T," 73
Big T Blues, 73
Billings, Josh, 102
Billy Banks' Rhythmmakers, 119
Billy Rose's Music Hall (New
    York), 181
"Bird." SEE Parker, Charlie
Birdland, 160, 197, 212, 213, 214,
    263, 266, 340, 343
Birdland All-Stars, 256
Birmingham Blues, 145
"Birth of the Blues," 76
Bix Beiderbecke Story, The, 100
Bix-Tram chase choruses, 98
Black and Blue, 147
Black and Tan Fantasy, 192
Black Bottom Stompers, 83
Black, Brown and Beige, 193, 196,
    198
Blackhawk Watchtower (Milan,
    Ill.), 96
Black Swan Jazz Masters, 219
Black Swan Record Company, 132,
    133
Black Swan Recording Co., 219
Black Swan Troubadors, 219
Blanton, Jimmy, 312, 316, 321
Blesh, Rudi, 13, 37, 38, 45, 91, 147,
    165, 339
Blu-Disc, 189
Blue Belles of Harlem, 195
Bluebird label, 87
Blue Books, the, 5, 6, 10
Blue Devil Blues, 234
Blue Devils, Walter Page's, 234, 239,
    247, 319
Blue Drag, 86
Blue Lou, 229
Blue Moon Inn, The (Washington,
    D.C.), 15
Blue 'n' Boogie, 333
Blue Note, 37, 330
Blue Rhythm Fantasy, 310

Blue Room, Lincoln (New York), 287
Blues for Fats, 149
Blues for Johnny, 36
Blues in C Sharp Minor, 310
Blues, The, 196
Blutopia, 195
Blythe, Jimmy, 38
Bobby Sox. SEE Scott, Bobby
Body and Soul, 89, 164, 169, 170, 206, 282
Bolden, Buddy, 62, 63, 308, 316
Bolling, Claude, 301
Bonano, Sharkey, 124
Boogie Woogie on the St. Louis Blues, 87
Booker T. Washington Theatre (St. Louis), 110, 113
Bop City (New York), 230
Borneman, Ernest, 340
Bostic, Earl, 329
Bostonians, 246
Boy in the Boat, The, 145
Boyer, Richard, 334
Boze, Sterling, 72, 113
Braff, Ruby, 73, 125
Brashear, Lorenzo, 219
"Brass Instrumentation in Be-Bop," 311
Braud, Wellman, 37
"Bricktop." SEE Smith, Ada
Brigode, Ace, 225
British Broadcasting Corporation, 176, 226
Broadway, the (Muskogee), 107
Broadway Jones' (New York), 221
"Broadway Rastus," 139
Broadway Syncopators, 222
Brockman, Gail, 88
Brodsky, Irv, 223
Bronson, Art, 246
Brookins, Tommy, 31
Brooks, George, 220
Brooks, Russell, 144
Broonzy, Big Bill, 127
Brown, Bessie, 220
Brown, Boyce, 35
Brown, Carlton, 123
Brown, Cleo, 34
Brown, John, 230

Brown, Les, 195
Brown, Pete, 171
Brown, Ray, 312, 341
Brown, Tom, 106
Brown, Vernon, 322
Brown Brothers, The, 112
Brown Sisters, 284
Brundy, Walter, 22
Brunies, George, 35
Brunswick records, 116, 119, 121, 155, 220
Bryan, Mike, 323
Bryant, Gladys, 220
Bryden, Beryl, 140
Bucket Got a Hole in It, 25, 57
Buckley's Novelty Orchestra, 97
Burns, Ralph, 195, 200
Bushell, Garvin, 219
Butterfield, Billy, 35
Bye, Bye, Blues, 336
Byas, Don, 240, 338
Byrd, Sammy, 113

Café Bohemia (New York), 308
Café Society Downtown (New York), 120, 230, 287, 329
Cake Walking Babies, 135
Calloway, Cab, 181, 225, 251, 336, 337
Camel Caravan, 322
Canadian Capers, 29
Candlelights, 102
Capitol, 230
Capitol Theatre (New York), 338
Careless Love, 25
Carew, Roy, 3, 7, 10, 15, 16
Carey, Jack, 26
Carey, Mutt, 26
Carle, Frankie, 74
Carmichael, Hoagy, 64, 73, 76, 90, 101, 102
Carnegie Hall (New York), 149, 193, 195, 197, 261, 290, 342
Carney, Harry, 199
Carolina Collegians, 67
Carolina Shout, 144
Carpenter, Charlie, 87, 257, 258, 266
Carter, Benny, 169, 224, 226, 227,

Carter, Benny (*continued*)
  251, 271, 298, 300, 305, 309,
  318, 329, 337
Carver, Wayman, 302
Cary, Dick, 125
Casa Loma, 167, 180, 181
Case, Russ, 194
Cash Box, 64
Catalano, Tony, 95
Catlett, Sid, 44, 228, 239, 302, 329
Cauldwell, Happy, 67, 68, 137, 166
Cavernism, 86
CBS, 54, 302
Cecil, Hotel (Harlem), 324
Celestin, Sunny, 27
Cemetery Blues, 130
Centennary of Progress, Chicago's,
  72
Central Café (Juarez, Mexico), 111
Central Plaza (New York), 307
Challis, Bill, 99, 102
Chambers, Elmer, 221
Charles, Ray, 343
Chauffer's Club (St. Louis), 29
"Check and Double Check," 189,
  192
Cherokee, 209
Cherry Blossom (Kansas City), 250
Chicago Breakdown, 83
Chicago Defender, 133
Chicago Musical College, 177
Chicago's Centennary of Progress,
  72
Chicago Theatre, 34
Chicken Shack (New York), 156
Chinatown, My Chinatown, 73, 301
Chittison, Herman, 299
"Chocolate Dandies," 221
"Chocolate Kiddies, The," 191
Chopin, 192
Christian, Charlie, 180, 184, 210,
  247, 306, 312, 316–331, 333
Christopher Columbus, 229
Cinderella Dance Palace (Broad-
  way), 98
Circle label, 37, 38
Clair De Lune, 101
Clap Hands, Here Comes Charlie,
  266
Clark, Carroll, 220

Clark, June, 70, 234
Clarke, Kenny, 210, 263, 302, 306,
  312, 319, 324, 326, 329, 330,
  333, 337
Clay, Shirley, 86
Clayton, Buck, 184, 236, 240, 284
Clef label, 212
Clift, Montgomery, 292
Club Alabam, 221, 222
Club DeLisa. see DeLisa
Club Elite, No. 2 (Chicago), 82,
  83
Club 65 (Chicago), 208
Cohn, Al, 265
Coker, Henry, 241
Cole, Cozy, 88, 282, 329
Cole, June, 154, 155, 167, 168
Cole, Nat (King), 51, 259, 302
Coleman, Bill, 329
Collier, Constance, 131
Collier's, 99
Collins, John, 312
Collins, Lee, 38
Collins, Shad, 240
Columbia, 65, 73, 116, 121, 220,
  221, 228, 282, 321, 322, 329
Columbia, English, 180, 226
Columbia Phonograph Company,
  132
Columbia Record Company, 130,
  133
Columbia Records, 121, 128, 135,
  340
Columbia's English label, 72
Commodore, 272, 288
Commodore Music Shop, 120
Como, Perry, 261
Concerning Jazz, 45
Concert House (Stockholm), 193
Condon, Eddie, 31, 35, 37, 46, 66,
  67, 68, 73, 119, 120, 121, 124,
  125, 138, 140, 178, 179, 342
Condon *Treasury of Jazz* album,
  116
Congress, Library of, recording, 7,
  10, 15
Confessin', 299, 346
Connie's Inn (New York), 138, 146,
  226
"Cookie," 299

Cooper, Al, 257
Cooper, Bob, 265
Cornet Chop Suey, 65
Cotton Club (Minneapolis), 248
Cotton Club (New York), 188, 189, 192, 197, 200, 227, 277, 335
Cotton Pickers, McKinney's, 154, 222, 278, 302
Cottrell, Louis, 22
Coulter, Glenn, 288, 289, 293
Covarrubias, Arnold, 323
"Covered Wagon, The," 112
Cowboy Band, Doc Ross and His, 65
Cox, Ida, 220, 329
Crawford, Jimmy, 230
Crawford, Joan, 109
Crazy Rhythm, 165
Creath, Charlie, 110
Creole Jazz Band, King Oliver, 30, 70
Creole Rhapsody, 198
Crosby, Bing, 53, 64, 76, 120, 317
Crosby, Israel, 228, 330
Cruze, James, 112
Cuffie, Ed, 241
Cunningham, Merce, 37
CY-BIX Orchestra, 96

Dale's Wail, 312
d'Alvarez, Marguerite, 131
Dandridge, Dorothy, 292
Daniels, Josephus, Secretary of the Navy, 5
Daphnis and Chloe, 200
Davenport Blues, 98, 101
Davis, Bud, 96
Davis, Miles, 211, 259, 308, 340
Davison, Wild Bill, 35
D.B. Blues, 255
Deal, Ray, 125
Dean, James, 52
Dear Old Southland, 154, 192
Debussy, 101, 200, 269, 270
Decca, 37, 76, 86, 121, 227
Dee Gee Records, 345
Deep Forest, 85
De Forrest, Maude, 220
De Franco, Buddy, 240, 340

De Lange, Eddie, 323
Delaney, Eric, 46
Delaunay, Charles, 204, 264, 296, 297, 298, 303, 306, 313, 342
DeLisa (Chicago), 85, 229
Delius, 200
de Paris, Wilbur, 9, 14, 16
Deppe, Lois, 82, 83
Desmond, Paul, 265
Dexter, Dave, Jr., 281, 282, 285
Dexter's band, 71
Dial, 203, 211, 212, 301
Diane, 66, 73
Dickerson, Carroll, 83, 84
Dickinson, Vic, 241, 299
Dillard, Bill, 318
Diminuendo and Crescendo in Blue, 194
Dippermouth Blues, 55, 224
Dirge for Indian Joe, 101
Disc, 38, 121
Dixie Belle, 95
Dixieland, 307
Dixieland Band, 110
Dixieland Band, 182
Dixieland Jazz Band, 173
Dixieland Rhythm Kings, 37
Dixon, Charlie, 222
Dizzy Crawl, The, 337
Dodds, Bill, 35
Dodds, Johnny, 13, 19, 20, 25, 29, 33, 34, 35, 83, 110, 174
Dodds, Irene, 33
Dodds, Warren ("Baby"), 13, 18–48, 110
Dominique, Natty, 34, 36, 37, 38, 46
Don't Be That Way, 185
Dorsey, Jimmy, 112, 119, 180, 183, 214, 245, 337
Dorsey, Tommy, 74, 119, 120, 180, 183, 214
Douglas Theatre (New York), 300, 302
Down Beat, 16, 67, 75, 85, 105, 120, 181, 206, 208, 209, 235, 246, 263, 288, 290, 291, 303, 337, 339
Downey, Down, 43
Downhearted Blues, 133

Down South Camp Meetin', 227
Drakes, Jessie, 266
Drum Is a Woman, A, 195
Dr. Heckle and Mr. Jibe, 72
Duchin [Eddie], 236
Duffy, William, 292
Duke Ellington, 187
"Dunn, Blind Willie," 317
Dupré, Marcel, 142
Durham, Ed, 241
Dusen, Frankie, 26
Dutrey, Honoré, 83
Dutrey, Sam, 110

Eager, Allen, 171, 265
Eagle Band, Frankie Dusen's, 26
East St. Louis Toddle-O, 191, 298
Ebony, 273, 291
Eckstine, Billy, 85, 86, 88, 208, 211,
    337, 341
Edgewater Beach Hotel (Illinois),
    100
Edison, Harry, 240, 259
Edmond's (Harlem), 219
Edwards (trombonist), 106
Eldridge, Carol, 313
Eldridge, Joe, 151, 155, 297, 298,
    302
Eldridge, Roy, 34, 151, 152, 155,
    156, 160, 162, 163, 228, 252,
    282, 296–315, 318, 324, 326,
    335, 336, 339, 344
Eldridge, Vi, 313
Elite club (Chicago, Ill.), 8
Elite Serenaders, 298
Ellington, Edward, 197
Ellington, Edward Kennedy (Duke),
    14, 16, 57, 86, 91, 134, 167,
    177, 180, 181, 183, 187–201,
    225, 233, 235, 296, 307, 317,
    324, 338, 339, 341
Ellington, Gay, 197
Ellington, Mercedes, 197
Ellington, Mercer, 190, 196
Ellington, Ruth, 191, 196
"Elliott," Roy, 298
Elman, Ziggy, 184, 322
Emerson, 220
Emerson Record Company, 133
"Emperor Jones," 137

"Empress of the Blues, The." SEE
    Smith, Bessie
Empty Bed Blues, 137
Encyclopedia of Jazz, 155
English Columbia, 180, 226
English Gramaphone Company,
    72
Entertainer's Cabaret (Chicago), 83
Epilogue, 101
Erlich, Jake, 292
Ertegun, Nesuhi, 340
Escudero, Bobby, 222, 223
Esoteric, 330
Esquire, 164, 165, 194, 339
Eureka Brass Band, 81
Evans, Carlisle, 94
Evans, Herschel, 167, 240, 248, 249,
    250, 251, 252, 253, 254, 268,
    319
Evans, Stomp, 166
Evergreen Review, 19, 22
Every Tub on Its Own Bottom, 111,
    241, 266

Fagan, Eleanora. SEE Holiday, Billie
Fairfax, Frank, 335
Faith, Percy, 188
Famous Door (New York), 120,
    138
Farewell Blues, 73
Farmer, Art, 266
Fantasy, 88
Farlow, Tail, 331
Fatool, Nick, 322
Fats Waller's Rhythm Club, 142,
    147
Faust, 34
Feather, Leonard, 155, 207, 211,
    213, 244, 246, 247, 263, 292
Fellman, Jim, 82
Fenton, Nick, 306, 330
Ferguson, Otis, 68, 71, 118
Ferrara, Don, 311
Few-clothes Café (New Orleans),
    24
Fidgety Feet, 95, 229
Fiedler, Arthur, 188
Finkelstein, Sidney, 43, 185, 271
Firebird, 101
Fireworks, 301

Index

Fish Market, 310
Fitzgerald, Ella, 296, 314, 326, 337
"Five Pennies, The," 118
Flashes, 102
Fleet, Biddy, 208
Flight of the Bumble Bee, 142
Florida Stomp, 309
Flying Home, 320, 323
Foggy Day, 267
Folkways, 39
Ford, Whitey, 263
Forty-Seventh and State, 74
Foster, Frank, 240
Foster, George ("Pops"), 27, 45, 46, 110
Fox, Ed, 87
Fox Terminal Theatre (Newark, N.J.), 145
Frazier, George, 126, 340
Frazier, "Mom," 327
Freebody Park (Newport, R.I.), 194
"Free for All," 179
Freeman, Bud, 31, 35, 66, 73, 178, 179, 245, 270, 329
Friar's Inn (Chicago), 96, 178
Friml, 142
Froeba, Frank, 72
Frye, Don, 11
Fuller, Walter, 86
Funeral March, Chopin's, 192

Gabe, Dan, 114, 115
Gabler, Milt, 120, 121
Gaillard, Slim, 263, 341
Gara, Larry, 19, 20, 22, 27, 29, 32, 34, 35, 36, 38, 39, 40, 43, 46
Garland, Eddie, 23
Garner, Erroll, 238
Garroway, Dave, 188
"Gay Divorcee, The," 284
Gee, Jack, 128
Genius, 161
Genius of Art Tatum, The, 160
Gennett Company, 12, 70, 83, 220
Gershwin, George, 131, 149, 159, 179
Getz, Stan, 164, 172, 194, 265
Gillespie, Dizzy, 45, 55, 87, 165, 210, 211, 264, 306, 308, 310,

Gillespie, Dizzy (*continued*) 316, 318, 319, 326, 329, 330, 332–347
Gillespie, Mrs. John. SEE Willis, Lorraine
Gillespie, Mrs. Lottie, 334, 335
Gin House Blues, The, 136
Giuffre, Jimmy, 195, 259, 265
Glaser, Joe, 78, 284, 289, 291
Gleason, Ralph J., 85, 265
Gleason, Jackie, 197
Gloomy Sunday, 287
God Bless the Child, 288
Godowski, 155
Goldkette, 74, 91, 99, 113, 114, 118, 119, 167, 224, 317
Gone With "What" Wind, 320
Gonsalves, Paul, 194, 240
Gonzales, Anita, 8, 11
Gonzales, Babs, 341
Gonzales, Luciano, 341
Goodman, Benny, 31, 43, 52, 55, 57, 72, 74, 87, 99, 107, 114, 117, 118, 122, 134, 173, 175–186, 188, 193, 194, 218, 227, 228, 229, 230, 236, 262, 271, 282, 303, 320–323, 325–329, 331, 339, 341
Goodman, Freddy, 177
Goodman, Harry, 177
Goodman Septet, 329, 330
Goodman Sextet, 329, 330
Gordon, Dexter, 265
Gough, Eleanora Fagan. SEE Holliday, Billie
Gould, Morton, 188
Gowans, Brad, 112
Grainger, Porter, 130, 131, 134
Grand Terrace, the (Chicago), 85, 86, 87, 227, 228, 252, 279
Grand Terrace Swing, 229
Grand Theater (Chicago), 131
Grant, Coot, 220
Granz, Norman, 160, 164, 212, 256, 267, 271, 274, 288, 307, 340, 343
Grauer, Bill, 339, 340
Gray, Wardell, 88, 240, 265
Green, Benny, 87, 337

Green, Charles "Big," 134, 135, 137, 221, 224, 225, 229
Green, Freddie, 237, 238, 239, 284, 286
Green, Ralph "Zeb," 190
Green, Raymond, 219
Green, Urbie, 171
Greer, Sonny, 191, 197, 233
Greystone (Detroit), 167
Griffin, Chris, 322
Grimes, Tiny, 157
Grofe, 99
Gryce, Gigi, 204, 207, 215, 216
Guarnieri, Johnny, 149, 229
Guide to Jazz, 174
Guide to Longplay Jazz Records, 159
Gulda, Friedrich, 340
Gully Low, 301
Guttridge, Len, 61
Guy, Freddy, 191
Guy, Joe, 292, 326, 330
Gypsy, The, 56, 57

Hackett, 73
Hagen, Cass, 118
Haggart, Bob, 35
Haig, Al, 341
Hall, Adelaide, 155
Hall, Edmond, 57, 329
Hall, Minor, 29
Hall, Tubby, 22, 83
Hallett, Mal, 74, 302
Hammond, John, 72, 132, 134, 180, 181, 182, 226, 227, 235, 236, 238, 239, 247, 249, 276, 282, 320, 321, 322, 323, 326, 327, 328, 340
Hampton, Lionel, 180, 184, 302, 322, 323, 329, 342
Handel, 171
Handy, W. C., 8, 15, 16, 137, 219
Hanighen, Bernie, 282, 283
Happy Birthday, 193
Hard Times, 336
Hardin, Lil, 30
Hardwicke, Otto "Toby," 191, 296, 302
Hardy, Emmet, 94
"Harlem Frolics, The," 131, 138
Harlem Laments, 86

Harper, Leonard, 146
Harris, Benny, 87, 337
Harris, Pat, 246
Harrison, Jimmy, 68, 69, 70, 218, 224, 229
Hart, Clyde, 329
Hassler, Bud, 103
Hatch, Wilbur, 97
Hatchett, Edith, 143
Hawes, Elizabeth, 62
Hawk in Hi Fi, 173
Hawk in Paris, The, 173
Hawkins, Coleman, 70, 80, 160, 163–174, 218, 221, 222, 225, 226, 227, 240, 243, 248, 252, 253, 260, 269, 270, 273, 296, 297, 298, 300, 305, 307, 308, 309, 314, 319, 329
Hawkins, Colette, 173
Hawkins, Dolores, 173
Hawkins, Erskine, 344
Hawkins, Mimi, 173
Hawkins, René, 173
Hayes, Edgar, 336
Hear Me Talkin' to Ya, 66, 70, 252, 283
Heckler's Hop, 311
Hefti, Neal, 241
Henderson, Fletcher, 14, 52, 63, 68, 70, 74, 116, 134, 135, 147, 164, 165, 166, 167, 168, 171, 174, 180, 181, 182, 184, 200, 218–231, 233, 248, 249, 251, 253, 297, 302, 303, 309, 322, 329
Henderson, Fletcher Hamilton, Sr., 219
Henderson, Horace, 226, 299
Henderson, Leora, 225, 227, 249
Henderson, Ozie, 219
Henderson, Rosa, 220
Henderson Stomp, 147, 229
Hentoff, Nat, 293
"Hep-Stations of 1945," 341
Herald Tribune, New York, 44
Herald Tribune Youth Forum, New York, 18
Herschman, Leo R., 76
Herman, Woody, 188, 195, 200, 265, 337
Herzog, Arthur, 288

Hess, Otto, 124
Hibbler, Al, 268
Hicks, Edna, 220
Hickory House (New York), 302
Higginbotham, J. C., 226, 329
High Hat club, 206
High Society, 24, 56, 124
Hightower, Willie, 22, 24, 25
Hi Ho Trailus Boot Whip, 310
Hill, Chippie, 36
Hill, Teddy, 210, 302, 309, 310, 318, 321, 324, 325, 326, 327, 328, 335, 336, 337
Hinchcliffe, Edwin, 123
Hines, Earl, 43, 80–89, 114, 141, 181, 210, 211, 228, 337, 338
Hines, Sam, 299
Hinton, Milt, 329, 337
"Hippity Hop," 234
His Rhythm (Waller band), 45
History of Jazz in America, A, 45, 154, 300
Hite, Les, 337
Hobo, You Can't Ride This Train, 50
Hobson, Wilder, 122, 123, 229
Hodeir, André, 243, 271, 309, 310, 312
Hodes, Art, 35, 37, 130
Hodges, Johnny, 200, 271, 341
Hoefer, George, Jr., 60, 65, 71, 72, 75, 76, 77
Holiday, Billie, 140, 158, 194, 243, 251, 253, 262, 263, 268, 276–295, 302, 321, 326, 341
Holiday, Clarence, 278
Hollywood (New York), 191
Hollywood Bar (Harlem), 153
Holman, Bill, 200
Holst, Gustav, 101, 200
Honeysuckle Rose, 141, 146, 329
Horn Palace (San Antonio), 61
Horne, Lena, 51, 188, 194, 199, 291, 326
Horowitz, 155
Hot Mustard, 147
Hot Five, Armstrong's, 51, 81
Hot Record Society, 73
Hot Seven, Armstrong's, 38, 83, 84
Hot Six, Louis Armstrong's, 84

Hotel Cecil (Harlem), 324
Hound Dog, 50
Howard, Darnell, 83, 86
Howard, Eddy, 329
Howard Theatre (Washington), 335
How High the Moon, 267
Hungarian Rhapsody, 34, 93
Hunkadola, 182
Hunter, Alberta, 133, 220
Hunter, Lloyd, 320
Husing, Ted, 191
Hutton, Ina Ray, 337
Hylton, Jack, 168
Hylton, Mrs. Jack, 164, 168

I Ain't Gonna Give Nobody None of My Jelly Roll, 104
Ida, 117, 120
If It Ain't Love, 146
I Got Rhythm, 252
I Gotta Right To Sing the Blues, 72
I Let A Song Go Out of My Heart, 192
I'll Be Seeing You, 292
I'm Gonna Stomp, 67
In a Mist, 97, 102
In a Summer Garden, 200
Indiana, 56, 57
Inside Bebop, 343
Inside Jazz, 343
In the Dark, 102
In the Mood, 198
In the Shade of the Old Apple Tree, 24
Isle of Capri Mambo, 195
It Had To Be You, 294
It's the Talk of the Town, 165
Ives, Charles, 271
Ivie Anderson's (Los Angeles), 158
Ivory Theatre (Chattanooga), 138
I Wished on the Moon, 282

Jack Hits the Road, 74
Jackson. SEE Teagarden, Jack
Jackson, Chubby, 342
Jackson, Dewey, 299
Jackson, Mahalia, 140
Jackson, Milt, 211, 259, 340, 341
Jackson, Preston, 22
Jackson, Tony, 6, 7, 10, 78

Jacquet, Illinois, 240
Jaffe, Nat, 162
James, Baby, 299
James, Harry, 184
James, Ruth Ellington, 198. SEE
    ALSO Ellington, Ruth
Janis, Conrad, 37
JATP, 164
Jazz: A People's Music, 43, 185, 271
"Jazz at the Philharmonic," 212,
    255, 259, 262, 264, 288, 296,
    303, 306, 307
Jazzbo Brown from Memphis Town,
    135
Jazz Hot, 68, 296, 303, 309
Jazz Hounds, Mamie Smith's, 164
Jazz: Its Evolution and Essence,
    271, 312
Jazz Journal, 19
Jazzmen, 20, 30, 38, 100, 114, 118
Jazz Record, The, 341
Jazz-Tango Dancing, 68
Jazztone, 173
"Jazz Train, The," 230
Jenkins, Gordon, 188, 346
Jelly Roll Blues, 8
Jerome, Jerry, 322
Jester-Pillar, 321
Jitterbug Waltz, 146
John, Kenny, 125
Johns, Irving, 134
Johnson, Bill, 8, 30
Johnson, Bobby, 134
Johnson, Budd, 86, 87, 184
Johnson, Bunk, 6, 22, 26, 36, 37, 62,
    339
Johnson, Charlie, 67, 302
Johnson, Freddy, 168
Johnson, James P., 8, 80, 88, 134,
    135, 137, 141, 144, 145, 147,
    148, 149, 156, 190, 221, 233,
    329
Johnson, Mrs. James P., 132, 144
Johnson, Jay, 340
Johnson, J. C., 230
Johnson, J. J., 69, 241
Johnson, Joe, 116
Johnson, J. Rosamunde, 137
Johnson, Lonnie, 34, 317
Jones, Davey, 29

Jones, Hank, 184
Jones, Isham, 31, 179, 181
Jones, Jo, 45, 206, 209, 238, 239,
    248, 252, 253, 258, 262, 266,
    267, 269, 284, 308, 312, 329
Jones, Maggie, 220, 234
Jones, Quincy, 239, 241
Jones, Reunald, 299
Jones, Richard M., 316
Jones, Thad, 241
Joplin, Scott, 24
Joy, Leonard, 169
"Jump for Joy," 193
Jumpin' at the Woodside, 236, 241
Jungle Blues, 179
Jungle Inn, The (Washington, D.C.),
    15
Junior Orpheum Circuit, 107
Just Friends, 212

Kahn, Roger Wolfe, 317
Kaminsky, Max, 73, 125, 339, 341
Kansas City Six, 272
Kansas City Stomps, 9
"Kattie Crippin and Her Kids," 234
Kaye, Sammy, 195
Keepnews, Orrin, 339, 340
"Keep Shufflin'," 147
Kelly, Burt, 33, 46
Kelly, Peck, 60, 61, 113
Kelly's Stable (New York), 169,
    312
Kent, Duke of, 197
Kenton, Stan, 174, 200, 307
Kentucky Club, 191
Kentucky Grasshoppers, The, 67
Keppard, Freddie, 8, 15, 33, 62
Kersey, Kenny, 312
Kessel, Barney, 264, 331
Killian, Al, 240
Kincaide, Deane, 227
King, Martin Luther, 127
King, Wayne, 111
"King of Swing." SEE Goodman,
    Benny
King Oliver's Creole Jazz Band, 8,
    30. SEE ALSO Oliver, Joe "King"
King Porter Stomp, 12, 17
King Porter Stomp, New, 229
Kingdom of Swing, The, 179

Kirby, John, 228, 249, 282
Kirk, Andy, 181, 249, 250, 320, 321
Kirkeby, Ed, 143, 146
Kirkpatrick, Don, 302
Klook. SEE Clarke, Kenny
Knapp, Orville, 109, 111
Knockin' a Jug, 68
Koenigswarter, Baroness Nica, 207, 214, 216
Konitz, Lee, 265
Kostelanetz, André, 188, 345
Kraslow, George, 102
Kress, Carl, 317
Kreuger, Bennie, 116, 178
Krupa, Gene, 32, 34, 35, 43, 72, 74, 118, 178, 179, 180, 183, 184, 236, 239, 282, 302, 303, 305
Kuhn, Rolf, 340
Kyle, Billy, 57

Ladnier, Tommy, 82, 134, 224, 229
Lady Be Good, 268
Lady Day. SEE Holiday, Billie
Lady Sings the Blues, 251
Lafayette Theatre (New York), 145, 283, 301
Laine, Jack, 62, 106, 113
Lamare, Nappy, 35
Lamb's Café (Chicago), 106
Lambert, Donald, 156
La Menthe, Ferdinand Joseph. SEE Morton, Jelly Roll
La Mer, 200
Land of the Loon, 101
Lane, Eastwood, 101
Lang, Eddie, 68, 73, 118, 134, 317
Lanin, Sam, 223
Lanza, Mario, 184
La Rocca, Nick, 63, 94, 95, 106
Laurinburg Institute (North Carolina), 334, 335
La Vere, Charlie, 72
Lawson, Yank, 35
Lazy River, 50
Lee, George E., 207, 248
Lee, Peggy, 188
Lee, Sonny, 110, 113, 116
Leonard, Harlan, 319
Leroy's (New York), 144

Lester Leaps In, 266
Let Me Off Uptown, 304
Let's Dance, 182
Levey, Stan, 337, 341
Levy, John, 291, 292
Lewis, Emma, 220
Lewis, George, 38
Lewis, John, 195, 244, 262, 266, **271**
Lewis, Meade Lux, 124, 287, **330**
Lewis, Ted, 112, 177
Liberian Suite, 195
Liberace, 184
Liebestraum, 142
Liederhouse, 82
Life, 124, 342
Lincoln, Abe, 225
Lincoln Gardens (Chicago), 30, **31**, 33
Lincoln Theatre, 143, 145, 234
Link, Harry, 146
Lion, Alfred, 330
Liston, Melba, 343
Liszt, 93, 142
Little Club (New York), 179
Little Gate. SEE Teagarden, Charlie
"Little Jazz." SEE Eldridge, Roy
"Liza and Her Shufflin' Six," 145
Log Cabin, Jerry's (Harlem), 263, 277, 281, 287
Logan, Dr. Arthur, 196
Lomax, Alan, 5, 7, 9, 10, 11, **14**
Lombardo, Guy, 188
London Suite, 146
Longshaw, Fred, 134, 136
Lost in a Fog, 165
Lost Your Head Blues, 136
Louis Armstrong and His Hot Seven, 38, 83, 84
Louis Armstrong and His Orchestra, 84
Louis Armstrong and His Savoy Ballroom Five, 84
Louis Armstrong's Hot Six, 84
Louis Armstrong Story, The, 65
Louis Armstrong's All-Stars, 62, **76**
Louis's Hot Five, 81
Love Is Just Around the Corner, **121**
Loveless Love, 73
Lover Man, 211
Loyocano, Arnold "Joe," 113

Lunceford, Jimmy, **87, 181, 183, 230**
Lush Life, 199
Lustig, Billy, 68
Lustig, Ray, 114
Lyric Theater (New Orleans), 129
Lyttelton, Humphrey, 46, 56

McConnell, Shorty, 88
McCoy, Clyde, 43, 72
McCoy, Viola, 220
McDonough, Dick, 72, 317
McGhee, Howard, 165, 305
McHugh, Jimmy, 195
McKay, Louis, 292
McKenzie, Red, 119
McKinney, Dr. Sam, 327, 328
McKinney, William, 14, 181
McKinney's Cotton Pickers, 154, 155, 222
McPartland, Jimmy, 35, 66, 178, 179
McPherson, Ozie, 220
McRae, Carmen, 286
McShann, Jay, 208, 209, 210
MacDowell, 101
Macero, Ted, 334
Mack, Sticky, 190
Mack the Knife, 54, 56
Madhouse, 86
Mahogany Hall Stomp, 68
Mahones, Gildo, 266
Makin' Friends, 61, 67
Mamie Smith's Jazz Hounds, 164
Man I Love, The, 165
Mandel, Johnny, 241
Mandy Lee Blues, 70
Manhattan's Kit Kat Club, 138
Mannone, Wingy, 65, 66, 72
Marable, Fate, 11, 28, 29, 95
Ma Rainey's Rabbit Foot Minstrels, 127
Mares, Paul, 35, 96
Marigold Gardens (Chicago), 114
Marin, R. J., 60
Marsala, Joe, 72
Marsh, Arno, 265
Marsh, Warne, 265
Marshall, Kaiser, 43, 70, 137, 222
Martin, Henry, 22, 23, 26
Martin, Mary, 64

Massaro, Salvatore. SEE Lang, Eddie
Matlock, Matty, 301
May, Billy, 200
Mays, Willie, 326
Me and My Gin, 136
Mean Old Bed Bug Blues, 135
Meet Me Tonight in Dreamland, **73**
Melancholy, 83
Melody Maker, 167, 180, 235, 244, 340
Melrose, Lester, 11, 12, 13, 16
Melrose, Walter, 11, 12, 13, 16
"Member of the Wedding, The," **230**
Memphis Blues, 25
Mendelssohn, 322
Mercer, Johnny, 78
Merrill, Charlie, 105, 107, 109
Metronome, 236, 311, 339, 341
Metronome All-Star, 329
Metropolitan Opera House, 194, 302
Meyers, Hazel, 220
Mezzrow, Milton (Mezz), 35, 36, 37, 45, 100, 333
Middleton, Velma, 53, 57
"Midnight Steppers, The," 138
Milenberg Joys, 12, 223
Miles, Josie, 220
Miley, Bubber, 133, 191, 192
Milhaud, 200
Miller, Glenn, 52, 71, 178, 179
Millinder, Lucky, 84, 337
Mills, Florence, 132
Mills, Irving, 192
Mills, Johnny, 299
Millstein, Gilbert, 293
Milne Municipal Boys' Home (New Orleans), 78
Minor, Don, 241
Minton's Playhouse, 148, 210, 232, 267, 306, 324, 325, 327, 328, 329, 330, 338
Miss Brown to You, 282
Mr. Henry Lee, 67
Mr. T. SEE Teagarden, Jack
Mister Jelly Roll, 5
Misty Morning, 317
Mitchell, George, 86
Mitchell, Whitey, 263
Moan, You Mourners, 135
Moldroon, Oliver, 298

Mole, Miff, 37, 68, 116, 117, 118, 223
Mondello, Toots, 74, 322
Monk, Thelonius, 170, 172, 210, 306, 319, 326, 329, 330, 333
Monologue, 194, 196
Mooche, The, 317
Mood Indigo, 192
Moore, Alice, 292
Moore, Breu, 265
Morgan, Lee, 344
Morris, Marlowe, 267
Morris, William, 87
Morrison, Allan, 273
Morton, Benny, 224, 226, 241, 269, 329
Morton, "Jelly Roll," 3–17, 38, 67, 80, 81, 124, 190, 341
Moszkowski, 142
Moten, Bennie, 209, 226, 235, 238, 248, 319
Moten, Buster, 235
Moulin Rouge (Paris), 324
Mound City Blue Blowers, 165
Moynahan, Jim, 101
Muggles, 84
Mulligan, Gerry, 26, 125
Mullins, Maizie, 144
Mundy, Jimmy, 74, 86
Muni, Paul, 276
Municipal Stadium (Philadelphia), 194
Murphy, Dudley, 137
Murphy, Turk, 54
Murray, Mack, 21
Murrow, Ed, 54, 175
Muscle Shoals Blues, 145
Muse, Red, 29
Music Box, The (Washington, D.C.), 15
Music Corporation of America, 74
Music for Torching, 293
Music Hall, Billy Rose's, 181
Music Inn (Berkshires), 18, 345
Music Lovers' Encyclopedia, 104
"Musician's Rest" (Minneapolis), 321
Muskat, 74
Muskrat Ramble, 65
Muskogee Blue, 121, 122

Musso, Vido, 184
Mussorgsky, 271
Mutual (radio), 37
My Fate Is in Your Hands, 146

NAACP, 190, 194, 198
Nance, Ray, 86, 200
National Biscuit Company, 227, 228
N.B.C., 154
Nelson, Big Eye Louis, 25
Nest, The (Chicago), 84, 114
Never Plead Guilty, 292
Newborn, Phineas, 238
New King Porter Stomp, 229
Newman, Jerry, 325, 328, 330, 331
Newman, Joe, 237, 241
"New Movements in Be-bop," 342
New Orleans, 288
New Orleans Rhythm Kings, 12, 35, 67, 96, 113, 178
Newport Jazz Festival, 55
Newton, Frankie, 73, 134, 287
New World A-Comin', 195
New York *Herald Tribune* Youth Forum, 18
New York Times, 54, 221
Nice Jazz Festival, 46
Nice Work If You Can Get It, 293
Nicholas, Albert, 37
Nichols, Ed, 100
Nichols, Red, 63, 108, 116, 118, 179, 223, 298, 300, 317
Nick's, 37
Night and Day, 284, 290
Nighthawk Syncopators, 297
Nighthawks, 299
Night in Tunisia, 344
91 Theatre (Atlanta, Ga.), 131
Nobody Knows You When You're Down and Out, 135
Noone, Jimmie, 12, 36, 84, 98, 114, 178
Nora Bayes Theatre, 221
NORK, 96, 178
Norvo, 236
Nunez, Alcide "Yellow," 105, 106, 111, 122

O'Brien, Floyd, 35
O'Connor, Father, 281

ODJB. SEE Original Dixieland Jazz Band
Okeh, 118, 132, 133, 145
Oliver, Joe (King), 8, 12, 26, 29, 30, 32, 33, 49, 55, 56, 62, 63, 70, 83, 84, 98, 114, 223, 224, 247, 299, 316, 317
Oliver, Sy, 74, 200, 241, 299
One and Two Blues, 136
One Hour, 165
One O'Clock Jump, 198, 236, 241, 266
On Revival Day, 135
Onyx Club (New York), 120, 155
Opera House (San Francisco), 200
Orchestra World, 123
Oriental Strut, 66
Original Creole Orchestra, 8
Original Dixieland Band, 98
Original Dixieland Jazz Band, 62, 94, 95, 98, 105, 106
Original Southern Trumpeter's, R. J. Marin's, 60
Orr, Dee, 114
Ory, Kid, 13, 16, 23, 25, 26, 30
Osborne, Mary, 320
Ostrich Walk, 95
Over the Rainbow, 160
Over the Waves, 24

Pace, Harry, 132, 219
Page, Oran "Hot Lips," 130, 148, 240, 319, 329, 340
Page, Walter, 234, 238, 239, 247, 248, 284, 319
Palace (New York), 192
Palace Theater (Chicago), 131
Palais Royale, 191
Palais Royal Orchestra, 298
Palladium (Hollywood), 304
Palmer, Bee, 94
Palmer, Roy, 24, 82
Palomar Ballroom (Los Angeles), 182
Panassie, Hugues, 88, 123, 174
Pantages vaudeville circuit, 83
Panther Room, Hotel Sherman, 77
Paps (drummer), 22
Paradise Gardens (Chicago), 130, 140

Paramount label, 133, 220
Paramount lot, 53
Paramount Theatre (New York), 194
Parenti, Tony, 66
Paris, Wilbur de, 9, 10, 14, 16
Parker, Chan, 203, 204, 208, 213, 214, 215
Parker, Charlie, 18, 45, 87, 88, 156, 172, 177, 194, 202–217, 259, 264, 265, 306, 308, 310, 316, 318, 319, 326, 328, 331, 333, 337, 338, 340, 341, 343, 346, 347
Parker, Doris, 205, 206, 207, 209, 212, 213, 215, 216
Parker, Pree, 213
Parlophone, 180, 226
Paseo Club, 248, 249
Pastor, Tony, 286
Payne, Bennie, 147
Pearls, The, 9, 12, 17
Peck Kelly's Bad Boys, 60, 61, 113
Peer, Ralph, 67
Pell, Dave, 265
Pennsylvania Hotel (New York), 304, 325, 329
Perkins, Bill, 265
Perkins, Dave, 22
Perkins, Gene, 108
Perkins, Fred, 108
Perry, Doc, 190
Persing, Colonel C. L., 109
Peterson, Art, 94, 97
Peterson, Charlie, 118, 124
Peterson, Chuck, 286
Peterson, Oscar, 238, 312
Petrouchka, 101
Pettiford, Oscar, 165, 320, 321, 337, 338, 339
Pettit, Buddy, 15
Picasso, 165
Pickin' the Cabbage, 336
Pierce, Nat, 241
Piron, Armand, 22
Piron, A. J., 223
Pitchin' a Bit Short, 73
Planets, The, 101, 200
Plantation Café (Chicago), 83
Plantation Club (Chicago), 114

Playmore (Kansas City, Mo.), 108

Plunketts' speakeasy, 119

Polka Dots and Moonbeams, 267

Pollack, Ben, 31, 32, 39, 67, 71, 74, 117, 178, 179

Ponce, Phil, 147

Porter, Cole, 188, 195, 284

Powell, Benny, 241

Powell, Bud, 160, 214, 259, 337

Powell, Mel, 325

Powell, Rudy, 254, 261, 336

Pozo, Chano. SEE Gonzales, Luciano

Presley, Elvis, 50, 184

Preston, Jerry, 281. SEE ALSO Log Cabin, Jerry's

Pretty Baby, 7, 78

Previn, André, 200

Prez. SEE Young, Lester Willis

Price, Sammy, 45

Prima, Leon, 113

Prima, Louis, 113, 121

Prince, Bob, 320

Procope, Russell, 249

Profit, Clarence, 156

QRS Piano Roll Company, 84, 145, 147

"Queen of the Blues, The." SEE Smith, Bessie

Queer Notions, 167

Quinichette, Paul, 172, 240, 265, 266

Rachmaninoff, 155

Ragas, 106

Rainey, Gertrude "Ma," 136, 220, 277, 292

Ramey, Gene, 206, 207, 215

Ramsey, Fred, Jr., 20, 30, 39, 124, 159

Raney, Jimmy, 328

Rappolo, Leon, 62, 63, 105, 113, 178

Ravel, 101, 200

Razaf, Andy, 146

Reardon, Caspar, 73

Record Changer, 165, 268, 311, 339, 340, 341

Red Hot Peppers, 4, 11, 12, 13, 38

Red Mill Café (Chicago), 82

Redman, Don, 134, 145, 146, 181, 218, 221, 222, 224, 227

Reinhardt, Django, 169, 318, 324, 326

Reminiscing in Tempo, 198

Renaissance (New York), 298

Renaud, Henri, 264

Rendezvous Café (Chicago), 101

Reno Club (Kansas City, Mo.), 248, 250

Reser, Harry, 72

Resnick, Ephie, 125

Reuben Harris's (New York), 156

Rhapsody in Blue, 159

Rhodes, Todd, 155

Rhythm Club (Harlem), 155, 300

Rhythm Kings, 63

Richards, Red, 125

Rifflin' the Scotch, 282

Rimski-Korsakov, 142

Ripley, Robert, 15

Riskin, Andy ("Itsy" or Itzey), 101, 114

Ritz Café (Oklahoma City), 322

Riverside, 70, 167, 340

Roach, Max, 18, 44, 45, 338

Roberts, Lucky, 233

Robichaux band, 21

Robin Hood Dell (Philadelphia), 194

Robinson, Floyd, 112

Robinson, Prince, 166

Robison, Carson, 65

Rock-a-Bye-Basie, 337

Rockin' Chair, 65, 73, 304

Rockwell, Tommy, 68

Rodgers, Gene, 169

Rodgers, Richard, 195

Rogers, Buddy, 182

Rogers, Shorty, 195

Rollins, Sonny, 172, 243

Rongetti, Nick, 124

Room 1411, 179

Roosevelt Theatre (New York), 144

Rose, Billy, 181, 227

Roseland Ballroom (New York), 52, 63, 68, 116, 166, 167, 221, 222, 224

Rose Room, 229, 323

Rosetta, 86
Ross, Allie, 222
Ross, Doc, and His Cowboy Band, 65
"Roy Elliott and his Palais Royal Orchestra from New York," 298
Royal, Marshall, 240
Royal Gardens (Chicago), 30, 31
Rug Cutter's Swing, 227
Rugolo, 200
Rushing, Jimmy, 234, 235, 254, 258, 261, 319
Rusin, Babe, 179
Russell, Bill, 36, 38, 40
Russell, Luis, 68
Russell, Mary, 103, 122
Russell, Pee Wee, 35, 62, 65, 66, 69, 73, 74, 100, 103–126, 188, 229
Russell, Ross, 203, 211, 212, 268, 306, 311
Russo, Bill, 69, 77
Rutherford, Anita, 147
Ryan, Jimmy, 37

Sacré du Printemps, 338
St. Cyr, Johnny, 13
St. Louis Blues, 25, 136
"St. Louis Blues," 137
St. Louis Club Orchestra, Herbert Berger's, 110
St. Louis Shuffle, 147
St. Louis Symphony Orchestra, 110
Salvador, Sal, 331
Sampson, Edgar, 74
Sandiford, Frank, 213, 217
Sarle, Tony, 110
Savannah [Georgia] Symphony Orchestra, 125
Savoy ballroom (Harlem), 63, 335
Savoy Ballroom (Chicago), 83
Savoy Ballroom Five, Louis Armstrong and His, 84
Schoebel, Elmer, 96
Schoenberg, 101
Schoeppe, Franz, 177
Scott, Bobby, 258, 259, 262
Scott, Bud, 316
Scott, Cecil, 300, 302

Scott, Hazel, 169
Scott, Howard, 221
Scott, Marion, 286
Scott, Ronnie, 259
Sedric, Gene, 141, 268
Seiver's Hotel, 106
Serenade to a Shylock, 73, 121
Seven Come Eleven, 320
Shaffner, Dean, 76
Shand, Terry, 61
Shavers, Charlie, 173, 335
Shaw, Artie, 183, 285, 286, 303, 304
Shayne, Freddie, 36
Sheehan's, Jack, 27
Sherock, Shorty, 304
Shields, Larry, 105, 106, 110, 124
Shining Trumpets, 13, 38, 91
Shoe Shine Boy, 266
Simeon, Omer, 4, 12, 86, 228
Simon, Dr. Gerry, 113
Simmons, John, 291
Simon, Bill, 265, 309
Simpkins, Arthur Lee, 85
Sims, Zoot, 265
Sinatra, Frank, 184, 268, 345
Sing, Sing, Sing, 185
Singleton, Zutty, 32, 83, 110, 124, 129, 223
Sir Charles. SEE Thompson, Charles
Sister Kate, 124, 133
Skip the Gutter, 301
Slow Boat to China, 230
"Smack," 322
Smalls' Paradise (Harlem), 67, 70, 296, 302
Smith, Ada, 191, 324
Smith, Bessie, 73, 98, 120, 127–140, 220, 277, 280, 283, 287, 324
Smith, Buster, 209, 319
Smith, Clara, 140, 220, 234
Smith, Clarence, 139
Smith, Floyd, 320
Smith, Hazel, 140
Smith, Jabbo, 299, 301
Smith, Joe, 134, 136, 137, 166, 218, 219, 221, 224, 225, 229
Smith, Laura, 140
Smith, Mamie, 133, 140, 164, 166
Smith, Tab, 240
Smith, Trixie, 140, 220

Smith, Willie the Lion, 144, 190, 233
Snake Rag, 70
Snookie's, 345
Snowden, Elmer, 191, 296, 302
Soft Winds, 229
Solitude, 192, 195
Solo Flight, 328, 329
Someday Sweetheart, 73
Sometimes I'm Happy, 228
Soper, Tut, 36
Sophisticated Lady, 192
Sousa, 59
South, Eddie, 158
"South's Greatest Trombone Wonder, The," 60
Southern Barbeque, 234
Southern Music Company, 67
Southmore (Chicago), 114
Spanier, Muggsy, 31, 57, 83, 178
Spanish Dance No. 1, 142
Spanish Days, 142
Sparbaro (Spargo), 106
Specht, Paul, 117, 118, 222
Spikes brothers, 11
Spring Cleaning, 148
Spring Song, Mendelssohn's, 322
Squeeze Me, 145
Stables, Burt Kelly's, 46
Stacy, Frank, 339
Stacy, Jess, 31, 35, 73, 83, 180, 182, 229
Stafford, George, 67
Stampede, 165, 298
Stardust Road, The, 101
Stark, Bobby, 225, 300
Starr, Milton, 138
Stars and Stripes Forever, The, 159
Stars Fell on Alabama, 73
Statler Hotel (New York). SEE Pennsylvania Hotel
Stealin' Apples, 229
Stearns, Marshall W., 72, 176, 338, 346
Stevens, Ashton, 142
Steward, Herbie, 265
Stewart, Rex, 224, 226, 298, 300
Stewart, Slam, 157
Stitt, Sonny, 172
Stokowski, Leopold, 197

Stompers, Fletcher Henderson, 299
Stompin' at the Savoy, 185, 195, 330
Stork Club (New York), 120
"Stormy Weather," 142
Story, Alderman Sidney, 5
Story of Jazz, The, 72
Storyville (Boston), 55, 125
Straight, Charlie, 98, 101
Straine, Mary, 220
Strange Fruit, 287
Stravinsky, 101, 338
Strayhorn, Billy, 194, 199, 200
Streckfus, 27, 28, 29
"Strike Up the Band," 179
Stuffy, 165
Sturgess, Ted, 312
Stuyvesant Casino (New York), 36, 124, 339
Sugar Foot Stomp, 224
Sulieman, Idrees, 266
Sullivan, Joe, 67, 72, 118, 120, 124, 140, 149, 282, 284
Summertime, 149, 285
Sunset Café (Chicago), 83
Sutton, Ralph, 149
Suzy Q, the (West Coast), 76
Swampy River, 197
Sweet and Lovely, 230
Sweets. SEE Edison, Harry
Swing Low, Sweet Spiritual, 77
Swing Records, 168
Swingin' the Blues, 236, 266
Sylvester, Bob, 292
Sylvester, Hannah, 220
Symphony Hall (Boston), 76

Tabou (France), 264
Take Me to That Land of Jazz, 121
Tan, 276
Tarto, Joe, 223
Tate, Buddy, 240
Tate, Erskine, 148
Tatum, Art, 120, 151–162, 169, 302, 305, 318, 339
Tatum Trio, Art, 157
Taxi War Dance, 269
Taylor, Billy, 15, 134, 154, 155, 158, 159, 160, 161, 173
Taylor, Deems, 188

Tea for Two, 322
Teagarden, Addie, 76
Teagarden, Clois, 60
Teagarden, Weldon John (Jack),
    35, 59–79, 88, 113, 118, 120,
    124, 125, 134, 140, 282, 341
Teagarden, Joe, 76
Teagarden, Norma, 60
Teschemacher, Frank, 31, 83, 114,
    118, 123, 178
Tenot, Frank, 260, 264, 268, 272
Terrace Gardens, 95, 97
Terry, Clark, 240
Texas Tea Party, 72
That's a Serious Thing, 67
That's My Desire, 53
That Thing, 308–309
*There'll Be a Hot Time in the Old
    Town Tonight,* 135
"This Is Jazz Series," 37
This Is Teagarden, 69, 77
Thompson, Charles, 263
Thompson, Edna, 190
Thompson, Lucky, 230, 240
Three Deuces (Chicago), 34, 154,
    155, 178, 302
3-2-1 Blues, 121, 122
Thundermug Stomp, 147
Tiger, 124
Tiger Rag, 95, 111
Tilghman, Tom, 153, 157, 158, 161,
    162
Time, 342
Times, New York, 54
Tin Can, 223
Tin Roof Blues, 57
Tippin' Out, 310
To a Water Lily, 101
T.O.B.A. circuit, 138, 234
Top and Bottom, 147
Topsy, 330
Tormé, Mel, 341
Tough, Dave, 31, 32, 35, 43, 74, 178
Towles, Nat, 320
Town Hall (New York), 124, 149,
    288
Traill, Sinclair, 19, 45
Tranthem, Cookie, 108
Travelin' All Alone, 282

Travelin' Light, 294
Treasury of Jazz, 121
Trent, Al, 320
Trepagnier, Ernest, 24
Tristano, Lennie, 45, 188
Trombone Cholly, 135
Trombone Club, 119
Trueheart, John, 282
Truman, President, 197
Trumbauer, Frankie, 65, 91, 98, 113,
    245, 253, 265
Trumbauer's Arcadia Ballroom Or-
    chestra, 114
Tucker, Bobby, 290, 291
Turner, Joe, 156, 287
Turpin, Charlie, 110
Turpin, Tom, 110
Twelfth Street Rag Mambo, 195
Tynan, John, 64, 77, 78

Ulanov, Barry, 45, 154, 156, 159,
    187, 236, 265, 271, 286, 300,
    311
Umbrella Man, The, 344
Underneath the Harlem Moon, 284
United Hot Clubs of America, 121
Uptown House, Clark Monroe's,
    172, 208
Uptown Theatre (Chicago), 178
Usher, David, 345

Vallee, Rudy, 118, 206
Val's Alley (Cleveland), 156
Vance, Dick, 230
Van Eps, George, 317
van Praag, Joost, 68
Van Vechten, Carl, 129–130, 131
Variety Stomp, 147
Vaughan, Sarah, 88, 268, 337
Vendome orchestra, Erskine Tate's,
    148
Venuti, Joe, 46, 73
Venuti-Lang All-Star Orchestra, 73
Victor, 4, 14, 36, 37, 67, 74, 86, 87,
    110, 142, 147, 179, 220, 228,
    229, 329
Victor Hugo (Theater), 323
Victor Studios, 169, 171
Vocalion, 73, 83, 86, 220, 229, 329

Wabash Stomp, 309
Waiter and the Porter and the Maid Upstairs, The, 64
Walder, Herman, 250
Walker, Frank, 128, 129, 133, 134, 136, 138
Wallace, Inez, 220
Waller, Adeline Lockett, 143
Waller, Edward, 143
Waller, Thomas "Fats," 72, 88, 141–150, 153, 156, 157, 191, 221, 233, 234, 242, 326
Wallington, George, 338
Walter Page's Blue Devils, 234
Ware, Efferge, 207
Warren, Earl, 240
Warwick, Carl "Bama," 335
Warwick Hall (Chicago), 83
Washington, Buck, 134
Washington, Isabelle, 220
Washington, Jack, 240, 319
Waters, Ethel, 131, 132, 135, 219, 220, 223, 230, 277, 284
Watters, Johnny, 82
Watts, Billy, 113
Weather, Boozy, 108
Weather Bird Rag, 84
Weatherford, Teddy, 82
Webb, Chick, 43, 181, 236, 239, 316
Webb, Speed, 299
Webster, Ben, 209, 210, 240, 246, 250, 251, 253, 268, 282, 307, 319, 329
Webster, Freddy, 87, 337
We Called It Music, 66, 124
Wee Baby Blues, 156
Weeping Willow Blues, 132
Wein, George, 55, 257, 266, 267
Welge, Walter "Cy," 96
Welk, Lawrence, 188
Welles, Orson, 16, 197
Wells, Dickie, 241, 302
We're in the Money, 120
Wess, Frank, 240
West End Blues, 56, 84, 279, 280
Weston, Randy, 204
Wettling, George, 31, 35, 43, 46, 83, 125, 178

What a Little Moonlight Will Do, 282
When It's Sleepy Time Down South, 57
When the Saints Go Marching In, 313
Where Has My Mother Gone?, 143
Whetsol, Arthur, 191
Whiffenpoof Song, 346
White, Gonzel, 234
White, Lulu, 6
White, Sonny, 286
Whiteman, Paul, 74, 75, 78, 91, 96, 99, 100, 101, 117, 191, 317
Whiteman Stomp, 147
WHN, 222
"Whoopee Girls, The," 138
Whoopee Makers, The, 67
Whyte, Zach, 299
Wild Man Blues, 83, 301
Wilder, Joe, 240
Wilkins, Ernie, 240
Williams, Clarence, 128, 133, 134, 145
Williams, Cootie, 63, 184, 329
Williams, George, 220
Williams, Mary Lou, 70, 74, 239, 250, 321, 341
Williams, Spencer, 142
Willis, Lorraine, 335, 336, 337, 338, 343, 345, 346, 347
Wilson, Dick, 250, 282, 319
Wilson, Edith, 222
Wilson, Gus, 299
Wilson, John S., 293
Wilson, Lena, 220
Wilson, Shadow, 87
Wilson, Teddy, 180, 184, 282, 284, 285, 299, 305, 329
Winburn, Anna Mae, 320
Winding, Kai, 65
Winding Boy, The. SEE Morton, Jelly Roll
Windsor, Duke of, 197
Winsted's "Broadway Rastus," 139
Winsten, Archer, 288
WLW (Cincinnati), 142, 147
Wolverine Blues, 12
Wolverines, 97, 98, 100, 101, 113

WQXBY (Kansas City, Mo.), 235
Wrappin' It Up, 227
WSPD (Ohio), 154

Young, Irma, 245
Young, Lee, 245, 246, 259
Young, Lester, 164, 171, 172, 206, 210, 227, 236, 240, 243–275, 283, 284, 286, 296, 306, 307, 308, 316, 319, 320
Young, Lester, Jr., 256
Young, Mary, 256
Young, Trummy, 57, 86

Young, William H. (Billy), 244, 245
Young, Yvette, 256
Young Man With a Horn, 232
Young Woman's Blues, 136
Your Mother's Son-in-Law, 282
Youth Forum, New York *Herald Tribune*, 18

Zacheis, Les, 97
Zeno, Henry, 22, 26
Zonky, 146
Zoot, 172
Zurke, Bob, 35